THE
BEST
OF
Gourmet

THE
BEST
OF
Gourmet

1995

FROM THE EDITORS OF GOURMET

PHOTOGRAPHS BY ROMULO A. YANES

CONDÉ NAST BOOKS · RANDOM HOUSE, NEW YORK

LIBRARY OF CONGRESS
CATALOGING-IN-PUBLICATION DATA

(Revised for vol. 10)
Main entry under title:
The Best of Gourmet: featuring the flavors of
Mexico/from the editors of Gourmet
    p.   cm.
Includes index.
    1.Cookery, Mexican. I.The Best of Gourmet
TX716-M48427 1995
641.5972-dc20   94-42992
ISBN 0-679-44146-8
ISSN 1046-1760

Most of the recipes in this work were published previously in *Gourmet* Magazine.

Manufactured in the United States of America

98765432
First Edition

All the informative text in this book was written by Diane Keitt and Judith Tropea.

The text of this book was set in Times Roman by Michael Shroyer and Media Projects Incorporated. The four-color separations were done by The Color Company, Seiple Lithographers, and Applied Graphic Technologies. The book was printed and bound at R. R. Donnelley and Sons. Stock is Citation Webb Gloss, Westvāco.

Front Jacket: "Mango Ice Cream" (page 290), "Buñuelos" (page 291).

Back Jacket: "Grilled Rib-Eye Steaks with Béarnaise Butter" (page 127), "Corn Boats with Zucchini and Pepper Jack Cheese" (page 177), "Potato Salad with Garlic Mayonnaise and Chives" (page 202).

Frontispiece: "Golden-Raisin Irish Soda Bread" (page 102), "Irish Brown Soda Bread" (page 102).

For Condé Nast Books

Jill Cohen, President
Ellen Maria Bruzelius, Direct Marketing
    Director
Kristine Smith-Cunningham, Advertising
    Promotion Manager
Tina Kessler, Direct Marketing
    Administrator
Jennifer Metz, Direct Marketing Associate
Diane Pesce, Prepress Services Manager
Serafino J. Cambareri, Quality Control
    Manager

For *Gourmet* Books

Diane Keitt, Editor
Judith Tropea, Associate Editor

For *Gourmet* Magazine

Gail Zweigenthal, Editor-in-Chief

Zanne Early Zakroff, Executive Food
    Editor
Kemp Miles Minifie, Senior Food Editor
Alexis M. Touchet, Associate Food Editor
Lori Longbotham, Food Editor
Amy Mastrangelo, Food Editor
Elizabeth Vought, Food Editor
Lori Walther, Food Editor
Peggy Anderson, Assistant Food Editor

Romulo A. Yanes, Photographer
Marjorie H. Webb, Stylist
Nancy Purdum, Stylist

Produced in association with
Media Projects Incorporated

Carter Smith, Executive Editor
Anne Wright, Project Editor
Shelley Latham, Project Editor
John W. Kern, Production Editor
Martina D'Alton, Associate Project Editor
Marilyn Flaig, Indexer
Michael Shroyer, Art/Production Director

ACKNOWLEDGMENTS

The editors of *Gourmet* Books would like to thank colleagues and freelancers who contributed so much to this tenth-anniversary edition.

Special thanks go to Zanne Early Zakroff, *Gourmet*'s Executive Food Editor, who acted as consultant, and to Karen Salsgiver and Laura Howell of Salsgiver Coveney Associates, Inc., for making some exciting changes to our book design.

This year the Cuisines of the World section features The Flavors of Mexico. Menus were created and styled by *Gourmet* food editors Alexis Touchet (Almuerzo), Lori Walther (An Oaxacan Dinner), and Liz Vought (A Mexican Buffet). Lori also developed and styled the Mango Ice Cream that appears on the jacket. Wines for the menus were assigned by *Gourmet*'s Wine Editor, Gerald Asher. All menu and regional photographs are courtesy of Romulo A. Yanes. Jeannie Oberholtzer was the prop stylist for the jacket and food photographs. Menu and recipe translations are by Jane Zanca. Line drawings by Susie Howard and Laura Hartman Maestro complement the section.

The recipes for this year's addendum — Quick and Easy Hors d'Oeuvres, Snacks, and Beverages — are the creation of Georgia Chan Downard, and they are accompanied by line drawings by Laura Hartman Maestro.

Many artists provided the line drawings that appear throughout the book. We would like to thank Carla Borea, Jean Chandler, Beverly Charlton, Suzanne Dunaway, Barbara Fiore, Vicky Harrison, Susie Howard, Zoe Mavridis, Jeanne Meinke, Rowena Perkins, Agni Saucier, Jim Saucier, Alexandra Schultz, and Meg Shields. We would also like to thank our book designer, Michael Shroyer, for once again working on this annual. Also, thank you to Hobby McKenney, Maura Walsh, and Toni Rachiele, and to Anne Wright, Shelley Latham, and John Kern at Media Projects, for their editorial assistance.

CONTENTS

9   INTRODUCTION

11   THE MENU COLLECTION

12   A Southern New Year's Day Buffet

16   New Year's Eve Supper For Two

18   Chicken Dinners in the Kitchen

22   Après-Skate Danish-Style

24   Bright Lights Big City Dinner

28   An Early Spring Dinner

30   Easter Dinner

35   Sunday Supper

36   A New Orleans Courtyard Dinner

40   A Pan-Asian Luncheon on Maui

44   A Taste of Thailand

49   Dinner from the Grill

50   Fourth of July Family Reunion Picnic

54   Cocktails after Tennis

56   A Moroccan Feast

60   Supper on the Porch

63   A Small Garden Wedding

66   A Hikers' Picnic

69   Oktoberfest

72   Autumn Dinner for Two

75   Thanksgiving Dinner

78   A Bird of a Different Feather

81   Christmas Dinner

84   A Caroling Party

87 A RECIPE COMPENDIUM

88 Hors d'Oeuvres, Canapés, Dips and Spreads

101 Breads

110 Soups

120 Fish and Shellfish

127 Meat

137 Poultry

150 Cheese, Egg, and Breakfast Dishes

156 Pasta and Grains

171 Vegetables

192 Salads and Salad Dressings

212 Sauces

218 Desserts

254 Beverages

258 CUISINES OF THE WORLD

The Flavors of Mexico

302 A GOURMET ADDENDUM

Quick and Easy Hors d'Oeuvres, Snacks, and Beverages

312 GUIDES TO THE TEXT

312 General Index

329 Index of 45-Minute Recipes

333 Index of Recipe Titles

339 Table Setting Acknowledgments

INTRODUCTION

With this edition, *The Best of Gourmet* celebrates its tenth anniversary. It's really gratifying to me that you have made this series so successful—there are now over one million books in print!

Anniversaries are special, and so we decided to celebrate in style by giving this tenth edition an updated look. You will notice that while we have kept the popular original format intact, we have changed the cover and some of the interior design elements.

Along with our bright, modern design, this year's menus and recipes are very contemporary as well. One of my favorite menus is our Dinner from the Grill, an inspired cookout of Grilled Rosemary Garlic Shrimp, Grilled Tortilla and Onion Cake, Wilted Red Cabbage and Bell Pepper Slaw, and Baked Alaska Peanut S'Mores. The presentation is colorful and inviting; the taste, light and delicious. All the dishes can be made without much fuss, and many can be prepared in advance.

Continuing this theme, we've included more than 100 recipes that can be completed in 45 minutes or less. From Turkey Cutlets Milanese with Watercress Salad to Scallion Biscuits to Kahlúa, Toasted Coconut, and Ice-Cream Parfaits, you will be able to find plenty of dishes to fit into your busy lifestyle. We've even created an all-new addendum filled with Quick and Easy Hors d'Oeuvres, Snacks, and Beverages, so that you will be able to entertain at a moment's notice. Be sure to use the Index of 45-Minute Recipes to make up your own menus with these quick dishes.

More surprises await, including a brand new section, The Flavors of Mexico. Outstanding photography, insightful information, and three menus specially developed by our own food editors take you to this seductive country for an exciting tour filled with flavor.

We hope you will enjoy all that this book has to offer. Come celebrate our best recipes and much, much more as we look forward to a second decade of *The Best of Gourmet*.

Gail Zweigenthal, Editor-in-Chief

Every month *Gourmet* magazine presents extraordinary menus that are captured in full-color photographs. The dishes are discussed by the food editors for months, as each is tested, tasted, and tested again until the flavor and presentation are just right. Then, on the appointed day, prop stylists, food stylist, and photographer spin their magic, and another *Gourmet* meal comes to life. The Menu Collection that follows is a photograph album of 24 such menus from the 1994 issues of the magazine.

Whether you are looking for an intimate dinner or a buffet for twelve, here you will find the perfect menu. For example, the Autumn Dinner for Two will make your guest feel very important indeed, because *everything* in this little meal is special. From the Sautéed Quail with Shiitake Port Sauce to the Caramelized Pear Charlottes with Persimmon, uncommon ingredients make for a memorable evening. The Southern New Year's Day Buffet, on the other hand, serves a crowd with ever-popular regional favorites such as Duck and Sausage Gumbo and Honey-Baked Ham.

When it comes to offering menus that dazzle, *Gourmet* excels. Our Bright Lights Big City Dinner begins with a light Lobster and Shrimp Bisque, continues with Baked Halibut with Warm Sherry Onion Vinaigrette gently herbed with fresh thyme, and concludes with unique Pavlovas with Kir Royale Sorbet and Kiwis. Or, perhaps, the Pan-Asian Luncheon on Maui, featuring Grilled Teriyaki Pork Chops with Pineapple Papaya Relish, will catch your eye.

For those times when only comfort food will do, however, turn to Chicken Dinners in the Kitchen, with a choice of hearty Chicken and Dumplings or Roast Chicken with Mashed-Potato Stuffing and Root Vegetables, or to a Sunday Supper of Old-Fashioned Meat Loaf and velvety-smooth Chocolate Cream Pie.

And, what would the holidays be without *Gourmet*? You'll find Roast Prime Ribs of Beef with Pink and Green Peppercorn Crust for Christmas Dinner; and Roast Turkey with Potato, Apple, and Prune Stuffing and Port Gravy for Thanksgiving. Or, why not try crispy duck breasts from the menu A Bird of a Different Feather?

Variety makes life interesting, and you will find plenty of choice here. As you leaf through page after page of delightful entertaining ideas, savor the possibilities.

A SOUTHERN
NEW YEAR'S DAY BUFFET

Crab-Meat Parmesan Canapés, p. 95

•

Duck and Sausage Gumbo, p. 143

Brown and White Rice, p. 144

Honey-Baked Ham

Black-Eyed Pea and Cabbage Slaw, p. 205

Thyme Corn Sticks, p. 105

Beaujolais Nouveau '93

Dixie Beer

•

Mocha Rum Cake, p. 221

Benne Seed Raisin Bars, p. 228

•

Serves 12

Crab-Meat Parmesan Canapés;
Thyme Corn Sticks

Duck and Sausage Gumbo

Mocha Rum Cake;
Benne Seed Raisin Bars

14

Chocolate Almond Sherry Cake
with Sherry Custard Sauce and Caramelized Pears

NEW YEAR'S EVE SUPPER

FOR TWO

Leek, Prosciutto, and Cheese Empanadas, p. 179

Mixed Greens with Walnut Vinaigrette, p. 195

•

Paella-Style Shellfish Pasta, p. 126

Veuve Clicquot La Grande Dame '85

•

*Chocolate Almond Sherry Cake with Sherry Custard Sauce
and Caramelized Pears, p. 219*

•

Serves 2

Leek, Prosciutto, and Cheese Empanadas;
Mixed Greens with Walnut Vinaigrette

CHICKEN DINNERS IN THE KITCHEN

Frisée Salad with Poached Eggs, p. 196

•

Chicken and Dumplings, p. 138

—or—

*Roast Chicken with Mashed-Potato Stuffing
and Root Vegetables, p. 137*

*Lolonis Private Reserve
Mendocino County Zinfandel '91*

•

Bread, Fruit, and Cheese

Prune Armagnac Gingerbread, p. 226

•

Serves 6

Frisée Salad with Poached Eggs;
Bread, Fruit, and Cheese

Chicken and Dumplings

Roast Chicken with Mashed-Potato Stuffing
and Root Vegetables

Curried Herring on Pumpernickel

APRÈS-SKATE DANISH-STYLE

Curried Herring on Pumpernickel, p. 96

Yellow Pea Soup, p. 118

Aalborg Akvavit

•

Glazed Smoked Pork Chops, p. 133

Green Beans, p. 173

Mustard Sauce, p. 213

Rye Bread

Carlsberg lager

•

Danish Applesauce Bread Crumb Pudding, p. 250

•

Serves 6

Yellow Pea Soup;
Glazed Smoked Pork Chops;
Green Beans; Mustard Sauce;
Rye Bread

BRIGHT LIGHTS
BIG CITY DINNER

Lobster and Shrimp Bisque, p. 116

•

Baked Halibut with Warm Sherry Onion Vinaigrette, p. 120

Lima Bean, Potato, and Garlic Purée with Potato Crisps, p. 174

Sautéed Spinach, p. 188

Castello della Sala Orvieto Classico '91

•

Pavlovas with Kir Royale Sorbet and Kiwis, p. 243

Château de Baun Sonoma County Brut Sparkling Wine

•

Serves 6

Pavlovas with Kir Royale Sorbet and Kiwis

Baked Halibut with Warm Sherry Onion Vinaigrette; Lima Bean,
Potato, and Garlic Purée with Potato Crisps; Sautéed Spinach

Mixed Baby Greens with Aniseed Vinaigrette
and Goat Cheese Crostini

AN EARLY SPRING DINNER

*Mixed Baby Greens with Aniseed Vinaigrette
and Goat Cheese Crostini, p. 194*

Marinated Lamb Chops, p. 136

Yellow Pepper Risotto, p. 169

Pencil-Thin Asparagus and Scallions, p. 171

La Casa Brunello di Montalcino '86

•

Lemon-Curd Strawberry Tart, p. 239

•

Serves 4

Marinated Lamb Chops; Yellow Pepper Risotto;
Pencil-Thin Asparagus and Scallions

EASTER DINNER

Grilled Portobello Mushrooms with Parmesan Crisps, p. 181

•

Crown Roast of Lamb, p. 135

Garlic Rosemary Jelly, p. 212

Minted Saffron Rice with Currants and Pine Nuts, p. 168

Glazed Baby Turnips and Carrots, p. 190

Chalk Hill Estate-Bottled Cabernet Sauvignon '90

•

Rhubarb Lemon Cake Roll, p. 227

White Chocolate Toasted Almond Semifreddo, p. 228

•

Serves 6

Crown Roast of Lamb; Minted Saffron Rice with
Currants and Pine Nuts; Glazed Baby Turnips
and Carrots; Garlic Rosemary Jelly

Grilled Portobello Mushrooms with Parmesan Crisp

Red Leaf Lettuce and Watercress Salad with Buttermilk Dressing

SUNDAY SUPPER

Old-Fashioned Meat Loaf, p. 131

Scalloped Potatoes, p. 186

Buttered Peas, p. 183

*Red-Leaf Lettuce and Watercress Salad with
Buttermilk Dressing, p. 197*

St. Francis Estate-Bottled Sonoma Valley Merlot '90

•

Chocolate Cream Pie, p. 234

•

Serves 4 to 6

Old-Fashioned Meat Loaf;
Scalloped Potatoes; Buttered Peas

A NEW ORLEANS
COURTYARD DINNER

Fried Crawfish Rémoulade, p. 124

Guenoc Chardonnay '92

•

Grilled Spiced Chicken Breasts, p. 138

Creole Sauce with Yellow Peppers, p. 139

Tasso Grits Batons, p. 167

Haricots Verts, p. 174

Ridge Vineyards Geyserville Zinfandel '90

•

Praline Pecan Tarts, p. 240

Strawberries

•

Serves 6

Grilled Spiced Chicken Breasts; Creole Sauce with
Yellow Peppers; Tasso Grits Batons; Haricots Verts

Praline Pecan Tarts; Strawberries

A PAN-ASIAN LUNCHEON
ON MAUI

Scallop and Corn Pot Stickers with Sesame Vinaigrette, p. 124

Grilled Teriyaki Pork Chops with Pineapple Papaya Relish, p. 134

Bean-Thread Noodles with Shiitake and Vegetables, p. 164

Sautéed Snow Peas, p. 183

Jekel Vineyards Arroyo Seco Johannisberg Riesling '91

•

Macadamia Coconut Cake, p. 224

•

Serves 6

Scallop and Corn Pot Stickers
with Sesame Vinaigrette

Macadamia Coconut Cake

Grilled Teriyaki Pork Chops with Pineapple
Papaya Relish; Bean-Thread Noodles with
Shiitake and Vegetables; Sautéed Snow Peas

43

A TASTE OF THAILAND

Spiced Shrimp Soup, p. 119

•

Roast Marinated Cornish Hens, p. 142

Sweet Chili Sauce, p. 143

Rice Noodles with Garlic and Herbs, p. 164

Minted Eggplant Rounds, p. 178

Cucumber Carrot Salad, p. 200

Van Duzer Willamette Valley Vineyards Dry Riesling '92

•

Sticky Rice with Mango, p. 253

•

Serves 6

Spiced Shrimp Soup

Sticky Rice with Mango

Roast Marinated Cornish Hen; Sweet Chili Sauce;
Rice Noodles with Garlic and Herbs;
Minted Eggplant Rounds

Baked Alaska Peanut S'mores

DINNER FROM THE GRILL

Grilled Rosemary Garlic Shrimp, p. 126

Grilled Tortilla and Onion Cake, p. 182

Wilted Red Cabbage and Bell Pepper Slaw, p. 204

Pieropan Soave Classico Superiore '92

•

Baked Alaska Peanut S'mores, p. 243

•

Serves 4

Grilled Rosemary Garlic Shrimp; Grilled Tortilla and Onion Cake;
Wilted Red Cabbage and Bell Pepper Slaw

FOURTH OF JULY
FAMILY REUNION PICNIC

Tomatillo and Yellow Tomato Salsa with Tortilla Chips, p. 99

Chipotle Mayonnaise Dip with Carrots, p. 98

Corona Beer

•

Grilled Turkey Burgers, p. 148

Homemade Tomato Ketchup, p. 214

Grilled Sausages, p. 135

*Tomato, Cucumber, and Avocado with
Lemon Vinaigrette,* p. 203

Herbed Tricolor Pasta Salad, p. 206

Cumin Corn on the Cob, p. 177

Sutter Home Cabernet Sauvignon '91

Pink Lemonade

•

*Orange and Sour-Cream Drop Shortcakes with
Assorted Berries,* p. 226

Date Walnut Yogurt Ice Cream, p. 244

•

Serves 12

Tomatillo and Yellow Tomato Salsa with Tortilla Chips;
Chipotle Mayonnaise Dip with Carrots

Clockwise from far left: Cumin Corn on the Cob; Herbed Tricolor Pasta Salad; Tortilla Chips; Tomato, Cucumber, and Avocado with Lemon Vinaigrette; Grilled Turkey Burgers; Grilled Sausages; Assorted Mustards; Homemade Tomato Ketchup

Lemon Fennel Shrimp with Tarragon

COCKTAILS AFTER TENNIS

Spicy Cumin Cheese Straws, p. 88

Tomato and Bacon Salad in Bibb Lettuce Cups, p. 95

Lemon Fennel Shrimp with Tarragon, p. 94

Antipasto-Stuffed Baguettes, p. 88

Orange Rum Rickeys, p. 255

Vodka Coolers, p. 256

•

Serves 8

Orange Rum Rickeys; Vodka Coolers;
Spicy Cumin Cheese Straws;
Tomato and Bacon Salad in Bibb Lettuce Cups

Orange and
Radish Salad;
French Bread

A MOROCCAN FEAST

*Hard-Cooked Eggs with Cumin,
Coarse Salt, and Cayenne*, p. 90

Black Olives with Harissa, p. 91

Cracked Green Olives with Herbs and Preserved Lemon, p. 92

French Bread　　　*Coriander Eggplant Salad*, p. 200

Orange and Radish Salad, p. 203

Red Onion, Parsley, and Preserved Lemon Salad, p. 201

Boissière Dry Vermouth with Club Soda

•

Moroccan Chicken and Almond Pies, p. 141

Fish Chermoula, p. 122

Simi Winery Sendal '91

•

Honey Nut Candies, p. 248　　　*Fresh Fruit*

Moroccan Mint Tea, p. 257

•

Serves 6

Moroccan Chicken and Almond Pies;
Black Olives with Harissa

Fish Chermoula

Honey Nut Candies;
Melon, Grapes, Dates;
Moroccan Mint Tea

Watermelon Sorbet with Chocolate Seeds

SUPPER ON THE PORCH

Grilled Rib-Eye Steaks with Béarnaise Butter, p. 127

Corn Boats with Zucchini and Pepper Jack Cheese, p. 177

Potato Salad with Garlic Mayonnaise and Chives, p. 202

Vine-Ripened Cherry Tomatoes

Alain Graillot Crozes-Hermitage '91

•

Watermelon Sorbet with Chocolate Seeds, p. 244

•

Serves 4

Grilled Rib-Eye Steaks with Béarnaise Butter;
Corn Boats with Zucchini and Pepper Jack
Cheese; Potato Salad with Garlic Mayonnaise
and Chives; Vine-Ripened Cherry Tomatoes

A SMALL GARDEN
WEDDING

Salmon Caviar Torte, p. 93

Green and White Crudités with Herbed Anise Dip, p. 98

*Cold Shrimp and Vegetable Spring Rolls with
Cashew Dipping Sauce, p. 94*

Smoked Chicken with Mango and Mint, p. 89

Dr. Fischer Ockfener Bockstein Spätlese '92

•

Lobster, Corn, Zucchini, and Basil Salad, p. 192

*Fillet of Beef with Arugula, Cherry Tomatoes,
and Roasted Garlic Vinaigrette, p. 127*

Wild Rice and Orzo with Toasted Walnuts, p. 170

Mesclun Salad, p. 196

Miniature Cloverleaf Rolls, p. 101

Kent Rasmussen Carneros Pinot Noir '91

•

Lemon Raspberry Wedding Cake, p. 222
Crème Fraîche Ice Cream, p. 224

•

Serves 12

Cold Shrimp and Vegetable Spring Rolls with
Cashew Dipping Sauce; Smoked Chicken with
Mango and Mint; Salmon Caviar Torte with Toast Points

Fillet of Beef with Arugula, Cherry Tomatoes, and
Roasted Garlic Vinaigrette; Lobster, Corn, Zucchini,
and Basil Salad; Wild Rice and Orzo with Toasted
Walnuts; Miniature Cloverleaf Rolls; Mesclun Salad

Granola and Dried Cranberry Chocolate Chip Cookies

A HIKERS' PICNIC

Chilled Yellow Pepper and Scallion Buttermilk Soup, p. 118

Azuki Bean and Vegetable Salad in Pita Bread, p. 197

•

Granola and Dried Cranberry Chocolate Chip Cookies, p. 231

Apples

•

Serves 6

Chilled Yellow Pepper and Scallion
Buttermilk Soup; Azuki Bean and
Vegetable Salad in Pita Bread

OKTOBERFEST

Beet and Fennel Soup, p. 112

Pumpernickel and Rye Breadsticks, p. 105

•

Roast Pork Loin with Beer Sauce, p. 132

Red Onion Sauerkraut, p. 183

Celery Root, Gruyère, and Apple Slaw with Horseradish, p. 204

Warm German Potato Salad, p. 202

*Beck's beer, Würzburger Hofbrau Fallfest Beer,
and/or your local microbrewery favorites*

•

Chocolate Almond Torte, p. 218

Sour Cherry Compote, p. 219

•

Serves 6

Beet and Fennel Soup;
Pumpernickel and Rye Breadsticks

Chocolate Almond Torte;
Sour Cherry Compote

Roast Pork Loin with Beer Sauce; Red Onion Sauerkraut;
Celery Root, Gruyère, and Apple Slaw with Horseradish;
Warm German Potato Salad

71

Caramelized Pear Charlotte with Persimmon

AUTUMN DINNER FOR TWO

Sautéed Quail with Shiitake Port Sauce, p. 146

Bulgur, Pine Nut, and Red Pepper Pilaf, p. 167

Broccoli Rabe with Sherry Vinegar, p. 175

Château Gruaud Larose Grand Cru Classé Saint-Julien '85

•

Caramelized Pear Charlottes with Persimmon, p. 246

Taylor Fladgate Ten-Year-Old Tawny Port

Serves 2

Sautéed Quail with Shiitake Port Sauce; Bulgur, Pine Nut,
and Red Pepper Pilaf; Broccoli Rabe with Sherry Vinegar

THANKSGIVING

DINNER

Herbed Goat Cheese, Roasted Beet,
and Watercress Salad, p. 198

Columbia Crest Columbia Valley Chardonnay '92

•

Roast Turkey with Potato, Apple,
and Prune Stuffing and Port Gravy, p. 146

Cranberry Quince Chutney, p. 212

Jerusalem Artichoke and Sage Gratin, p. 172

Roasted Carrots and Parsnips, p. 175

Balsamic-Glazed Pearl Onions, p. 182

Sautéed Persimmons and Green Beans
with Chives, p. 173

Ravenswood Dickerson Vineyard
Napa Valley Zinfandel '91

•

Pear and Pumpkin Pie, p. 234

Ginger Crème Anglaise, p. 217

Chocolate, Orange, and Chestnut Pavé, p. 249

Ficklin Vintage California Port '83

•

Serves 8

Roast Turkey with Potato, Apple, and Prune
Stuffing; Jerusalem Artichoke and Sage Gratin;
Port Gravy; Roasted Carrots and Parsnips;
Cranberry Quince Chutney; Sautéed Persimmons and
Green Beans with Chives; Balsamic-Glazed Pearl Onions

Grape and Rosemary Focaccia

A BIRD OF

A DIFFERENT FEATHER

Red-Wine–Braised Duck Legs with Roasted Pears and Onions, p. 145

Bedell Cellars Merlot '91

—*or*—

Crispy Duck Breasts with Pear and Green Peppercorn Sauce, p. 144

Harvest Wild Rice, p. 170

Sautéed Kale with Cracklings and Garlic Bread Crumbs, p. 178

Grape and Rosemary Focaccia, p. 101

Reichsgraf von Kesselstatt Josephshöfer Riesling Spätlese '92

•

Thyme-Scented Apple Galette, p. 237

•

Serves 4

Red-Wine–Braised Duck Legs with Roasted Pears
and Onions; Harvest Wild Rice; Sautéed Kale with
Cracklings and Garlic Bread Crumbs

CHRISTMAS DINNER

Warm Salad of Seared Scallops, Haricots Verts, and
Bell Peppers in Walnut Vinaigrette, p. 193

Casteller Herrenberg Müller-Thurgau '92
Fürstlich Castell'sches Domäenamt

•

Roast Prime Ribs of Beef with Pink and Green Peppercorn
Crust and Red-Wine Pan Sauce, p. 128

Potato and Porcini Gratin, p. 183

Broccoli and Cauliflower with
Horseradish Bread Crumbs, p. 174

Rosemary Popovers, p. 105

Sterling Vineyards Winery Lake Carneros Pinot Noir '92

•

Chocolate Praline Croquembouche, p. 240

Blandy's 10-Year-Old Malmsey Madeira

•

Serves 8

Warm Salad of Seared Scallops,
Haricots Verts, and Bell Peppers
in Walnut Vinaigrette

Roast Prime Ribs of Beef with Pink and
Green Peppercorn Crust and Red-Wine Pan Sauce;
Potato and Porcini Gratin; Broccoli and Cauliflower with
Horseradish Bread Crumbs; Rosemary Popovers

Nose-Warmer Punch; Crisp Spiced Nuts

A CAROLING PARTY

Crisp Spiced Nuts, p. 90

Nose-Warmer Punch, p. 255

•

Hearty Goulash Soup, p. 114

Viennese Cucumber Salad, p. 199

Marinated Vegetables with Mustard Dill Dressing, p. 190

Fess Parker Santa Barbara County Syrah '92

•

Austrian Sweet Cheese Crêpes Baked in Custard, p. 251

Apricot Caramel Sauce, p. 252

•

Serves 12

Hearty Goulash Soup; Viennese Cucumber Salad

A RECIPE
COMPENDIUM

Here we have it all — tasty hors d'oeuvres, heartwarming soups, moist muffins, unusual pizzas, flavorful meats and poultry, succulent fish and shellfish, comforting pastas, innovative vegetables, crisp salads, refreshing beverages, and, of course, glorious desserts. This section holds over 450 of the best recipes that appeared in *Gourmet* magazine during 1994, including all the dishes from *Gourmet*'s Menus and Cuisine Courante (pictured in The Menu Collection), as well as favorites from the magazine's other food columns — In Short Order, Twice as Good, The Last Touch, and Forbidden Pleasures. Recipes from special articles also appear.

Most people think you need hours in the kitchen to prepare exciting food, but In Short Order dishes prove that marvelous fare for two can be made in 45 minutes or less. Who would guess that Yellow Squash and Bell Pepper Soup; Seared Salmon with Horseradish Mustard Vinaigrette; Crispy Cauliflower with Olives, Capers, and Parsley; or Individual Coconut Rum Chocolate Cakes can be made so quickly! Other time-savers come from Twice as Good, where leftovers from one fabulous meal are used to make another — our Rump Roast with Vegetables can be transformed into our savory Deviled Beef Miroton a few days later.

Sometimes a perfect little addition turns an ordinary meal into something special, and recipes from The Last Touch fit the bill. For example, flavored oils can make all the difference — Lemon Spiced Oil adds a zing to rice dishes, Pesto Oil makes mashed potatoes memorable, and Chipotle Pepper Oil warms up roasted chicken.

When you are ready to throw caution to the wind, Forbidden Pleasures recipes offer naughty splurges, such as the ever-so-decadent Raspberry Chocolate Meringue Icebox Cake. This sweet indulgence is filled with bittersweet chocolate, raspberries, and heavy cream. And, finally, our feature articles showcase seasonal dishes, including hearty baked pastas for cold winter nights, cool soups for sizzling summers, and tempting apple pies and tarts for crisp autumn days.

Take time to peruse this exceptional collection of versatile recipes. Pick your favorites, gather your friends, and enjoy.

HORS D'OEUVRES, CANAPÉS, DIPS AND SPREADS

HORS D'OEUVRES

Anchovy Puffs

a 2-ounce can flat anchovies, rinsed, patted dry, and minced
3 tablespoons mayonnaise
2 sheets (1 pound) frozen puff pastry, thawed
an egg wash made by beating 1 large egg with 1 tablespoon water

In a small bowl with a fork mash anchovies with mayonnaise. On a lightly floured surface roll out both sheets of pastry into 14-inch squares and trim edges to form 13-inch squares. Brush off excess flour and spread anchovy mayonnaise evenly over 1 pastry sheet. Cover with remaining pastry sheet and press sheets together gently.

Preheat oven to 375° F. and lightly grease baking sheets.

With a 3- to 4-inch decorative cutter, such as a fish, cut pastry into shapes. Reserve scraps and cut into bite-size pieces to bake separately. (To eliminate scraps, forego decorative shapes altogether and simply cut pastry into squares.)

Arrange pastries on prepared baking sheets and brush tops with egg wash. With the edge of a cookie cutter or the back of a sharp knife score fish. Bake pastries in oven until puffed and golden, 12 to 15 minutes. Makes about 24 anchovy puffs plus scraps.

Antipasto-Stuffed Baguettes

2 small thin *baguettes* (each about 16 by 2 by 1 inch)
about ¼ cup bottled olive paste or *tapenade**
4 ounces mild goat cheese
¼ pound thinly sliced Genoa salami or smoked turkey
2 cups packed *arugula* leaves, washed well and spun dry
a 7-ounce jar roasted red peppers, drained, rinsed, and patted dry
a 13- to 14-ounce can whole artichoke hearts, drained, rinsed, patted dry, and chopped

*available at specialty foods shops and some supermarkets

Cut top third off each *baguette* horizontally with a serrated knife and remove soft crumb from tops and bottoms, leaving shells about ½ inch thick.

Spread about 1 tablespoon olive paste or *tapenade* on inside of each bottom shell and top with goat cheese, spreading it evenly. Fold salami or turkey slices in half and fit them in an even layer over cheese in each shell. Arrange half of *arugula* on each meat layer and top with a layer of roasted peppers. Divide artichoke hearts between bottom shells and spread inside of top shells with remaining olive paste.

Fit top shells over bottom shells and press *baguettes* together, re-forming loaves. Wrap each *baguette* tightly in foil and chill at least 3 hours or overnight.

Cut each *baguette* diagonally into 12 slices with a serrated knife and secure each slice with a wooden pick. Makes 24 hors d'oeuvres.

Spicy Cumin Cheese Straws

4 ounces extra-sharp Cheddar cheese, shredded fine (about 1¼ cups)
½ teaspoon ground cumin
¼ teaspoon cayenne, or to taste
1 sheet (about ½ pound) frozen puff pastry, thawed
an egg wash made by beating 1 large egg with 2 teaspoons water
1 tablespoon cuminseed
coarse sea salt to taste

In a small bowl toss together cheese, ground cumin, and cayenne.

On a lightly floured surface roll out pastry into a 14- by 12-inch rectangle and brush with some egg wash. Cut pastry in half crosswise, forming two 12- by 7-inch rectangles. Sprinkle cheese mixture over 1 rectangle and top with other rectangle, egg-wash side down, pressing it firmly to force out any air pockets. Roll pastry out slightly to make layers adhere (rectangle should be about 12½ by 7½ inches). Brush pastry with some remaining egg wash and sprinkle evenly with cuminseed and sea salt.

With a pastry wheel or sharp knife cut pastry into strips about 7½ inches long and ½ inch wide. Twist strips and arrange on a baking sheet, pressing ends onto sheet to keep strips twisted. *Cheese straws may be prepared up to this point 2 weeks ahead. Freeze cheese straws on baking sheets 1 hour, or until frozen, and transfer to a resealable freezer bag. Do not thaw cheese straws before proceeding.*

Preheat oven to 425° F. and grease 2 baking sheets.

Arrange half of cheese straws about 1 inch apart on 1 baking sheet and bake in middle of oven 10 to 12 minutes, or until pale golden. Bake remaining cheese straws in same manner.

Serve cheese straws warm or at room temperature. Makes about 24 cheese straws.

PHOTO ON PAGE 55

Smoked Chicken with Mango and Mint

2½ tablespoons white-wine vinegar
⅓ cup olive oil
1½ pounds smoked boneless chicken breasts*,
    skinned and cut into ¾-inch pieces
3 to 4 firm-ripe mangoes
about 48 fresh mint leaves
about 48 wooden picks

Garnish: mint sprigs

*available at some specialty foods shops

In a small bowl whisk together vinegar, oil, and salt and pepper to taste. In a resealable plastic bag combine chicken with oil mixture and marinate, chilled, at least 8 hours or overnight.

Cut mangoes by slicing just to sides of each pit and with a ¾-inch melon-ball cutter scoop flesh from mango halves. (There should be about 48 mango pieces.) *Mango may be scooped 8 hours ahead and chilled, covered.*

Just before serving, assemble hors d'oeuvres by threading 1 chicken piece, 1 mint leaf, and 1 mango piece on each pick and arrange on a platter. Sprinkle hors d'oeuvres with freshly ground black pepper if desired and garnish with mint sprigs. Makes about 48 hors d'oeuvres.

PHOTO ON PAGE 63

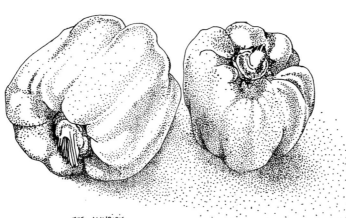

ZOE MAVRIDIS

Pepper Jack Crackers

1 stick (½ cup) unsalted butter, softened
½ pound pepper Jack cheese, grated coarse
1 large egg, separated
1 teaspoon salt, or to taste
¾ teaspoon cayenne, or to taste
1 cup all-purpose flour

Preheat oven to 375° F. and grease 2 baking sheets.

In a food processor blend together butter and cheese until smooth. Add egg yolk, salt, and cayenne and blend until combined. Add flour and blend until mixture just forms a dough.

Working in batches, transfer dough to a pastry bag fitted with a ⅞-inch-wide ribbon tip and pipe dough in long strips 2 inches apart on baking sheets. (Alternatively, working in batches, dough may be transferred to a cookie press fitted with a ribbon disk and pressed out in long strips 2 inches apart on baking sheets.) Dough strips may break in places but repairs are not necessary, as strips will be cut later.

In a small bowl whisk together egg white and a pinch salt until just combined. Brush each strip of dough with some egg white and bake in batches in middle of oven until golden brown, about 10 to 15 minutes. While crackers are still hot, slice diagonally into 1½-inch-long pieces and cool completely on racks. *Crackers keep in airtight containers 5 days.* Makes about 95 crackers.

*Hard-Cooked Eggs with Cumin,
Coarse Salt, and Cayenne*

1 tablespoon cuminseed
1 teaspoon coriander seeds
6 hard-cooked large eggs, halved
2 tablespoons coarse salt, or to taste
1 tablespoon cayenne, or to taste

In a small skillet dry-roast cuminseed and coriander seeds over moderate heat, shaking the skillet, until fragrant, being careful not to burn them. In a mortar with a pestle, an electric spice grinder, or a cleaned coffee grinder grind seeds fine.

Arrange egg halves on a platter and sprinkle with some of cumin mixture, salt, and cayenne. Serves 6.

Crisp Spiced Nuts

2 large egg whites
1½ teaspoons salt
¾ cup sugar
2 teaspoons Worcestershire sauce
2 tablespoons paprika (preferably Hungarian sweet*)
1½ teaspoons cayenne
1½ cups whole blanched almonds (about ½ pound)
1½ cups hazelnuts (about ½ pound)
1½ cups pecans (about ½ pound)
¾ stick (6 tablespoons) unsalted butter, melted and cooled

*available at specialty foods shops and many supermarkets

Preheat oven to 325° F.

In a bowl with an electric mixer beat whites with salt until very foamy and gradually beat in sugar, Worcestershire sauce, paprika, and cayenne. Stir in nuts and butter, combining well, and spread in a large shallow baking pan.

Bake nuts in middle of oven, stirring every 10 minutes, until crisp and golden, about 30 to 40 minutes. Spread nuts on a sheet of foil and cool. Break up nut clusters. *Nuts may be made 1 week ahead and kept in an airtight container at room temperature.* Makes about 4½ cups.

PHOTO ON PAGE 84

Hot Curried Party Mix

6 cups mixed Chex cereals (rice, whole-grain, and corn)
1½ cups sesame sticks* if desired
1½ cups small thin pretzels
1 cup pecans
1 cup roasted peanuts
½ stick (¼ cup) unsalted butter
1 tablespoon soy sauce
2 teaspoons curry powder
2 teaspoons sugar
½ to ¾ teaspoon cayenne
¼ teaspoon salt

*available at natural foods stores and many supermarkets

Preheat oven to 250° F.
In a large bowl toss together cereals, sesame sticks, pretzels, and nuts. In a small saucepan melt butter with soy sauce over moderately low heat and whisk in curry powder, sugar, cayenne, and salt. Drizzle butter mixture over cereal, tossing well, and spread in a shallow roasting pan. Bake mixture 1 hour and transfer to a bowl to cool completely. *Party mix keeps in an airtight container 1 month.* Makes about 12 cups.

Sweet-and-Spicy Nuts

2 cups unsalted mixed nuts such as pecans and whole almonds
1½ tablespoons unsalted butter
2 tablespoons firmly packed brown sugar
1½ tablespoons granulated sugar
½ teaspoon cayenne
½ teaspoon freshly ground black pepper
1 teaspoon salt

In a heavy skillet cook nuts in butter over moderate heat, stirring, 2 minutes. In a bowl stir together sugars, cayenne, black pepper, and salt and sprinkle mixture over nuts. Continue to cook nuts, stirring constantly, until sugar caramelizes, about 8 minutes. Transfer nuts to a sheet of foil and cool. Break nuts apart. *Nuts may be made 3 days ahead and kept in an airtight container.* Makes 2 cups.

Black Olives with Harissa

1 pound oil-cured black olives (preferably Moroccan)*
For harissa
1 teaspoon cuminseed
½ teaspoon coriander seeds
½ teaspoon caraway seeds
2 hot red dried chilies*, stemmed but not seeded (about 2 inches in length)
2 garlic cloves
½ teaspoon coarse salt, or to taste
1 medium red bell pepper, roasted (procedure follows) and chopped coarse
1 tablespoon olive oil

*available at Middle Eastern or Mediterranean markets, some specialty foods shops, or by mail order from Kalustyan's, 123 Lexington Avenue, New York, NY 10016, tel. (212) 685-3451

In a colander rinse olives under cold water 1 minute and in a bowl cover with cold water. Soak olives 4 hours to remove excess salt and drain well.
Make harissa:
In a mortar with a pestle, an electric spice grinder, or a cleaned coffee grinder grind seeds fine. If using mortar and pestle, add chilies, garlic, and salt and pound to a paste. If using a spice or coffee grinder, transfer seeds to a small food processor and add chilies, garlic, and salt. Grind mixture to a paste. Add pepper and oil and pound or purée to a coarse paste.
In a large bowl stir together *harissa* and olives and marinate, covered and chilled, at least 6 hours or overnight. *Olives may be prepared 1 week ahead and chilled, covered.*
Serve olives at room temperature. Makes 3 cups.

PHOTO ON PAGE 57

To Roast Peppers

Using a long-handled fork, char peppers over an open flame or on a rack set over an electric burner, turning, until skins are blackened, 4 to 6 minutes. (Or broil peppers on rack of a broiler pan under a preheated broiler about 2 inches from heat, turning every 5 minutes, 15 to 20 minutes, or until skins are blistered and charred.) Transfer peppers to a bowl and let stand, covered, until cool enough to handle. Keeping peppers whole, peel them, starting at blossom end. Cut off pepper tops and discard seeds and ribs. (Wear rubber gloves when handling chilies.)

Cracked Green Olives with Herbs and Preserved Lemon

1 pound small to medium brine-cured green olives
    (preferably cracked)*
¼ cup chopped fresh coriander
3 tablespoons chopped fresh mint leaves
peel of ½ preserved lemon**, cut
    into julienne strips, plus 3 tablespoons
    preserved lemon juice or
    fresh lemon juice to taste
2 tablespoons olive oil
2 garlic cloves,
    minced
¼ teaspoon ground coriander
a pinch dried hot red pepper flakes

*available at Middle Eastern and Mediterranean
    markets, specialty foods shops, or by mail order
    from Kalustyan's, 123 Lexington Avenue,
    New York, NY 10016, tel. (212) 685-3451
**available by mail order from The Gardener,
    1836 Fourth Street, Berkeley, CA 94710,
    tel. (510) 548-4545, or recipe follows

If using uncracked whole olives, crush lightly with flat side of a large knife on a cutting board. In a large bowl cover olives with cold water and soak 4 hours to remove excess salt. Drain olives well. In a bowl stir together olives and remaining ingredients and marinate, covered and chilled, at least 6 hours or overnight. *Olives may be prepared 1 week ahead and chilled, covered.*

Serve olives at room temperature. Makes 3 cups.

Paula Wolfert's Seven-Day Preserved Lemons

4 large (about 6 ounces each) lemons (preferably
    thin-skinned), scrubbed
⅔ cup kosher salt
1 cup fresh lemon juice (from about 5 large
    lemons)
olive oil

Dry lemons well and cut each into 8 wedges. In a bowl toss wedges with salt and transfer to a glass jar (about 6-cup capacity). Add lemon juice and cover jar with a tight-fitting glass lid or plastic-coated lid. Let lemons stand at room temperature 7 days, shaking jar each day to redistribute salt and juice. Add oil to cover lemons and store, covered and chilled, up to 6 months. Makes 4 preserved lemons.

Herbed Olives

3 cups (about ¾ pound) mixed black and green
    brine-cured olives, such as Kalamata, *picholine*,
    and Gaeta
3 tablespoons olive oil
1 to 1½ tablespoons minced fresh rosemary
    and/or thyme leaves or 1 to 1½ teaspoons
    dried, crumbled
1 teaspoon freshly grated lemon zest
2 garlic cloves, sliced thin lengthwise
½ teaspoon fennel seeds, or to taste, crushed
¼ teaspoon dried hot red pepper flakes, or to taste

In a container with a tight-fitting lid combine all ingredients with salt and pepper to taste and chill, shaking occasionally, at least 1 day and up to 1 week.

Serve olives at room temperature. Makes 3 cups.

Oven-Fried Potato Chips with Thyme

6 tablespoons vegetable oil
3 russet (baking) potatoes (about 1½ pounds)
1½ teaspoons dried thyme, crumbled

Preheat oven to 400° F. and brush 2 large baking sheets well with some oil.

Peel potatoes and with a *mandoline* or other hand-held slicing device cut lengthwise into ⅛-inch-thick slices. Immediately arrange potatoes in one layer on baking sheets and brush with remaining oil.

Bake potatoes in middle of oven until golden, 12 to 15 minutes, and while still warm transfer with a metal spatula to racks. Sprinkle with thyme and salt to taste. *Chips may be made 3 days ahead. Cool chips completely and keep in an airtight container at room temperature.* Serves 4.

Salmon Caviar Torte

6 tablespoons mayonnaise
¾ stick unsalted butter, melted and cooled
8 hard-cooked large eggs, chopped fine
½ cup finely chopped celery
⅓ cup finely chopped red onion
1½ tablespoons fresh lemon juice, or to taste
¼ cup finely chopped scallion greens
¼ cup minced fresh chives
¼ cup minced fresh dill
8 ounces cream cheese, softened
½ cup sour cream
6 ounces salmon caviar

Garnish: dill sprigs
Accompaniments: pumpernickel toast points and
　　rye toast points

In a bowl whisk together mayonnaise and butter and stir in eggs, celery, onion, lemon juice, and salt and pepper to taste. Spread mixture in an oiled 9-inch springform pan and sprinkle evenly with scallion greens, chives, and dill.

In a small bowl stir together cream cheese and sour cream until smooth. Drop dollops of cream-cheese mixture over herbs and spread carefully (keeping herb layer intact) to form an even topping. *Chill torte, covered, at least 8 hours and up to 1 day.*

Just before serving, run a thin knife around edge of pan and remove side. Transfer torte to a serving plate and spread caviar over top. Garnish torte with dill sprigs and serve with toast points. Serves 12.

PHOTO ON PAGE 62

Spicy Shortbread Bites

2 tablespoons paprika
2½ teaspoons coarse salt
1⅛ teaspoons cayenne
7 tablespoons unsalted butter,
　　softened
2 tablespoons sugar
1 cup all-purpose flour
1 teaspoon curry powder
½ teaspoon ground cumin

Preheat oven to 350° F.

In a small bowl whisk together paprika, 2 teaspoons salt, and 1 teaspoon cayenne and set aside.

In a bowl with an electric mixer beat butter with sugar until light and fluffy. In another bowl whisk together remaining ½ teaspoon salt, remaining ⅛ teaspoon cayenne, flour, curry powder, and cumin. Beat flour mixture into butter mixture until just combined.

On a lightly floured surface knead dough about 8 times, or until it just comes together. Divide dough into 4 equal pieces. On a sheet of wax paper roll each piece of dough into a ¾-inch-thick log. Sprinkle one quarter of spice mixture along the length of each log and roll in mixture to coat completely.

Wrap each log in wax paper. Freeze dough just until firm, 15 to 20 minutes. *Shortbread dough may be made 1 week ahead and frozen. Before proceeding with recipe, remove dough from freezer and let stand about 15 minutes, or until slightly softened to facilitate slicing.*

Remove logs carefully from wax paper and slice into ½-inch-thick rounds. Place rounds ¼ inch apart on ungreased baking sheets and bake in batches in middle of oven 15 minutes, or until browned lightly.

Gently loosen shortbread bites with a spatula from baking sheet (do not remove from sheet) and cool completely. Carefully transfer shortbread bites to a serving dish (they will be fragile) and serve as an hors d'oeuvre. Makes about 140 shortbread bites.

Cold Shrimp and Vegetable Spring Rolls with Cashew Dipping Sauce

1 pound large shrimp (about 15), shelled and deveined
¾ cup finely shredded carrot
¼ cup finely chopped scallion greens
1 teaspoon rice vinegar, or to taste
twelve 6½-inch rounds of rice paper*
¾ cup fresh coriander leaves
¾ cup finely shredded Bibb lettuce
¾ cup alfalfa sprouts

Garnish: coriander sprigs
Accompaniment: cashew dipping sauce
   (recipe follows)

*available at Asian markets

In a saucepan of boiling salted water cook shrimp until just cooked through, 1 to 2 minutes, and drain. Let shrimp cool and cut into ¼-inch pieces.

In a small bowl toss carrot with scallion greens, vinegar, and salt and pepper to taste.

Fill a small shallow baking pan or cake pan with warm water. Working with 4 sheets rice paper at a time, immerse them in water and let stand until very pliable, about 45 seconds. Carefully arrange soaked sheets in a single layer on paper towels to drain. Working with 1 soaked sheet at a time and keeping remaining sheets covered with dampened paper towels, put sheet on a clean dry work surface and arrange about 1 tablespoon coriander leaves in a horizontal line across bottom, leaving a 1-inch border on bottom edge and on each side. Top coriander with about 2 tablespoons shrimp pieces and top shrimp with about 1 tablespoon carrot mixture. Sprinkle about 1 tablespoon lettuce, about 1 tablespoon sprouts, and salt and pepper to taste over carrot mixture. Roll up filling tightly in sheet, folding in 2 sides of sheet to completely enclose filling, and continue rolling.

Make more spring rolls in same manner with remaining 3 soaked sheets. Transfer assembled rolls to a tray and cover with dampened paper towels. Repeat procedure with remaining 8 rice paper sheets and filling ingredients. Tightly cover tray with plastic wrap (keeping dampened paper towels directly on spring rolls). *Spring rolls may be made 6 hours ahead and chilled.*

Just before serving, with a serrated knife cut spring rolls in half diagonally. Arrange spring rolls on a platter and garnish with coriander sprigs. Serve spring rolls with cashew dipping sauce. Makes 24 hors d'oeuvres.

PHOTO ON PAGE 62

Cashew Dipping Sauce

1 cup unsalted roasted cashews (about ¼ pound)
1 tablespoon vegetable oil
¾ cup plain yogurt
2 garlic cloves, minced
1 tablespoon fresh lemon juice, or to taste
1 tablespoon soy sauce, or to taste
cayenne to taste

In a food processor blend cashews with oil, scraping down sides, until mixture forms a paste. Add remaining ingredients and salt and black pepper to taste and blend until smooth. *Dipping sauce may be made 4 days ahead and chilled, covered. Return dipping sauce to room temperature before serving.* Makes about 1½ cups.

Lemon Fennel Shrimp with Tarragon

1 pound medium shrimp (about 32)
4 tablespoons fresh lemon juice
2 teaspoons fennel seeds, crushed
a pinch dried hot red pepper flakes if desired
6 tablespoons olive oil
3 large garlic cloves, crushed
½ lemon, sliced thin
2 teaspoons finely chopped fresh tarragon leaves

Garnish: tarragon sprig

In a large saucepan of salted boiling water cook shrimp 1 minute, or until just cooked through. In a colander drain shrimp and rinse under cold water until cool. Shell and if desired devein shrimp.

In a bowl or plastic container whisk together lemon juice, fennel seeds, red pepper flakes, and salt and pepper to taste and add oil in a stream, whisking.

Stir in shrimp, garlic, and sliced lemon and marinate, covered and chilled, stirring occasionally, at least 6 hours or overnight. Stir in chopped tarragon. Serve shrimp garnished with tarragon sprig. Serves 8 as an hors d'oeuvre.

PHOTO ON PAGE 54

Tomato and Bacon Salad in Bibb Lettuce Cups

4 vine-ripened tomatoes, seeded and chopped fine
   (about 2 cups)
6 slices bacon, cooked until crisp and crumbled
¼ cup finely chopped sweet onion, or to taste
2 tablespoons olive oil (preferably extra-virgin)
2 teaspoons balsamic vinegar, or to taste
24 outer Bibb lettuce leaves (about 4 heads),
   washed and patted dry
about ¼ cup finely shredded fresh basil leaves

Garnish: fresh basil sprigs

In a bowl toss together tomatoes, bacon, onion, oil, vinegar, and salt and pepper to taste. Spoon mixture into lettuce leaves and sprinkle with shredded basil.

Serve lettuce cups on a platter garnished with basil sprigs. Makes 24 hors d'oeuvres.

PHOTO ON PAGE 55

Pepper-Vodka–Soaked Cherry Tomatoes with Seasoned Sea Salt

1 pint vine-ripened cherry tomatoes
½ cup pepper-flavored vodka
3 tablespoons coarse or fine sea salt
1 tablespoon lemon pepper

Poke 6 holes with a wooden pick or skewer in each tomato and put in a shallow bowl. Pour vodka over tomatoes and let stand, covered, tossing occasionally, 1 hour, or until soaked to desired taste.

In a small bowl stir together salt and pepper.

Serve tomatoes with seasoned salt for dipping. Makes 2 cups.

CANAPÉS

Crab-Meat Parmesan Canapés

12 slices homemade-type white bread,
   crusts discarded and bread cut into
   4 triangles
1 cup fresh lump crab meat, picked over
⅔ cup mayonnaise
⅔ cup freshly grated Parmesan cheese
4 scallions, chopped fine
1 teaspoon fresh lemon juice,
   or to taste

Preheat oven to 400° F.

Toast bread on a baking sheet in oven until golden, about 5 minutes. In a bowl stir together remaining ingredients with salt and pepper to taste. *Toasts and crab-meat mixture may be made 1 day ahead.*

Reduce oven temperature to 375° F.

Spread crab-meat mixture on toasts and arrange on baking sheet. *Canapés may be assembled 30 minutes ahead.* Bake canapés in middle of oven until puffed, about 10 minutes. Makes 48 canapés.

PHOTO ON PAGE 13

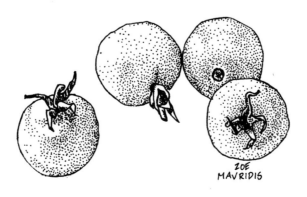

ZOE
MAVRIDIS

Curried Herring on Pumpernickel

⅓ cup drained bottled herring in wine sauce
3 tablespoons mayonnaise
¼ teaspoon curry powder, or to taste
2 tablespoons minced red onion
2 tablespoons minced scallion green
1 tablespoon unsalted butter, softened
6 slices party-type pumpernickel bread,
  2½ inches square

Garnish: 24 snow-pea shoots* or other sprouts

*available at specialty produce markets

Cut away and discard dark flesh on herring. Chop herring into ¼-inch pieces and pat dry between paper towels. In a bowl stir herring together with mayonnaise, curry powder, onion, scallion, and salt to taste. *Curried herring may be made 1 day ahead and chilled, covered.*

Spread butter on bread and cut each slice into 4 triangles. Divide herring among triangles and garnish with shoots. Serves 6.

PHOTO ON PAGE 22

Peppered Chicken Liver, Sage, and Fried Onion Bruschetta

2 tablespoons vegetable oil
1 small onion, halved lengthwise and sliced thin
½ pound chicken livers, trimmed and halved
2 large garlic cloves, sliced
2 large fresh sage leaves, minced, or ¼ teaspoon
  dried, crumbled
1 teaspoon freshly ground black pepper, or to taste
1 teaspoon coarse salt
a pinch of ground allspice, or to taste
16 toasts (recipe follows)

Garnish: 16 small fresh sage leaves

In a large skillet heat oil over moderately high heat until hot but not smoking and in it sauté onion, stirring, until golden. Transfer onion with a slotted spoon to paper towels to drain.

Pat chicken livers dry. Add garlic to skillet and cook over moderate heat, stirring, until pale golden.

Add chicken livers and sauté over moderately high heat until golden and just springy to the touch, about 1½ to 2 minutes on each side. Stir in minced or crumbled sage, pepper, salt, and allspice and in a food processor coarsely purée. Mound about 2 teaspoons chicken liver mixture on oiled side of each toast and top with onions. Garnish with sage leaves. Makes 16 *bruschetta.*

To Make Toasts

a 24-inch-long loaf of crusty Italian bread
1 garlic clove
¼ cup extra-virgin olive oil

Prepare grill or preheat broiler.

With a serrated knife cut bread crosswise into ½-inch-thick slices. Grill slices on a rack set about 4 inches over glowing coals 1 to 1½ minutes on each side, or until golden brown and crisp outside but still soft inside. Alternatively, slices may be broiled in batches under a broiler about 4 inches from heat 1 to 1½ minutes, or until golden. Rub toasts with garlic on one side and lightly brush same side with oil. *Toasts may be made 1 week ahead and kept in an airtight container.* Makes about 45 toasts.

Mozzarella, Greens, and Garlic Bruschetta

1¼ pounds *arugula*, spinach, or escarole
6 garlic cloves, minced and mashed to a paste with
  ½ teaspoon coarse salt
2 tablespoons olive oil
½ cup coarsely shredded mozzarella cheese
16 toasts (recipe precedes)

Discard coarse stems from greens and wash leaves thoroughly. Chop greens coarse (there should be about 6 cups).

In a heavy skillet cook garlic paste in oil over moderately low heat, stirring, 1 minute. Add greens and salt and pepper to taste and sauté over moderately high heat, stirring, until wilted and tender, about 3 minutes. Pour off excess liquid. Transfer greens mixture to a bowl and cool to warm. Stir in mozzarella and mound about 1 tablespoon on oiled side of each toast. Makes 16 *bruschetta.*

Tomato and Ricotta Salata Bruschetta

2 large shallots, sliced thin
1 tablespoon olive oil (preferably extra-virgin)
2 cups chopped seeded vine-ripened tomato
2 ounces *ricotta salata* (firm salted sheep's milk cheese) or feta, cut into fine dice (about ⅓ cup)
2 tablespoons minced fresh chives, or to taste
2 teaspoons balsamic vinegar, or to taste
16 toasts (page 96)

In a skillet cook shallots in oil over moderate heat, stirring, until softened. Stir in tomato and salt and pepper to taste and cook, stirring, 30 seconds, or until just heated through. In a bowl toss together tomato mixture with cheese, chives, vinegar, and salt and pepper to taste and mound about 1 tablespoon mixture on oiled side of each toast. Makes 16 *bruschetta*.

TEA SANDWICHES

Cheddar Chutney Tea Sandwiches

a 9-ounce jar Major Grey's chutney (about ½ cup), pieces chopped
½ pound sharp Cheddar cheese (preferably white), grated coarse (about 2 cups)
½ cup sour cream

3 ounces cream cheese, softened
12 very thin slices homemade-type whole-wheat bread
½ cup minced fresh coriander leaves
⅓ cup mayonnaise

In a bowl stir together chutney, Cheddar, sour cream, cream cheese, and salt and pepper to taste until combined well.

Make 6 sandwiches with filling and bread, pressing together gently. With a 1½-inch round cutter cut 4 rounds from each sandwich.

Put coriander on a small plate and spread edges of rounds with mayonnaise to coat well. Roll edges in coriander. *Sandwiches may be made 2 hours ahead and chilled, wrapped in plastic wrap.* Makes 24 tea sandwiches.

*Chicken Salad Tea Sandwiches
with Smoked Almonds*

3 cups chicken broth or water
2 whole boneless chicken breasts with skin (about 1½ pounds), halved
1 cup mayonnaise
⅓ cup minced shallot
1 teaspoon minced fresh tarragon leaves
24 very thin slices homemade-type white bread
½ cup finely chopped smoked almonds (about 2 ounces)

In a deep 12-inch skillet bring broth or water to a boil and add chicken breasts in one layer. Reduce heat and poach chicken at a bare simmer, turning once, 7 minutes. Remove skillet from heat and cool chicken in cooking liquid 20 minutes. Discard skin and shred chicken fine.

In a bowl stir together chicken, ½ cup of mayonnaise, shallot, tarragon, and salt and pepper to taste.

Make 12 sandwiches with chicken salad and bread, pressing together gently. With a 2-inch round cutter cut 2 rounds from each sandwich.

Put almonds on a small plate and spread edges of rounds with remaining ½ cup mayonnaise to coat well. Roll edges in almonds. *Sandwiches may be made 2 hours ahead and chilled, wrapped in plastic wrap.* Makes 24 tea sandwiches.

*Minted Radish Tea Sandwiches
with Lemon Mayonnaise*

1 cup mayonnaise
2 tablespoons sour cream
1 tablespoon freshly grated lemon zest
2 teaspoons coarse-grained mustard
2 teaspoons fresh lemon juice,
  or to taste
24 very thin slices homemade-type white bread
1 cup mint leaves (from about
  1 large bunch)
16 radishes, trimmed and sliced as thin
  as possible

In a small bowl stir together mayonnaise, sour cream, zest, mustard, lemon juice, and salt and pepper to taste.

Spread bread generously with lemon mayonnaise. Top half of slices with a layer of mint and top mint with overlapping rows of radish. Top radish with remaining bread and press together gently. Trim crusts and cut sandwiches in half diagonally. *Sandwiches may be made 2 hours ahead and chilled, wrapped in plastic wrap.* Makes 24 tea sandwiches.

DIPS AND SPREADS

Chipotle Mayonnaise Dip with Carrots

1 cup mayonnaise
1 cup sour cream
2 canned *chipotle* chilies in *adobo* sauce,* minced
  to a paste (about 1 tablespoon), plus ½ teaspoon
  adobo sauce
24 small carrots, trimmed, or 12 large carrots,
  cut into sticks

*available at Hispanic markets and some specialty
  foods shops

In a bowl whisk together mayonnaise, sour cream, chili paste, *adobo* sauce, and salt to taste. *Dip may be made 2 days ahead and chilled, covered.*
Serve dip with carrots. Makes 2 cups.

PHOTO ON PAGE 51

Green and White Crudités with Herbed Anise Dip

For dip
½ cup plain yogurt
½ cup sour cream
½ cup mayonnaise
1½ teaspoons white-wine vinegar, or to taste
1½ teaspoons coarse-grained mustard, or to taste
1 large garlic clove, minced and mashed to a paste
  with ½ teaspoon salt
1 teaspoon aniseed, crushed
2 teaspoons Pernod, or to taste
1½ tablespoons minced fresh tarragon leaves
1½ tablespoons minced fresh chervil leaves
  if desired

12 cups assorted *crudités* such as blanched
  broccoli and cauliflower flowerets, green beans,
  snow peas, raw sliced celery, fennel, green
  bell peppers, cucumber, *daikon*, and
  Belgian endive leaves

Make dip:
In a bowl whisk together all dip ingredients except herbs with salt and pepper to taste. Chill dip, covered, at least 4 hours and up to 4 days. Just before serving, stir in tarragon and chervil.

Arrange *crudités* decoratively on a tiered serving plate or in a basket and serve with dip. Serves 12.

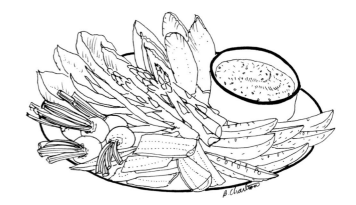

Roasted Red Pepper and Eggplant Dip
with Pita Wedges

a ¾-pound eggplant
2 pounds red bell peppers
4 tablespoons olive oil (preferably extra-virgin)
    plus additional for coating the vegetables
4 large garlic cloves, minced
3 tablespoons fresh lemon juice, or to taste
1 small fresh *jalapeño* chili, seeded and minced
    (wear rubber gloves)
pita loaves, cut into wedges

Preheat oven to 400° F.

Coat eggplant and bell peppers lightly with additional oil and arrange in a jelly-roll pan. Roast vegetables, turning once or twice, 30 minutes, or until eggplant is very soft and peppers are charred. Transfer peppers to a metal bowl and let steam, covered tightly with plastic wrap, until cool enough to handle.

Peel and seed bell peppers and pat dry between paper towels. Peel eggplant and put flesh in a food processor. Add bell peppers, remaining 4 tablespoons oil, garlic, lemon juice, *jalapeño*, and salt and pepper to taste and combine well.

Transfer mixture to a heavy saucepan and simmer, stirring frequently, 15 to 20 minutes, or until thickened and reduced to about 2 cups.

Cool dip and chill, covered, at least 1 day and up to 1 week.

Serve dip with *pita* wedges. Makes about 2 cups.

Tomatillo and Yellow Tomato Salsa
with Tortilla Chips

For chips
vegetable oil for frying tortillas
twelve 6-inch corn tortillas, each cut into 8 wedges
For salsa
2 tablespoons vegetable oil
6 tomatillos*, husks discarded and the fruit rinsed
    under warm water and chopped fine
4 vine-ripened large yellow tomatoes or yellow
    bell peppers (or a mix of both), chopped fine
1 large onion, chopped fine
1 to 2 *jalapeño* chilies, minced
    (wear rubber gloves)
¼ cup chopped fresh coriander

*available at specialty produce markets and many
supermarkets

Make chips:
In a kettle heat ¾ inch oil to 375° F. on a deep-fat thermometer and fry tortilla wedges, a dozen at a time, until crisp and most of bubbling subsides, about 1 minute, transferring chips with a slotted spoon to paper towels to drain. Sprinkle chips with salt to taste. *Tortilla chips may be made 1 day ahead and kept in airtight containers.*
Make salsa:
In a bowl combine well oil, tomatillos, tomatoes or bell peppers, onion, *jalapeños,* coriander, and salt to taste and chill *salsa,* covered, at least 1 hour or overnight.

Serve *salsa* with chips. Makes 8 dozen chips and about 6 cups *salsa.*

PHOTO ON PAGE 51

Anchoïade
(Provençal Anchovy Vegetable Spread)

⅓ cup blanched whole almonds
a 2-ounce can flat anchovies, rinsed and
    patted dry
3 garlic cloves
1 shallot, quartered
3 tablespoons olive oil
1 tablespoon red-wine vinegar
¼ teaspoon *herbes de Provence* or dried Italian
    seasoning, crumbled
1 tomato, seeded and chopped fine
    (about ¾ cup)
1 red bell pepper, chopped fine (about ¾ cup)
3 tablespoons finely chopped fresh parsley leaves

Accompaniment: French bread toasts

In a food processor grind fine almonds with anchovies and garlic. With motor running add shallot, oil, vinegar, and herbs and blend well. Add tomato, bell pepper, and parsley and pulse motor until just combined (do not purée smooth). Anchoïade *may be made 1 day ahead and chilled, covered.*

Serve *anchoïade* at room temperature on toasts. Makes about 2 cups.

Cherry and Pecan Cream Cheese Spread

1 cup dried sour cherries*
1 cup water
two 8-ounce packages cream cheese, softened
½ cup chopped toasted pecans
1 tablespoon fresh lime juice
½ teaspoon fresh thyme leaves
¼ teaspoon freshly grated lime zest

Accompaniment: scones or crackers

*available at specialty foods shops

In a small heavy saucepan simmer cherries in water until liquid is reduced to about 1 tablespoon. Remove pan from heat and cool mixture.

In a bowl whisk together cream cheese, pecans, lime juice, thyme, zest, cherry mixture, and salt and pepper to taste until spread is combined well. *Spread may be made 2 days ahead and chilled, covered.*

Serve spread with scones or crackers. Makes about 3 cups.

Dilled Feta Ricotta Spread

8 ounces feta cheese, crumbled (about 1⅓ cups)
1 cup whole-milk ricotta cheese
¼ cup finely chopped scallion
¼ cup pine nuts, toasted lightly and cooled
2 tablespoons chopped fresh dill, or to taste
2 teaspoons fresh lemon juice, or to taste

Accompaniment: crackers or toast points

In a food processor blend cheeses until smooth. Add remaining ingredients and pulse until combined well but still chunky. *Spread may be made 3 days ahead and chilled, covered.*

Serve spread chilled or at room temperature with crackers or toast points. Makes about 2 cups.

Salmon Rillettes

3 cups water
1 pound skinless fresh salmon fillet
1 pound smoked salmon,
  chopped fine
½ cup (1 stick) unsalted butter,
  softened
3 shallots, minced
⅓ cup chopped fresh parsley leaves
2 tablespoons fresh lemon juice
2 teaspoons Dijon mustard
2 teaspoons drained capers
2 teaspoons Cognac or other brandy
2 teaspoons freshly grated lemon zest

Accompaniment: whole-wheat French or Italian
  bread, sliced

In a skillet bring water to a boil and add fresh salmon. Reduce heat and poach salmon at a bare simmer, turning once, about 4 minutes, or until just cooked through. Transfer salmon to a bowl and cool.

Flake fresh salmon and add smoked salmon, butter, shallots, parsley, lemon juice, mustard, capers, Cognac or other brandy, zest, and salt and pepper to taste. Stir mixture until combined well and pack into a 1-quart terrine or bowl. Rillettes *may be made 4 hours ahead and chilled, covered.*

Serve salmon *rillettes*, chilled slightly, with bread. Makes about 4 cups.

BREADS

YEAST BREADS

Grape and Rosemary Focaccia

½ pound seedless red grapes
two ¼-ounce packages active dry yeast
  (5 teaspoons)
½ teaspoon sugar
1½ cups lukewarm water
4¼ cups bread flour
1 teaspoon table salt
¼ cup olive oil
2 tablespoons fresh rosemary leaves
coarse salt to taste
freshly ground black pepper to taste

Preheat oven to 300° F.

In a baking dish large enough to hold grapes in one layer cook grapes in middle of oven 30 minutes, or until soft and sticky, and cool slightly.

In a standing electric mixer fitted with paddle attachment beat together yeast, sugar, and water and let stand 5 minutes, or until foamy. Add flour, table salt, and oil and combine well.

With dough hook knead dough 2 minutes, or until soft and slightly sticky. Form dough into a ball and let rest on a floured surface, covered with an inverted bowl, 10 minutes.

On lightly floured surface roll dough into an 18- by 8-inch oval. Arrange oval diagonally on a greased large baking sheet and sprinkle with grapes, rosemary, coarse salt, and pepper. Let dough rise, covered loosely with plastic wrap, in a warm place 1 hour, or until almost doubled in bulk.

Preheat oven to 375° F.

Bake *focaccia* in middle of oven 1 hour, or until golden, and cool on baking sheet on a rack. Serve *focaccia* warm or at room temperature.

PHOTO ON PAGE 78

Miniature Cloverleaf Rolls

¾ cup milk
3 tablespoons sugar
3 tablespoons unsalted butter
1½ teaspoons salt
a ¼-ounce package (2½ teaspoons) active dry yeast
1 large egg
2½ to 3 cups all-purpose flour
an egg wash made by beating 1 large egg with
    2 teaspoons water
poppy seeds and/or lightly toasted sesame seeds
    for sprinkling

In a small saucepan heat milk with sugar, butter, and salt over low heat until mixture is lukewarm, or registers between 110° F. and 115° F. on a candy thermometer, and transfer to a bowl.

Sprinkle yeast over milk mixture and let stand until foamy, about 5 minutes. Whisk in egg and stir in 2½ cups flour, stirring until mixture forms a dough.

On a floured surface knead dough, kneading in enough of remaining ½ cup flour to form a soft dough, 8 to 10 minutes. Form dough into a ball and transfer to a well-buttered bowl. Turn dough to coat with butter. Cover bowl with plastic wrap and let dough rise in a warm place until doubled in bulk, about 1 hour.

Butter 32 miniature (⅛-cup) muffin tins.

Turn dough out on a floured surface. Working with about one third of dough at a time, cut off pieces about the size of large marbles. Form pieces into balls and put 3 balls into each prepared tin. Let rolls rise, covered loosely, in a warm place until almost doubled in bulk, 30 to 40 minutes.

While rolls are rising, preheat oven to 400° F.

Brush rolls lightly with egg wash and sprinkle with seeds. Bake rolls in middle of oven until golden, about 10 minutes. *Rolls may be made 2 weeks ahead and frozen, double-wrapped in resealable plastic bags, with excess air pressed out. Reheat rolls, wrapped in foil, in middle of a preheated 350° F. oven 15 to 20 minutes, or until heated through.* Makes 32 rolls.

PHOTO ON PAGES 64 AND 65

Scallion Biscuits

1 tablespoon unsalted butter
1 scallion, minced
1 cup all-purpose flour
1 tablespoon sugar
1¼ teaspoons baking powder
¾ teaspoon salt
3 tablespoons vegetable shortening
⅓ cup milk

Preheat oven to 450° F.

In a small skillet or saucepan melt butter over moderate heat and cook scallion, seasoned with salt, until softened but not browned.

In a bowl whisk together flour, sugar, baking powder, and salt. Blend in shortening with pastry blender or fingertips until mixture resembles coarse meal and stir in milk to form a soft dough. In bowl knead dough gently with lightly floured hands 8 times.

On an ungreased small baking sheet pat dough into a 4-inch square and cut into quarters. Separate quarters on baking sheet and brush each with some scallion butter. Bake biscuits 15 minutes, or until tops are golden, and serve warm. Makes 4 biscuits.

Irish Brown Soda Bread

1¼ cups unbleached all-purpose flour plus
   additional for sprinkling
1 cup whole-wheat flour
½ cup old-fashioned rolled oats
¼ cup toasted wheat germ
1½ teaspoons baking soda
1 teaspoon salt
½ stick (¼ cup) cold unsalted butter, cut into bits
1⅓ cups buttermilk or plain yogurt

Preheat oven to 425° F. and sprinkle a baking sheet lightly with flour.

In a large bowl whisk together flours, oats, wheat germ, baking soda, and salt. Add butter and toss to coat with flour. With fingertips rub in butter until mixture resembles coarse meal. Add buttermilk or yogurt and stir until dough is moistened evenly.

On a floured surface knead dough 1 minute, sprinkling lightly with additional flour to prevent sticking (dough should remain soft). Shape dough into a ball.

On prepared baking sheet pat dough out into a 7-inch round. Sprinkle dough with additional flour and with fingertips spread lightly over round. With a sharp knife cut a shallow X in top of round.

Bake bread in middle of oven 30 minutes. Cool bread on a rack 2 hours before slicing.

FRONTISPIECE

Golden-Raisin Irish Soda Bread

2 cups unbleached all-purpose flour plus additional
   for sprinkling
¼ cup wheat bran (not bran cereal) or toasted
   wheat germ
1 teaspoon baking soda
½ teaspoon salt
½ stick (¼ cup) cold unsalted butter, cut into bits
1 cup golden raisins
1 cup buttermilk or plain yogurt

Preheat oven to 400° F. and sprinkle a baking sheet lightly with flour.

In a large bowl whisk together flour, bran or wheat germ, baking soda, and salt. Add butter and toss to coat with flour. With fingertips rub in butter until mixture resembles coarse meal. Add raisins and toss until coated. Add buttermilk or yogurt and stir until dough is moistened evenly.

On a floured surface knead dough 1 minute, sprinkling lightly with additional flour to prevent sticking (dough should remain soft). Shape dough into a ball.

On prepared baking sheet pat dough out into a 6-inch round. Sprinkle round with additional flour and with fingertips spread lightly over round. With a sharp knife cut a shallow X in top of round.

Bake bread in middle of oven 35 to 45 minutes, or until golden brown. Wrap bread in a kitchen towel and cool on a rack 1 hour. Unwrap bread and cool 1 hour more.

FRONTISPIECE

Bacon, Gruyère, and Scallion Muffins

6 slices bacon
1½ cups all-purpose flour
2 teaspoons baking powder
1½ teaspoons sugar
½ teaspoon salt
1 cup grated Gruyère cheese (about 4 ounces)
⅓ cup finely chopped scallion
¾ cup milk
1 large egg
1 tablespoon Dijon mustard

Preheat oven to 425° F. and butter twelve ⅓-cup muffin tins.

In a skillet cook bacon over moderately low heat until crisp and transfer to paper towels to drain, reserving ¼ cup bacon fat. Crumble bacon.

In a bowl whisk together flour, baking powder, sugar, salt, Gruyère, scallion, and bacon. In a small bowl whisk together milk, egg, mustard, and reserved bacon fat. Add milk mixture to flour mixture, stirring until just combined (do not overmix).

Divide batter evenly among prepared muffin tins and bake in middle of oven 15 to 20 minutes, or until golden and a tester comes out clean. Makes 12 muffins.

Feta Corn Muffins

1 cup yellow cornmeal
⅔ cup all-purpose flour
1 teaspoon baking powder
½ teaspoon baking soda
½ teaspoon salt
1 tablespoon finely chopped fresh sage leaves
1 cup crumbled feta cheese
   (about 6 ounces)
1 cup milk
1 large egg
½ stick (¼ cup) unsalted butter, melted

Preheat oven to 425° F. and butter twelve ⅓-cup muffin tins generously.

In a large bowl whisk together cornmeal, flour, baking powder, baking soda, and salt. Add sage and feta and toss well.

In a bowl whisk together milk, egg, and butter.

Add egg mixture to dry ingredients, stirring until batter is just combined (do not overmix).

Divide batter among prepared muffin tins. Bake muffins in middle of oven about 18 to 20 minutes, or until golden and springy to touch.

Turn muffins out onto racks to cool. Makes 12 muffins.

ZOE ELIZABETH MAVRIDIS

Spicy Roasted Red Pepper Corn Muffins

1¼ cups yellow cornmeal
½ cup all-purpose flour
1 tablespoon sugar
1½ teaspoons baking powder
1 teaspoon baking soda
1 teaspoon salt
1 cup grated extra-sharp Cheddar cheese
   (about 4 ounces)
¾ cup buttermilk
1 large egg
½ stick (¼ cup) unsalted butter, melted and cooled
2 tablespoons minced seeded pickled *jalapeño*
   chilies (wear rubber gloves)
a 7-ounce jar roasted red peppers, drained, rinsed,
   patted very dry between paper towels, and
   chopped fine

Preheat oven to 425° F. and butter twelve ⅓-cup muffin tins.

In a bowl whisk together cornmeal, flour, sugar, baking powder, baking soda, salt, and Cheddar. In a small bowl whisk together buttermilk, egg, butter, and chilies. Add buttermilk mixture to cornmeal mixture, stirring until just combined, and stir in roasted peppers (do not overmix).

Divide batter evenly among prepared tins and bake in middle of oven 15 to 20 minutes, or until golden and a tester comes out clean. Makes 12 muffins.

Limpa Muffins

1½ cups all-purpose flour
1 cup rye flour*
1 tablespoon baking powder
1 teaspoon salt
1¼ teaspoons aniseed
1¼ teaspoons caraway seeds
1 cup milk
1 large egg
1 teaspoon freshly grated orange zest
½ stick (¼ cup) unsalted butter,
   melted
2½ tablespoons unsulfured molasses

*available at natural foods stores and specialty
   foods shops

Preheat oven to 425° F. and butter twelve ⅓-cup muffin tins.

In a bowl whisk together flours, baking powder, salt, aniseed, and caraway seeds. In a small bowl whisk together milk, egg, zest, butter, and molasses. Add milk mixture to flour mixture, stirring until just combined (do not overmix).

Divide batter evenly among prepared muffin tins and bake in middle of oven 15 to 20 minutes, or until a tester comes out clean. Makes 12 muffins.

Pecan Anadama Muffins

1⅓ cups all-purpose flour
⅔ cup yellow cornmeal
1½ teaspoons baking powder
¾ teaspoon baking soda
1 teaspoon salt
¼ cup dried currants
½ cup chopped pecans,
   toasted lightly

1 cup sour cream
2 large eggs
½ stick (¼ cup) unsalted butter,
    melted and cooled
¼ cup unsulfured molasses

Preheat oven to 400° F. and butter twelve ⅓-cup muffin tins.

In a bowl whisk together flour, cornmeal, baking powder, baking soda, salt, currants, and pecans. In a small bowl whisk together sour cream, eggs, butter, and molasses. Add sour cream mixture to flour mixture, stirring until just combined (do not overmix).

Divide batter evenly among prepared muffin tins and bake in middle of oven 15 to 20 minutes, or until a tester comes out clean. Makes 12 muffins.

Rosemary Popovers

1⅓ cups all-purpose flour
½ teaspoon salt
4 large eggs
1⅓ cups milk
5 tablespoons melted drippings from a rib roast
    or melted unsalted butter
4 teaspoons minced fresh rosemary leaves

Preheat oven to 350° F.

In a blender blend flour, salt, eggs, milk, and 4 tablespoons drippings or butter, scraping down sides, 30 seconds.

Brush eight 1-cup popover tins or ⅔-cup custard cups with some remaining fat and heat in middle of oven 5 minutes, or until hot. Fill tins or cups half full with batter and sprinkle top of each popover with about ½ teaspoon rosemary. Bake popovers 45 minutes, or until golden brown and crisp. Makes 8 rosemary popovers.

PHOTO ON PAGES 82 AND 83

Thyme Corn Sticks

vegetable shortening for greasing molds
3 large eggs
1¼ sticks (10 tablespoons) unsalted butter,
    melted and cooled

⅓ cup vegetable oil
2 cups plain yogurt
1 cup all-purpose flour
2 cups stone-ground yellow cornmeal
1½ tablespoons baking powder
2 teaspoons salt
2 teaspoons sugar
1 tablespoon minced fresh thyme leaves or
    1 teaspoon dried, crumbled

Preheat oven to 400° F. Grease 5- by 1½-inch corn-stick molds generously with shortening and on a baking sheet heat in oven for 10 minutes.

While molds are heating, in a large bowl whisk together eggs, butter, oil, and yogurt. In a bowl whisk together remaining ingredients. Add flour mixture to egg mixture and combine batter well.

Remove molds from oven carefully and pour ¼ cup batter into each mold. Bake corn sticks in batches in middle of oven until a tester comes out clean, about 15 to 17 minutes, and remove from molds. *Corn sticks may be made 3 days ahead and kept chilled in resealable plastic bags. Reheat corn sticks on a baking sheet in 400° F. oven about 5 minutes.* Makes 24 corn sticks.

PHOTO ON PAGE 13

Pumpernickel and Rye Breadsticks

5 tablespoons unsalted butter
2 teaspoons caraway seeds
1 teaspoon coarse salt plus additional to taste
2 slices pumpernickel bread
2 slices rye bread

Preheat oven to 350° F.

In a small saucepan melt butter with caraway seeds and 1 teaspoon salt. Brush bread on both sides with butter mixture and slice lengthwise into ½-inch-wide strips. On a baking sheet sprinkle breadsticks with additional salt and bake in lower third of oven, turning once, until golden brown and crisp, about 15 minutes. Transfer breadsticks to a rack and cool completely. *Breadsticks may be made 2 days ahead and kept in a resealable plastic bag.* Makes about 24 breadsticks.

PHOTO ON PAGES 68 AND 69

PIZZA

Shrimp Creole and Smoked Mozzarella Pizzas

1 medium onion, chopped
1 small green bell pepper,
   chopped
1 celery rib, chopped
1 large garlic clove, minced
1 tablespoon vegetable oil
a 14- to 16-ounce can whole peeled tomatoes
   including their juice, chopped
¼ teaspoon dried thyme,
   crumbled
cayenne to taste
1 pound small shrimp (about 48), shelled and
   deveined
yellow cornmeal for sprinkling pan
1 recipe pizza dough (recipe follows)
¼ pound smoked mozzarella cheese*, grated
   (about 1 cup)

*available at specialty foods shops and some
   supermarkets

In a medium heavy saucepan cook onion, bell pepper, celery, and garlic in oil, covered, over moderately low heat, stirring, until celery is softened, about 10 minutes. Add tomatoes and juice, thyme, and cayenne and simmer, uncovered, stirring, until mixture is very thick, about 20 minutes. Season with salt and pepper. *Sauce may be made 1 day ahead and chilled, covered.*

Stir in shrimp and cook sauce, stirring, until shrimp are cooked through, the liquid they give off is evaporated, and the sauce is thickened.

Preheat oven to 500° F.

Sprinkle cornmeal on an oiled 14-inch black steel pizza pan or black steel baking sheet. Roll out dough on a lightly floured surface into a 14-inch round and fit into pan. Sprinkle dough with half of mozzarella and top with shrimp Creole, spreading mixture evenly, and remaining cheese.

Bake pizza in lower third of an electric oven or on floor of a gas oven 10 minutes, or until crust is golden. Makes one 14-inch pizza, serving 4 as an entrée.

Pizza Dough

½ teaspoon sugar
⅔ cup warm water (110° to 115° F.)
a ¼-ounce package (2½ teaspoons) active dry yeast
2 to 2¼ cups unbleached flour
½ teaspoon salt
olive oil for oiling bowl

In a large bowl dissolve sugar in water. Sprinkle yeast over water and let stand until foamy, about 5 minutes. Stir in 2 cups flour and salt and blend mixture until it forms a dough. Knead dough on a floured surface, incorporating as much of remaining ¼ cup flour as necessary to prevent dough from sticking, until smooth and elastic, about 5 minutes.

(Alternatively, dough may be made in a food processor. Proof yeast as described above. In the food processor process yeast mixture with 2 cups flour and salt until mixture forms a ball, adding more water, 1 teaspoon at a time, if too dry or some of remaining ¼ cup flour, 1 tablespoon at a time, if too wet, and knead dough by processing it 15 seconds more.)

Put dough, prepared by either method, in a deep oiled bowl and turn to coat with oil. Let dough rise, covered with plastic wrap, in a warm place 1 hour, or until doubled in bulk, and punch down. Dough is now ready to be formed into pizza. Makes enough dough for one 14-inch pizza.

Deep-Dish Sausage and Tomato Pizza

For dough
½ teaspoon sugar
1 cup warm water (110° to 115° F.)
a ¼-ounce package (2½ teaspoons) active dry yeast
2¼ to 2½ cups unbleached flour
½ cup yellow cornmeal
¾ teaspoon salt
2 tablespoons olive oil plus additional for
   oiling bowl

1 pound Italian sausage, casings discarded
a 14- to 16-ounce can peeled whole tomatoes,
   drained and chopped
1 teaspoon dried oregano, crumbled
2 cups grated whole-milk mozzarella cheese
   (about ½ pound)

Make dough:

In a large bowl dissolve sugar in water. Sprinkle yeast over water and let stand until foamy, about 5 minutes. Stir in 2¼ cups flour, cornmeal, salt, and 2 tablespoons oil and blend until mixture forms a dough. Knead dough on a floured surface, incorporating as much of remaining ¼ cup flour as necessary to prevent dough from sticking, until smooth and elastic, about 5 minutes.

(Alternatively, dough may be made in a food processor. Proof yeast as described above. In the food processor process yeast mixture with 2¼ cups flour, cornmeal, salt, and 2 tablespoons oil until mixture forms a ball, adding more water, 1 teaspoon at a time, if too dry or some of remaining ¼ cup flour, 1 tablespoon at a time, if too wet, and knead dough by processing it 15 seconds more.)

Put dough in a deep oiled bowl and turn to coat with oil. Let dough rise, covered with plastic wrap, in a warm place 1 hour, or until doubled in bulk.

While dough is rising, in a heavy skillet cook sausage over moderately high heat, breaking up lumps, until no longer pink and stir in tomatoes, oregano, and salt and pepper to taste. Transfer sausage mixture to paper towels to drain and cool.

Preheat oven to 500° F.

Punch down dough and knead 4 times. In an oiled 10½-inch cast-iron skillet, press dough with oiled fingers until it comes 2 inches up the side and is an even thickness on bottom. Let dough rise, covered loosely with plastic wrap, in a warm place 15 minutes.

Sprinkle dough with half of mozzarella and top with sausage mixture and remaining cheese. Bake pizza in lower third of an electric oven or on floor of a gas oven 15 minutes. Reduce oven temperature to 400° F. and bake 10 minutes more, or until crust is golden. Serves 4 as an entrée.

Parsley Pesto and Feta Phyllo Pizza

For pesto
3 cups packed fresh parsley leaves,
    preferably flat-leafed (about 3 bunches),
    rinsed and spun dry
2 large garlic cloves,
    chopped
⅓ cup freshly grated Parmesan cheese
⅓ cup pine nuts, toasted until golden and cooled
⅓ cup olive oil

¾ stick (6 tablespoons) unsalted butter, melted and
    kept warm
10 sheets *phyllo,* stacked between 2 sheets of wax
    paper and covered with a kitchen towel
9 tablespoons freshly grated Parmesan cheese
    (about 2 ounces)
¾ cup crumbled feta cheese (about ¼ pound)

Preheat oven to 400° F.
Make pesto:

In a food processor blend well *pesto* ingredients. Pesto *may be made 3 days ahead and chilled, surface covered with plastic wrap.*

Lightly brush a large baking sheet with some butter and put 1 sheet *phyllo* on butter. Lightly brush *phyllo* with some remaining butter and sprinkle with 1 tablespoon Parmesan. Put another sheet *phyllo* over cheese, pressing firmly so that it adheres to bottom layer. Butter, sprinkle with Parmesan, and layer remaining phyllo in same manner, ending with a sheet of *phyllo.* Lightly brush top sheet with remaining butter. Fold in all sides ¼ inch, pressing to top sheet, and fold up a ¼-inch border, crimping corners.

Spread *pesto* on *phyllo* crust and sprinkle with feta.

Bake pizza in middle of oven until crust is golden, about 15 minutes. Serves 4 as an entrée or 8 as an hors d'oeuvre.

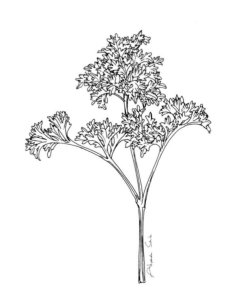

Butternut Squash, Bacon, and Rosemary Phyllo Pizza

a 1½-pound butternut squash
1 tablespoon vegetable oil
½ cup water
¾ stick (6 tablespoons) unsalted butter,
    melted and kept warm
10 sheets *phyllo*, stacked between 2 sheets wax
    paper and covered with a kitchen towel
9 tablespoons freshly grated Parmesan cheese
    (about 2 ounces)
6 slices bacon, cut into ½-inch pieces,
    cooked until crisp,
    and drained
1 tablespoon fresh rosemary leaves,
    minced
6 scallion greens,
    chopped
1 small red onion, sliced thin and separated
    into pieces

Quarter squash lengthwise and discard seeds. Peel squash carefully and cut into ¾-inch pieces. In a large heavy skillet cook squash in oil over moderate heat, stirring occasionally, 2 minutes. Add water and salt to taste and simmer, covered, until squash is just tender, about 10 minutes. Simmer squash, uncovered, until almost all water is evaporated, about 5 minutes. In a food processor purée squash with salt and pepper to taste. *Squash purée may be made 1 day ahead and chilled, covered.*

Preheat oven to 400° F.

Lightly brush a large baking sheet with some butter and put 1 sheet *phyllo* on butter. Lightly brush *phyllo* with some remaining butter and sprinkle with 1 tablespoon Parmesan. Put another sheet of *phyllo* over cheese, pressing it firmly so that it adheres to bottom layer. Butter, sprinkle with cheese, and layer remaining *phyllo* in the same manner, ending with a sheet of *phyllo*. Lightly brush top sheet with remaining butter. Fold in all sides ¼ inch, pressing to top sheet, and fold up a ¼-inch border, crimping corners.

Spread squash purée evenly on *phyllo* crust and top with bacon, rosemary leaves, scallion greens, and red onion.

Bake pizza in middle of oven until crust is golden, about 15 minutes. Serves 4 as an entrée or 8 as an hors d'oeuvre.

Broccoli Rabe and Chick-Pea Pita Pizzas

2 large garlic cloves, sliced thin
¼ cup extra-virgin olive oil
a 19-ounce can chick-peas, rinsed and drained
½ cup water
1 large bunch broccoli rabe, coarse and hollow
    stems discarded and the rest chopped
    (about 9 cups)
½ teaspoon dried hot red pepper flakes
three 6-inch *pita* loaves, halved horizontally to
    form 6 rounds
½ cup freshly grated Parmesan cheese
    (about 2 ounces)

Preheat oven to 400° F.

In a large heavy skillet cook garlic in oil over moderate heat, stirring, until pale golden. Transfer garlic and 1 tablespoon oil to a food processor. Add chick-peas, ¼ cup water, and salt and pepper to taste and blend mixture until smooth.

Heat oil remaining in skillet over moderately high heat until hot but not smoking and cook broccoli rabe, turning it with tongs, until wilted. Add remaining ¼ cup water and pepper flakes and simmer, covered partially, until broccoli rabe is crisp-tender and almost all liquid is evaporated, about 2 minutes.

Spread rough sides of *pita* with chick-pea purée and top with broccoli rabe and Parmesan.

Arrange *pita* pizzas on a large baking sheet and bake in middle of oven 10 minutes, or until edges are golden. Serves 6 as an entrée or 10 to 12 as an hors d'oeuvre.

Potato, Anchovy, and Jarlsberg Pita Pizzas

a ½-pound russet (baking) potato
1¾ cups grated Jarlsberg cheese (about 6 ounces)
8 flat anchovy fillets, patted dry and chopped fine
½ cup minced onion (about 1 small)
three 6-inch *pita* loaves, halved horizontally to
    form 6 rounds
¼ cup extra-virgin olive oil
2 tablespoons drained bottled capers, minced

Preheat oven to 400° F.

Peel potato and in a food processor fitted with a grating disk or with a hand-held grater grate potato coarse. In a bowl toss together potato, Jarlsberg, anchovies, onion, and salt and pepper to taste.

Brush rough sides of *pita* with oil and top with potato mixture.

Arrange *pita* pizzas on a large baking sheet and bake in middle of oven until edges are golden, about 14 minutes. Sprinkle *pita* pizzas with capers. Serves 6 as an entrée or 10 to 12 as an hors d'oeuvre.

Arugula and Prosciutto Tortilla Pizzas

a ¼-pound piece of prosciutto, cut into ¼-inch dice
   (about ⅔ cup)
1 medium red onion, chopped fine (about 1 cup)
¼ cup olive oil
2 bunches *arugula*, coarse stems discarded and the
   rest washed well, spun dry, and chopped
four 8½-inch flour tortillas
⅔ cup freshly grated Parmesan cheese
   (about 3 ounces)

Preheat oven to 400° F.

In a medium heavy skillet cook prosciutto and onion in oil over moderate heat, stirring, until onion is softened. Remove skillet from heat and stir in *arugula* and salt and pepper to taste.

Arrange flour tortillas on 2 baking sheets and top with *arugula* mixture and Parmesan.

Bake tortilla pizzas on upper and lower racks of oven, switching position of baking sheets halfway through baking, until edges are golden, about 10 minutes. Serves 4 as an entrée or 8 to 10 as an hors d'oeuvre.

Tomatillo and Pepper Jack Tortilla Pizzas

four 8½-inch flour tortillas
2 cups grated pepper Jack cheese (about 6 ounces)
¾ pound *tomatillos**, husks discarded and the flesh
   rinsed under warm water and chopped fine
   (about 2½ cups)
½ cup packed fresh coriander, chopped fine
½ cup finely chopped onion (about 1 small)

*available at Hispanic markets, specialty produce
   shops, and some supermarkets

Preheat oven to 400° F.

Divide tortillas between 2 baking sheets and sprinkle with half of pepper Jack. Top cheese with *tomatillos*, coriander, onion, and salt to taste and sprinkle with remaining cheese.

Bake pizzas on upper and lower racks of oven, switching position of baking sheets halfway through baking, until edges are golden, about 14 minutes. Serves 4 as an entrée or 8 to 10 as an hors d'oeuvre.

SOUPS

Southwestern Pinto Bean Soup

1 pound dried pinto beans,
   picked over
3 medium onions, chopped fine
5 garlic cloves, minced
¼ cup vegetable oil
2 red bell peppers, chopped
1 tablespoon chili powder
2 teaspoons ground cumin
6 cups water
½ pound cured *chorizo* (Spanish sausage)*,
   sliced ¼ inch thick, if desired
a 28- to 32-ounce can whole tomatoes,
   drained and puréed coarse
2 cups chicken broth
½ cup canned mild enchilada sauce
   (not *salsa*), or to taste
3 tablespoons fresh lime juice, or to taste
⅓ to ½ cup chopped fresh coriander

*available at Hispanic markets and some specialty
   foods shops and supermarkets

In a bowl soak beans in water to cover by 2 inches overnight or quick-soak (procedure follows) and drain.

In a heavy kettle sauté onions and garlic in oil over moderately high heat, stirring, until pale golden. Add bell peppers and cook over moderate heat, stirring, until softened. Add chili powder and cumin and cook, stirring, 30 seconds. Add drained beans and the 6 cups water and simmer, covered partially, until tender, about 1 to 1¼ hours.

While soup is simmering, in a skillet brown *chorizo,* in batches if necessary, over moderately high heat and transfer to paper towels to drain. Add *chorizo* to soup with tomatoes, broth, enchilada sauce, and salt to taste and simmer, covered partially and stirring occasionally, 30 minutes. *Soup may be made 4 days ahead (cool uncovered before chilling covered).*

Just before serving, stir in lime juice and coriander. Makes about 10 cups.

To Quick-Soak Dried Beans

In a large saucepan combine dried beans, picked over and rinsed, with triple their volume of cold water. Bring water to a boil and cook beans, uncovered, over moderate heat 2 minutes. Remove pan from heat and let beans soak 1 hour.

White Bean, Wheat Berry, and Escarole Soup

1 pound dried baby lima beans or other dried
   white beans, picked over
2 ham hocks
⅔ cup wheat berries*
8 cups water
2 cups chicken broth
2 medium onions, chopped
3 carrots, chopped
3 celery ribs, chopped
1 bay leaf
1 teaspoon dried rosemary, crumbled
1 head escarole (about 1 pound), chopped coarse
3 garlic cloves, minced

*available at natural foods stores and some
   specialty foods shops

In a bowl soak beans in water to cover by 2 inches overnight or quick-soak (procedure precedes) and drain.

In a heavy kettle (at least 5 quarts) simmer ham hocks and wheat berries in the 8 cups water and broth, covered, 1 hour. Add drained beans and bring to a boil. Reduce to a simmer and skim froth. Add onions, carrots, celery, bay leaf, and rosemary and simmer, covered, until beans are tender, about 1 hour.

Transfer ham hocks with a slotted spoon to a cutting board. Discard fat and bones and chop meat.

In a blender or food processor purée 3 cups soup. Stir purée into soup with chopped meat and escarole and simmer, uncovered, 15 minutes. Stir in garlic and salt and pepper to taste. *Soup may be made 4 days ahead (cool uncovered before chilling covered).* Makes about 15 cups.

Chinese Beef Noodle Soup

2½ pounds beef short ribs, cut between bones
    into pieces
7 cups water
⅓ cup soy sauce
¼ cup Scotch or medium-dry Sherry
1 tablespoon sugar
six ¼-inch-thick diagonal slices fresh gingerroot
8 scallions, trimmed
3 large garlic cloves, chopped
a 3-inch cinnamon stick
1 teaspoon aniseed
¼ teaspoon dried hot red pepper flakes
½ pound turnips, peeled and cut into ¾-inch cubes
6 ounces egg noodles
1 teaspoon Asian (toasted) sesame oil if desired

In a heavy kettle (at least 5 quarts) combine short ribs, water, soy sauce, Scotch, and sugar and bring to a boil. Reduce to a simmer and skim froth. Add gingerroot, 5 scallions, flattened with the side of a large knife, garlic, cinnamon, aniseed, and pepper flakes and simmer, covered, 2 hours, or until rib meat is tender. Let ribs cool, uncovered, in broth 30 minutes and transfer with a slotted spoon to a cutting board. Chop meat, discarding fat and bones.

Strain broth through a fine sieve into a large saucepan and add meat. If finishing and serving soup immediately, spoon off fat. *For best results, chill soup, covered, overnight and discard fat.*

Add turnips and simmer, covered, 10 minutes. Add noodles and simmer, covered, stirring occasionally, until tender, about 7 minutes. *Soup may be prepared up to this point 2 days ahead (cool uncovered before chilling covered). Reheat gently.*

Slice remaining 3 scallions thin and stir into soup. Stir in sesame oil (if using). Makes about 10 cups.

Cold Beet and Celery Soup

1 cup finely chopped onion
2 cups thinly sliced celery
2 tablespoons olive oil
2 teaspoons sugar
1½ pounds beets, peeled and cut into 1-inch pieces
1 tablespoon red-wine vinegar plus additional
    to taste
3 cups low-salt chicken broth
ice water for thinning soup

Garnish: sour cream seasoned with bottled horseradish, and minced fresh chives

In a heavy saucepan cook onion and celery in oil with sugar and salt and pepper to taste over moderately low heat, stirring, until softened and add beets, 1 tablespoon vinegar, and broth. Simmer mixture, covered, 35 to 40 minutes, or until beets are very tender.

In a blender purée mixture in batches until very smooth, transferring as puréed to a bowl. Chill soup, covered, at least 6 hours or overnight.

Thin soup with ice water and season with additional vinegar and salt and pepper.

Garnish soup with sour cream and chives. Makes about 7 cups.

Beet and Fennel Soup

5 medium beets
2 tablespoons vegetable oil
2 large onions, sliced
¼ teaspoon fennel seeds
3 fennel bulbs (sometimes called anise), sliced thin
  (about 6½ cups)
¼ cup water
3 cups low-salt chicken broth
2 tablespoons fresh orange juice
¼ cup Gilka (German caraway seed liqueur)
  if desired

Garnish: beet matchsticks and fennel leaves
Accompaniment: pumpernickel and rye
  breadsticks (page 105)

Preheat oven to 400° F.

Trim beets, leaving 1 inch of stems attached, and scrub well. Wrap beets tightly in foil and roast in middle of oven until tender, about 1½ hours. Unwrap beets carefully and let stand until cool enough to handle. Peel beets. Cut half of 1 beet into 1-inch-long matchsticks for garnish and chop remaining beets.

In a large heavy saucepan heat oil over moderate heat until hot but not smoking and cook onions with fennel seeds, stirring, until softened, about 15 minutes. Add sliced fennel and water and cook, covered, stirring occasionally, until fennel is very soft, 15 to 20 minutes. Stir in chopped beets and broth and simmer, uncovered, 15 minutes. In a blender purée soup in batches, transferring it as puréed to another saucepan. *Soup may be prepared up to this point 2 days ahead and chilled, covered.* Reheat soup until hot, thinning with water if necessary. Stir in orange juice, liqueur if using, and salt and pepper to taste.

Garnish soup with beet matchsticks and fennel leaves and serve with breadsticks. Serves 6.

PHOTO ON PAGES 68 AND 69

Cold Curried Carrot and Coconut Milk Soup

¾ cup finely chopped scallion (about 1 bunch)
1 small onion, chopped (about ⅔ cup)
1 tablespoon finely grated peeled fresh gingerroot
2 tablespoons unsalted butter
1 tablespoon curry powder
1½ pounds carrots, peeled and sliced thin
  (about 4 cups)
2½ cups low-salt chicken broth
1 to 1½ cups canned unsweetened coconut milk*
1 tablespoon fresh lime juice plus additional
  to taste
ice water for thinning soup

Garnish: trimmed scallions

*available at Asian markets and some specialty
  foods shops

In a large heavy saucepan cook scallion, onion, and gingerroot in butter with curry powder and salt and pepper to taste over moderately low heat until softened and add carrots and broth. Simmer mixture, covered, 20 minutes, or until carrots are very soft.

In a blender purée mixture in batches with coconut milk until very smooth, transferring as puréed to a bowl. Stir in 1 tablespoon lime juice and chill soup at least 6 hours or overnight.

Thin soup with ice water and season with additional lime juice and salt and pepper.

Garnish soup with trimmed scallions. Makes about 6½ cups.

Cumin Corn Chowder

1 onion, chopped
1 tablespoon vegetable oil
2 cups fresh corn (cut from about 4 ears)
3 cups water
¼ teaspoon ground cumin
½ pound tofu (preferably silken)
1 garlic clove, chopped fine

In a heavy saucepan cook onion in oil over moderately low heat, stirring, until softened. Add corn, water, and cumin and simmer 10 minutes.

Chop tofu if not using silken. In a blender purée tofu, garlic, and all but about 1 cup soup in 2 batches, transferring it as puréed to a bowl, and stir into remaining soup.

Season soup with salt and pepper and heat over moderate heat, stirring, until hot. Serves 2.

Cold Cucumber Mint Soup

3 cucumbers, peeled, seeded, and chopped, plus
   1 cup peeled, seeded, and finely diced
   cucumber
1 cup plain yogurt
⅔ cup sour cream
½ teaspoon English-style dry mustard, or to taste
¼ cup chopped fresh mint leaves

Garnish: cucumber slices and mint sprigs

In a blender purée chopped cucumbers, yogurt, sour cream, mustard, and salt and pepper and transfer to a bowl. Chill soup at least 6 hours or overnight.

Stir in finely diced cucumber and chopped mint and garnish soup with cucumber slices and mint sprigs. Makes about 4½ cups.

Smoked Fish Chowder

3 slices bacon, chopped
2 medium onions, chopped
1½ pounds russet (baking) potatoes
2 celery ribs, chopped
1½ cups chicken broth
1½ cups water
a 10-ounce package frozen baby lima beans
a 10-ounce package frozen corn
2 teaspoons cornstarch
1½ cups half-and-half or milk
1 to 2 teaspoons Worcestershire sauce
1 pound finnan haddie (smoked haddock), cut into
   1-inch pieces, or 2 smoked trout, skinned,
   boned, and flaked into 1-inch pieces
3 tablespoons minced fresh parsley leaves or
   fresh dill

In a heavy kettle (at least 5 quarts) cook bacon over moderate heat, stirring, until crisp. Add onions and cook, stirring, until softened. Peel potatoes and cut into ¾-inch cubes. Add potatoes, celery, broth, and water and simmer, covered, 10 minutes. Add lima beans and corn and simmer, covered, 5 minutes.

In a small bowl dissolve cornstarch in half-and-half or milk and stir into simmering soup with Worcestershire sauce. Bring soup to a boil, stirring, and add fish. (If using smoked trout, no further cooking is necessary; if using finnan haddie or fresh fish, simmer, covered, 5 minutes, or until it just flakes.) Stir in parsley or dill. *Soup may be made 2 days ahead (cool uncovered before chilling covered). Reheat gently.* Makes about 12 cups.

Spicy Gazpacho

2½ pounds vine-ripened tomatoes,
   chopped
1 medium green bell pepper, chopped
1 medium red bell pepper, chopped
1 small fresh *jalapeño* chili, or to taste, seeded and
   chopped (wear rubber gloves)
1 small onion, chopped
1 medium cucumber, peeled, seeded,
   and chopped
3 large garlic cloves, minced and mashed to a
   paste with ¾ teaspoon salt
enough white bread, crusts removed and bread
   torn into pieces, to measure 2 cups
   (about 4 slices)
3 tablespoons red-wine vinegar, or to taste
3 tablespoons olive oil
ice water for thinning soup

Garnish: croutons, and finely diced tomato, green
   bell pepper, red bell pepper, and cucumbers

In a blender purée chopped tomatoes, bell peppers, *jalapeño,* onion, cucumber, garlic paste, bread, vinegar, oil, and salt and pepper to taste. Force purée through a coarse sieve into a bowl and chill soup at least 6 hours or overnight.

Thin soup with ice water and serve garnished with croutons and finely diced vegetables. Makes about 6½ cups.

Hearty Goulash Soup

5 slices bacon, chopped
3 pounds boneless chuck, trimmed and
    cut into ½-inch cubes
2 tablespoons vegetable oil
4 medium onions (about 1½ pounds),
    chopped fine
3 garlic cloves, minced
3 tablespoons paprika (preferably Hungarian
    sweet*)
1½ teaspoons caraway seeds
⅓ cup all-purpose flour
¼ cup red-wine vinegar
¼ cup tomato paste
5 cups beef broth
5 cups water
½ teaspoon salt
2 red bell peppers,
    chopped fine
4 large russet (baking) potatoes
    (about 2½ pounds)

*available at specialty foods shops and many
    supermarkets

In an 8-quart heavy kettle cook bacon slices over moderate heat, stirring, until crisp and transfer with a slotted spoon to a large bowl. In fat remaining in kettle brown chuck cubes in small batches over high heat, transferring them as browned with slotted spoon to bowl.

Reduce heat to moderate and add oil. Add onions and garlic and cook, stirring, until golden. Stir in paprika, caraway seeds, and flour and cook, stirring, 2 minutes. Whisk in vinegar and tomato paste and cook, whisking, 1 minute. (Mixture will be very thick.) Stir in broth, water, salt, bell peppers, bacon, and chuck and bring to a boil, stirring. Simmer soup, covered, stirring occasionally, 45 minutes.

Peel potatoes and cut into ½-inch pieces. Add potatoes to soup and simmer, covered, stirring occasionally until tender, about 30 minutes. Season soup with salt and pepper. *Soup may be made 3 days ahead and cooled, uncovered, before chilling, covered. Reheat soup, thinning with water if desired.* Makes about 16 cups, serving 12.

PHOTO ON PAGES 84 AND 85

Lemon Zucchini Vichyssoise

1 large leek (white and pale green parts only),
    chopped fine and washed well (about 1½ cups)
¾ cup finely chopped onion
1 tablespoon minced garlic
2 tablespoons olive oil
a ½-pound russet (baking) potato
1½ pounds zucchini, sliced thin (about 4 cups)
3 cups low-salt chicken broth
⅓ cup heavy cream
1 tablespoon fresh lemon juice plus additional
    to taste
ice water for thinning soup

Garnish: lemon slices

In a large heavy saucepan cook leek, onion, and garlic with salt and pepper to taste in oil over moderately low heat, stirring, until leek is softened. Peel potato and cut into 1-inch pieces. Add potato, zucchini, and broth to leek mixture. Simmer mixture, covered, 15 minutes, or until potato is very tender.

In a blender purée mixture in batches until very smooth, transferring as puréed to a bowl. Stir in cream, 1 tablespoon lemon juice, and salt and pepper to taste and chill soup at least 6 hours or overnight.

Thin soup with ice water and season with additional lemon juice and salt and pepper.

Garnish soup with lemon slices. Makes 6 cups.

Hearty Lentil and Ham Soup

1 leftover smoked ham bone or 2 smoked
    ham hocks
1 pound lentils (about 2½ cups), picked over
    and rinsed
½ pound mushrooms, chopped (about 3½ cups)
3 onions, chopped coarse
1 cup chopped carrot
1 cup chopped celery
1 cinnamon stick
1 bay leaf
3½ cups beef broth
8 cups water

In a 6- to 8-quart kettle combine all ingredients and simmer soup, covered partially, stirring occasionally,

1½ hours. Discard bay leaf and cinnamon stick and remove meat from bone or hocks. Chop meat and stir into soup. Makes about 3½ quarts.

Lentil, Kale, and Sausage Soup

a 2½-inch piece smoked *kielbasa*, sliced thin
1 teaspoon vegetable oil if necessary
2 garlic cloves, minced
1 small onion, sliced thin
½ cup lentils, picked over
1½ cups water
1½ cups chicken broth
½ small bunch kale, stems and center ribs
   discarded and leaves sliced thin (about 2 cups)
1 tablespoon balsamic or red-wine vinegar

In a 3-quart heavy saucepan brown sausage over moderate heat and transfer to paper towels to drain. If there is more than 1 teaspoon fat in pan pour off excess; if there is less add enough oil to measure 1 teaspoon fat. Cook garlic in fat, stirring, until golden. Add onion and cook, stirring, until softened.

Add lentils, water, broth, and sausage and simmer, covered, 30 minutes. Add kale and simmer, uncovered, until tender, 5 to 7 minutes. Stir in vinegar and salt and pepper to taste. Makes about 3 cups.

Lettuce and Pea Soup

1 cup chopped onion
2 tablespoons vegetable oil
5 cups sliced romaine
   (about 1 head)
1½ cups chicken broth plus, if desired,
   additional to thin soup
1 cup cooked fresh or thawed frozen peas
½ teaspoon sugar
¾ teaspoon chopped fresh marjoram leaves or
   ¼ teaspoon dried, crumbled
a pinch freshly grated nutmeg
¼ cup sour cream

In a saucepan cook onion in oil over moderate heat, stirring, until softened, about 10 minutes. Stir in romaine and cook, stirring, until wilted. Stir in 1½ cups broth, peas, sugar, marjoram, nutmeg, and salt and pepper to taste and simmer soup 10 minutes.

In a blender purée soup in batches until smooth, adding additional broth to thin to desired consistency. If serving soup hot return it to pan and whisk in sour cream. Heat soup, stirring, until just heated through, but do not let boil. If serving soup cold transfer it to a bowl and whisk in sour cream. Set bowl in a larger bowl of ice and cold water and chill soup, stirring occasionally, 15 minutes, or until cool. Serves 2.

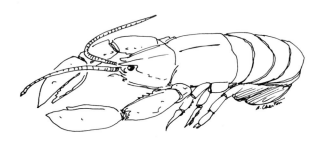

Lobster and Shrimp Bisque

16 cups water
1½ cups dry white wine
two 1¼-pound live lobsters
¾ pound large shrimp (about 18), shelled,
    reserving shells, and deveined if desired
2 medium onions
1 fennel bulb, chopped (about 2 cups)
4 large carrots, chopped
1 celery rib, chopped
2 bay leaves
¾ teaspoon dried thyme, crumbled
¼ cup fresh parsley sprigs
¼ teaspoon black peppercorns
zest of 1 navel orange, removed in strips with
    a vegetable peeler
3 garlic cloves, minced
2 tablespoons olive oil
¼ teaspoon saffron threads
a 28- to 32-ounce can whole tomatoes, drained
    and chopped
¼ cup heavy cream
1½ tablespoons Pernod, or to taste
1 tablespoon fresh lemon juice, or to taste

Garnish: fennel bulb leaves

In a large (5- to 6-quart) kettle combine water and
1 cup wine and bring to a boil. Plunge lobsters into
liquid headfirst and return liquid to a boil. Simmer
lobsters, covered, 9 minutes. With tongs plunge lobsters immediately into cold water to stop cooking, reserving cooking liquid.

Working over a bowl to catch the juices, twist off
tails and claws and reserve juices. Discard tomalley,
head sacs, and any roe and remove meat from tails
and claws, reserving it separately.

To reserved cooking liquid add lobster shells, reserved lobster juices and shrimp shells, 1 onion, quartered, 1 cup fennel, half the carrots, celery, 1 bay leaf,
thyme, parsley, peppercorns, and zest. Simmer mixture gently, uncovered, skimming froth occasionally,
1¼ hours.

Strain stock through large sieve set into a large
bowl and pour into cleaned kettle. Boil stock until reduced to about 6 cups and return to bowl. *Stock,
cooked lobster, and shelled raw shrimp keep, covered
separately and chilled, 1 day.*

In a kettle cook remaining onion, chopped fine, remaining 1 cup fennel, remaining carrots, remaining
bay leaf, garlic, and salt and pepper to taste in oil
over moderate heat, stirring, until vegetables are soft.

Add remaining ½ cup wine and boil until almost
evaporated. Add saffron, tomatoes, and shellfish
stock and simmer, covered, 20 minutes. Add shrimp
and reserved lobster claw meat (reserving tail meat)
and simmer 2 minutes, or until shrimp are cooked
through. Remove soup from heat and remove 6
shrimp, reserving them. Discard bay leaf.

In a blender purée soup in batches until smooth,
transferring as it is puréed to a very fine sieve set
over a saucepan. Force soup through sieve, pressing
hard on solids, and whisk in cream, Pernod, and salt
and pepper to taste. Heat bisque over moderate heat
until hot (do not boil) and stir in lemon juice.

Chop fine reserved shrimp and lobster tail meat
and divide among heated soup bowls. Ladle soup
over shellfish and garnish with fennel leaves. Makes
about 7 cups.

PHOTO ON PAGES 24 AND 25

Minestrone with Garlic and Parmesan Croutons

2 tablespoons olive oil
1 small onion, cut into ¼-inch-thick slices
1 carrot, cut into ¼-inch-thick slices
1 small red potato, cut into ½-inch dice
a 14- to 16-ounce can peeled whole tomatoes
    including their juice
1¼ cups low-salt chicken broth

1 ounce (about 2 tablespoons) dried *ditalini* or
    other small macaroni-type pasta
1 large garlic clove, sliced
2 slices homemade-type white bread, cut into
    ½-inch cubes
1 teaspoon minced fresh parsley leaves
1 tablespoon freshly grated Parmesan cheese
1 small zucchini (about 6 ounces), washed and
    cut into ½-inch dice
1 cup chopped romaine lettuce

In a large saucepan heat 1 tablespoon oil over moderately high heat until hot but not smoking and sauté onion, carrot, and potato with salt to taste until vegetables are lightly browned. Add tomatoes and their liquid, broth, and pasta and simmer, stirring to break up tomatoes, 10 minutes, or until pasta and vegetables are tender.

In a skillet sauté garlic in remaining tablespoon oil over moderately high heat until golden and discard with a slotted spoon. In garlic-flavored oil fry bread, seasoned with salt, over moderate heat, stirring occasionally, until golden on all sides. Remove skillet from heat and add parsley and Parmesan, tossing croutons to coat well.

Add zucchini and half the croutons to tomato mixture and simmer, stirring occasionally, 5 minutes, or until zucchini is almost tender and croutons are dissolved. Stir in romaine and cook 1 minute.

Serve soup sprinkled with remaining croutons. Makes about 4½ cups.

Mushroom Barley Soup

1 ounce dried *shiitake* mushrooms or other dried
    mushrooms such as *porcini,* morels, or
    chanterelles if desired
1 cup boiling-hot water if using dried mushrooms
6 garlic cloves, chopped fine
¼ cup olive oil
3 medium onions, chopped fine
2 pounds white mushrooms, sliced thin
1 tablespoon soy sauce
½ cup medium-dry Sherry
5 cups chicken broth
5 cups water
1 cup pearl barley

8 carrots, sliced diagonally ½ inch thick
½ teaspoon dried thyme, crumbled
½ teaspoon dried rosemary, crumbled
⅓ cup minced fresh parsley leaves

In a small bowl soak dried mushrooms (if using) in the boiling water 20 minutes and transfer to a cutting board, reserving liquid. Discard stems of *shiitakes* (if using) and slice mushrooms thin. Strain reserved liquid through a fine sieve lined with a dampened paper towel into another small bowl.

In a heavy kettle (at least 5 quarts) cook garlic in oil over moderate heat, stirring, until golden. Add onions and cook, stirring, until pale golden. Add white mushrooms, dried mushrooms (if using), and soy sauce and sauté over moderately high heat, stirring, until liquid mushrooms give off is evaporated. Add Sherry and boil until evaporated.

Add broth, water, strained mushroom-soaking liquid, barley, carrots, and dried herbs to mushroom mixture and simmer, covered, 1 hour. Season soup with salt and pepper. *Soup may be prepared up to this point 4 days ahead (cool uncovered before chilling covered.)*

Just before serving, stir in parsley. Makes 12 cups.

Split-Pea Soup with Caramelized Onions and Cuminseed

1 cup dried split peas
½ teaspoon dried basil, crumbled
1 bay leaf
2 cups water
2 cups chicken broth
2 cups chopped onion
½ teaspoon cuminseed
3 tablespoons olive oil

In a heavy saucepan simmer peas, basil, and bay leaf in water and broth, covered partially, until peas are tender, about 35 minutes, and discard bay leaf.

While peas are cooking, in a heavy skillet sauté onion and cuminseed in oil over moderately high heat, stirring, until golden brown.

In a blender purée soup in batches until just smooth and transfer to a bowl. Stir in onion mixture and salt and pepper to taste. Makes about 4 cups.

Yellow Pea Soup

2 cups dried whole yellow peas* or yellow split
    peas, picked over
8 leeks (white parts only), chopped coarse, washed
    well, and drained
12 cups water
1 smoked ham hock
2 thyme sprigs or ½ teaspoon dried thyme,
    crumbled
½ pound celery root
4 carrots, quartered lengthwise and sliced thin

*available by mail order from Old Denmark
    Scandinavian Food Specialties, 133 East 65th
    Street, NYC 10021, tel. (212) 744-2533

In a large bowl soak peas overnight in enough cold
water to cover by 2 inches and drain.

In a 7½-quart heavy kettle combine leeks, the 12
cups water, peas, ham hock, and thyme and simmer
mixture, uncovered, until peas are very tender, about
30 minutes.

In a blender purée 4 cups soup in batches and return to kettle.

Peel celery root and cut into ¼-inch dice. Add celery root to soup and simmer, stirring occasionally, 20
minutes. Add carrots and simmer, stirring occasionally, until tender, about 15 minutes.

Remove meat from ham hock and discard skin and
bones. Chop meat coarse and stir into soup with salt
and pepper to taste. *Soup may be made 3 days in advance. Cool soup uncovered and keep covered and
chilled. Thin soup with water if too thick.* Makes
about 12 cups.

PHOTO ON PAGE 23

Chilled Yellow Pepper and Scallion Buttermilk Soup

3 bunches scallions
3 large yellow bell peppers (about 1½ pounds),
    chopped
1 tablespoon vegetable oil
3 cups water
2 cups buttermilk

Chop white and pale green parts of scallions and
slice greens thin. In a large heavy saucepan cook
chopped scallions and bell peppers in oil over moderately low heat, stirring occasionally, until softened.
Add water and simmer 15 minutes, or until peppers
are very tender.

In a blender purée mixture and in a bowl stir together purée, buttermilk, scallion greens, and salt and
pepper to taste. Chill soup, covered. *Soup may be
made 1 day ahead and chilled, covered.* Makes about
6 cups.

PHOTO ON PAGE 67

Cioppino
(San Francisco-Style Seafood Soup)

4 garlic cloves, minced
¼ cup olive oil
1 medium onion, chopped fine
½ teaspoon dried hot red pepper flakes
1 green bell pepper, chopped
1 tablespoon red-wine vinegar
1½ cups dry white wine
1 teaspoon dried oregano, crumbled
1 bay leaf
a 28- to 32-ounce can whole tomatoes including
    juice, puréed coarse
1 tablespoon tomato paste
2 pounds live hard-shelled crabs
12 small hard-shelled clams, scrubbed well
½ pound medium shrimp, shelled, leaving tails and
    first joint intact
½ pound sea scallops
1 pound scrod or other white fish fillet, cut into
    1-inch pieces
2 tablespoons minced fresh parsley leaves

In a heavy kettle (at least 5 quarts) cook garlic in
oil over moderate heat, stirring, until pale golden.
Add onion and cook, stirring, until softened. Add
pepper flakes and bell pepper and cook, stirring, until
softened. Add vinegar and boil until evaporated. Add
wine, oregano, and bay leaf and simmer 5 minutes.
Stir in tomato purée and paste and bring to a boil.

Add crabs and clams and simmer, covered, 15 to
20 minutes, checking often and transferring clams as
they open to a bowl (discard unopened ones).

Transfer crabs with tongs to a cutting board and remove top shells, adding any crab liquid to soup.

Halve or quarter crabs (depending on size) and re-serve, with any additional liquid, in a bowl.

Add shrimp, scallops, and fish to soup and simmer, covered, 5 minutes, or until seafood is just cooked through. Stir in gently crabs, their liquid, and clams and sprinkle with parsley. Serves 6.

Spiced Shrimp Soup

1 pound (about 26) medium shrimp (preferably
    with heads)
4 stalks fresh lemongrass*, outer leaves discarded
    and root ends trimmed
6 cups water
¼ cup finely chopped well-washed coriander roots
    and/or stems
½ teaspoon salt, or to taste
½ teaspoon freshly ground black pepper
a 1-inch cube peeled fresh gingerroot, cut into fine
    julienne strips
¼ cup Asian fish sauce (preferably *naam pla**)
¼ cup fresh lime juice
1 small fresh red or green Thai chili* or *serrano*
    chili, or to taste, seeded and sliced very thin
    (wear rubber gloves)

Garnish: fresh coriander leaves, thinly sliced
    kaffir lime leaves*, and small fresh red Thai
    chilies

*available at Asian markets, some specialty
    foods shops, by mail order from
    Adriana's Caravan, Brooklyn, NY,
    tel. (800) 316-0820 or (718) 436-8565, or
    Uwajimaya, 519 Sixth Avenue South, Seattle,
    WA 98104, tel. (206) 624-6248

Rinse shrimp well and shell, reserving shell and heads.

Cut 3 lemongrass stalks into 1-inch sections and crush lightly with flat side of a heavy knife. In a saucepan combine crushed lemongrass with reserved shrimp shells and heads, water, coriander roots, salt, and pepper and simmer, uncovered, 20 minutes. Strain broth through a fine sieve into another saucepan.

Thinly slice lower 6 inches of remaining lemongrass stalk, discarding remainder of stalk, and combine with broth and gingerroot. Simmer broth 5 minutes. Add shrimp and simmer 1 minute, or until shrimp are just firm to touch. Stir in fish sauce, lime juice, and chili.

Serve soup warm or at room temperature, garnished with coriander leaves, lime leaves, and chilies. Makes about 6 cups.

PHOTO ON PAGE 45

Yellow Squash and Bell Pepper Soup

¼ cup chopped onion
2 tablespoons unsalted butter
1 large yellow bell pepper, thinly sliced (about
    1½ cups)
¾ pound yellow summer squash, sliced thin
    crosswise (about 3 cups)
¼ teaspoon minced garlic
1 cup low-salt chicken broth
2 tablespoons chopped fresh coriander

In a large skillet cook onion in butter over moderate heat, stirring, until softened. Add bell pepper and cook, covered, stirring occasionally, until pepper is softened, about 5 minutes. Stir in squash and garlic and cook, covered, stirring occasionally, until squash is tender, about 10 minutes. Stir in broth and bring mixture to a simmer. In a blender purée soup until smooth and transfer to a saucepan. Cook soup over moderate heat until just heated through, stirring in enough water to thin to desired consistency, and season with salt and pepper.

Serve soup sprinkled with coriander. Makes about 2½ cups.

FISH AND SHELLFISH

FISH

Broiled Flounder with Bread Crumb Topping

¼ cup finely chopped onion
¼ cup finely chopped green bell pepper
1 garlic clove,
  minced
2 teaspoons vegetable oil
2 tablespoons fine dry bread crumbs
2 flounder fillets (each about
  6 ounces)
2 tablespoons mayonnaise

In a heavy skillet cook onion, bell pepper, and garlic in oil over moderately low heat, stirring occasionally, until vegetables are softened and stir in bread crumbs and salt and pepper to taste.

Preheat broiler.

On a work surface arrange flounder skinned sides up and spread top with mayonnaise. Sprinkle flounder with bread crumb mixture and on oiled rack of a broiler pan broil about 6 inches from heat until cooked through, about 6 minutes. Serves 2.

Baked Halibut with Warm Sherry Onion Vinaigrette

1½ cups finely chopped onion
3 tablespoons minced shallot
1 large garlic clove,
  minced
1 tablespoon unsalted butter
4 tablespoons Sherry vinegar*
1 plum tomato, seeded and
  chopped fine
⅓ cup finely diced red bell pepper
½ cup olive oil
1½ teaspoons minced fresh thyme plus
  1 thyme sprig

4 Kalamata or other brine-cured large black olives,
  pitted and chopped fine
2 tablespoons minced fresh parsley leaves
three 10- to 12-ounce pieces of halibut fillet,
  halved crosswise
2 tablespoons dry white wine
¼ cup fish stock or bottled clam juice

Garnish: fresh thyme sprigs

*available at specialty foods shops and some
  supermarkets

In a heavy skillet cook onion, 1½ tablespoons shallot, and garlic in butter with salt and pepper to taste over moderate heat, stirring, until onion is pale golden, about 10 minutes.

Stir in vinegar and cook, covered, 5 minutes. Stir in tomato and cook, covered, stirring occasionally, 10 minutes. Stir in bell pepper and ¼ cup oil and cook, covered, stirring occasionally, 5 minutes. Stir in minced thyme and olives and cook, uncovered, stirring, 2 minutes. Stir in parsley and remaining ¼ cup oil and keep vinaigrette warm.

Preheat oven to 425° F. and butter a baking dish just large enough to hold fillets in one layer.

Sprinkle remaining 1½ tablespoons shallot in baking dish and in it arrange fillets, seasoned with salt and pepper. Add thyme sprig, wine, and stock or clam juice and cover fillets with a buttered piece of wax paper. Bake fish in middle of oven 10 to 15 minutes (depending upon thickness of fillets), or until just cooked through.

Transfer baked fillets to a large platter and keep warm. Pour cooking liquid through a fine sieve set over skillet with vinaigrette. Cook vinaigrette over moderate heat, stirring, until warm and cooking liquid is incorporated.

Serve fish, garnished with thyme sprigs, with warm vinaigrette. Serves 6.

PHOTO ON PAGE 26

Seared Salmon with Horseradish Mustard Vinaigrette

two 6-ounce pieces salmon fillet
1 teaspoon coarse salt
½ teaspoon freshly ground black pepper
3 tablespoons olive oil
2 teaspoons white-wine vinegar
2 teaspoons Dijon mustard
2 teaspoons drained bottled horseradish

Pat salmon dry and coat with salt and pepper. In a heavy skillet (preferably cast iron) heat 1 tablespoon oil over moderately high heat until hot but not smoking and sear salmon, skin sides down, 5 minutes. Reduce heat to moderately low. Turn salmon and cook 4 minutes more, or until it just flakes.

While salmon is cooking, in a small bowl whisk together vinegar, mustard, horseradish, remaining 2 tablespoons oil, and salt and pepper to taste until emulsified.

Serve vinaigrette over salmon. Serves 2.

Broiled Salmon Fillet with Mustard Dill Sauce

a 2½- to 3-pound salmon fillet
soy sauce for rubbing salmon

Garnish: fresh bay leaves and thyme sprigs
Accompaniment: mustard dill sauce (recipe follows)

Preheat broiler.

Rinse salmon and pat dry. Arrange salmon, skin side down, in a foil-lined jelly-roll pan and rub thoroughly with soy sauce. Season salmon with salt and pepper and broil about 4 inches from heat 12 to 15 minutes, or until just cooked through. Transfer salmon to a platter and garnish with herbs.

Serve salmon warm or at room temperature with mustard dill sauce. Serves 6.

Mustard Dill Sauce

½ cup coarse-grained mustard
¼ cup water
½ cup heavy cream
¼ cup olive oil
4 teaspoons sugar
½ cup chopped fresh dill, or to taste

In a bowl combine well all ingredients and season with pepper. *Sauce may be made 1 day ahead and chilled, covered. Let sauce come to room temperature and whisk before serving.* Makes about 1½ cups.

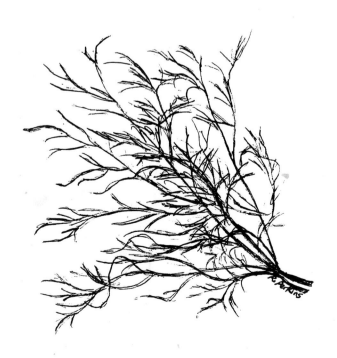

Fish Chermoula
(Fish with Moroccan Seasoning)

For chermoula
½ teaspoon coriander seeds
12 whole black peppercorns
¼ teaspoon dried hot red pepper flakes
large pinch of saffron threads, crumbled
½ teaspoon coarse salt
1 teaspoon paprika
1 medium onion, minced (about1 cup)
⅓ cup finely chopped fresh parsley leaves
2 tablespoons minced preserved lemon peel*
    plus 2 tablespoons preserved lemon juice or
    fresh lemon juice to taste
2 tablespoons olive oil
2 tablespoons finely chopped fresh coriander
1 garlic clove, minced

6 skinless small fish fillets such as sea bass,
    red snapper, or any other firm white lean fish
    (about 1¾ pounds)
2 tablespoons unsalted butter
½ cup water
4 fennel bulbs (sometimes called anise, about
    3 pounds), trimmed and cut lengthwise into
    thin strips

Garnish: fennel leaves

*available by mail order from The Gardener,
    1836 Fourth Street, Berkeley, CA 94710,
    tel. (510) 548-4545, or recipe, page 92

Make chermoula:
With a mortar and pestle, an electric spice grinder, or a cleaned coffee grinder grind fine coriander seeds, peppercorns, red pepper flakes, and saffron. Transfer spice mixture to a small bowl and stir in remaining chermoula ingredients.

Lightly oil a shallow baking dish just large enough to hold fillets in one layer. Arrange fillets, seasoned with salt and pepper, in dish and top evenly with chermoula. Chill fillets, covered, 1 hour.

Preheat oven to 350° F.

In a large heavy skillet melt butter in water over moderately high heat. Add fennel and cook, covered, stirring occasionally, 10 minutes. Cook fennel, uncovered, stirring occasionally, until tender, 5 to 10 minutes more, and season with salt and pepper.

While fennel is cooking, bake chilled fish in oven until it just flakes, 10 to 15 minutes.

Serve each fillet on a bed of fennel and garnish with fennel leaves. Serves 6.

PHOTO ON PAGE 58

Red Snapper and Eggplant with
Red Bell Pepper Sauce

For sauce
1 tablespoon olive oil
2 large red bell peppers, sliced thin
¾ teaspoon minced garlic
2 teaspoons fresh lemon juice, or to taste

olive oil for brushing pan and eggplant
1 small eggplant (preferably Asian, about 6 inches
    long and 2½ inches wide)
two 6- to 7-ounce red snapper fillets, skinned
1 tablespoon thinly sliced fresh mint leaves

Garnish: thinly sliced fresh mint leaves

Make sauce:
In a large skillet heat oil over moderately high heat until hot but not smoking and cook peppers and

garlic, stirring, 10 minutes, or until peppers are tender. Transfer pepper mixture to a blender and blend with lemon juice until smooth. Season sauce with salt and pepper and keep warm.

Preheat broiler and lightly brush a small shallow baking pan with oil.

Cut four ¼-inch-thick lengthwise slices from eggplant, reserving remainder for another use. Rinse fish fillets and pat dry. Season fillets with salt and pepper to taste and arrange, skinned side down, in prepared baking pan. Sprinkle each fillet with ½ tablespoon mint leaves. Arrange 2 eggplant slices on each fillet, covering mint completely and overlapping eggplant slices slightly, and brush them lightly with oil. Broil fillets about 4 inches from heat until fillets are just cooked through and eggplant is golden, about 5 minutes.

Divide sauce between 2 plates and arrange fillets, brushed with pan juices, on top of sauce. Garnish fillets with mint leaves. Serves 2.

Snapper with Browned Butter and Capers

2 tablespoons unsalted butter
1 shallot, minced
2 teaspoons fresh lemon juice
2 tablespoons minced fresh parsley leaves
1 tablespoon drained bottled capers,
  minced
2 teaspoons finely chopped lemon pulp
1 teaspoon freshly grated lemon zest
two ½-pound red snapper fillets

Garnish: lemon slices

Preheat oven to 350° F.

In a small skillet melt butter over moderate heat until it begins to brown and stir in shallot. Cook mixture until shallot is softened but not browned, about 2 minutes. Remove skillet from heat and stir in lemon juice.

In a small bowl stir together parsley, capers, lemon pulp, and zest.

Put fish fillets in a jelly-roll pan, skin sides down, and sprinkle with salt and pepper to taste. Brush fillets with butter mixture and sprinkle with parsley mixture. Bake fillets in middle of oven until just

cooked through, about 12 minutes. Garnish fillets with lemon slices. Serves 2.

Fillet of Sole with Pine Nuts and Chives

1½ tablespoons pine nuts
2 tablespoons unsalted butter
1½ teaspoons minced fresh chives or
  scallion greens
two 6-ounce fillets of sole
seasoned all-purpose flour for dredging

Accompaniment: lemon wedges

In a large non-stick skillet sauté pine nuts in 1 tablespoon butter over moderately high heat, stirring, until golden. Add chives or scallion greens. Remove skillet from heat and transfer mixture with slotted spoon to a dish.

Season sole with salt and pepper and dredge in flour, shaking off excess. In the skillet heat remaining tablespoon butter over moderately high heat until foam subsides and sauté sole until it just flakes, about 1 minute on each side. Transfer sole to plates and spoon pine nut mixture over it.

Serve sole with lemon. Serves 2.

Olive and Fennel Tuna Melts

two 6⅛-ounce cans solid white tuna, drained well
⅓ cup mayonnaise
⅔ cup finely chopped fennel bulb
5 Kalamata or other brine-cured black olives,
  pitted and chopped
1 tablespoon minced fresh parsley leaves
1 tablespoon fresh lemon juice, or to taste
4 slices rye bread, toasted lightly
4 ounces grated sharp Cheddar cheese

Preheat broiler.

Into a bowl flake tuna and stir in mayonnaise, fennel, olives, parsley, lemon juice, and salt and pepper to taste. Divide tuna salad among toast and top with Cheddar. In a shallow baking pan broil sandwiches under broiler about 4 inches from heat until cheese is bubbling, 1 to 2 minutes. Makes 4 sandwiches.

Fried Crawfish Rémoulade

1½ tablespoons drained bottled horseradish
1½ tablespoons Creole mustard* or Dijon mustard
3 tablespoons distilled white vinegar
1 teaspoon paprika
½ teaspoon salt
cayenne to taste
⅓ cup vegetable oil plus additional for frying
2 scallions, chopped fine
1 celery rib, chopped fine
1 pound shelled crawfish tails*, thawed if frozen
   and drained
seasoned all-purpose flour for dredging
4 cups shredded romaine
2 cups shredded *radicchio*

*available by mail order from Community
   Kitchens, Ridgely, MD, tel. (800) 535-9901

In a bowl whisk together horseradish, mustard, vinegar, paprika, salt, and cayenne and add ⅓ cup of oil in a stream, whisking until emulsified. Stir in scallions and celery. Rémoulade *may be made 1 day ahead and chilled, covered.*

In a bowl dredge crawfish in seasoned flour and shake in a sieve to remove excess flour. In a kettle heat 1½ inches of additional oil to 390° F. on a deep-fat thermometer and fry crawfish in 4 batches 45 seconds, or until golden. Transfer crawfish with a slotted spoon to paper towels to drain.

In a bowl toss together romaine and *radicchio* and divide among 6 plates. Arrange crawfish on lettuce and serve with *rémoulade.* Serves 6 as a first course.

PHOTO ON PAGE 37

Fried Oyster Po' Boys

For tartar sauce
1 cup mayonnaise
¼ cup minced sweet pickle
1 hard-boiled large egg, forced through a
   coarse sieve
2 tablespoons minced shallot
2 tablespoons drained bottled capers
½ teaspoon dried tarragon, crumbled
2 tablespoons Creole mustard* or Dijon mustard
2 tablespoons minced fresh parsley leaves
1 teaspoon fresh lemon juice

24 shucked oysters, drained
yellow cornmeal, seasoned with freshly ground
   black pepper and cayenne, for coating
vegetable oil for deep-frying
2 loaves soft-crusted French bread
sliced tomatoes
shredded iceberg lettuce

*available by mail order from Community
   Kitchens, Ridgely, MD, tel. (800) 535-9901

Make tartar sauce:
In a bowl stir together sauce ingredients.

In a heavy-duty plastic bag, working in batches of 6, coat oysters with cornmeal, knocking off excess. In a heavy kettle heat 1½ inches of oil to 375° F. on a deep-fat thermometer and fry oysters in batches of 6, turning occasionally, until golden and just cooked through, about 1½ minutes. Transfer oysters with a slotted spoon to paper towels to drain.

Halve loaves crosswise and horizontally, cutting all the way through, and spread each piece with about 2 tablespoons tartar sauce. Divide tomatoes, lettuce, and oysters among bottom pieces of bread and top with remaining bread, pressing together gently. Makes 4 sandwiches.

Scallop and Corn Pot Stickers with Sesame Vinaigrette

For pot stickers
½ pound sea scallops
¼ teaspoon salt
¼ cup soft tofu (preferably silken)
¼ cup cooked corn
¼ cup minced red bell pepper
3 tablespoons minced scallion
2 tablespoons finely chopped fresh coriander
eighteen 3- to 4-inch round won ton or
   dumpling or *gyoza* wrappers*,
   thawed if frozen

cornstarch for dusting tray
For vinaigrette
3 tablespoons rice vinegar
1 tablespoon soy sauce
1 tablespoon Asian (toasted) sesame oil
2 tablespoons black* or white sesame seeds,
  toasted lightly

1 tablespoon vegetable oil
⅓ cup water

Garnish: fresh coriander leaves

*available at Asian markets and many
  specialty foods shops and
  supermarkets

Make pot stickers:

Discard small tough muscle from side of each scallop and in a food processor purée half of scallops with salt. With motor running add tofu in a stream and blend until just combined.

Transfer scallop mousse to a small bowl. Chop fine remaining scallops and stir into mousse with corn, bell pepper, scallion, and coriander.

Put about 1 tablespoon filling in center of 1 wrapper and moisten edge of wrapper. Gather edge of wrapper up and around filling, pleating edge. Gently squeeze middle of pot sticker to form a waist, keeping filling level with top of wrapper. (Pot sticker will resemble a sack filled to top.)

Make 17 more pot stickers in same manner and arrange on a tray dusted lightly with cornstarch. *Pot stickers may be made up to this point 1 day ahead and chilled, covered with plastic wrap.*

Make vinaigrette:

In a bowl whisk together vinaigrette ingredients.

In a large non-stick skillet heat oil over moderately high heat until hot but not smoking and fry pot-sticker bottoms until golden, about 1 minute. Add water and steam pot stickers, covered, 3 to 4 minutes, or until filling is springy to touch. Remove lid and cook pot stickers until liquid is evaporated and bottoms are recrisped.

Serve steamed pot stickers with sesame vinaigrette and garnish with coriander leaves. Serves 6 as a first course.

PHOTO ON PAGES 40 AND 41

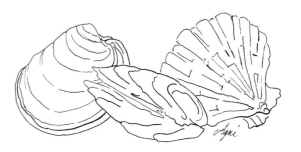

*Grilled Sea Scallops and Tomatoes
with Olive Vinaigrette*

¼ cup chopped pitted Kalamata or other
  brine-cured black olives
1 tablespoon finely chopped bottled roasted
  red pepper
½ teaspoon minced garlic
1 teaspoon Dijon mustard
1 tablespoon red-wine vinegar
¼ teaspoon fresh lemon juice
¼ cup olive oil (preferably extra-virgin)
½ pound sea scallops, rinsed and drained
2 medium vine-ripened tomatoes, cut into wedges
2 cups *arugula,* stems discarded and leaves
  washed well and spun dry

In a blender blend olives, roasted pepper, garlic, mustard, vinegar, lemon juice, and salt and pepper to taste until smooth. With motor running add 3 tablespoons oil in a stream and blend vinaigrette until emulsified.

Discard small tough muscle from side of each scallop if necessary and in a bowl toss scallops with remaining tablespoon oil and salt and pepper to taste.

Heat a well-seasoned ridged grill pan over high heat until hot and grill scallops until just cooked through, 2 to 3 minutes on each side. Transfer scallops to a plate and keep warm. Grill tomatoes over high heat until tender and lightly charred, 1 to 2 minutes on each side.

Toss *arugula* with half the vinaigrette and divide between 2 plates. Top *arugula* with scallops and tomatoes and serve with remaining vinaigrette if desired. Serves 2.

Crisp Curried Shrimp

2 tablespoons all-purpose flour
½ teaspoon curry powder
⅛ teaspoon cayenne pepper
¾ pound large shrimp (about 12), shelled and
    deveined
2 tablespoons olive oil
1 bunch scallions, cut into 2-inch lengths

Accompaniment: lemon wedges

In a bowl stir together flour, curry powder, cayenne, and salt to taste. Add shrimp to flour mixture, tossing to coat.

In a large heavy skillet heat oil over moderately high heat until hot but not smoking and sauté scallions until well browned and almost tender.

Add shrimp to scallions and sauté, stirring occasionally, about 4 minutes, or until shrimp are opaque throughout.

Serve shrimp with lemon. Serves 2.

Grilled Rosemary Garlic Shrimp

¼ cup finely chopped garlic, mashed to a paste
    with 1 teaspoon coarse salt
2 tablespoons minced fresh rosemary leaves
3 tablespoons olive oil plus oil for brushing shrimp
16 jumbo shrimp (about 10 per pound)
four 12-inch bamboo skewers

Garnish: fresh rosemary sprigs
Accompaniment: lemon wedges

In a large bowl stir together garlic, rosemary, and 3 tablespoons oil and add shrimp. Marinate shrimp, covered and chilled, at least 4 hours or overnight.

In a shallow dish soak skewers in water to cover 30 minutes and prepare grill.

To grill, thread 4 shrimp on each skewer and brush with additional oil. Grill shrimp on an oiled rack set 5 inches over glowing coals 3 to 4 minutes on each side, or until just cooked through.

(Alternatively, brush shrimp with additional oil and grill in a hot well-seasoned ridged grill pan, covered, over moderately high heat 3 to 4 minutes on each side, or until cooked through.)

Garnish shrimp with rosemary sprigs and serve with lemon. Serves 4.

PHOTO ON PAGE 48

Paella-Style Shellfish Pasta

2 cups chicken broth
¾ cup dry white wine
½ teaspoon crumbled saffron threads
3 tablespoons olive oil
6 ounces *fideos* (thin Spanish noodles in coils) or
    thin spaghetti, either pasta broken into 2-inch
    lengths
6 large shrimp (16 to 20 per pound), shelled
6 large sea scallops
6 New Zealand cockles or Manila clams, scrubbed
½ of a 9-ounce package frozen artichoke hearts,
    thawed
1 teaspoon minced fresh chives

Preheat oven to 400° F.

In a saucepan bring broth and wine to a boil and stir in saffron. Keep mixture at a simmer. In a heavy ovenproof skillet measuring 8 inches across the bottom heat oil over moderately high heat until hot but not smoking and sauté uncooked pasta, stirring, until golden, about 2 minutes. Pour simmering broth mixture over pasta and simmer 5 minutes.

Nestle shellfish and artichoke hearts into pasta and bake, uncovered, in middle of oven until liquid is reduced to a syrupy glaze (pasta should be tender but crisp on top), about 20 minutes.

Sprinkle pasta with chives. Serves 2.

MEAT

BEEF

blender or food processor blend together with mustard, vinegars, and salt and pepper to taste until smooth. With motor running add oil in a very thin stream and blend until emulsified. *Vinaigrette may be made 4 days ahead and chilled in a tightly sealed jar. Shake vinaigrette well or reblend before serving.*

Slice fillet thin. Arrange fillet, *arugula*, and red cherry tomatoes decoratively on a platter and serve with vinaigrette. Serves 12.

PHOTO ON PAGES 64 AND 65

Fillet of Beef with Arugula, Cherry Tomatoes, and Roasted Garlic Vinaigrette

a trimmed 4- to 4½-pound fillet of beef, tied,
    at room temperature
For vinaigrette
3 heads garlic, unpeeled
2 teaspoons Dijon mustard
¼ cup red-wine vinegar
¼ cup balsamic vinegar
1½ cups olive oil

6 cups *arugula*, washed thoroughly and spun dry
3 cups vine-ripened red cherry tomatoes, halved
3 cups vine-ripened yellow cherry tomatoes,
    halved

Preheat oven to 500° F.

Pat fillet dry and season with salt and pepper. In an oiled roasting pan roast fillet in middle of oven until a meat thermometer registers 130° F. for medium-rare meat, 20 to 25 minutes, and let cool to room temperature. *Fillet may be roasted 2 days ahead and chilled, wrapped well.*

Make vinaigrette:

Preheat oven to 400° F.

Cut top ¼ inch off each head garlic and wrap heads together in foil. Roast garlic 40 to 50 minutes, or until very soft, and let cool. Squeeze roasted garlic from each head (there should be about ⅓ cup) and in a

Grilled Rib-Eye Steaks with Béarnaise Butter

For béarnaise butter
3 tablespoons unsalted butter, softened
2 teaspoons finely chopped fresh tarragon leaves
2 teaspoons minced shallot
½ teaspoon fresh lemon juice, or to taste
⅛ teaspoon salt

four 1-inch-thick rib-eye steaks
vegetable oil for rubbing on steaks

Make béarnaise butter:

On a small plate with a fork blend all béarnaise butter ingredients together well and transfer to a sheet of wax paper. Using wax paper as an aid, shape butter into a 4-inch-long log and wrap. Chill butter 1 hour, or until firm. *Béarnaise butter may be made 5 days ahead and chilled, wrapped tightly.*

Prepare grill.

Bring steaks to room temperature and rub lightly with oil. Season steaks with salt and pepper and grill on a rack set 5 to 6 inches over glowing coals 4 to 5 minutes on each side for medium-rare meat. (Alternatively, steaks may be grilled in a hot well-seasoned ridged grill pan over moderately high heat.)

Serve steaks topped with thin slices of béarnaise butter. Serves 4.

PHOTO ON PAGE 61

Grilled Rib-Eye Steaks with Cucumber Relish

For relish
1½ cups diced seeded cucumber
3 tablespoons finely chopped red onion
½ teaspoon finely chopped *jalapeño* chili,
    or to taste (wear rubber gloves)
¼ cup plain yogurt
½ teaspoon minced garlic
1 teaspoon fresh lemon juice

two 1-inch-thick rib-eye steaks at room
    temperature
freshly ground black pepper

Prepare grill.
Make relish:
In a small bowl combine relish ingredients with
salt to taste.

Season steaks with salt and generously with pepper. Grill steaks on an oiled rack set 5 to 6 inches
over glowing coals 4 to 5 minutes on each side for
medium-rare meat. (Alternatively, steaks may be
grilled in a hot well-seasoned ridged grill pan over
moderately high heat.)
Serve steaks with relish. Serves 2.

Roast Prime Ribs of Beef with Pink and Green Peppercorn Crust and Red-Wine Pan Sauce

a 4-rib standing rib roast (about 7½ to 8 pounds
    trimmed)
For crust
2 teaspoons whole allspice berries, crushed
3 tablespoons pink peppercorns*, crushed lightly
3 tablespoons freeze-dried green peppercorns,
    crushed lightly
3 tablespoons unsalted butter, softened
2 tablespoons all-purpose flour
1 tablespoon firmly packed brown sugar
1 tablespoon Dijon mustard
1½ teaspoons salt
For sauce
⅔ cup dry red wine
2 cups low-salt beef broth
1½ tablespoons cornstarch
1 tablespoon Worcestershire sauce
1 tablespoon water

Garnish: rosemary sprigs

*available at specialty foods shops

Let rib roast stand at room temperature 1 hour.
Preheat oven to 500° F.
Make crust:
In a small bowl combine crust ingredients, stirring
to form a paste.
Pat beef dry and sprinkle with salt and pepper. In a
roasting pan roast beef, ribs side down, 30 minutes.
Transfer beef to a platter and discard drippings unless
needed for another use.
Reduce oven temperature to 350° F.
Return beef to roasting pan, ribs side down, and
spread with peppercorn paste. Roast beef 1 to 1¼
hours more, or until a meat thermometer inserted in
fleshy section registers 135° F. for medium-rare meat.
Transfer beef to a cutting board and discard strings
if necessary. Let beef stand, covered loosely, at least
20 minutes and up to 30 minutes before carving.
Make sauce:
Skim fat from drippings in roasting pan. To pan
add wine and deglaze over moderately high heat,
scraping up brown bits. Boil mixture until reduced by
about half and transfer to a saucepan. Add broth and
boil 5 minutes.
In a bowl dissolve cornstarch in Worcestershire
sauce and water and add to pan in a stream, whisking.
Bring sauce to a boil, whisking, and boil 1 minute.
Season sauce with salt and pepper.
Garnish rib roast with rosemary sprigs and serve
with sauce. Serves 8.

PHOTO ON PAGES 82 AND 83

Grilled Spicy Skirt Steak

a ¾- to 1-pound skirt steak, trimmed
1 tablespoon chili powder
1 teaspoon ground cumin
1 large garlic clove, minced and mashed to a
    paste with 1 teaspoon coarse salt
2 teaspoons Worcestershire sauce
1 teaspoon sugar
¾ teaspoon freshly ground black pepper
¼ teaspoon allspice
1 tablespoon vegetable oil

Accompaniment: flour tortillas, warmed

Prepare grill.

Cut steak into large pieces to fit on a grill or ridged grill pan.

In a small bowl stir together chili powder, cumin, garlic paste, Worcestershire sauce, sugar, pepper, allspice, and oil and rub all over meat. Marinate meat in a resealable plastic bag, chilled, 20 minutes.

Grill steak on a well-oiled rack set about 4 inches over glowing coals 3 to 5 minutes on each side, or until just springy to touch, for medium-rare meat. (Alternatively, steak may be grilled in a hot well-seasoned ridged grill pan over moderately high heat.) Let steak stand on a cutting board 5 minutes and cut across grain on the diagonal into thin slices.

Serve steak with tortillas. Serves 2 generously.

Balsamic-Glazed Sirloin Steak

¾ pound ½-inch-thick boneless sirloin steak
2 teaspoons sesame seeds
2 teaspoons vegetable oil
2 garlic cloves, minced
⅛ teaspoon dried hot red pepper flakes
3 tablespoons medium-dry Sherry
1 tablespoon soy sauce
2 teaspoons balsamic vinegar
1 teaspoon honey
1 tablespoon cold unsalted butter

Pat steak dry and season lightly with salt and pepper. Spread 1 teaspoon sesame seeds evenly on one side of steak.

In a large heavy skillet heat oil over moderately high heat until it begins to smoke and add steak, sesame seed-side down. Spread remaining teaspoon sesame seeds on top of steak. Cook steak 1½ minutes on each side for medium-rare meat and transfer with a slotted spatula to a small platter. Keep steak warm.

Pour off almost all fat from skillet and add garlic and red pepper flakes. Cook garlic mixture over moderate heat, stirring, 10 seconds and add Sherry. Boil mixture until almost all liquid is evaporated and remove skillet from heat. Add soy sauce, vinegar, and honey and bring to a simmer, stirring. Add butter and cook, stirring, over low heat until incorporated. Spoon glaze over steak. Serves 2.

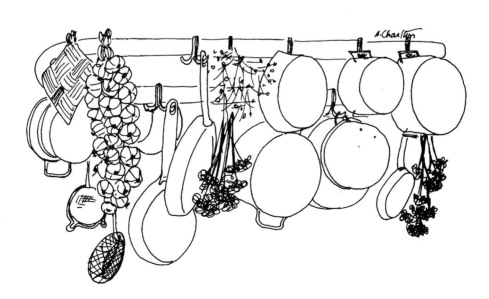

The following recipe has been designed to produce leftovers that can be used to make Deviled Miroton (recipe below).

Rump Roast with Vegetables

3 pounds large boiling potatoes (about 6 to 8)
6 carrots, cut crosswise into thirds
a 3- to 3½-pound boneless beef rump roast, tied,
    at room temperature
1 yellow onion, sliced
a 10-ounce carton red or white pearl onions,
    blanched in boiling water 2 minutes and peeled
2 heads elephant garlic or regular garlic, separated
    into cloves (unpeeled)
3 tablespoons vegetable oil
For gravy
3 cups beef broth
3½ tablespoons all-purpose flour
¼ cup water
2 teaspoons balsamic or other red-wine vinegar

Peel boiling potatoes and in a saucepan combine with salted water to cover. Bring water to a boil and simmer potatoes, covered, 10 minutes. Add carrots and simmer, covered, 5 minutes. Drain vegetables and cool. Quarter potatoes.

Preheat oven to 450° F.

Pat rump roast dry and season with salt and pepper. Put meat in a roasting pan, fat side up, and scatter sliced onion around it.

In another roasting pan toss pearl onions, garlic, carrots, and potatoes with oil and season with salt and pepper. Roast vegetables in upper third of oven, stirring once, 20 minutes.

Put meat in lower third of oven and roast meat and vegetables, stirring vegetables once, 20 minutes. Reduce temperature to 300° F. and roast meat and vegetables until a meat thermometer registers 130° F. for medium-rare meat and vegetables are golden, about 20 to 25 minutes. Transfer meat and vegetables to a platter and keep warm, covered loosely with foil.

Make gravy:

Add broth to meat-roasting pan and deglaze pan over high heat, scraping up brown bits. In a small bowl whisk together flour and water and add to simmering broth in a stream, whisking. Add vinegar and simmer, whisking, 3 minutes. Strain gravy through a fine sieve and reserve 1 cup for making deviled miroton (recipe follows).

Serve roast, sliced thin, with gravy, reserving narrower half of roast, unsliced, for making deviled miroton. Serves 4 to 6.

Deviled Miroton
(Gratin of Sliced Beef and Mustard Gravy)

2 large onions, sliced thin
3½ tablespoons olive oil
1½ tablespoons all-purpose flour
½ cup dry red wine
2 teaspoons tomato paste
1 cup beef broth

1 cup beef gravy (reserved from rump roast,
    recipe precedes)
2 tablespoons Dijon mustard
12 thin slices (about 1¼ pounds) leftover roast
    beef (such as rump roast, recipe precedes)
1⅓ cups fresh bread crumbs

In a large heavy skillet cook onions in 2 tablespoons oil over moderate heat, stirring, until golden
and add flour. Cook mixture over moderately low
heat, stirring, 2 minutes and stir in wine and tomato
paste. Bring mixture to a boil, stirring, and stir in
broth and gravy. Simmer sauce, stirring, 3 minutes
and stir in mustard.

Preheat oven to 400° F.

Spoon half of sauce into a 2-quart shallow flameproof baking dish and arrange beef on it, overlapping
slices. Spread remaining sauce over beef.

In a bowl toss bread crumbs well with remaining
1½ tablespoons oil and sprinkle over sauce. Bake
miroton in upper third of oven until just bubbling
around edges, about 5 to 10 minutes. (If crumbs are
not golden, put *miroton* under broiler 1 to 2 minutes.)
Serves 4 to 6.

Orange-Flavored Beef and
Snow Pea Stir-Fry with Noodles

1 teaspoon cornstarch
2 teaspoons soy sauce
¾ cup beef broth
1 teaspoon freshly grated orange zest
½ teaspoon sugar
6 ounces Asian egg noodles or thin spaghetti
1½ tablespoons vegetable oil
¾ pound boneless sirloin, cut into ¼-inch-thick
    strips
1 garlic clove, minced
1 teaspoon minced peeled fresh gingerroot
6 ounces snow peas, trimmed and cut lengthwise
    into ¼-inch-wide strips

In a bowl dissolve cornstarch in soy sauce and stir
in broth, zest, and sugar.

In a kettle of salted boiling water cook noodles
until tender and drain well.

While noodles are cooking, in a heavy skillet

measuring about 10 inches across the top heat 1 tablespoon of oil over moderately high heat until hot but
not smoking. Stir-fry beef, patted dry and seasoned
with salt and pepper, until browned, about 45 seconds, and transfer to a bowl. Add the remaining
½ tablespoon oil to skillet and stir-fry garlic, gingerroot, and snow peas 30 seconds. Stir cornstarch mixture and add to snow peas, stirring. Simmer mixture
until thickened and stir in beef with any juices accu-
mulated in bowl and salt and pepper to taste. In a
large bowl toss beef mixture with noodles. Serves 2.

Old-Fashioned Meat Loaf

2 cups finely chopped onion
1 tablespoon minced garlic
1 celery rib, chopped fine
1 carrot, chopped fine
½ cup finely chopped scallion
2 tablespoons unsalted butter
2 teaspoons salt
1½ teaspoons freshly ground black pepper
2 teaspoons Worcestershire sauce
⅔ cup ketchup
1½ pounds ground chuck
¾ pound ground pork
1 cup fresh bread crumbs
2 large eggs, beaten lightly
⅓ cup minced fresh parsley leaves

Accompaniment: ketchup, if desired

Preheat oven to 350° F.

In a large heavy skillet cook onion, garlic, celery,
carrot, and scallion in butter over moderate heat, stirring, 5 minutes. Cook vegetables, covered, stirring
occasionally, until carrot is tender, about 5 minutes
more. Stir in salt, pepper, Worcestershire sauce, and
⅓ cup of ketchup and cook, stirring, 1 minute.

In a large bowl combine well vegetables, meats,
bread crumbs, eggs, and parsley. In a shallow baking
pan form mixture into a 10- by 5-inch oval loaf and
spread remaining ⅓ cup ketchup over loaf.

Bake meat loaf in oven 1 hour, or until a meat thermometer inserted in center registers 155° F.

Serve meatloaf with ketchup. Serves 4 to 6.

PHOTO ON PAGES 34 AND 35

Steak Sandwiches with Tomato Pesto

2 garlic cloves, chopped
6 tablespoons olive oil
⅓ cup drained bottled dried tomatoes packed in oil
⅓ cup packed fresh basil leaves
1 teaspoon balsamic vinegar
1 pound sliced medium-rare steak (about 2 cups)
eight ½-inch-thick slices sourdough bread,
    toasted lightly

In a small saucepan cook garlic in oil over moderately low heat, stirring, until softened and cool. In a small food processor or blender purée tomatoes, basil, oil mixture, and vinegar until *pesto* is smooth.

In a bowl toss steak with half of *pesto* and spread remaining *pesto* on bread. Divide steak among 4 bread slices and top with remaining 4 slices. Makes 4 sandwiches.

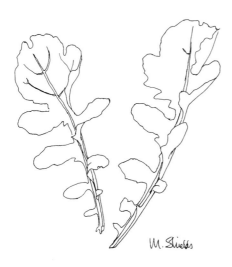

M. Shields

Herbed Hamburgers with Arugula

¾ pound ground beef
1 teaspoon minced fresh thyme leaves
1 teaspoon vegetable oil
mayonnaise to taste
2 onion rolls or hamburger buns, split
2 tablespoons finely chopped red onion
¾ cup washed, spun dry, and chopped *arugula*

In a bowl gently combine beef and thyme and form into two ¾-inch-thick patties. In a heavy skillet

(preferably cast iron) heat oil over moderately high heat until hot but not smoking and reduce heat to moderate. Cook patties 3½ minutes on each side for medium-rare meat and drain on paper towels.

Spread mayonnaise on insides of rolls or buns and make sandwiches with onion, *arugula*, and patties. Serves 2.

PORK

Peppered Pork Tenderloin with Cherry Salsa

½ pound dark sweet cherries, pitted and chopped
    (about 1 cup)
2 teaspoons fresh lime juice
¼ teaspoon freshly grated lime zest
1 tablespoon finely chopped red onion
1 teaspoon finely chopped seeded fresh *jalapeño*
    chili (wear rubber gloves)
1½ teaspoons finely chopped fresh coriander
¾ pound pork tenderloin, trimmed of
    excess fat
2 tablespoons crushed black peppercorns
1 tablespoon olive oil

Preheat oven to 425° F.

In a bowl stir together cherries, lime juice, zest, onion, *jalapeño*, and coriander.

Season pork with salt and press peppercorns into it. In a large heavy skillet heat oil over moderately high heat until hot but not smoking and brown pork on all sides.

Transfer pork to a shallow baking dish and roast in oven until a meat thermometer registers 155° F., about 20 minutes. Transfer pork to a cutting board and let stand 5 to 10 minutes. Slice pork into ½-inch-thick medallions and serve with *salsa.* Serves 2.

Roast Pork Loin with Beer Sauce

For marinade
½ cup Dijon mustard
1 large onion, chopped
½ cup honey
3 cups beer (not dark), preferably German

a 3½-pound boneless pork loin, tied
    (3 to 3½ inches wide)
2 tablespoons vegetable oil
a *beurre manié* made by rubbing together
    1 tablespoon softened unsalted butter and
    1 tablespoon all-purpose flour

Make marinade:

In a large saucepan stir together marinade ingredients. Bring marinade just to a boil, stirring (marinade
will rise and foam), and remove pan from heat. In a
blender purée marinade in 2 batches, transferring it as
puréed to a bowl. Cool marinade to room temperature
and spoon off any remaining foam.

In a large heavy resealable plastic bag combine
pork and marinade and seal bag, pressing out any excess air. Put bag in a baking pan and marinate pork,
chilled, turning bag once or twice, at least 8 hours
and up to 24. Let pork in marinade come to room
temperature, about 40 minutes. Transfer marinade to
a saucepan and bring just to a boil.

Preheat oven to 375° F.

Pat pork dry with paper towels and season with
salt and pepper. In a flameproof roasting pan heat oil
over moderately high heat until hot but not smoking
and brown pork on all sides. Roast pork in middle of
oven, basting frequently with some marinade, until a
meat thermometer registers 155° F. for slightly pink
meat, 1 to 1½ hours. Transfer pork to a cutting board,
reserving juices in roasting pan and discarding string,
and let stand, covered loosely with foil, about 15
minutes.

While pork is standing, skim and discard fat from
pan and add remaining marinade. Deglaze roasting
pan over moderately high heat, scraping up brown
bits. Bring sauce just to a boil and strain through a
fine sieve into another pan. Bring sauce to a simmer
and whisk in *beurre manié*, bit by bit, whisking until
sauce is combined well and thickened slightly.

Serve pork, sliced, with sauce. Serves 6.

PHOTO ON PAGE 70

Boneless Pork Loin Chops with Onion Marmalade

two 1-inch-thick boneless pork loin chops
    (about 6 ounces each)
½ teaspoon dried rosemary, crumbled

1 tablespoon olive oil
1 large onion (about ¾ pound), halved lengthwise
    and sliced thin crosswise
¼ cup water
2 tablespoons balsamic vinegar
2 tablespoons red-currant jelly

Trim excess fat from pork chops and sprinkle with
rosemary and salt and pepper to taste. In a heavy
10-inch skillet heat oil over moderately high heat
until hot but not smoking and sauté pork chops until
browned on both sides, about 5 minutes. Transfer
pork chops with tongs to a plate.

In drippings remaining in skillet sauté onion until
it begins to brown. Add water, vinegar, and jelly and
bring to a boil, stirring until jelly melts. Simmer mixture, covered, over moderate heat until onion is tender, about 5 minutes.

Return pork to skillet and cook, uncovered, turning
once, until cooked through and almost all liquid is
evaporated, about 5 minutes. Serves 2.

Glazed Smoked Pork Chops

¼ cup red currant jelly
1 teaspoon cider vinegar
a center-cut smoked pork loin
    (about 8 chops)*

Accompaniment: mustard sauce (page 213)

*available at some butchers and by mail order
    from Nodine's Smokehouse, Goshen, CT,
    tel. (800) 222-2059, in CT (800) 626-3021

Preheat oven to 350° F.

In a small saucepan melt jelly with vinegar over
moderate heat, stirring, and in a roasting pan brush
pork all over with jelly. Cover pork with foil and
roast in oven 1 hour. Remove foil and brush pork
with pan juices.

Reduce oven temperature to 325° F.

Roast pork, uncovered, 15 minutes more. Let pork
stand 15 minutes.

Serve pork, cut into chops, with mustard sauce.
Serves 6.

PHOTO ON PAGE 23

Garlic Orange Pork Chops

four ½-inch-thick pork chops
1 tablespoon vegetable oil
1 large garlic clove,
  minced
½ cup fresh orange juice
¼ cup dry white wine
1 to 2 tablespoons fresh lemon juice

Pat pork dry and season with salt and pepper. In a skillet heat oil over moderately high heat until hot but not smoking and brown chops until golden. Add garlic, orange juice, wine, and lemon juice and simmer, covered partially, until pork is tender, 10 to 15 minutes. Serves 2.

Grilled Teriyaki Pork Chops with
Pineapple Papaya Relish

For marinade
⅔ cup soy sauce
⅓ cup firmly packed light brown sugar
⅓ cup water
¼ cup rice vinegar
3 garlic cloves, chopped fine

a 2-inch piece fresh gingerroot, peeled and
  chopped fine

six 1-inch-thick rib pork chops, bones frenched by
  butcher if desired

Accompaniment: pineapple papaya relish
  (recipe follows)

Make marinade:
In a saucepan combine marinade ingredients and bring to a boil, stirring until sugar is dissolved. Cool marinade completely.

Put chops in a large resealable plastic bag and pour marinade over them. Seal bag, pressing out excess air, and set in a shallow dish. Marinate meat, chilled, turning bag once or twice, overnight.

Pour marinade into a saucepan and boil 5 minutes. Grill chops on an oiled rack set about 4 inches over glowing coals 7 to 8 minutes on each side, or until just cooked through, basting with marinade during last 5 minutes of cooking. (Alternatively, meat may be grilled in a hot well-seasoned ridged grill pan or broiled.)

Serve pork chops with relish. Serves 6.

PHOTO ON PAGE 42

Pineapple Papaya Relish

2 cups finely diced fresh pineapple
1 cup finely diced fresh papaya
½ cup finely diced red bell pepper
½ cup finely diced Maui, Vidalia, or other
    sweet onion
1 garlic clove, minced
1 small fresh hot green chili such as a *serrano* or
    Thai chili, seeded and minced (wear rubber
    gloves)
2 tablespoons shredded fresh mint leaves

In a bowl combine all ingredients with salt to taste
and let stand at room temperature 1 hour. *Relish may
be made 1 day ahead and chilled, covered.*

Serve pineapple papaya relish at room temperature. Makes about 3 cups.

PHOTO ON PAGE 42

Grilled Sausages

about 2 pounds fresh beef and lamb sausage links
    with rosemary*
about 2 pounds smoked whiskey fennel pork
    sausage links*

Accompaniments
homemade tomato ketchup (page 214)
assorted mustards
12 to 16 small French loaves or
    hot dog buns

*available by mail order from Aidells Sausage
    Company, 1575 Minnesota Street,
    San Francisco, CA 94107,
    tel. (415) 285-6660

Prepare grill.

Grill fresh sausages on an oiled rack set 5 to 6
inches over glowing coals, turning them, 10 to 15
minutes, or until cooked through (170° F. on an
instant-read thermometer). Grill smoked sausages on
rack, turning them, 5 to 8 minutes, or until heated
through.

Serve sausages with ketchup and mustards on
bread. Serves about 12.

PHOTO ON PAGES 52 AND 53

LAMB

Crown Roast of Lamb

a 16-chop frenched and trimmed crown
    roast of lamb (about 4 pounds),
    at room temperature
2 tablespoons balsamic vinegar
1 cup dry red wine
2½ cups beef broth
2 tablespoons arrowroot
3 tablespoons water
minted saffron rice with currants and pine nuts
    (page 168)
glazed baby turnips and carrots
    (page 190)

Garnish: mint sprigs
Accompaniment: garlic rosemary jelly
    (page 212)

Preheat oven to 425° F.

Rub lamb well with salt and pepper to taste
and cover ends of bones with foil. Put lamb in an
oiled roasting pan and roast in middle of oven 25 to
30 minutes, or until a meat thermometer inserted into
the thickest part of the meat inside the crown registers 130° to 135° F. for medium-rare meat. Transfer
lamb to a platter and let stand, covered loosely, 15
minutes.

While lamb is standing, spoon off excess fat from
pan juices. Set roasting pan over moderately high
heat and add vinegar and wine. Deglaze pan, scraping
up browned bits, and boil liquid until reduced to
about ¼ cup. Add broth and bring to a boil.

In a small bowl whisk arrowroot and water until
smooth and add to boiling broth mixture, whisking.
Simmer sauce, whisking, 2 minutes, or until slightly
thickened, and season with salt and pepper. Keep
sauce warm, covered.

Remove foil from bones and spoon some rice into
crown, serving remaining rice on side. Arrange
glazed vegetables around roast and strain sauce
through a fine sieve into a sauceboat. Garnish platter
with mint sprigs and serve with jelly. Serves 6.

PHOTO ON PAGE 33

*Lamb Medallions with White-Bean Potato Purée
and Red-Wine Sauce*

1 medium russet (baking) potato (about ½ pound)
1 cup drained canned white beans
1½ tablespoons olive oil
1 large garlic clove, minced and mashed to a paste
    with ¼ teaspoon salt
four 1-inch-thick loin lamb chops, boned and tied
all-purpose flour seasoned with salt and pepper
    for dredging
3 tablespoons finely chopped shallot (about
    2 large)
¼ cup dry red wine
½ teaspoon Dijon mustard
⅓ cup chicken or beef broth
3 tablespoons heavy cream
1 tablespoon minced fresh parsley leaves

In a small saucepan combine potato, peeled and cut into ½-inch pieces, with water to cover and boil until tender, about 10 minutes. Add beans and simmer 2 minutes. Drain mixture well, reserving about ⅓ cup cooking water, and force through a ricer or food mill back into pan. Stir in ½ tablespoon oil, about one third garlic paste, salt and pepper to taste, and enough reserved cooking water to reach desired consistency and keep warm.

In a shallow dish dredge lamb medallions in flour, shaking off excess. In a heavy skillet heat remaining tablespoon oil over moderately high heat until hot but not smoking and sauté lamb about 3 minutes on each side for medium-rare meat. Transfer lamb to a plate and keep warm.

To skillet add shallot and remaining garlic paste and cook over moderately low heat, stirring, until softened. Deglaze skillet with wine over high heat, scraping up browned bits, and boil until reduced by about half. Stir in mustard, broth, and cream and simmer until thickened. Stir in parsley.

Divide purée between 2 plates and top with lamb and sauce. Serves 2.

Marinated Lamb Chops

¼ cup olive oil
1 tablespoon balsamic vinegar
4 garlic cloves,
    minced
8 frenched 1-inch-thick rib lamb chops
    (about 1 pound total)

In a small bowl whisk together oil, vinegar, garlic, and salt and pepper to taste. On a plate or in a shallow dish coat lamb chops on both sides with marinade and let marinate at room temperature, turning once, 30 minutes.

Preheat broiler.

Broil chops on rack of a broiler pan 2 inches from heat 7 minutes, turning after 5 minutes, for medium-rare meat. Serves 4.

PHOTO ON PAGES 28 AND 29

Lamb and Sweet Potato Stew

1 pound boneless lamb shoulder, cut into
    ½-inch pieces
1½ tablespoons all-purpose flour
1 tablespoon olive oil
1 garlic clove,
    minced
¼ cup red wine
1 cup water
½ cinnamon stick
a ½-pound sweet potato, peeled and
    cut into 1-inch pieces

In a bowl toss lamb with flour and salt and pepper to taste. In a 10-inch skillet heat oil over moderately high heat and sauté garlic, stirring, 1 minute. Add lamb and brown, stirring, about 2 minutes. Add wine and boil 1 minute. Add water and cinnamon stick and scatter sweet potato on top. Simmer stew, covered, about 30 minutes, or until lamb is tender, and season with salt and pepper. Serves 2.

POULTRY

*Roast Chicken with Mashed-Potato Stuffing
and Root Vegetables*

For mashed-potato stuffing
3 pounds russet (baking) potatoes
   (about 6 large)
1 garlic head, separated into cloves and peeled
   (about 14 cloves)
1 bay leaf
½ cup milk
3 tablespoons unsalted butter, softened
1 tablespoon fresh thyme leaves

a 5-pound whole chicken, giblets reserved for
   another use
2 tablespoons unsalted butter,
   softened
12 shallots, peeled
2 garlic heads, outer skins discarded and
   heads intact
1 tablespoon vegetable oil
6 thin carrots (about 1 pound), peeled and cut into
   1-inch pieces
2 small turnips (about 1 pound), peeled and each
   cut into 8 wedges
6 thin parsnips (about 1 pound), peeled and cut
   into 2-inch pieces
1 small celery root (about ¾ pound), peeled and
   cut into 8 wedges
8 fresh thyme sprigs

Garnish: chopped fresh parsley leaves

Make mashed-potato stuffing:
Peel potatoes and cut into ½-inch pieces. In a saucepan of boiling salted water cook potatoes with garlic and bay leaf until tender, about 15 minutes. Drain potato mixture, return it to pan, and cook over high heat, shaking pan, until any excess liquid is evaporated, about 30 seconds. Remove pan from heat and discard bay leaf. Add milk, butter, and thyme. Mash potatoes and garlic with a potato masher until smooth and stir in salt and pepper to taste.

Preheat oven to 450° F.

Rinse chicken inside and out and pat dry completely. Fill cavity loosely with some of stuffing and reserve remaining stuffing in a small baking dish. Truss chicken and rub all over with butter. Season chicken with salt and pepper and arrange, breast side down, on a rack set in a large shallow roasting pan. In a small bowl toss shallots and garlic with oil and add to roasting pan.

Roast chicken in lower third of oven for 30 minutes. Turn chicken breast side up and baste with pan juices. Arrange vegetables and thyme sprigs in pan and season with salt and pepper. Roast chicken and vegetables, stirring and basting frequently, 1 hour, or until a meat thermometer inserted in fleshy part of thigh registers 180° F. During last 30 minutes of roasting bake reserved stuffing, covered with foil.

Let chicken stand 10 minutes before carving. Discard thyme sprigs. Serve chicken, stuffing, and vegetables sprinkled with parsley. Serves 6.

PHOTO ON PAGE 21

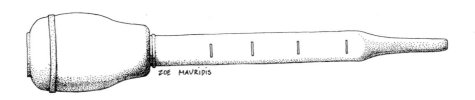

ZOE MAVRIDIS

Chicken and Dumplings

4 pounds chicken parts
1 cup all-purpose flour, seasoned with salt
   and pepper
2 tablespoons unsalted butter
1 tablespoon vegetable oil
6 leeks (white and pale green parts only),
   sliced thin crosswise and washed thoroughly
   (about 2 cups)
6 shallots, sliced thin (about 1 cup)
6 carrots, peeled, halved lengthwise, and sliced
2 celery ribs with leaves, sliced
1 small bay leaf
½ teaspoon dried thyme leaves, crumbled
3½ cups low-salt chicken broth
½ cup apple cider or juice
For dumplings
1½ cups all-purpose flour
½ cup yellow cornmeal
1 tablespoon baking powder
½ teaspoon salt
2 tablespoons minced fresh dill
1 cup plus 3 tablespoons half-and-half

1 cup green peas, defrosted if frozen

Dredge chicken parts in seasoned flour, shaking off excess, and put on a rack.

In a large heavy kettle melt butter with oil over moderately high heat until foam subsides and brown chicken in batches (do not crowd), transferring it to a plate as done, about 5 minutes on each side.

Stir in leeks and shallots and cook 3 minutes, scraping the bottom of the pan and stirring occasionally. Stir in carrots, celery, bay leaf, and thyme and cook 3 minutes. Stir in broth, cider, and chicken and bring liquid to a boil. Reduce heat and simmer, covered partially, until chicken is cooked through, 10 to 15 minutes.

Make dumplings while chicken is cooking:

Into a bowl sift together flour, cornmeal, baking powder, and salt and stir in dill. With a fork stir in half-and-half until dough is just blended.

With a large soup spoon scoop out 12 dumplings and arrange over chicken mixture. Simmer chicken and dumplings, covered, 9 minutes. Sprinkle in peas and cook until dumplings are done, about 3 minutes

more. (Dumplings are done when a wooden pick inserted in center comes out clean.) Discard bay leaf. Serves 6.

PHOTO ON PAGE 20

Chicken Breasts with Horseradish-Scallion Crust

1½ teaspoons Dijon mustard
¼ cup mayonnaise
1 whole boneless chicken breast with skin, halved
1 tablespoon olive oil
2 tablespoons chopped scallion
½ teaspoon minced garlic
½ cup fine fresh bread crumbs
2 tablespoons drained bottled horseradish
½ teaspoon chopped fresh tarragon leaves, or a
   pinch dried, crumbled

Preheat oven to 425° F.

In a small bowl whisk together mustard and mayonnaise until combined well.

Pat chicken dry and season with salt and pepper. Heat oil in a 10-inch non-stick skillet over moderately high heat until hot but not smoking and brown chicken, about 5 minutes on each side. Transfer chicken to a shallow baking dish and pour off all but about 2 teaspoons oil from skillet.

Add scallion to skillet and cook over moderate heat, stirring, until softened. Stir in garlic and cook 30 seconds.

Remove skillet from heat and stir in bread crumbs, horseradish, tarragon, and salt and pepper to taste. Spread mayonnaise mixture on skin side of each chicken breast and top evenly with bread crumb mixture. Bake chicken in middle of oven 10 minutes, or until cooked through, and let stand 5 minutes before serving. Serves 2.

Grilled Spiced Chicken Breasts

2 teaspoons coriander seeds
2 bay leaves
2 teaspoons black peppercorns
4 whole cloves
3 large whole boneless chicken breasts with skin
   (about 10 ounces each), halved
1½ teaspoons salt

Garnish: fresh thyme sprigs
Accompaniment: Creole sauce with yellow
   peppers (recipe follows)

In an electric spice grinder or blender grind fine coriander seeds, bay leaves, peppercorns, and cloves. Pat chicken dry and rub ground spices and salt all over it. Grill chicken on an oiled rack 4 inches above glowing coals 5 minutes on each side, or until cooked through. (Alternatively, grill chicken in a hot well-seasoned ridged grill pan.)

Garnish chicken with thyme sprigs and serve with Creole sauce with yellow peppers. Serves 6.

PHOTO ON PAGE 38

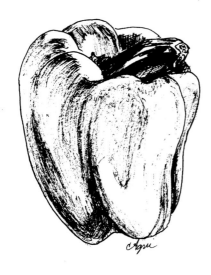

Creole Sauce with Yellow Peppers

2 medium onions, chopped
1 yellow bell pepper, chopped
1 celery rib, chopped
4 garlic cloves, minced
2 tablespoons olive oil
a 28-ounce to 32-ounce can plum tomatoes,
   drained and chopped
1 cup chicken broth
1 teaspoon minced fresh thyme leaves

In a heavy saucepan cook onions, bell pepper, celery, and garlic in oil over moderately low heat, stirring occasionally, until celery is softened. Add tomatoes, broth, and thyme and simmer sauce 25 minutes, or until most of liquid is evaporated. Season sauce with salt and pepper. *Sauce may be made 1 day ahead and chilled, covered.* Makes about 2½ cups.

PHOTO ON PAGE 38

Roasted Chicken Breast and Vegetables with Prunes

1 tablespoon unsalted butter
1 whole chicken breast,
   split
½ teaspoon dried thyme leaves,
   crumbled
2 carrots, cut into ¼-inch slices
1 onion, cut into ½-inch wedges
three ¼-inch-thick lemon slices
6 pitted prunes
⅔ cup low-salt chicken broth
2 tablespoons dry white wine
1½ teaspoons all-purpose flour
1 teaspoon minced fresh parsley leaves

Garnish: parsley sprigs

Put butter in small flameproof roasting pan and put pan in oven. Preheat oven to 450° F.

Pat chicken dry and sprinkle with thyme and salt and pepper to taste. Put chicken, skin sides down, in hot butter and arrange carrots, onion, and lemon around chicken. Season vegetables with salt.

Roast chicken and vegetables 10 minutes. Turn chicken skin sides up and put 3 prunes under each half. Roast chicken and vegetables, stirring vegetables once halfway through cooking time, 15 minutes more, or until chicken is cooked through and vegetables are tender. Remove pan from oven and with slotted spoon transfer chicken, vegetables, lemon, and prunes to a platter.

In a measuring cup or small bowl stir together chicken broth, wine, flour, and parsley. Add mixture to pan and boil over high heat, stirring and scraping up browned bits, 1 minute, or until sauce is thickened slightly.

Pour sauce over chicken and vegetables and garnish with parsley sprigs. Serves 2.

2 or 3 squares caraway corn bread (recipe
   follows), split horizontally
2 tablespoons minced red onion

Accompaniment: two-cabbage slaw (page 204)

In a saucepan cook onion in oil over moderate
heat, stirring, until golden. Add garlic and cook, stirring, 30 seconds. Stir in ketchup, water, juice, molasses, horseradish, cumin, red pepper flakes, and allspice and simmer, stirring twice, 15 minutes.

Stir in chicken and simmer until just heated
through, about 1 minute.

On 2 or 3 plates spoon chicken and sauce over bottom halves of corn bread squares and sprinkle with
red onion. Top barbecue with top halves of corn
bread squares and serve with slaw. Serves 2 or 3.

Caraway Corn Bread

1 cup all-purpose flour
⅓ cup yellow cornmeal
1 tablespoon sugar
2 teaspoons baking powder
1 teaspoon salt
¼ teaspoon baking soda
2 teaspoons caraway seeds
2 large eggs
1 cup milk
⅓ cup sour cream
5 tablespoons butter, melted and cooled slightly

Preheat oven to 425° F. and generously grease an
8-inch square baking pan.

In a bowl whisk together flour, cornmeal, sugar,
baking powder, salt, baking soda, and 1 teaspoon caraway seeds.

In a small bowl whisk together eggs, milk, sour
cream, and butter.

Add milk mixture to cornmeal mixture and stir
until just combined.

Spread batter in prepared pan and sprinkle with remaining 1 teaspoon caraway seeds. Bake corn bread
in middle of oven 20 minutes, or until sides begin to
pull away from edges of pan.

Cool corn bread in pan on a rack 5 minutes and cut
into 4 squares. Makes four 4-inch squares.

Chicken Barbecue

1 yellow onion,
   minced
2 tablespoons vegetable oil
2 large garlic cloves,
   minced
1 cup ketchup
½ cup water
2 tablespoons fresh lemon juice
2 tablespoons unsulfured molasses
1 teaspoon drained bottled horseradish
½ teaspoon ground cumin
¼ teaspoon dried hot red pepper flakes
⅛ teaspoon ground allspice
2 cups diced cooked chicken such as rotisserie
   chicken

Moroccan Chicken and Almond Pies

For almond sugar
½ cup blanched whole almonds, toasted and
    cooled
3 tablespoons granulated sugar
1 teaspoon cinnamon
For filling
¼ teaspoon saffron threads,
    crumbled
2 tablespoons hot water
1 medium onion, chopped (about 1¼ cups)
2 garlic cloves, cut into thin strips
3 tablespoons unsalted butter
¾ teaspoon ground ginger
2 teaspoons *ras el hanout**
½ teaspoon freshly ground black pepper
2 pounds chicken parts (about 1 whole breast,
    2 thighs, and 2 legs)
1½ cups low-salt chicken broth
3 large eggs, beaten lightly
¼ cup plus 2 tablespoons chopped fresh parsley
    leaves
3 tablespoons chopped fresh coriander
1½ tablespoons fresh lemon juice, or to taste

9 tablespoons unsalted butter
18 sheets (about 1½ packages) *phyllo* (preferably
    Number 4 ultra-thin)
confectioners' sugar and cinnamon for sprinkling

*available by mail order from Kalustyan's,
    123 Lexington Avenue, New York, NY 10016,
    tel. (212) 685-3451, or recipe (page 142)

Make almond sugar:
In a food processor grind fine almonds, granulated sugar, and cinnamon. *Almond sugar may be made 1 day ahead and kept covered in a cool dark place.*
Make filling:
In a small bowl combine saffron with hot water and let stand 10 minutes.

In a heavy 4-quart kettle sauté onion and garlic in butter over moderately high heat, stirring occasionally, until onion is golden, about 4 minutes. Reduce heat to moderate and add ginger, *ras el hanout,* and pepper. Cook mixture, stirring, 3 minutes.

Add chicken parts, broth, and saffron mixture and simmer, covered, turning the chicken once, until chicken is very tender and cooked through, 25 to 35 minutes. Let chicken stand in cooking liquid off heat 30 minutes. Transfer chicken to a plate, reserving cooking liquid and solids, and, when cool enough to handle, shred chicken, discarding skin and bones.

Measure reserved cooking liquid and solids and if necessary boil, stirring occasionally, until reduced to about 1¾ cups. Reduce heat to moderate and add eggs in a stream, whisking. Cook mixture, stirring, until eggs are set, about 3 minutes. Remove kettle from heat and pour egg mixture into a coarse sieve set over a bowl. Let mixture drain undisturbed 10 minutes before discarding liquid. Transfer egg mixture to a bowl. Stir in chicken, parsley, coriander, lemon juice, and salt and pepper to taste and chill. *Filling may be made 1 day ahead and chilled, covered.*

Prehcat oven to 425° F. and butter 2 large shallow baking pans.

In a small saucepan melt butter and keep warm but not hot.

Cut *phyllo* sheets in half lengthwise and stack between 2 sheets wax paper. Cover wax paper sheets with a kitchen towel. On a work surface arrange a half sheet of *phyllo* with short side facing you and brush with melted butter. On this, layer and brush 3 more half sheets of *phyllo* in the same manner.

Sprinkle 1 tablespoon almond sugar on short side of *phyllo* nearest you to cover about a 2½- by 4-inch area, leaving a 1-inch border on 3 edges. Put ⅓ cup chicken mixture over almond sugar and spread out slightly. Top chicken mixture with 1 more tablespoon almond sugar and roll up filling in *phyllo*, folding in sides after first roll. Transfer pie, seam side down, to baking pan and brush with melted butter. Chill pie immediately.

Form 8 more pies in the same manner with remaining *phyllo*, butter, almond sugar, and chicken mixture, chilling each pie as it is made. *Pies may be prepared up to this point 4 hours ahead and chilled, covered lightly with plastic wrap once cold.*

Bake chilled pies in oven until tops and ends are puffed and browned, 15 to 20 minutes. Cool pies slightly on a rack. Sprinkle pies with confectioners' sugar and cinnamon and serve warm. Makes 9 pies to serve 6 with second helpings.

PHOTO ON PAGE 57

Ras el Hanout
(Moroccan Spice Blend)

½ teaspoon aniseed
1 teaspoon fennel seeds
8 whole allspice berries
seeds from 8 cardamom pods
8 whole cloves
15 whole black peppercorns
1 stick cinnamon, broken in half
1 tablespoon sesame seeds
1 teaspoon coriander seeds
½ teaspoon cuminseed
a pinch dried hot red pepper flakes
a pinch ground mace
1 tablespoon ground ginger
1 teaspoon freshly ground nutmeg

In a spice grinder or cleaned coffee grinder grind fine aniseed, fennel seeds, allspice berries, cardamom seeds, cloves, peppercorns, cinnamon stick, sesame seeds, coriander seeds, cuminseed, and red pepper flakes. In a small bowl stir together ground spice mixture, mace, ginger, and nutmeg until combined well. Ras el hanout *may be kept in a tightly closed jar in a cool dark place up to 6 months.* Makes ¼ cup.

Cobb Salad Pitas

½ teaspoon Dijon mustard
1 tablespoon red-wine vinegar
3 tablespoons olive oil
1 small avocado (preferably California)
2½ cups diced cooked chicken (2 whole breasts)
½ cup chopped seeded vine-ripened tomato
4 slices bacon, cooked until crisp and crumbled
½ cup crumbled Roquefort cheese
   (about 2 ounces)
2 cups shredded romaine
four 7-inch *pita* loaves, halved crosswise
1 hard-boiled large egg, forced through
   a coarse sieve

In a bowl whisk together mustard, vinegar, and salt and pepper to taste and add oil in a stream, whisking until emulsified. Peel, pit, and finely chop avocado and add to dressing. Add chicken, tomato, bacon, and cheese and toss lightly.

Divide romaine among *pita* halves. Divide chicken mixture among *pita* halves and sprinkle with egg. Makes 8 sandwiches, serving 4.

ASSORTED FOWL

Roast Marinated Cornish Hens

For marinade-sauce
4 stalks fresh lemongrass*, outer leaves discarded
   and root ends trimmed
⅔ cup chopped well-washed coriander roots
   and/or stems
½ cup chopped shallot
8 large garlic cloves
¼ cup chopped peeled fresh gingerroot
¼ cup palm sugar* or firmly packed
   brown sugar
2 tablespoons curry powder
2 teaspoons freshly ground black pepper
¼ teaspoon salt
¼ cup Asian fish sauce (preferably *naam pla**)
1 cup well-stirred canned unsweetened coconut
   milk*

three 1¼- to 1½-pound Cornish hens, butterflied
   (backbone and breastbone removed)
1 cup well-stirred canned unsweetened coconut
   milk*

Accompaniment: sweet chili sauce (recipe follows)
   if desired

*available at Asian markets, some specialty foods shops, and by mail order from Adriana's Caravan, Brooklyn, NY, tel. (800) 316-0820 or (718) 436-8565 or Uwajimaya, 519 Sixth Avenue South, Seattle, WA 98104, tel. (206) 624-6248

Make marinade-sauce:
Thinly slice lower 6 inches of lemongrass stalks, discarding remaining stalks. In a food processor or blender finely grind together sliced lemongrass, coriander, shallot, garlic, and gingerroot. Add sugar,

curry powder, pepper, salt, fish sauce, and coconut milk and purée.

Quarter each hen and divide between 2 large resealable plastic bags. Divide marinade between bags and seal bags, pressing out excess air. Put bags in a large shallow dish and marinate hens, chilled, turning bag once or twice, overnight.

Preheat oven to 450° F. and line a large shallow roasting pan with foil.

Remove hens from marinade, reserving marinade, and arrange hens, skin sides up, in prepared pan. Roast hens 20 to 25 minutes, or until just cooked through.

While hens are roasting, in a small saucepan combine reserved marinade and coconut milk. Cook sauce at a slow boil, stirring occasionally, 5 minutes and strain through a fine sieve into another small saucepan to keep warm.

Serve hens with marinade sauce and/or sweet chili sauce for dipping if desired. Serves 6.

PHOTO ON PAGE 46

Sweet Chili Sauce

¾ cup sugar
½ cup water
⅔ cup rice or white-wine vinegar
4 large garlic cloves, minced
¾ teaspoon dried hot red pepper flakes
¾ teaspoon salt

In a small saucepan combine all ingredients and simmer, stirring occasionally, 10 minutes. Cool sauce to room temperature. *Sauce may be made 3 days ahead and chilled, covered.*

Serve sauce at room temperature. Makes 1½ cups.

PHOTO ON PAGE 46

Duck and Sausage Gumbo

two 5½-pound ducks, excess fat discarded and
   ducks cut into serving pieces
2 pounds *kielbasa* (Polish smoked sausage),
   cut into ¼-inch-thick rounds
12 cups chicken broth
6 cups water
⅓ cup all-purpose flour

2 onions, chopped
2 celery ribs, chopped
1 red bell pepper, chopped
1 green bell pepper, chopped
1 teaspoon cayenne, or to taste
2 cups thinly sliced scallion greens

Accompaniment: brown and white rice
   (page 144)

Prick duck skin all over with tip of a knife. In a heavy skillet brown *kielbasa* and duck in batches over moderately high heat, transferring as browned to paper towels to drain. Combine *kielbasa* and duck with broth and water in a 6-gallon kettle and bring to a simmer.

Pour off all but ¼ cup fat from skillet. Add flour and cook *roux* over moderately low heat, stirring constantly, until a shade darker than peanut butter, about 30 minutes. Add onions, celery, and bell peppers and cook, stirring occasionally, until vegetables are crisp-tender. Add vegetable mixture to kettle and stir until *roux* is dissolved.

Simmer gumbo, uncovered, 2 hours and cool completely. Bone duck, discarding skin and bones. Chill gumbo overnight. *Gumbo may be made 2 days ahead and chilled, covered.* Discard fat on surface and reheat gumbo with cayenne, scallions, and salt to taste over moderate heat.

Serve duck and sausage gumbo over rice. Makes about 20 cups, serving 12.

PHOTO ON PAGE 14

Brown and White Rice

1½ cups long-grain brown rice
1½ cups long-grain white rice

To a kettle of boiling salted water add brown rice, stirring, and boil 15 minutes. Drain rice in a large colander and rinse. Put colander over a kettle of boiling water and steam brown rice, covered with a kitchen towel and a lid, until fluffy and dry, about 25 minutes. Cook white rice in same manner, boiling 10 minutes and steaming 15 minutes. In a bowl toss brown and white rice together. *Rice may be made 3 days ahead and chilled in resealable plastic bags. Steam rice to reheat.*

Makes about 9 cups, serving 12.

*Crispy Duck Breasts with
Pear and Green Peppercorn Sauce*

1½ pounds boneless duck breast* (4 boneless breast halves, cut from two 5½- to 6-pound ducks)
1 firm-ripe Bosc pear
¾ cup apple juice
½ teaspoon cornstarch
2 tablespoons Calvados or Armagnac

1 tablespoon green peppercorns packed in brine, drained and crushed lightly
1 tablespoon duck or veal *demiglace** or ½ extra-large vegetarian vegetable bouillon cube
1 teaspoon fresh thyme leaves or ¼ teaspoon dried, crumbled

Garnish: fresh thyme sprigs

*available at many butcher shops and specialty foods shops and by mail order from D'Artagnan, tel. (800) 327-8246 or, in New Jersey, (201) 792-0748

Trim excess fat from duck breasts. Heat a 12-inch heavy skillet over high heat until very hot. Pat breasts dry and season with salt. Put breasts, skin sides down, in skillet and reduce heat to moderate. Cook breasts 20 minutes, or until skin is crisp and mahogany-colored, removing fat from skillet as it is rendered with a metal bulb baster (or very carefully pouring it off). Turn breasts and cook about 2 minutes for medium-rare or to desired doneness. Transfer breasts to a plate and keep warm, covered loosely.

While duck breasts are cooking, peel pear and cut into ¼-inch dice. Pour off all but about 1 tablespoon

fat from skillet and sauté pear until lightly browned, about 1 minute. In a measuring cup stir together apple juice and cornstarch. To pear add Calvados or Armagnac. Stir in cornstarch mixture, peppercorns, *demiglace* or bouillon cube, and thyme and simmer, stirring, 2 minutes, or until slightly thickened.

Serve duck breasts, sliced, with sauce spooned over them and garnish with thyme sprigs. Serves 4.

Red-Wine-Braised Duck Legs with Roasted Pears and Onions

4 large duck legs* (about 2¾ pounds total,
    cut from two 5½- to 6-pound ducks)
a 750-ml. bottle light fruity red wine such as
    Pinot Noir (about 3¼ cups)
a *bouquet garni* of 10 lightly crushed juniper
    berries**, 3 whole cloves, a 4- by 1-inch strip
    orange zest, and 1 bay leaf tied together in a
    cheesecloth bag
1 tablespoon vegetable oil
1 large carrot, cut into ¼-inch dice
1 large celery rib, cut into
    ¼-inch dice
1 large onion, cut into ¼-inch dice
2 large fresh parsley sprigs plus 1 tablespoon
    minced fresh parsley leaves
For roasted pears and onions
3 medium onions, halved
    or quartered
2 ripe Bosc pears
2 tablespoons unsalted butter
1 tablespoon fresh lemon juice
2 teaspoons honey
¼ teaspoon salt

a *beurre manié* made by rubbing together
    2 tablespoons softened unsalted butter and
    2 tablespoons all-purpose flour

Garnish: fresh parsley sprigs

*available at some butcher shops and by mail
    order (in package of 6 legs) from D'Artagnan,
    tel. (800) 327-8246 or, in New Jersey,
    (201) 792-0748
**available in spice section of supermarkets

Trim excess fat from duck legs. In a large bowl marinate duck legs in wine with *bouquet garni*, covered and chilled, 2 hours.

Transfer legs to a plate, reserving wine and *bouquet garni*. In a heavy kettle large enough to hold legs in one layer heat oil over moderately high heat until hot. Pat legs dry with paper towels and season with salt. Cook legs, skin sides down, 20 minutes, or until skin is crisp and mahogany-colored, removing fat from kettle as it is rendered with a metal bulb baster (or very carefully pouring it off). Turn legs and cook until browned on other side, about 2 minutes, transferring as browned to a plate.

Pour off all but about 2 tablespoons fat from kettle and sauté vegetables with salt to taste, stirring occasionally, until tender and lightly browned, about 15 minutes. Add duck legs, skin sides up, with parsley sprigs and reserved wine and *bouquet garni* and simmer, covered, 1½ hours, or until tender. *Braised duck legs may be prepared up to this point 2 days ahead and chilled, covered. Reheat mixture over low heat, adding ⅓ cup water, before proceeding with duck preparation.*

Make roasted pears and onions during last hour of duck braising:
Preheat oven to 400° F.

In a shallow baking pan large enough to hold onions and pears in one layer melt butter in oven and swirl pan to coat. Add onion halves, cut sides down, or quarters and bake 30 minutes. Halve pears lengthwise. Add pears, cut sides down, to pan and bake 20 minutes, or until pears and onions are tender and lightly browned. In a cup stir together lemon juice, honey, and salt and add to onions and pears, tossing to coat.

Transfer duck legs to a warm plate and keep warm, covered with foil. Discard parsley sprigs and *bouquet garni* and strain liquid into a 1-quart measuring cup, reserving vegetables. Let liquid stand until fat rises to top and skim and discard fat. Return liquid to kettle and simmer until reduced to about 2 cups. Add *beurre manié*, a little at a time, whisking, and boil 2 minutes. Stir reserved vegetables and minced parsley into sauce and heat through if necessary.

Serve duck legs, with sauce spooned over them and garnished with parsley sprigs, with roasted pears and onions. Serves 4.

PHOTO ON PAGES 78 AND 79

Sautéed Quail with Shiitake Port Sauce

4 semi-boneless quail*
4 teaspoons Worcestershire sauce
2 tablespoons plus 1 teaspoon olive oil
¼ teaspoon dried thyme, crumbled
1 cup all-purpose flour
2 tablespoons paprika
1 tablespoon unsalted butter
4 fresh large *shiitake* mushrooms, stems discarded
    and caps sliced thin
1 small garlic clove, minced
1 cup chicken broth
¼ cup Tawny Port
¼ teaspoon balsamic vinegar

*available at butcher shops, some supermarkets,
    and by mail order from D'Artagnan, tel. (800)
    327-8246 or, in New Jersey, (201) 792-0748

Sprinkle each quail with ½ teaspoon Worcester-shire sauce, 1 teaspoon oil, thyme, and salt and pepper to taste and rub gently into cavity and skin. In a resealable plastic bag set in a shallow pan marinate quail, chilled, at least 4 hours or overnight.

Preheat oven to 300° F. and line a plate with wax paper.

Pat quail dry inside and out and in a shallow dish combine flour, paprika, and salt and pepper to taste. Dredge quail in mixture, 1 at a time, shaking off excess, and transfer to prepared plate.

Heat a large heavy skillet (preferably cast iron) over moderately high heat until hot and add remaining 1 tablespoon oil and butter. Heat fat until foam begins to subside and sauté quail until golden brown and cooked through, about 3 to 5 minutes on each side. Transfer quail to a shallow baking pan and keep warm in oven.

In fat remaining in skillet sauté mushrooms with garlic, stirring, until liquid mushrooms give off is evaporated and add broth, Port, and remaining 2 teaspoons Worcestershire sauce. Simmer sauce until thickened and reduced to about ¾ cup, about 15 minutes, and stir in vinegar and salt and pepper to taste.

On a cutting board halve quail and stir any quail juices from pan and board into sauce. Serves 2.

PHOTO ON PAGE 73

Roast Turkey with Potato, Apple, and Prune Stuffing and Port Gravy

a 12- to 14-pound turkey, neck and giblets
    (excluding liver) reserved for making gravy
potato, apple, and prune stuffing (recipe follows)
1 stick (½ cup) unsalted butter, softened
1 cup water
1 cup turkey giblet stock (page 147) or
    chicken broth
For gravy
1 cup Tawny Port, preferably reserved from
    stuffing (recipe follows)
4 tablespoons all-purpose flour
4 cups turkey giblet stock or chicken broth
2 tablespoons fresh lemon juice

Garnish: fresh thyme and flat-leafed parsley sprigs
    and apple slices

Preheat oven to 425° F.

Rinse turkey and pat dry inside and out. Season turkey inside and out with salt and pepper and pack neck cavity loosely with some stuffing. Fold neck skin under body and fasten with a skewer. Fill body cavity loosely with some remaining stuffing and truss turkey. Transfer remaining stuffing to a buttered 3-quart baking dish and reserve it, covered and chilled.

Spread turkey with butter and on a rack in a roasting pan roast in oven 30 minutes.

Reduce oven temperature to 325° F.

Baste turkey with pan juices. Add water to pan and roast, basting every 20 minutes, 2½ to 3 hours more, or until a meat thermometer inserted in fleshy part of a thigh registers 180° F. and juices run clear when thigh is pierced.

During last 1½ hours of roasting, drizzle reserved stuffing with stock or broth and bake, covered, in 325° F. oven 1 hour. Bake stuffing, uncovered, 30 minutes more. Transfer turkey to a heated platter, reserving juices in roasting pan, and discard string. Keep turkey warm, covered loosely with foil.

Make gravy:

Skim fat from roasting pan juices, reserving ¼ cup fat, and deglaze pan with Port over moderately high heat, scraping up browned bits. Bring Port to a boil and remove pan from heat. In a saucepan whisk together reserved fat and flour and cook *roux* over moderately low heat, whisking, 3 minutes. Add Port mixture and stock or broth in a stream, whisking, and simmer, whisking occasionally, 10 minutes. Stir in lemon juice and salt and pepper to taste and transfer gravy to a heated gravy boat.

Garnish turkey and stuffing with herbs and apple slices. Serves 8.

PHOTO ON PAGES 76 AND 77

Potato, Apple, and Prune Stuffing

2 cups Tawny Port
1½ cups pitted prunes (about 9 ounces), chopped
enough homemade-type white bread (about
    7 slices), cut into ½-inch pieces, to measure
    4½ cups
3 large russet (baking) potatoes (about 2 pounds)
2 tablespoons olive oil
2 Granny Smith apples
1 stick (½ cup) unsalted butter
4 large celery ribs, chopped (about 1½ cups)
2 small onions, chopped (about 2 cups)
2 tablespoons finely chopped fresh thyme leaves
¾ cup chopped fresh parsley leaves

Preheat oven to 375° F.

In a small saucepan bring Port with prunes to a boil and remove pan from heat. Cover mixture and macerate 1 hour. Drain prunes through a sieve into a bowl, pressing on solids, and reserve Port for gravy (within preceding turkey recipe) and prunes for stuffing.

In a shallow baking pan spread bread pieces in one layer and bake in middle of oven, stirring occasionally, until golden, 10 to 15 minutes. Transfer bread to a large bowl.

Increase oven temperature to 425° F.

Peel potatoes and cut into ½-inch cubes. In shallow baking pan toss potatoes with oil and roast in bottom third of oven, turning occasionally, until browned and crisp, about 20 minutes. Add potatoes to bread.

Peel apples and cut into ½-inch pieces. In a large heavy skillet melt butter over moderate heat and cook celery, onions, thyme, and apples, stirring, until vegetables are softened, about 15 minutes. Remove skillet from heat and stir in reserved prunes, combining well. Stir vegetable mixture into bread mixture with parsley and salt and pepper to taste and cool com-

pletely. *Stuffing may be made 1 day ahead and chilled, covered. (To prevent bacterial growth do not stuff turkey cavities ahead.)* Makes about 11 cups, enough to stuff a 12- to 14-pound turkey with extra to bake on the side.

PHOTO ON PAGES 76 AND 77

Turkey Giblet Stock

neck and giblets (excluding liver) from a
    12- to 14-pound turkey
5 cups chicken broth
5 cups water
1 celery rib, chopped
1 carrot, chopped
1 onion, quartered
1 bay leaf
½ teaspoon dried thyme, crumbled
1 teaspoon whole black peppercorns

In a large saucepan combine neck, giblets, broth, water, celery, carrot, and onion and bring to a boil, skimming froth. Add remaining ingredients and cook at a bare simmer 2 hours, or until liquid is reduced to 5 cups. Strain stock through a fine sieve into a bowl. *Stock may be made 2 days ahead. Cool stock completely, uncovered, and keep chilled or frozen in an airtight container.* Makes 5 cups.

147

Turkey Cutlets Milanese with Watercress Salad

For turkey cutlets
¾ pound turkey cutlets (about ¼-inch thick)
all-purpose flour seasoned with salt and pepper
   for dredging
2 large eggs
¾ cup fine fresh bread crumbs
¾ cup finely shredded Parmesan cheese
2 tablespoons olive oil
For salad
1 bunch watercress, coarse stems discarded and
   leaves washed well and spun dry
¼ cup thinly sliced red onion
1½ tablespoons olive oil
1 teaspoon fresh lemon juice
⅛ teaspoon salt

Accompaniment: lemon wedges

Make turkey cutlets:
Pat turkey dry and spread seasoned flour on a plate. In a small shallow bowl beat eggs lightly and in another small shallow bowl stir together bread crumbs and Parmesan.

Dredge cutlets in flour, shaking off excess, and dip in egg, letting excess drip off. Coat cutlets with bread crumb mixture and put on a wax-paper–lined tray. Chill cutlets 15 minutes.

In a 12-inch non-stick skillet heat oil over moderately high heat until hot but not smoking and sauté cutlets 1½ to 2 minutes on each side, or until golden and just cooked through. Remove skillet from heat.
Make salad:
In a bowl combine watercress and onion and drizzle with oil, tossing to coat. Add lemon juice and salt and toss well.

Transfer cutlets with a slotted spatula to paper towels to drain briefly and arrange on plates. Top cutlets with salad and serve with lemon wedges. Serves 2.

Turkey Meatball Stroganov

½ pound ground turkey
1 small onion, chopped fine
1 small garlic clove,
   minced
½ teaspoon salt

½ teaspoon freshly ground black pepper
½ cup fresh bread crumbs
1 large egg yolk
1 tablespoon olive oil
¼ pound mushrooms, sliced thin
   (about 2 cups)
¼ cup medium-dry Sherry
1 cup low-salt chicken broth
1 teaspoon Worcestershire sauce
a *beurre manié* made by rubbing together
   1 tablespoon softened unsalted butter and
   1 tablespoon all-purpose flour
1 to 2 tablespoons minced fresh dill

Accompaniments
buttered egg noodles
sour cream

In a small bowl stir together well turkey, 2 tablespoons onion, garlic, salt, pepper, bread crumbs, and egg yolk and form into meatballs about 1 inch in diameter.

In a heavy skillet heat oil over moderately high heat until hot but not smoking and cook meatballs, shaking skillet, until browned well, about 4 minutes. Transfer meatballs with a slotted spoon to paper towels to drain.

To skillet add remaining onion and salt and pepper to taste and cook over moderate heat, stirring, until onion is softened. Add mushrooms and cook, stirring, until liquid mushrooms give off is evaporated. Add Sherry and boil until almost completely reduced. Add broth and Worcestershire sauce and bring to a boil. Add *beurre manié*, a little at a time, whisking, and boil 2 minutes. Add meatballs and simmer, covered, 5 minutes. Stir in dill.

Serve meatball Stroganov with egg noodles and sour cream. Serves 2.

Grilled Turkey Burgers

For burgers
1 cup chopped scallion (about 1 bunch)
3 large garlic cloves, minced
1 tablespoon Worcestershire sauce
2 tablespoons drained bottled capers, minced
4½ pounds ground turkey

Accompaniments
homemade tomato ketchup (page 214)
assorted mustards
12 onion rolls or hamburger buns

Make burgers:

In a bowl stir together scallion, garlic, Worcestershire sauce, capers, and salt and pepper to taste. Add turkey, combining mixture well, and form into twelve 1-inch-thick patties. *Burgers may be prepared up to this point 1 day ahead and chilled, covered.*

Prepare grill.

Grill burgers on an oiled rack set 5 to 6 inches over glowing coals 6 minutes on each side, or until cooked through.

Serve burgers with ketchup and mustards on bread. Serves 12.

PHOTO ON PAGES 52 AND 53

Turkey Burgers with Mushroom Gravy

¾ pound ground turkey
2 teaspoons Worcestershire sauce
1 teaspoon Dijon mustard
3 teaspoons olive oil
1 small onion, chopped
½ pound mushrooms, sliced
¼ teaspoon dried sage, crumbled
¾ cup chicken broth
2 teaspoons all-purpose flour

Accompaniment: cranberry sauce

In a bowl stir together turkey, Worcestershire sauce, and mustard and form into two ¾-inch-thick burgers. Season burgers with salt and pepper.

In a large heavy skillet heat 2 teaspoons oil over moderately high heat until hot but not smoking and sauté burgers until cooked through, about 6 minutes on each side. Transfer burgers to a plate.

To skillet add onion and remaining teaspoon oil

and cook over moderate heat, stirring, 3 minutes. Add mushrooms and sage and cook, stirring, until liquid mushrooms give off is evaporated. In a small bowl whisk together broth and flour until flour is dissolved and stir into mushrooms. Simmer gravy, stirring, 5 minutes and spoon over burgers.

Serve burgers with cranberry sauce. Serves 2.

Turkey Watercress Club Sandwiches

1 tablespoon olive oil
2 tablespoons fresh lemon juice
¾ teaspoon freshly ground black pepper
1 garlic clove, minced
¾ pound turkey cutlets (each about ⅓ inch thick)
¾ cup watercress leaves plus about 1 cup
    tender sprigs
⅓ cup mayonnaise
twelve ½-inch-thick slices brioche or challah,
    toasted lightly
12 slices bacon, cooked until crisp
3 small tomatoes,
    sliced

In a shallow dish whisk oil and 1 tablespoon of lemon juice with pepper and garlic and add turkey. Marinate turkey, turning once, 30 minutes. Discard marinade. Heat a well-seasoned ridged grill pan over moderately high heat until hot and grill turkey 3 minutes on each side, or until just cooked through. Cool turkey on a cutting board and cut into 4 portions.

In a small food processor or blender purée watercress leaves and mayonnaise until smooth and blend in remaining tablespoon lemon juice and salt and pepper to taste.

Spread watercress mayonnaise on 8 toast slices and top 4 with turkey and salt and pepper to taste. Top turkey with 4 remaining mayonnaise-spread toasts, mayonnaise sides up, and top each portion with bacon, tomatoes, and watercress sprigs. Top with remaining toasts. Makes 4 sandwiches.

CHEESE, EGG, AND BREAKFAST DISHES

Feta with Rosemary Pepper Honey

½ cup honey
¼ cup water
2 teaspoons chopped fresh rosemary leaves
1 teaspoon black peppercorns, cracked coarse
1 pound feta cheese, rinsed and patted dry

In a small saucepan combine honey, water, rosemary, and peppercorns and simmer, swirling pan occasionally, until reduced to about ½ cup. Cool honey to room temperature.

Cut feta into thin slices and serve drizzled with honey mixture. Serves 8 as a dessert.

Sautéed Feta with Tomato Sauce

8 ounces feta cheese
¼ cup all-purpose flour
¾ cup fresh bread crumbs (about 2 slices
    homemade-type white bread)

1 large egg
1 cup prepared tomato sauce
2 tablespoons olive oil
½ large lemon
freshly ground black pepper
    to taste

Freeze feta, wrapped in plastic wrap, 30 minutes (to facilitate slicing). Cut feta into ⅓-inch-thick slices and gently pat dry between paper towels.

Spread flour and bread crumbs on 2 separate plates. In a shallow bowl beat egg lightly. Working with 1 slice at a time, dredge feta gently in flour, brushing off excess, and dip in egg, letting excess drip off. Coat feta with bread crumbs and transfer to a wax-paper–lined tray. Chill feta 15 minutes.

In a small saucepan bring tomato sauce to a bare simmer and keep warm.

In a large non-stick skillet heat oil over moderately high heat until hot but not smoking and sauté feta in batches 1 to 2 minutes on each side, or until golden. Transfer feta with a slotted spatula to plates. Squeeze lemon over feta to taste and sprinkle with pepper.

Serve feta with tomato sauce. Serves 6 to 8 as a first course.

EGG DISHES

Stuffed Eggs with Vinegar Sauce on Toast

4 hard-cooked large eggs, peeled
2 tablespoons *crème fraîche* or sour cream
1 tablespoon cider vinegar
1 small garlic clove, minced
2 teaspoons chopped fresh parsley leaves
1 tablespoon unsalted butter
4 shallots, sliced thin
¼ cup chicken broth
8 slices toasted French bread

Garnish: chopped fresh parsley leaves

Cut eggs in half lengthwise and remove yolks. Press yolks through a fine sieve into a small bowl and reserve 1 tablespoon yolk on a small plate, covered. In small bowl with yolks stir together *crème fraîche* or sour cream, 1 teaspoon vinegar, garlic, 1 teaspoon parsley, and salt and pepper to taste.

Fill whites with yolk mixture and smooth tops.

In a small non-stick skillet heat butter over moderate heat and cook eggs, cut sides down, without turning, until heated through, about 3 minutes. Remove eggs from skillet with a slotted spoon and keep warm. Whisk in remaining 2 teaspoons vinegar, shallots, and broth and cook, whisking, until reduced slightly, about 1 minute. Add reserved sieved egg yolk and whisk until smooth. Add remaining teaspoon parsley and season with salt and pepper.

Spoon sauce over toasted bread slices and top with eggs. Garnish with parsley. Serves 2 as a brunch main course.

Herbed Egg Salad Sandwiches

4 hard-cooked large eggs, peeled and chopped
2 tablespoons mayonnaise
2 tablespoons sour cream
2 tablespoons minced fresh herbs such as parsley, chives, and/or tarragon
1 scallion, minced
2 teaspoons fresh lemon juice, or to taste
1 teaspoon Dijon mustard

a pinch freshly grated lemon zest
8 slices whole-grain bread

In a bowl stir together all ingredients except bread with salt and pepper to taste until combined well.

Make 4 sandwiches, pressing bread slices together gently. Serves 4.

Lentil and Red Pepper Frittata

⅔ cup lentils, picked over and rinsed
3 red bell peppers, sliced
1 large garlic clove, minced
2 tablespoons unsalted butter
12 large eggs
¼ cup finely chopped fresh parsley leaves
1½ cups coarsely grated Gruyère cheese
   (about 6 ounces)

Add lentils to a large saucepan of salted water and bring water to a boil. Cook lentils at a bare simmer until tender, about 15 to 20 minutes.

While lentils are cooking, in a large skillet cook bell peppers and garlic in butter over moderate heat, stirring, until peppers are softened. Remove skillet from heat and stir in lentils, drained well, and salt and pepper to taste.

Preheat oven to 375° F.

In a large bowl whisk together eggs and parsley. Spread lentil mixture in a buttered 6- to 8-cup gratin dish and pour egg mixture over it. Shake dish gently to distribute eggs evenly and top with Gruyère. Bake *frittata* in middle of oven until puffed, golden, and just set in middle, about 30 to 35 minutes.

Serve hot or at room temperature, cut into wedges. Serves 6.

Peach, Strawberry, and Banana Bruschetta

sixteen ½-inch-thick slices crusty Italian or
    French bread
2 tablespoons melted unsalted butter
1½ tablespoons sugar
1½ teaspoons cinnamon, or to taste
1 peach, peeled, pitted, and cut into fine dice
½ banana, cut into fine dice
8 large strawberries, cut into fine dice
5 to 6 tablespoons plain yogurt
honey for drizzling

Preheat oven to 375° F.

Arrange bread slices in one layer in a shallow baking pan and bake in middle of oven until golden,
about 10 minutes. Brush toasts with butter on one
side. *Toasts may be made 1 week ahead and kept in
an airtight container.*

In a small bowl stir together 1 tablespoon sugar
and cinnamon and sprinkle evenly over buttered side
of each toast. Broil toasts about 5 inches from heat
under preheated broiler 30 seconds, or until tops are
bubbling, and cool.

In a bowl stir together fruit and remaining ½ tablespoon sugar and mound about 1 tablespoon on each
toast. Top each toast with about 1 teaspoon yogurt
and drizzle with honey. Makes 16 *bruschetta.*

Cranberry-Stuffed French Toast

four 1-inch-thick diagonal slices Italian or
    French bread
4 tablespoons cranberry sauce (any kind)
2 large eggs
½ cup milk
1 tablespoon unsalted butter
confectioners' sugar for sprinkling

Accompaniment: pure maple syrup

Put bread slices, cut sides down, on a work surface
and make a horizontal lengthwise opening in each by
cutting to within ¼ inch of opposite side. Spread 1

tablespoon cranberry sauce in each opening and
gently press closed.

In a flat-bottomed dish just large enough to hold
bread slices in one layer whisk together eggs, milk,
and a pinch of salt. Add stuffed bread slices and soak,
turning once or twice, until custard is absorbed, 15 to
20 minutes.

In a 9- to 10-inch non-stick skillet heat butter over
moderate heat until foam subsides and cook bread
slices 5 to 7 minutes on each side, or until golden and
crisp. Transfer French toast with a slotted spatula to
paper towels to drain briefly and sprinkle with sugar.

Serve French toast with maple syrup. Serves 2.

*Gingerbread Pancakes with
Currant Pear Maple Syrup*

For syrup
½ cup pure maple syrup
1 medium firm-ripe pear, peeled, cored, and sliced
1½ tablespoons dried currants or raisins
For pancake batter
½ cup all-purpose flour
¼ teaspoon baking soda
¼ teaspoon salt
½ teaspoon ground ginger
¼ teaspoon cinnamon
a pinch of ground cloves
3 tablespoons molasses
1 large egg
½ cup sour cream or buttermilk
1 tablespoon unsalted butter, melted, plus
    additional for brushing griddle

Accompaniment: sour cream

Make syrup:
In a small saucepan combine syrup ingredients and
simmer, covered, until pear is tender, about 5 minutes. Keep syrup warm while making pancakes.
Make pancake batter:
Preheat oven to 200° F.
In a bowl whisk together flour, baking soda, salt,
and spices. In a small bowl whisk together molasses,
egg, ½ cup sour cream or buttermilk, and 1 tablespoon melted butter and add to flour mixture, stirring
until just combined.

Heat a griddle over moderate heat until hot enough to make drops of water scatter over surface and brush with additional butter. Drop batter by ¼-cup measures onto griddle and cook pancakes until golden, 1 to 2 minutes on each side. Transfer pancakes as cooked to a heatproof plate and keep warm in oven.

Serve pancakes with syrup and sour cream. Makes about six 4-inch pancakes.

Maple-Glazed Breakfast Apple Tarts

an 8-ounce package cream cheese,
   softened
¼ cup confectioners' sugar
1 teaspoon vanilla
2 medium Empire, Gala, or Golden Delicious
   apples
¼ cup granulated sugar
a 17¼-ounce package (2 sheets) frozen puff pastry,
   thawed
1 large egg, beaten lightly with 1 tablespoon water
½ cup pure maple syrup

In a small bowl stir together cream cheese, confectioners' sugar, and vanilla until smooth.

Peel, halve, and core apples and cut into ¼-inch slices. In a bowl toss apples with 2 tablespoons granulated sugar.

Preheat oven to 375° F.

On a lightly floured surface roll 1 sheet puff pastry into a 15- by 11-inch rectangle. From a long side, cut four ⅓-inch-wide strips. From a short side, cut two ⅓-inch-wide strips. Reserve pastry strips. Halve lengthwise what remains of rectangle and put halves on a baking sheet.

Just inside pastry rectangles' edges, brush ⅓-inch-wide borders of egg wash, reserving remaining egg wash. Arrange reserved pastry strips on borders so that they are flush with edges of rectangles, trimming strips to fit. Spread cream-cheese mixture inside borders on rectangles and top with apples.

On a lightly floured surface roll remaining sheet puff pastry into a 14- by 10-inch rectangle and halve lengthwise. Cut several 2½-inch diagonal slits down middle of each rectangle (do not cut within 1 inch of edges).

Brush pastry borders of apple-topped tarts with some remaining egg wash and top each with 1 pastry rectangle. Press edges gently but firmly together to seal. Brush remaining egg wash over pastry tops and sprinkle with remaining 2 tablespoons granulated sugar. Bake tarts in middle of oven 30 minutes, or until puffed and golden.

In a small saucepan simmer maple syrup 10 minutes, or until reduced to about ⅓ cup. Brush hot syrup glaze over warm tarts.

Serve tarts warm or at room temperature. Makes two 14- by 5-inch tarts.

BREAKFAST SAUCES AND SYRUPS

Honeyed Apple Cider Sauce

1½ cups apple cider
⅓ cup honey
⅓ cup sugar
1 large Granny Smith apple,
    peeled, cored, and cut
    into ¼-inch dice
2 tablespoons cornstarch
⅛ teaspoon cinnamon
⅛ teaspoon freshly grated nutmeg
2 tablespoons fresh lemon juice
1½ tablespoons unsalted butter

In a small heavy saucepan combine cider, honey, and sugar and simmer, uncovered, stirring, until sugar is dissolved. Add apple and simmer, covered, until tender, about 5 minutes. In a small bowl whisk together cornstarch, spices, lemon juice, and a pinch of salt until smooth and whisk into cider mixture. Simmer sauce, whisking, until thickened, about 1 minute. Remove pan from heat and whisk in butter.

Serve sauce warm. *Sauce keeps, covered and chilled, 1 week.* Makes about 2½ cups.

Vanilla Apricot Sauce

1 vanilla bean, split lengthwise
1 cup sugar
2 cups water
3 ounces dried apricots, chopped
    (about ⅔ cup)
1½ tablespoons fresh lemon juice,
    or to taste

In a small heavy saucepan combine vanilla bean, sugar, and water and simmer, stirring, until sugar is dissolved. Add apricots and simmer, covered, 15 minutes. Scrape seeds from vanilla bean with a knife into pan, reserving bean for another use, and purée mixture in a blender. Force sauce through a fine sieve into the pan and stir in lemon juice.

Serve sauce warm. *Sauce keeps, covered and chilled, 1 week.* Makes about 2¼ cups.

Brown Sugar Pecan Sauce

¾ cup firmly packed dark brown sugar
½ cup water
2 tablespoons light corn syrup
½ cup heavy cream
½ cup finely chopped toasted pecans
½ teaspoon vanilla

In a small heavy saucepan combine sugar, water, and corn syrup and simmer, stirring occasionally, 5 minutes. Stir in cream, pecans, and vanilla and simmer until thickened slightly, about 5 minutes.

Serve sauce warm. *Sauce keeps, covered and chilled, 2 weeks.* Makes about 2 cups.

Three-Berry Syrup

1½ cups cranberries
a 10-ounce package frozen raspberries in light
    syrup, thawed
½ cup sugar
¼ cup water
a 10-ounce package frozen sliced strawberries in
    syrup, thawed and drained, reserving syrup
1½ tablespoons fresh lemon juice, or to taste

In a heavy saucepan simmer cranberries and raspberries including their syrup, covered, until cranberries have burst, about 10 minutes. Force mixture through a fine sieve into a bowl, pressing hard on solids, and return liquid to pan. Stir in sugar, water, strawberry syrup, and lemon juice and simmer, uncovered, until sugar is dissolved and mixture has thickened slightly, 5 to 10 minutes. Stir in strawberries and simmer until heated through, about 2 minutes. *Syrup keeps, covered and chilled, 1 week.*

Serve syrup warm or at room temperature. Makes about 2½ cups.

Coffee Syrup

1½ cups firmly packed light brown sugar
¼ cup light corn syrup
½ cup water
1½ tablespoons instant coffee powder
1 tablespoon unsalted butter
½ teaspoon vanilla

In a small heavy saucepan combine sugar, corn syrup, and water and boil over moderate heat, stirring, until sugar is dissolved. Whisk in coffee powder and a pinch of salt and simmer 2 minutes. Whisk in butter and vanilla.

Serve syrup warm. *Syrup keeps, covered and chilled, 1 week.* Makes about 1½ cups.

Chocolate Maple Syrup

1½ cups pure maple syrup
3 tablespoons unsweetened cocoa powder,
 or to taste
½ stick (¼ cup) unsalted butter, cut into pieces

In a small heavy saucepan heat maple syrup over moderate heat until hot. Whisk in cocoa powder, butter, and a pinch of salt and simmer, whisking, 1 minute.

Serve syrup warm. *Syrup keeps, covered and chilled, 1 week.* Makes about 1¾ cups.

Spiced Rum Raisin Maple Syrup

⅓ cup raisins
3 tablespoons dark rum
1¼ cups pure maple syrup
¼ cup firmly packed light brown sugar
2 tablespoons water
1 cinnamon stick,
 broken in half
4 whole cloves
freshly grated nutmeg to taste

In a small bowl combine raisins with rum and let stand 15 minutes. In a small heavy saucepan combine maple syrup, sugar, water, cinnamon stick, cloves, nutmeg, and a pinch of salt and simmer, covered, stirring occasionally, 10 minutes. Add raisin mixture and simmer, covered, 2 minutes. Discard cinnamon stick and cloves.

Serve syrup warm. *Syrup keeps, covered and chilled, 1 week.* Makes about 2 cups.

PASTA AND GRAINS

Four-Cheese Baked Bow Ties

½ stick (¼ cup) unsalted butter
¼ cup all-purpose flour
1½ cups milk
a 28- to 32-ounce can whole Italian tomatoes,
  drained, reserving 1¼ cups juice, and
  chopped fine
1 pound bow-tie pasta
1½ cups coarsely grated mozzarella cheese
  (about 6 ounces)
½ cup crumbled Gorgonzola cheese
  (about 2 ounces)
½ cup diced Italian Fontina cheese
  (about 2 ounces)
1⅓ cups freshly grated Romano cheese
  (about 4 ounces)
½ cup finely chopped fresh parsley leaves
  (preferably flat-leafed)

Preheat oven to 375° F. and butter a 3- to 4-quart gratin dish or other shallow baking dish.

In a heavy saucepan melt butter over moderately low heat. Add flour and cook *roux*, whisking, 3 minutes. Add milk and reserved tomato juice in a stream, whisking, and bring to a boil, whisking. Stir in tomatoes and salt and pepper to taste and simmer until thickened, about 3 minutes.

In a kettle of salted boiling water cook bow-tie pasta until just *al dente*, about 8 minutes, and in a colander drain well.

In a bowl stir together pasta, sauce, mozzarella, Gorgonzola, Fontina, 1 cup Romano, and parsley and transfer to prepared dish. Sprinkle pasta with remaining ⅓ cup Romano. *Pasta may be made up to 6 hours ahead and chilled, covered. Bring pasta to room temperature before baking.*

Bake bow ties in middle of oven 30 to 35 minutes,

or until golden and bubbling, and let stand 10 minutes before serving. Serves 6 as an entrée.

Bow Ties with Peas, Lemon, and Mint

⅓ cup finely chopped shallot
1 tablespoon unsalted butter
2 teaspoons fresh lemon juice
¼ cup dry white wine or vermouth
¾ cup low-salt chicken broth
¼ cup heavy cream
½ cup cooked fresh peas or thawed frozen
¼ teaspoon freshly grated lemon zest
3 tablespoons freshly grated Parmesan cheese
½ pound bow-tie pasta
¼ cup julienne strips fresh mint leaves

In a saucepan cook shallot in butter over moderate heat, stirring, until softened. Add lemon juice and wine or vermouth and boil liquid until reduced to about 2 tablespoons. Stir in broth and boil liquid until reduced to about ¾ cup. Add cream and boil liquid until reduced to about ¾ cup. Stir in peas, zest, and Parmesan and cook sauce until peas are heated through.

While sauce is cooking, in a kettle of salted boiling water cook pasta until *al dente* and drain well. In a bowl toss pasta with sauce and mint. Serves 2.

Spinach, Ricotta, and Prosciutto Cannelloni

two 10-ounce boxes frozen chopped spinach
a 15-ounce container ricotta cheese
1½ cups freshly grated Parmesan cheese
3 large eggs
¼ pound thinly sliced prosciutto, chopped fine
¼ cup minced fresh parsley leaves (preferably
  flat-leafed)
ten 7-inch squares instant (no-boil) lasagne*
about 6 cups winter tomato sauce (recipe follows)

*available at specialty foods shops and many
  supermarkets

Cook spinach according to package instructions and drain well. Squeeze spinach dry by handfuls and chop fine. In a bowl stir together spinach, ricotta, 1 cup Parmesan, eggs, prosciutto, parsley, and salt and pepper to taste.

Preheat oven to 375° F. and oil a 13- by 9-inch baking dish.

In a large bowl of cold water soak lasagne squares until softened, about 15 minutes. Drain squares and pat dry between paper towels.

Spread 1 cup tomato sauce on bottom of prepared dish. Working with 1 square at a time, spread about ⅓ cup filling along one edge and roll up to enclose filling, leaving ends open.

Arrange cannelloni as formed, seam sides down, in one layer in baking dish. Spoon 2 cups sauce evenly over cannelloni, covering them, and sprinkle with remaining ½ cup Parmesan. *Pasta may be made up to 6 hours ahead and chilled, covered. Bring pasta to room temperature before baking.*

Bake cannelloni in middle of oven 30 minutes and let stand 10 minutes before serving.

Serve cannelloni with remaining tomato sauce, heated. Serves 6 as an entrée.

Winter Tomato Sauce

1½ cups finely chopped onion
⅓ cup finely chopped carrot
⅓ cup finely chopped celery
3 large garlic cloves, minced
1 tablespoon dried basil, crumbled
1 tablespoon dried oregano,
  crumbled
1 bay leaf
3 tablespoons olive oil
⅔ cup dry red wine
3 tablespoons tomato paste
two 28- to 32-ounce cans whole Italian
  tomatoes, drained, reserving juice,
  and chopped

In a heavy 5-quart saucepan cook onion, carrot, celery, garlic, basil, oregano, bay leaf, and salt and pepper to taste in oil over moderate heat, stirring, until vegetables are softened and add wine. Boil wine until most is evaporated and stir in tomato paste and tomatoes with reserved juice.

Simmer sauce, covered, over moderately low heat, stirring occasionally, 35 minutes and simmer, uncovered, stirring occasionally, 15 to 20 minutes, or until thickened. Discard bay leaf. *Sauce may be made 2 days ahead and chilled, covered.* Makes 6 cups.

minute. Add broth and raisins and simmer until broccoli rabe is just tender, about 3 minutes. Add butter, stirring until incorporated.

Drain pasta and return to kettle. Add broccoli rabe mixture and sausage and heat through if necessary.

Serve pasta with Parmesan. Serves 2.

Golden Onion and Zucchini Lasagne

1½ pounds onions, sliced thin (about 6 cups)
½ teaspoon dried thyme, crumbled, or
    1½ teaspoons chopped fresh thyme leaves
7 tablespoons unsalted butter
½ cup dry white wine
1 pound zucchini, scrubbed and sliced ¼ inch thick
    (about 3½ cups)
¼ cup all-purpose flour
2½ cups milk
freshly grated nutmeg to taste
three 7-inch squares instant (no-boil) lasagne*
1½ cups freshly grated Parmesan cheese
    (about 5 ounces)

*available at specialty foods shops and many
    supermarkets

In a large heavy skillet cook onions with dried thyme (if using) and salt and pepper to taste in 2 tablespoons butter, covered, over moderately low heat, stirring occasionally, 30 minutes, or until very tender and pale golden. Cook, uncovered, stirring, 15 minutes and add wine. Simmer mixture until most of wine is evaporated. Stir in fresh thyme (if using) and transfer to a bowl.

Preheat oven to 375° F. and butter an 8-inch square baking dish.

In the cleaned skillet cook half of zucchini slices in one layer in 1 tablespoon butter over moderate heat until tender, about 2 minutes on each side, and transfer to another bowl. Cook remaining zucchini in 1 tablespoon butter in same manner.

In a small heavy saucepan melt remaining 3 tablespoons butter over moderately low heat. Add flour and cook *roux*, whisking, 3 minutes. Add milk in a stream, whisking, and bring to a boil, whisking. Add nutmeg and salt and pepper to taste and simmer sauce, whisking, until thickened, about 2 minutes.

Cavatelli with Italian Sausage and Broccoli Rabe

½ pound (about 2 cups) dried *cavatelli* or other
    small shell-shaped pasta
½ pound (about 3 links) sweet Italian sausage
1 bunch (about ¾ pound) broccoli rabe, tough and
    hollow stems discarded, washed well
1 garlic clove, minced
1¼ cups low-salt chicken broth
¼ cup golden raisins
1 tablespoon unsalted butter

Accompaniment: freshly grated Parmesan cheese

In a kettle of boiling salted water cook pasta until *al dente*.

While pasta is cooking, squeeze sausage from its casings into a large heavy skillet and sauté over moderately high heat, stirring to break up chunks, until no longer pink. With slotted spoon transfer sausage to a bowl, reserving drippings in skillet.

Cut broccoli rabe into 1-inch pieces and sauté in drippings, stirring occasionally, until it begins to brown. Add garlic and sauté, stirring frequently, 1

Spread a few tablespoons sauce on bottom of baking dish. Over sauce in dish layer in this order: 1 lasagne square, half of onions, half of zucchini, a third sauce, and a third Parmesan. Repeat. Top with remaining lasagne square, remaining sauce and remaining Parmesan. *Pasta may be made up to 6 hours ahead and chilled, covered. Bring pasta to room temperature before baking.*

Bake lasagne in middle of oven 25 to 30 minutes, or until golden, and let stand 10 minutes before serving. Serves 6 to 8 as a first course or side dish.

Sausage and Wild Mushroom Lasagne with Red Pepper Tomato Sauce

For red pepper tomato sauce
1 pound hot and/or sweet Italian sausage, removed from casings
2 tablespoons olive oil
1 pound white mushrooms, sliced
2 cups finely chopped onion
3 large garlic cloves, minced
¾ teaspoon dried rosemary, crumbled
a pinch dried hot red pepper flakes
4 red bell peppers, sliced thin
2 pounds plum tomatoes, chopped
2 tablespoons balsamic vinegar, or to taste
For wild mushroom mixture
1½ ounces dried *porcini* mushrooms*
1½ cups hot water
½ stick (¼ cup) unsalted butter
¼ cup all-purpose flour
2½ cups milk
freshly grated nutmeg to taste

six 7-inch squares instant (no-boil) lasagne*
2 cups coarsely grated mozzarella cheese (about 8 ounces)
2 cups freshly grated Parmesan cheese (about 6 ounces)

*available at specialty foods shops and many supermarkets

Make red pepper tomato sauce:
In a heavy skillet measuring at least 12 inches across the top cook sausage over moderate heat, stirring and breaking it up, until cooked through and transfer with a slotted spoon to a bowl. Pour off all but 1 tablespoon fat from skillet and add 1 tablespoon oil, white mushrooms, and salt and pepper to taste. Cook white mushrooms over moderate heat, stirring, until all liquid given off is evaporated and add to sausage. Add remaining tablespoon oil to skillet and cook onion with garlic, rosemary, red pepper flakes, and salt and pepper to taste until softened. Stir in bell peppers and tomatoes and cook, covered, over moderately low heat, stirring occasionally, until peppers are very soft, about 20 minutes. In a blender or food processor purée tomato pepper mixture in batches, transferring to a large saucepan as puréed, and stir in vinegar. Add sausage mixture to sauce and simmer, uncovered, 5 minutes.

Preheat oven to 375° F. and oil a 13- by 9-inch baking dish.

Make wild mushroom mixture:
In a small bowl soak *porcini* in the hot water 30 minutes and drain liquid through a sieve lined with a rinsed and squeezed paper towel into a measuring cup. Reserve ½ cup soaking liquid and chop *porcini* fine. In a heavy saucepan melt butter over moderately low heat. Add flour and cook *roux*, whisking, 3 minutes. Add milk and reserved soaking liquid in a stream, whisking, and bring to a boil, whisking. Stir in *porcini*, nutmeg, and salt and pepper to taste and simmer over low heat, whisking occasionally, until thickened, about 5 minutes.

In a large bowl of cold water soak lasagne squares until softened, about 15 minutes. Drain squares and pat dry between paper towels. In a small bowl toss together grated mozzarella and Parmesan. Spread enough red pepper tomato sauce in prepared dish to coat bottom. Over sauce in dish layer ingredients in this order: 2 lasagne sheets (cut to fit in one layer), a third wild mushroom mixture, a third cheese, and a third remaining red pepper tomato sauce. Repeat twice, reversing order of red pepper tomato sauce and cheese at end of last round of layering so that cheese is on top. *Pasta may be made up to 6 hours ahead and chilled, covered. Bring pasta to room temperature before baking.*

Bake lasagne in middle of oven 35 to 40 minutes, or until golden, and let stand 10 minutes before serving. Serves 6 to 8 as an entrée.

Macaroni and Cheese

7 tablespoons unsalted butter
¼ cup plus 2 tablespoons all-purpose flour
4 cups milk
1½ teaspoons dry mustard
⅛ teaspoon cayenne, or to taste
1 pound elbow macaroni
3 cups coarsely grated extra-sharp Cheddar cheese
   (about 12 ounces)
1⅓ cups freshly grated Parmesan cheese
   (about 4 ounces)
1 cup fresh bread crumbs

Preheat oven to 350° F. and butter a 3- to 4-quart gratin dish or other shallow baking dish.

In a heavy saucepan melt 6 tablespoons butter over moderately low heat. Add flour and cook *roux*, whisking, 3 minutes. Add milk in a stream, whisking, and bring to a boil, whisking. Add mustard, cayenne, and salt and pepper to taste and simmer sauce, whisking occasionally, until thickened, about 2 minutes.

In a kettle of salted boiling water cook macaroni until just *al dente*, about 7 minutes, and drain well. In a large bowl stir together macaroni, sauce, Cheddar, and 1 cup Parmesan and transfer to prepared dish.

In a small bowl stir together bread crumbs and remaining ⅓ cup Parmesan and sprinkle evenly over macaroni. Cut remaining 1 tablespoon butter into bits and scatter over topping. *Pasta may be made up to 6 hours ahead and chilled, covered. Bring pasta to room temperature before baking.*

Bake macaroni in middle of oven 25 to 30 minutes, or until golden and bubbling. Serves 6 to 8 as an entrée or 8 to 10 as a side dish.

Lemon Dill Baked Orzo with Gruyère

1 tablespoon freshly grated lemon zest
½ cup finely chopped shallot
½ cup finely chopped celery
2 tablespoons unsalted butter
2 tablespoons olive oil
3 tablespoons all-purpose flour
2 cups chicken broth
1 pound *orzo* (rice-shaped pasta)
¼ cup minced fresh dill

2 cups coarsely grated Gruyère cheese
   (about 6 ounces)

Preheat oven to 400° F. Butter a 2-quart gratin dish or other shallow baking dish and sprinkle with 2 teaspoons zest.

In a heavy saucepan cook shallot and celery in butter and oil over moderate heat, stirring, until celery is softened. Add flour and cook mixture, stirring, 3 minutes. Add broth in a stream, whisking, and bring to a boil, whisking. Add remaining 1 teaspoon zest and salt and pepper to taste and simmer sauce, whisking, until thickened, about 3 minutes.

In a kettle of salted boiling water cook *orzo* until just *al dente*, about 6 minutes, and drain well. In a large bowl stir together *orzo*, sauce, dill, and Gruyère and transfer to prepared dish. *Pasta may be made up to 6 hours ahead and chilled, covered. Bring pasta to room temperature before baking.*

Bake *orzo* in middle of oven 30 minutes, or until bubbling and slightly crusty. Serves 6 as a side dish.

Rosemary Lemon Orzo Pilaf

¾ cup *orzo* (rice-shaped pasta)
½ tablespoon unsalted butter
½ teaspoon chopped fresh rosemary leaves
½ cup chicken broth
¾ cup water
2 teaspoons fresh lemon juice
¼ teaspoon salt

In a 1-quart heavy saucepan sauté *orzo* in butter over moderately high heat, stirring, until browned lightly and stir in remaining ingredients. Bring liquid to a boil and cover. Reduce heat to low and cook 15 minutes, or until liquid is absorbed. Remove pan from heat and let stand, covered, 5 minutes. Serves 2.

Duck Confit and Mashed Potato Ravioli with White Truffle Sauce

2 russet (baking) potatoes (about 1 pound)
2 tablespoons sour cream
about 14 ounces *confit* of duck leg*
   (2 whole legs)
3 tablespoons unsalted butter

1 garlic clove,
   minced
56 wonton wrappers**,
   thawed if frozen
28 flat-leafed parsley leaves
2 tablespoons white truffle oil***
2 tablespoons white truffle paste***

Garnish: flat-leafed parsley leaves

*available at specialty foods shops, some
   supermarkets, and by mail order from
   D'Artagnan, tel. (800) 327-8246, or, in
   New Jersey, (201) 792-0748
**available at Asian markets and many specialty
   foods shops and supermarkets
***available at specialty foods shops and by mail
   order from Aux Délices des Bois, New York,
   NY, tel. (800) 666-1232, fax. (212) 334-1231

Peel and quarter potatoes and in a saucepan combine with cold water to cover by 2 inches. Simmer potatoes 15 to 20 minutes, or until soft, and drain in a colander. Return potatoes to pan and steam, covered, over moderate heat, shaking pan, 30 seconds to evaporate any excess liquid. Force hot potatoes through a ricer or medium disk of a food mill into a bowl and beat in sour cream and salt and pepper to taste.

Remove skin from duck legs and cut into ¼-inch strips. In a small heavy skillet cook skin in 1 tablespoon butter over moderately low heat, stirring occasionally, until crisp and transfer cracklings with a slotted spoon to paper towels to drain.

Remove meat from duck legs and chop fine. Add garlic to fat remaining in skillet and cook over moderately low heat, stirring occasionally, until softened. Add meat to skillet and cook over moderate heat, stirring occasionally, until heated through. Stir in salt and pepper to taste. Stir meat mixture into potato mixture and cool. *Filling may be made 1 day ahead and chilled, covered.*

Put 1 wrapper on a lightly floured surface and mound 1 tablespoon filling in center. Top filling with 1 parsley leaf. Lightly brush edges of wrapper with water and put a second wrapper over first, pressing down around filling to force out air and sealing edges well. Trim excess dough with a round cutter or sharp knife. Make more ravioli with remaining wrappers, filling, and parsley in same manner, transferring as formed to a dry kitchen towel and turning occasionally to dry slightly.

In a kettle of gently boiling salted water cook ravioli in 2 batches 2 minutes, or until they rise to surface and are tender. (Do not let water boil vigorously once ravioli have been added.) Transfer ravioli as cooked with a slotted spoon to a dry kitchen towel to drain and keep warm.

While ravioli are cooking, in the small heavy skillet cook remaining 2 tablespoons butter over moderate heat, swirling skillet occasionally, until nut brown in color. Remove skillet from heat and stir in truffle oil and paste.

Arrange 4 or 5 ravioli on each of 6 heated plates and spoon truffle sauce on top. Top each serving with cracklings and garnish with parsley leaves. Makes 28 ravioli, serving 6 as a first course.

Cook chard and garlic, stirring, until chard is tender, about 2 minutes. Transfer chard mixture to a bowl and cool. To chard mixture add cheeses, 2 tablespoons bacon, and salt and pepper to taste.

Bring a saucepan of salted water to a gentle boil.

Put a won ton wrapper on a lightly floured surface and mound 1 tablespoon filling in center of wrapper. Brush edges of wrapper with water and put a second wrapper over first, pressing down around filling to force out air. Seal edges well and transfer ravioli to a kitchen towel. Make more ravioli with remaining wrappers and filling in same manner, turning them occasionally to dry slightly. Cook ravioli in water at a gentle boil 6 to 8 minutes, or until they rise to surface and are tender. (Do not let water boil vigorously once ravioli have been added.) With a slotted spoon transfer ravioli as cooked to a kitchen towel to drain.

Divide ravioli between 2 plates and spoon sauce over them. Sprinkle ravioli with remaining tablespoon bacon. Serves 2 as a main course.

Pasta with Roasted Eggplant, Ricotta, and Basil

¾ pound eggplant, cut into 1-inch pieces
   (about 4 cups)
2 tablespoons olive oil
1 medium onion, chopped fine (about 1 cup)
2 garlic cloves, minced
1 medium red bell pepper, sliced thin
   (about 1 cup)
½ pound vine-ripened plum tomatoes, seeded
   and chopped (about 4)
2 teaspoons balsamic vinegar, or to taste
½ pound *rotelle* or ziti
¼ cup ricotta cheese
¼ cup chopped fresh basil leaves
freshly grated Parmesan cheese to taste

Preheat oven to 450° F.

In a jelly-roll pan toss eggplant with 1 tablespoon oil and salt and pepper to taste and roast in oven, shaking pan occasionally, until golden and tender, 15 to 20 minutes.

While eggplant is roasting, in a heavy skillet cook onion, garlic, and bell pepper with salt and pepper to taste in remaining tablespoon oil over moderate heat, stirring, until softened.

M. Shields

*Swiss Chard, Bacon, and Ricotta Ravioli
with Tomato Sauce*

For filling
3 slices bacon
3 cups chopped Swiss chard, stems discarded,
   leaves washed and chopped (about ½ pound)
½ teaspoon minced garlic
½ cup ricotta cheese
2 tablespoons freshly grated Parmesan cheese

24 won ton wrappers*, thawed if frozen
1 cup prepared tomato sauce, heated

*available at Asian markets and most
   supermarkets

Make filling:
In a large heavy skillet cook bacon over moderate heat until crisp and with a slotted spatula transfer to a cutting board. Chop bacon fine. Remove all but 1 tablespoon fat from skillet and heat remaining fat over moderately high heat until hot but not smoking.

162

Add tomatoes and simmer, covered, stirring occasionally, until tomatoes and pepper are tender, 10 to 15 minutes.

Stir in vinegar and roasted eggplant.

In a kettle of boiling salted water cook pasta until *al dente*. Reserve ¾ pasta cooking water and drain pasta well. In a bowl toss pasta well with sauce, ricotta, basil, Parmesan, salt and pepper to taste, and enough reserved cooking water to reach desired consistency. Serves 2.

Rotini with Lentils and Spinach

1 onion, chopped coarse
1 large garlic clove, minced
2 tablespoons olive oil
⅔ cup lentils, picked over and rinsed
1½ cups water
¼ teaspoon dried tarragon, crumbled
¼ teaspoon dried oregano, crumbled
¼ teaspoon dried hot red pepper flakes,
   or to taste
a 14- to 16-ounce can whole tomatoes including
   the juice
1 tablespoon ketchup
1 pound fresh spinach, washed well, spun dry, and
   chopped, or a 10-ounce package frozen
1 pound *rotini* or other spiral pasta

Accompaniment: freshly grated Parmesan cheese

In a large saucepan cook onion and garlic in oil over moderate heat, stirring, until onion is softened. Stir in lentils, water, herbs, and red pepper flakes and simmer 10 minutes. Add tomatoes with juice, ketchup, and salt and pepper to taste and simmer, breaking up tomatoes with a wooden spoon, 20 minutes. Add spinach and cook sauce, stirring, until spinach is tender, about 2 minutes.

In a kettle of salted boiling water cook pasta until *al dente* and drain in a colander. In a large bowl toss pasta with sauce. Serve pasta with Parmesan. Serves 4.

Spaghetti with Anchovy Olive Sauce

5 large garlic cloves, sliced thin
⅓ cup olive oil
a 2-ounce can flat anchovies, drained, patted dry,
   and chopped
¾ cup pimiento-stuffed olives,
   rinsed, drained well,
   and chopped fine
1 cup finely chopped fresh flat-leafed parsley
   leaves
1 pound spaghetti

In a heavy skillet (measuring at least 12 inches across top) cook garlic in oil over moderate heat, stirring, until pale golden. Add anchovies and cook, mashing them, until they dissolve into oil, about 1 minute. Stir in olives and parsley and remove skillet from heat.

In a kettle of salted boiling water cook spaghetti until *al dente*. Reserve 1 cup pasta cooking water and drain spaghetti in a colander. Add spaghetti and ½ cup of reserved cooking water to sauce. Heat pasta over moderate heat, stirring and tossing it and adding more reserved cooking water as necessary, until it is coated well with sauce. Serves 4 to 6.

Spaghetti with Pepperoni, Peas, and Browned Onions

½ pound spaghetti
1 cup chopped onion
1 tablespoon vegetable oil
⅓ cup chopped sliced pepperoni
¾ cup frozen peas, thawed
2 tablespoons minced flat-leafed parsley leaves
2 tablespoons freshly grated Parmesan cheese,
   or to taste

In a large saucepan of salted boiling water cook spaghetti until *al dente*.

While spaghetti is cooking, in a 10- to 12-inch skillet sauté onion in oil over moderately high heat, stirring, until golden. Add pepperoni and peas and sauté, stirring, 1 minute.

Reserve ⅓ cup pasta cooking water and drain spaghetti. Add spaghetti to pepperoni mixture with parsley and reserved cooking water and cook over low heat, tossing, 1 minute. Remove skillet from heat and stir in Parmesan and salt and pepper to taste. Serves 2.

Baked Ziti with Turkey Meatballs

For meatballs
1 pound ground turkey
1 large garlic clove,
    minced
¾ cup fresh bread crumbs
½ cup finely chopped onion
3 tablespoons pine nuts, toasted, cooled, and
    chopped
½ cup minced fresh parsley leaves (preferably
    flat-leafed)
1 large egg, beaten lightly
1 teaspoon salt
1 teaspoon black pepper
4 tablespoons olive oil

1 pound ziti or *penne*
1½ cups coarsely grated mozzarella cheese
    (about 6 ounces)
1 cup freshly grated Romano cheese
    (about 3 ounces)
about 6 cups winter tomato sauce (page 157)
a 15-ounce container ricotta cheese

Make meatballs:

In a bowl stir together well turkey, garlic, bread crumbs, onion, pine nuts, parsley, egg, salt, and pepper and form into meatballs about 1 inch in diameter. In a large heavy skillet heat 2 tablespoons oil over moderately high heat until hot but not smoking and cook half of meatballs, shaking skillet, until browned and cooked through, about 4 minutes. Transfer meatballs to paper towels to drain and brown remaining meatballs in remaining 2 tablespoons oil in same manner.

Preheat oven to 375° F. and oil a 3- to 4-quart gratin dish or other shallow baking dish.

In a kettle of salted boiling water cook pasta until just *al dente*, about 8 minutes, and drain well. In a small bowl toss together mozzarella and Romano.

Spoon about 1½ cups tomato sauce and half of meatballs into prepared dish and spoon half of pasta on top. Spread half remaining sauce and half cheese mixture over pasta. Top with remaining meatballs and drop dollops of ricotta over meatballs. Spread remaining pasta over ricotta and top with remaining sauce and remaining cheese mixture. *Pasta may be made up to 6 hours ahead and chilled, covered. Bring pasta to room temperature before baking.*

Bake ziti in middle of oven 30 to 35 minutes, or until golden, and let stand 10 minutes before serving. Serves 6 to 8 as an entrée.

*Bean-Thread Noodles
with Shiitake Mushrooms and Vegetables*

6 ounces bean-thread (cellophane) noodles*
¼ pound fresh *shiitake* mushrooms, stems
    discarded and caps sliced thin
½ cup thinly sliced onion
a 1½-inch cube fresh gingerroot, peeled and cut
    into julienne strips
2 tablespoons vegetable oil
2 cups chicken broth
1 cup water
½ cup shredded carrot
3 scallions, cut into 1-inch sections and sections
    cut into julienne strips

*available at Asian markets and many specialty
    foods shops and supermarkets

In a bowl soak noodles in warm water to cover 15 minutes. Drain noodles and cut into 3-inch lengths.

In a large heavy saucepan cook mushrooms, onion, and gingerroot in oil over moderate heat, stirring, until mushrooms are tender. Add broth, water, carrot, noodles, and salt to taste and simmer, stirring occasionally, until liquid is absorbed, about 5 to 10 minutes. Stir in scallions. Serves 6.

PHOTO ON PAGE 42

Rice Noodles with Garlic and Herbs

1 cup plus 2 tablespoons vegetable oil
½ cup thinly sliced shallot
⅓ cup thinly sliced garlic
¼ cup tamarind (from a pliable block)*
½ cup warm water
3 tablespoons Asian fish sauce (preferably
    naam pla)
3 tablespoons rice vinegar
1½ tablespoons firmly packed brown sugar
¼ cup water

¾ pound dried flat rice noodles* (about
¼ to ½ inch wide)
1 small onion, sliced thin
1 small red bell pepper, cut into thin strips
¾ pint vine-ripened cherry tomatoes, quartered
¼ cup thinly sliced fresh Thai basil leaves* or
regular basil leaves
¼ cup chopped fresh coriander

*available at Asian markets, some specialty foods
shops, and by mail order from Adriana's
Caravan, Brooklyn, NY, tel. (800) 316-0820
or (718) 436-8565 or Uwajimaya, 519 Sixth
Avenue South, Seattle, WA 98104,
tel. (206) 624-6248

In an 8- or 9-inch skillet heat 1 cup oil over moderate heat until hot but not smoking and fry shallot, stirring, until golden, 1 to 2 minutes. Transfer shallot with a slotted spoon to paper towels to drain. Fry garlic in same hot oil in same manner.

In a small bowl stir together tamarind and warm water, mashing tamarind gently, and strain mixture through a fine sieve set over a bowl, pressing hard on solids. Stir in fish sauce, vinegar, sugar, and water.

In a large bowl soak noodles in cold water to cover 15 minutes. Drain noodles and in a kettle of boiling salted water cook until just tender, 1 to 2 minutes. In a colander drain noodles and rinse under cold water. Drain noodles well.

In a large skillet cook onion and bell pepper in remaining 2 tablespoons oil over moderate heat, stirring, until softened and add tomatoes, noodles, and sauce. Cook mixture, stirring, until heated through. Add herbs, garlic, and shallot and toss noodles well. Serves 6.

PHOTO ON PAGE 46

Cold Chinese-Style Sesame Noodles
with Cucumber

2 tablespoons dark (Asian) sesame oil
1 tablespoon soy sauce
1 tablespoon white-wine vinegar or unseasoned
rice vinegar
¼ teaspoon sugar
¼ teaspoon salt, or to taste

⅛ teaspoon dried hot red pepper flakes
6 ounces *capellini*
½ seedless cucumber, cut lengthwise into thin
spears and crosswise into thin slices (about
1 cup)
1 scallion, minced, or 1 tablespoon minced fresh
coriander
1½ teaspoons sesame seeds, toasted lightly
and cooled

In a small bowl stir together oil, soy sauce, vinegar, sugar, salt, and red pepper flakes until sugar and salt are dissolved.

In a large saucepan of salted boiling water cook *capellini* until tender and drain in colander. Rinse noodles under cold water until cool and drain well.

In a large bowl toss noodles with sauce, cucumber, and scallion or coriander until combined well and divide between 2 plates. Sprinkle noodles with sesame seeds. Serves 2.

*Soba with Pea Shoots,
Shiitake Mushrooms, and Leeks*

4 small leeks, white and pale green parts only,
    halved lengthwise, sliced thin crosswise,
    washed thoroughly, and patted dry (about
    1½ cups)
3 tablespoons vegetable oil
½ pound fresh *shiitake* mushrooms, stems
    discarded and caps sliced
4 scallions, sliced thin
2 tablespoons soy sauce, or to taste
2 teaspoons rice vinegar, or to taste
an 8- or 9-ounce package *soba* (buckwheat
    noodles)*
½ pound pea shoots,** washed well and spun dry

*available at Asian markets and health foods
    stores
**available seasonally at some Asian, specialty
    produce, and farmers markets

In a large skillet cook leeks in oil over moderately
low heat, stirring, until softened, about 10 minutes.
Stir in mushrooms and cook 5 minutes. Stir in scallions, soy sauce, and vinegar and cook 1 minute.

In a kettle of salted boiling water cook noodles 5
minutes or according to package directions. Put pea
shoots in a colander and drain cooked noodles over
shoots to wilt them. Rinse mixture in cold water and
drain well.

In a bowl toss noodles with pea shoots and stir in
cooked vegetables. Season mixture with salt and pepper and serve at room temperature. Serves 4.

PASTA SAUCES

Jalapeño Sunflower Seed Pesto

a 3-inch fresh *jalapeño* chili, chopped
    (wear rubber gloves)
⅓ cup raw unsalted sunflower seeds*, toasted
    lightly and cooled
1½ cups packed fresh coriander, rinsed and
    spun dry
1½ cups packed fresh parsley leaves (preferably
    flat-leafed), rinsed and spun dry
2 large garlic cloves, chopped
½ teaspoon salt
⅓ cup extra-virgin olive oil plus additional to
    cover *pesto*

*available at natural foods stores, specialty foods
    shops, and some supermarkets

In a food processor blend well all ingredients except additional oil. Transfer *pesto* to a jar with a tight-
fitting lid, covering *pesto* with a layer of additional
oil to prevent discoloration. Pesto *keeps, covered and
chilled, 2 weeks.* Makes about 1 cup.

To use pesto: Pour off layer of oil from *pesto.* In a
kettle of boiling salted water boil 1 pound pasta until
al dente. Reserve ⅔ cup of hot cooking water and
drain pasta in a colander. In a heated serving bowl stir
together ¾ cup *pesto* and reserved cooking water.
Add pasta to *pesto* and toss until coated well. Serves
4 to 6.

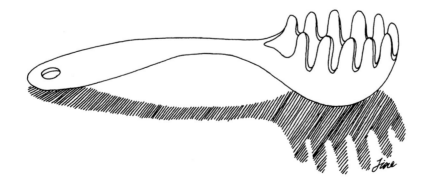

Spicy Sichuan Peanut Sauce

1 cup peanut butter
¼ cup soy sauce
¼ cup Asian sesame oil
3 tablespoons rice vinegar
    (not seasoned)
2 tablespoons finely chopped garlic
2 tablespoons grated peeled fresh gingerroot
1½ teaspoons Asian chili paste* or 1 teaspoon
    dried hot red pepper flakes,
    or to taste
1 tablespoon hoisin sauce*,
    or to taste
1½ to 2 tablespoons fresh lime juice
¾ cup water

*available at Asian markets, some specialty foods
    shops, and supermarkets

In a blender or food processor blend all ingredients
with salt to taste until smooth. Transfer sauce to a jar
with a tight-fitting lid. *Peanut sauce keeps, covered
and chilled, 1 week.* Makes about 2½ cups.

To use peanut sauce: Boil 1 pound Asian noodles
or spaghetti until *al dente* and drain in a colander.
Rinse noodles under cold water until cool and drain.
Toss noodles with about ¾ cup sauce and finely
chopped scallion to taste. Serves 4 to 6.

GRAINS

Bulgur, Pine Nut, and Red Pepper Pilaf

1 small onion,
    chopped fine
1 tablespoon vegetable oil
1 cup plus 2 tablespoons chicken broth
3 tablespoons finely diced red bell pepper
¾ cup bulgur*
2 tablespoons pine nuts,
    toasted lightly
2 teaspoons minced fresh chives

*available at natural foods stores and many
    supermarkets

In a small heavy saucepan cook onion in oil over
moderate heat, stirring, until softened.

Stir in broth, bell pepper, and bulgur and bring liquid to a boil. Cook mixture, covered, over low heat
12 minutes, or until liquid is absorbed.

Remove pan from heat and let stand, covered, 5
minutes. Stir in pine nuts, chives, and salt and pepper
to taste. Serves 2 generously.

PHOTO ON PAGE 69

Tasso Grits Batons

3 cups water
¾ cup quick-cooking grits
2 tablespoons unsalted butter
½ cup finely chopped *tasso** (Cajun-cured smoked
    pork, about 2 ounces)
all-purpose flour for dredging
2 large eggs beaten with 2 tablespoons
    water
unseasoned fine dry bread crumbs
    for dredging
oil for frying

*available by mail from Community Kitchens,
    Ridgely, MD, tel. (800) 535-9901

In a 2-quart heavy saucepan bring water to a boil.
Add grits in a stream, stirring, and cook, covered,
over moderately low heat, stirring occasionally, 5
minutes, or until thickened. Stir in butter, *tasso*, and
salt to taste and spread grits in baking dish, 13 by 9
by 2 inches. Cool grits and chill, covered, overnight.
*Tasso grits may be made 2 days ahead and chilled,
covered.*

Have flour, eggs, and bread crumbs ready in separate shallow dishes. Cut grits into twenty-four 4- by
½-inch batons and dredge in flour. Dip batons in egg
and dredge in bread crumbs. *Batons may be prepared
up to this point 8 hours ahead and chilled, uncovered, on a baking sheet.*

In a deep skillet or heavy kettle heat 1½ inches oil
to 375° F. on a deep-fat thermometer and fry batons
in batches, turning, until golden, about 1 minute.
Transfer batons with a slotted spoon to paper towels
to drain. Serves 6.

PHOTO ON PAGE 38

Lentils and Curried Rice with Fried Onions

2 teaspoons vegetable oil plus oil for frying
1 pound onions, sliced thin
1 cup lentils, picked over
    and rinsed
1 cup unconverted long-grain rice
2 cups water
2 teaspoons curry powder
⅛ teaspoon cayenne
1 teaspoon salt
½ cup loosely packed flat-leafed parsley leaves

In a large skillet heat ¼ inch oil over moderately high heat until hot but not smoking. Fry onions in batches, stirring occasionally, until golden brown. Transfer onions with a slotted spoon to a tray and sprinkle with salt to taste.

Add lentils to a large saucepan of salted water and bring water to a boil. Cook lentils at a bare simmer until just tender, about 15 minutes.

While lentils are cooking, in a small (1½- to 2-quart) saucepan cook rice in 2 teaspoons oil over high heat, stirring, for 1 minute. Add water, curry powder, cayenne, and salt and boil rice, uncovered, stirring occasionally, until surface is covered with steam holes and grains on top appear dry. Reduce heat as much as possible and cover pan with a tight-fitting lid. Cook rice 15 minutes more. Remove pan from heat and let rice stand, covered, 5 minutes. Transfer rice to a bowl and fluff with a fork. Add lentils, drained in a sieve and rinsed gently, and parsley and toss mixture well.

Top mixture with onions. *Mixture may be made 1 day ahead and chilled, covered.* Serve mixture warm or at room temperature. Serves 6 as a side dish.

Coconut Gingerroot Rice

2 tablespoons vegetable oil
1 tablespoon julienne strips peeled fresh
    gingerroot
1½ cups long-grain rice, rinsed well in
    several changes of water
    and drained
1¾ cups water
⅓ cup canned unsweetened coconut milk
1 small bay leaf

½ teaspoon salt
Tabasco to taste
2 scallions, minced
2 tablespoons minced fresh coriander

In a medium saucepan heat oil over moderately high heat until hot but not smoking and sauté gingerroot, stirring frequently, 2 minutes. Add rice and cook, stirring, 2 minutes. Add water, coconut milk, bay leaf, salt, and Tabasco and bring mixture to a boil. Reduce heat to low and cook mixture, covered, 20 minutes, or until rice is tender and liquid is absorbed.

Remove pan from heat and sprinkle rice with scallions and coriander. Let rice stand 5 minutes and fluff with a fork. Discard bay leaf. Serves 4.

Minted Saffron Rice with Currants and Pine Nuts

2 tablespoons vegetable oil
1 teaspoon cuminseed
1 cinnamon stick
1 bay leaf
1 cup finely chopped onion
2 cups long-grain rice
2¼ cups water
⅓ cup currants
¼ teaspoon crumbled saffron
    threads
1½ teaspoons salt
½ cup pine nuts,
    toasted lightly
¼ cup finely chopped fresh mint leaves

In a large heavy saucepan heat oil over moderate heat until hot but not smoking and cook cuminseed, cinnamon stick, and bay leaf, stirring, until mixture is fragrant and cuminseed is several shades darker (be careful not to burn it).

Add onion and cook, stirring, until softened. Add rice and cook, stirring, 1 minute. Add water, currants, saffron, and salt and bring to a boil, covered. Reduce heat to very low and simmer rice, covered, 20 minutes, or until liquid is absorbed.

Let rice stand 5 minutes. Discard cinnamon stick and bay leaf and stir in pine nuts and mint. Serves 6.

PHOTO ON PAGE 33

Boursin and Fennel Seed Risotto

1¾ cups low-salt chicken broth
¾ cup water
1 tablespoon unsalted butter
¾ cup unconverted long-grain rice
¼ teaspoon fennel seeds
3 tablespoons dry vermouth or dry white wine
2 tablespoons Boursin cheese
2 tablespoons minced fresh chives

In a small saucepan bring broth and water to a simmer and keep at a bare simmer.

In a heavy saucepan melt butter over moderately high heat and stir in rice and fennel seeds, stirring until coated with butter. Add vermouth or wine and cook, stirring, until absorbed. Add about ½ cup simmering broth and cook, stirring constantly, until absorbed. Continue cooking and adding broth, ½ cup at a time, stirring constantly and letting each portion be absorbed before adding next. (After last broth addition rice should be *al dente* and creamy.)

Remove pan from heat and stir in Boursin, chives, and salt and pepper to taste. Serves 2.

Yellow Pepper Risotto

3 yellow bell peppers,
   chopped
1 tablespoon water
5 tablespoons unsalted butter
1 cup finely diced zucchini
4 cups low-salt chicken broth
6 shallots, minced (about 1 cup)
1 garlic clove, minced
1 cup Arborio rice*
⅓ cup dry white wine
1 cup freshly grated Parmesan cheese
2 tablespoons minced flat-leafed parsley
   leaves

*available at specialty foods shops and some
   supermarkets

In a skillet cook bell peppers in water and 2 tablespoons of butter, covered partially, over moderate heat, stirring occasionally, until very soft, about 20 minutes. Purée peppers in a food processor or blender and strain through a coarse sieve into a small bowl. Season purée with salt and pepper.

In the cleaned skillet cook zucchini in 1 tablespoon remaining butter over moderate heat, stirring, until crisp-tender, about 2 minutes, and season with salt and pepper.

In a saucepan heat broth and keep at a bare simmer.

In a heavy 2- to 3-quart saucepan cook shallot and garlic in remaining 2 tablespoons butter over moderately low heat until very soft but not browned, about 5 minutes. Stir in rice and cook over moderate heat, stirring constantly, until edges become translucent, about 5 minutes. Add wine and cook, stirring constantly, until wine is absorbed. Add about ½ cup simmering broth and cook, stirring constantly, until broth is absorbed. Continue adding broth, about ½ cup at a time, and cooking, stirring constantly and letting each addition be absorbed before adding the next, until rice is *al dente*, about 20 minutes.

Remove pan from heat and stir in pepper purée, zucchini, Parmesan, 1 tablespoon parsley, and salt and pepper to taste. Sprinkle risotto with remaining tablespoon parsley. Serves 4.

PHOTO ON PAGE 29

Harvest Wild Rice

3 cups chicken broth
3 cups water
½ pound dried *flageolets** or Great Northern
    beans, picked over
¾ cup wild rice (about 4 ounces)
2 large leeks, white and pale green
    parts only
2 tablespoons unsalted butter
¼ pound fresh *shiitake* mushrooms,
    sliced thin
¼ cup hazelnuts, toasted and skinned
    (procedure follows) and
    chopped coarse
¼ cup dried cranberries*

*available at specialty foods shops

In a large saucepan simmer broth, water, and beans, covered, 45 minutes. Stir in wild rice and simmer, covered, 45 minutes, or until beans and rice are tender. Drain rice mixture and return to pan.

Cut leeks crosswise into ½-inch slices and in a bowl soak in water, agitating occasionally to dislodge any sand, 5 minutes. Lift leeks out of water and drain in a colander. In a non-stick skillet sauté leeks in butter over moderately high heat, stirring occasionally, until almost tender, about 5 minutes. Add mushrooms with salt to taste and cook, stirring occasionally, 2 minutes, or until vegetables are tender. Stir leek mixture into rice mixture. *Rice mixture may be prepared up to this point 1 day ahead and chilled, covered. Reheat mixture, adding water to prevent it from sticking to skillet, before proceeding.*

Stir hazelnuts and cranberries into rice mixture and serve warm. Serves 4.

PHOTO ON PAGES 78 AND 79

To Toast and Skin Hazelnuts

Preheat oven to 350° F.

In a baking pan toast hazelnuts in one layer in oven 10 to 15 minutes, or until colored lightly and skins blister. Wrap nuts in a kitchen towel and let steam 1 minute. Rub nuts in towel to remove as much of skins as possible and cool.

Wild Rice and Orzo with Toasted Walnuts

1½ cups wild rice
6 cups water
1 teaspoon salt
6 tablespoons walnut oil* or extra-virgin olive oil
1 pound *orzo* (rice-shaped pasta)
3 tablespoons fresh lemon juice plus additional
    to taste
⅔ cup finely chopped scallion
1 cup chopped toasted walnuts

*available at specialty foods shops

In a large saucepan combine rice with water and salt and simmer, covered, until tender, 40 to 45 minutes. Drain rice well and transfer to a large bowl. Toss rice with 2 tablespoons oil.

In a saucepan of boiling salted water cook *orzo* until *al dente*. Rinse *orzo* under cold water and drain well. To rice mixture add *orzo* with remaining 4 tablespoons oil, 3 tablespoons lemon juice, and salt and pepper and toss well. *Mixture may be prepared up to this point 1 day ahead and chilled, covered.* Just before serving, stir in scallion and walnuts and season with additional lemon juice and salt and pepper.

Serve mixture at room temperature. Makes about 12 cups.

PHOTO ON PAGE 64

VEGETABLES

Asparagus Amandine

¾ pound asparagus, trimmed
½ cup water
1 tablespoon unsalted butter
2 tablespoons sliced almonds,
   toasted lightly
fresh lemon juice to taste

Cut asparagus diagonally into ½-inch pieces. In a skillet measuring about 10 inches across top simmer asparagus in water and butter, uncovered, until asparagus is crisp-tender and liquid is reduced to a glaze, about 3 minutes. Stir in almonds, lemon juice, and salt and pepper to taste. Serves 2.

Roasted Asparagus with Balsamic Vinegar

1 pound fresh asparagus (12 to 14 medium stalks),
   trimmed and peeled
1½ teaspoons olive oil
   (preferably extra-virgin)
1 tablespoon balsamic vinegar

Preheat oven to 500° F.
In a large shallow baking pan toss asparagus with oil and salt and pepper to taste until coated well. Roast asparagus, shaking pan every 2 minutes, until tender and lightly browned, about 10 minutes. Remove pan from oven and drizzle vinegar over asparagus, shaking pan to combine well. Serves 2.

Pencil-Thin Asparagus and Scallions

¾ pound pencil-thin asparagus (about 30 stalks),
   trimmed and lower stalks peeled
15 pencil-thin whole scallions, trimmed and
   cut to length of asparagus, plus whites of
   2 scallions, minced
2 tablespoons unsalted butter

In a kettle of boiling salted water cook asparagus until crisp-tender, about 5 minutes. Remove asparagus with tongs and immediately plunge into a bowl of ice and cold water. In water in kettle cook whole scallions until crisp-tender, about 4 minutes. Remove scallions with tongs and immediately plunge into bowl of ice and cold water. Pat dry asparagus and scallions between paper towels. *Asparagus and scallions may be prepared up to this point 1 day ahead and chilled, covered.*

In a large non-stick skillet sauté minced scallion in butter over moderately high heat until softened, about 2 minutes. Stir in asparagus, whole scallions, and salt and pepper to taste and sauté, stirring occasionally, until heated through, about 5 minutes. Serves 4.

PHOTO ON PAGE 29

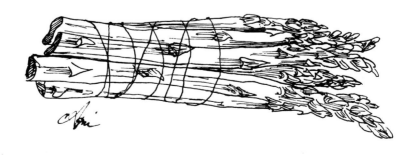

Stuffed Artichokes with Red Pepper Vinaigrette

2 large artichokes (each about ¾ pound)
½ lemon
¼ cup water
¼ cup plus 2 tablespoons minced red bell pepper
¼ cup minced onion
1 garlic clove, minced
4 tablespoons olive oil
¾ cup fine dry bread crumbs
¼ cup thinly sliced scallion greens
⅓ cup freshly grated Parmesan cheese
¼ teaspoon dried thyme, crumbled
cayenne to taste
2 tablespoons fresh lemon juice
2 teaspoons white-wine vinegar

Cut off stems of artichokes with a stainless-steel knife and discard. Break off tough outer leaves and cut off top fourth of artichokes. Snip off tips of leaves with scissors and rub cut edges with lemon half.

In a 4-quart microwave-safe glass bowl with a lid arrange artichokes, bottoms up, and add water. Microwave at high power (100%), covered, 10 minutes, or until bases are tender, and let stand, covered, 5 minutes.

Preheat oven to 375° F.

While artichokes are cooking, in a small heavy saucepan cook ¼ cup bell pepper, onion, and garlic in 1 tablespoon of oil over moderately low heat, stirring, until softened. In a bowl stir together vegetables, bread crumbs, scallion, cheese, thyme, cayenne, lemon juice, 1 tablespoon of remaining oil, and salt and pepper to taste.

Pull out centers of artichokes, leaving bases intact, and scrape out chokes with a small spoon. Spread leaves of artichokes gently and stuff each artichoke with some of stuffing, filling centers and spaces between leaves.

Arrange artichokes in a baking dish just large enough to hold them and add enough water to cover bottom of dish. Drizzle 1 tablespoon of remaining oil over artichokes and bake 12 minutes.

In a small bowl whisk together vinegar, remaining tablespoon oil, remaining 2 tablespoons bell pepper, and salt and pepper to taste.

Serve artichokes with vinaigrette spooned around them. Serves 2.

Jerusalem Artichoke and Sage Gratin

4 pounds Jerusalem artichokes (sunchokes)*
2 cups milk
5 tablespoons unsalted butter
1 large onion, chopped
2 garlic cloves, minced
3 tablespoons chopped fresh sage leaves
½ cup freshly grated Parmesan cheese
2½ cups fresh bread crumbs

Garnish: fried sage leaves (procedure within sage
  and garlic mashed potatoes recipe, page 184)

*available at specialty produce markets and
  some supermarkets

Peel Jerusalem artichokes and cut into 1-inch pieces. In a stainless-steel or enameled saucepan combine artichokes, milk, and enough water to cover artichokes by 1 inch and simmer until tender, about 30 minutes. (Milk will help prevent artichokes from discoloring.)

While artichokes are cooking, in a skillet heat 2 tablespoons butter over moderately high heat until foam subsides and sauté onion, garlic, and 1 tablespoon sage until onion is golden, about 6 minutes.

Preheat oven to 425° F. Butter a 2-quart gratin dish.

Drain artichokes and in a food processor purée with onion mixture and Parmesan until smooth. Spoon purée into prepared gratin dish. In large skillet melt remaining 3 tablespoons butter over moderate heat and sauté bread crumbs with remaining 2 tablespoons sage until golden, about 5 minutes. Season bread crumbs with salt and pepper and sprinkle evenly over purée. *Gratin may be prepared up to this point 2 days ahead and chilled, covered.*

Bake gratin in middle of oven until hot and bread crumbs are a shade darker, about 20 minutes, and garnish with fried sage leaves. Serves 8.

PHOTO ON PAGE 76

Boston Baked Bean Gratin

2 slices bacon, cut into ½-inch pieces
½ cup chopped onion
an 8-ounce can whole tomatoes, drained and
  chopped

172

2 tablespoons molasses
1 tablespoon Worcestershire sauce
a pinch dried hot red pepper flakes
a 16-ounce can pink or black beans, rinsed and
    drained
1 tablespoon vegetable oil
1 teaspoon Dijon mustard
¼ cup dry bread crumbs

In a 7- to 8-inch flameproof skillet cook bacon over moderate heat until crisp and spoon off all but 1 tablespoon fat. Add onion and cook, stirring, until softened. Stir in tomatoes, molasses, Worcestershire sauce, red pepper flakes, beans, and salt to taste and simmer until liquid is thickened, about 5 minutes.
Preheat broiler.
In a small bowl stir together oil and mustard and add crumbs, tossing to combine ingredients well. Sprinkle crumbs over beans and broil about 4 inches from heat until topping is crisp and golden, 1 to 2 minutes. Serves 2.

Green Beans

1¼ pounds green beans, trimmed

Accompaniment: mustard sauce (page 213)

In a saucepan of boiling salted water cook beans until crisp-tender, about 6 minutes, and drain well.
Serve beans with mustard sauce. Serves 6.

PHOTO ON PAGE 23

Stewed Green Beans

1 tablespoon olive oil
¾ pound green beans,
    trimmed and cut
    into 2-inch pieces
1 small onion, diced
¼ cup plus 2 tablespoons water
2 medium plum tomatoes, seeded and
    chopped coarse
1 teaspoon fresh lemon juice

In a large non-stick skillet heat oil over moderately high heat until hot but not smoking and sauté beans and onion with salt to taste, stirring occasionally, 8 to 10 minutes, or until beans begin to brown.
Add ¼ cup water and cook until water is evaporated and skillet is almost dry. Add tomatoes, lemon juice, and salt to taste and cook, stirring occasionally, until tomatoes are browned. Add remaining 2 tablespoons water and cook until it is evaporated and tomatoes are very soft. Serves 2.

Sautéed Persimmons and Green Beans with Chives

1½ pounds green beans, trimmed and cut
    diagonally into ½-inch pieces
3 tablespoons olive oil
3 ripe Fuyu (not Hachiya) persimmons* (about
    1 pound), cut into ¼-inch-thick slices and
    each slice cut into 1-inch pieces
½ cup 1-inch pieces fresh chives

*available at specialty produce markets

In a kettle of boiling salted water cook beans until just tender, 2 to 4 minutes, and drain. Plunge beans into a bowl of ice and cold water to stop cooking and drain. *Beans may be prepared up to this point 1 day ahead and chilled, covered.*
In a large heavy skillet heat oil over moderately high heat until hot but not smoking and sauté persimmons until lightly browned and softened, about 4 minutes. Add beans and ¼ cup chives and sauté, stirring gently, until hot.
Transfer mixture to a platter and sprinkle remaining ¼ cup chives on top. Serves 8.

PHOTO ON PAGE 77

Haricots Verts

1 pound *haricots verts* (French green beans;
   available at specialty produce markets)

In a kettle of boiling salted water cook beans 3
minutes, or until crisp-tender, and drain well. Season
beans with salt and pepper. Serves 6.

PHOTO ON PAGE 38

*Lima Bean, Potato, and Garlic Purée with
Potato Crisps*

1 pound russet (baking) potatoes
4 large garlic cloves, peeled
two 10-ounce packages frozen baby lima beans
3 tablespoons unsalted butter, softened

Accompaniment: potato crisps (recipe follows)

In a large saucepan combine potatoes, peeled and
cut into 1-inch pieces, and garlic with enough water
to cover by 1 inch and simmer, covered, 8 minutes.
Add lima beans and simmer 8 minutes more, or until
potatoes are tender.

Reserve about ¾ cup cooking liquid. Drain mixture
in colander and force through food mill fitted with
medium disk into a bowl. Stir in butter, salt and pepper to taste, and enough reserved liquid to reach desired consistency. *Purée keeps, covered and chilled,
1 day.*

Serve purée topped with potato crisps. Serves 6.

PHOTO ON PAGE 26

Potato Crisps

olive oil for brushing potato
1 large russet (baking) potato

Preheat oven to 400° F. and brush a baking sheet
well with oil.

Peel potato and trim to form a rectangle about 3 by
1½ by 1 inch. Halve rectangle through 1-inch side to
form 2 rectangles about 3 by 1½ by ½ inches. With a
mandoline or other hand-held slicing device slice
potato 1⁄16 inch thick on the long narrow side of each
rectangle to form strips about 3 by ½ inches. On oiled
sheet arrange strips, 4 at a time, overlapping ends to
form squares. Brush each square with oil and sprinkle
with salt to taste.

Bake crisps in middle of oven 10 minutes, or until
golden brown. Transfer crisps to rack to cool. *Potato
crisps keep in an airtight container 3 days.* Makes
about 12 potato crisps.

PHOTO ON PAGE 26

*Broccoli and Cauliflower with Horseradish
Bread Crumbs*

1½ bunches broccoli
   (about 1½ pounds)
1 large head cauliflower
   (about 2 pounds)
1 tablespoon vegetable oil
3 tablespoons unsalted butter
2 cups very coarse dry bread crumbs
2 tablespoons drained bottled horseradish

Trim broccoli, reserving stems for another use, and cut flowerets into 1-inch pieces. (There should be about 5 cups.)

Trim cauliflower and cut flowerets into 1-inch pieces. (There should be about 5 cups.)

In a large saucepan of boiling salted water cook vegetables until crisp-tender, 3 to 5 minutes. in a colander drain vegetables and refresh under cold water to stop cooking. Drain vegetables well. *Vegetables may be prepared up to this point 1 day ahead and chilled, covered.*

In a large heavy skillet heat oil and 2 tablespoons butter over moderately high heat until foam begins to subside and sauté bread crumbs, stirring, until golden. Stir in horseradish and salt to taste and sauté, stirring, until crisp. *Bread crumbs may be prepared 3 days ahead and kept in an airtight container.*

Preheat oven to 350° F.

In skillet melt remaining tablespoon butter over moderate heat and in it toss vegetables with salt and pepper to taste. Sprinkle vegetables with bread crumbs and toss to combine. Transfer mixture to a baking dish and bake, uncovered, 10 minutes, or until just heated through. Serves 8.

PHOTO ON PAGE 83

Broccoli Rabe with Sherry Vinegar

½ pound broccoli rabe
1 tablespoon olive oil
2 tablespoons water
1½ teaspoons Sherry vinegar*

*available at specialty foods shops and some
  supermarkets

Discard yellow leaves and hollow or coarse stems from broccoli rabe. Cut off top 5 inches of broccoli rabe and reserve remaining stems for another use.

In a large heavy skillet heat oil over moderately high heat until hot but not smoking and sauté broccoli rabe, stirring occasionally, until crisp-tender, about 4 minutes. Add water and cook, covered, 2 minutes, or until tender.

Remove skillet from heat and stir in vinegar and salt and pepper to taste. Serves 2.

PHOTO ON PAGE 73

Roasted Carrots and Parsnips

2 pounds parsnips (about 6 medium), peeled
    and cut into 2-inch-long sticks, each about
    ¼ inch thick
1 pound carrots (about 6 medium),
    peeled and cut into 2-inch-long sticks,
    each about ¼ inch thick
3 tablespoons olive oil

Garnish: carrot tops

Preheat oven to 425° F.

Divide parsnip sticks and carrot sticks between 2 shallow baking pans and toss each pan of vegetables with 1½ tablespoons olive oil. Spread vegetables in one layer and season with salt and pepper to taste. Roast parsnips and carrots in oven, switching position of pans in oven halfway through baking and stirring occasionally, about 20 to 25 minutes, or until browned and crisp. Garnish vegetables with carrot tops. Serves 8.

PHOTO ON PAGES 76 AND 77

Crispy Cauliflower with Olives, Capers, and Parsley

2 tablespoons finely chopped Kalamata
    olives (about 6) or other brine-cured
    black olives
2 teaspoons drained capers,
    finely chopped
1 tablespoon red-wine vinegar
3 tablespoon extra-virgin olive oil
4 cups 1-inch cauliflower flowerets
    (about 1 head)
2 tablespoons chopped fresh parsley leaves
    (preferably flat-leafed)

In a small bowl stir together olives, capers, vinegar, and 2 tablespoons oil.

In a large non-stick skillet heat remaining tablespoon oil over moderately high heat until hot but not smoking and cook cauliflower, covered, stirring occasionally, 10 minutes. Uncover skillet and sauté cauliflower until tender and browned, 5 to 10 minutes more. Transfer cauliflower to a bowl and toss with olive mixture and parsley. Season cauliflower with salt and pepper. Serves 2.

175

Swiss Chard with Olives and Raisins

¾ pound (about ½ large bunch) Swiss chard,
    washed well and drained
½ onion, chopped fine
1 tablespoon olive oil
¼ cup water
2 tablespoons golden raisins,
    chopped fine
6 Kalamata or other large brine-cured black olives,
    pitted and chopped fine

Cut stems and thick center ribs from Swiss chard leaves. Discard center ribs and chop coarse stems and leaves separately.

In a 9-inch heavy skillet cook onion in oil over moderate heat, stirring, until softened. Add stems, 2 tablespoons water, raisins, and salt to taste and cook, covered, over moderately low heat until stems are softened, about 5 minutes. Add leaves, olives, and remaining 2 tablespoons water and cook, covered, over moderate heat until leaves are wilted, about 3 minutes. Remove lid and cook, stirring occasionally, until most of liquid is evaporated and leaves are tender. Serves 2.

Sautéed Chick-Peas with Cinnamon and Fresh Coriander

a 19-ounce can chick-peas, rinsed and drained
    (about 2 cups)
2 tablespoons plus 2 teaspoons olive oil
    (preferably extra-virgin)
2 cinnamon sticks, halved
2 teaspoons fresh lemon juice,
    or to taste
¼ cup fresh coriander

Dry chick-peas completely between layers of paper towels.

In a deep 12-inch heavy skillet (preferably nonstick) heat 2 tablespoons oil with cinnamon sticks over moderately high heat until cinnamon is fragrant and sauté chick-peas, shaking skillet, until browned and crisp, about 10 minutes. Transfer chick-peas to a bowl and toss with remaining 2 teaspoons oil, lemon juice, coriander, and salt and pepper to taste. Serve chick-peas warm or at room temperature. Serves 2.

Hummus and Vegetable Lahvash Sandwiches

about 2 cups *hummus* (recipe follows)
a 16- to 18-inch round very thin pliable *lahvash*
    (mountain shepherd bread)*
½ cup sliced seedless cucumber
1 large carrot, cut into ribbonlike strands with a
    vegetable peeler (about 1 cup)
1 small sweet onion, sliced thin
½ cup finely shredded radish (about 6)
½ cup alfalfa sprouts
1 tablespoon sesame seeds, toasted

Garnish: alfalfa sprouts and toasted sesame seeds

*available at Middle Eastern groceries, specialty
    foods shops, and some supermarkets and
    by mail order from Damascus Bakeries,
    56 Gold Street, Brooklyn, NY 11201,
    tel. (718) 855-1456

Spread *hummus* evenly on *lahvash* and top with cucumber, carrot, onion, radish, sprouts, and sesame seeds. Roll *lahvash* up tightly jelly-roll fashion and trim ends. Cut roll crosswise into 8 pieces.

Garnish sandwiches with sprouts and sesame seeds. Makes 8 sandwiches, serving 4.

Hummus

2 large garlic cloves, minced and mashed to a
    paste with ½ teaspoon salt
a 16- to 19-ounce can chick-peas, rinsed and
    drained
⅓ cup well-stirred *tahini* (sesame seed paste)*
2 tablespoons fresh lemon juice
2 tablespoons olive oil
1 teaspoon ground cumin
3 tablespoons water
3 tablespoons minced fresh parsley leaves

*available at specialty foods shops, natural foods
    stores, and some supermarkets

In a food processor blend together garlic paste, chick-peas, *tahini*, lemon juice, oil, and cumin, scraping down side, until smooth. Add water, parsley, and salt and pepper to taste and pulse until just combined.

Hummus *may be made 2 days ahead and chilled, covered.* Makes about 2 cups.

Cumin Corn on the Cob

12 ears corn, shucked
extra-virgin olive oil to taste
1 teaspoon ground cumin
coarse salt to taste
freshly ground black pepper to taste

In a kettle combine corn with enough cold water to cover. Bring water to a boil and remove kettle immediately from heat. *Corn may be cooked 30 minutes ahead and kept warm in the cooking water.*

Drain corn well and transfer to a platter. Drizzle corn with oil and sprinkle with cumin, salt, and pepper. Serves 12.

PHOTO ON PAGES 52 AND 53

Corn Boats with Zucchini and Pepper Jack Cheese

4 ears corn, unhusked
2 tablespoons olive oil
1 medium zucchini, cut into ⅓-inch dice
1 cup finely chopped red onion
1 cup coarsely grated Monterey Jack cheese
  with hot peppers
2 tablespoons finely crushed corn tortilla chips

Pull a lengthwise strip of corn husk (about 1 to 1½ inches wide) from each ear to expose a strip of kernels and discard husk strip. Carefully peel back remaining husks, keeping them attached to stem ends, and snap ears from stem ends. Discard silk from husks. Tear a thin strip from a tender inner piece of each husk and use it to tie loose end of each husk together, forming a boat. Cut corn kernels from ears and discard cobs.

In a large heavy skillet heat oil over moderately high heat until hot but not smoking and sauté zucchini, stirring occasionally, until browned lightly and just tender, 2 to 3 minutes. Transfer zucchini with a slotted spoon to a bowl and season with salt.

In oil remaining in skillet sauté corn kernels and onion with salt to taste over moderately high heat, stirring, 4 minutes and cook, covered, over low heat until corn is crisp-tender, 2 to 3 minutes. Add corn mixture to zucchini and season with salt.

Cool filling and stir in cheese. Spoon filling into husk boats. *Corn boats may be prepared up to this point 1 day ahead and chilled, covered.*

Preheat oven to 375° F.

Arrange boats on a baking sheet and sprinkle filling with tortilla crumbs. Bake boats in upper third of oven until cheese is melted and filling is heated through, 15 to 20 minutes.

Serve corn boats warm or at room temperature. Serves 4.

PHOTO ON PAGE 61

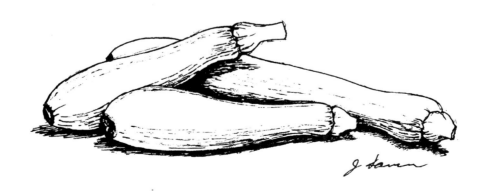

Minted Eggplant Rounds

6 Asian (long, thin) eggplants* (about 2 pounds)
vegetable oil for brushing eggplant
⅓ cup fresh lime juice
⅓ cup Asian fish sauce (preferably *naam pla***)
2 tablespoons sugar
4 large garlic cloves,
    minced
¼ cup finely chopped fresh mint leaves

*available at Asian and specialty produce markets
    and some supermarkets
**available at Asian markets, some specialty
    foods shops, and by mail order from Adriana's
    Caravan, Brooklyn, NY, tel. (800) 316-0820 or
    (718) 436-8565 or Uwajimaya, 519 Sixth
    Avenue South, Seattle, WA 98104, tel.
    (206) 624-6248

Preheat broiler.

Cut eggplants crosswise into ¾-inch slices and arrange on baking sheets. Brush both sides lightly with oil and broil in batches about 4 inches from heat until golden brown, 3 to 4 minutes on each side.

While eggplant is broiling, stir together lime juice, fish sauce, sugar, garlic, and mint until sugar is dissolved.

Serve eggplant drizzled with sauce. Serves 6.

PHOTO ON PAGE 46

Eggplant Parmigiana Rounds

all-purpose flour for dredging
2 large eggs, beaten lightly
¾ cup dry bread crumbs, seasoned with salt
    and pepper
a 1-pound eggplant, cut into ½-inch-thick rounds
vegetable oil for frying
1 cup tomato sauce
¼ pound mozzarella cheese, sliced thin

Have ready in 3 separate bowls flour, eggs, and bread crumbs. Dredge eggplant in flour and coat with egg, letting excess drip off. Dredge eggplant in bread crumbs.

In a heavy skillet heat ¼ inch oil over moderately high heat until hot but not smoking and fry eggplant

rounds in batches 3 minutes on each side, transferring them with a slotted spoon to paper towels to drain.

Preheat broiler.

Arrange rounds on a baking sheet and top with tomato sauce and mozzarella. Broil rounds about 2 inches from heat until cheese is melted, 3 minutes. Serves 2.

Sautéed Kale with Cracklings and Garlic Bread Crumbs

¼ cup uncooked duck fat, or 3 slices bacon
    plus 1 tablespoon olive oil
½ cup fresh bread crumbs
1 small garlic clove, minced
⅛ teaspoon salt
1 large bunch kale (about 1¼ pounds), rinsed and
    stems and tough ribs discarded

Chop duck fat or bacon into small pieces. In a large heavy skillet cook duck fat or bacon over moderate heat, stirring occasionally, until crisp and transfer to paper towels to drain. Pour half of fat from skillet into a heatproof container and reserve.

In fat remaining in skillet cook bread crumbs and garlic with salt, stirring occasionally, until golden and transfer to paper towels.

Wipe skillet clean and heat reserved fat (adding oil if using bacon fat) over moderately high heat until hot but not smoking. Sauté kale with salt to taste, turning with tongs to coat, until kale just wilts, about 2 minutes, and toss with cracklings or bacon and bread crumb mixture. Serves 4.

PHOTO ON PAGES 78 AND 79

Warm Leeks Vinaigrette

8 leeks (each about 1 inch in diameter), trimmed
    and cleaned thoroughly
2 tablespoons olive oil
2 tablespoons dry red wine
½ cup plus 2 tablespoons chicken broth
2 teaspoons red-wine vinegar
½ teaspoon Dijon mustard

In a 10-inch skillet sauté leeks in oil over moderately high heat, turning, until golden, about 10 minutes. Stir in wine and ½ cup chicken broth and cook leeks, covered, turning occasionally, until tender when pierced, about 10 minutes. Transfer leeks to a serving plate.

Whisk remaining 2 tablespoons broth and vinegar into skillet and boil, stirring, until thickened slightly. Remove skillet from heat and whisk in mustard and salt and pepper to taste. Pour vinaigrette over leeks. Serves 2.

Leek, Prosciutto, and Cheese Empanadas

¾ cup chopped well-rinsed white and pale green
  part of leek (about ½ pound untrimmed)
2 tablespoons chopped sliced prosciutto or ham
  (about 2 thin slices)
1 tablespoon olive oil
3 tablespoons water
2 tablespoons grated Manchego* or
  mild white Cheddar cheese
1 sheet (about ½ pound) frozen puff pastry, thawed
an egg wash made by beating together 1 large egg
  and 1 teaspoon water

*available at cheese shops and specialty
  foods shops

Preheat oven to 425° F.

In a small heavy skillet cook leek and prosciutto in oil over moderate heat, stirring, until leek is softened. Add water and cook, covered, over low heat until leek is soft, about 10 minutes. Pour off any excess water. Remove skillet from heat and add salt and pepper to taste. Let filling cool completely and stir in cheese.

Roll out puff pastry on lightly floured surface into a 12-inch square and with a 4-inch round cutter cut out 4 rounds.

Divide filling among rounds, mounding it in center, and brush edges of rounds with water. Fold rounds in half, pressing edges together firmly, and crimp edges with tines of fork to seal. Empanadas *may be prepared up to this point 1 day ahead and chilled, covered.*

Arrange *empanadas* on a dampened baking sheet and brush with egg wash. Prick the top of each *empanada* several times with fork (for steam vents). Bake *empanadas* in upper third of oven until puffed and golden, 12 to 15 minutes. Makes 4 *empanadas*.

PHOTO ON PAGE 17

Lentil Burgers with Yogurt Mint Sauce

1¼ cups lentils, picked over
  and rinsed
½ cup rolled oats
2 garlic cloves, minced
2 teaspoons ground coriander seeds
2 teaspoons ground cumin
1 large egg, beaten lightly
½ cup plain yogurt
⅓ cup chopped fresh mint leaves
vegetable oil for frying
6 *pita* loaves, halved to form pockets
6 soft-leafed lettuce leaves

Add lentils to a large saucepan of salted water and bring water to a boil. Cook lentils at a bare simmer until tender, about 15 to 20 minutes.

In a blender or food processor grind oats into meal. Drain lentils in a sieve and in a bowl combine with garlic, coriander, cumin, and 3 tablespoons ground oats. Mash lentils coarse with a potato masher. Stir in egg and salt and pepper to taste and form mixture into six 3-inch burgers, each ½ inch thick. Coat burgers with remaining ground oats and chill, uncovered, 15 minutes.

In a small bowl stir together yogurt, mint, and salt and pepper to taste.

In a large skillet heat ¼ inch oil over moderately high heat until hot but not smoking and fry burgers, in batches if necessary, until browned and crisp, about 3 to 4 minutes on each side.

Serve burgers in *pitas* with lettuce and yogurt mint sauce. Serves 6.

179

Lentils with Bitter Greens

½ cup dried lentils, picked over and rinsed
1½ cups low-salt chicken broth
½ cup water
1½ tablespoons extra-virgin olive oil
1 tablespoon red-wine vinegar
2 teaspoons fresh lemon juice
1 small bunch *arugula*, coarse stems discarded,
    the rest washed and spun dry
½ head (about ¼ pound) *radicchio*
1 medium Belgian endive
2 ounces crumbled feta cheese (about ⅓ cup)

In a saucepan simmer lentils in broth and water, covered, 20 minutes, or until tender, and drain. Toss lentils with olive oil, vinegar, and lemon juice and cool almost to room temperature.

Chop *arugula*, *radicchio*, and endive into ¼-inch pieces and add to lentils. Add feta and salt and coarsely ground black pepper to taste, tossing well. Serves 2.

Refried Red Lentils

1 cup red lentils*, picked over
3 cups water
1 teaspoon ground cumin
1 teaspoon chili powder
1 teaspoon salt
1 cup chopped onion
¼ cup olive oil

1 large garlic clove, minced
2 teaspoons fresh lime juice
2 tablespoons finely chopped fresh coriander

Accompaniment: toasted *pita* triangles or tortilla
    chips if desired

*available at natural foods stores, East Indian
    markets, and some supermarkets

In a large bowl wash lentils in several changes cold water until water runs clear and drain in a sieve. In a saucepan combine lentils, water, cumin, chili powder, and salt and boil lentils, whisking frequently, until smooth, about 35 minutes.

While lentils are boiling, in a skillet cook onion in oil over moderate heat, stirring, until it begins to turn golden. Add garlic and cook mixture, stirring, 5 minutes. Add lentil purée, lime juice, coriander, and salt and pepper to taste and combine well.

Serve mixture as a dip with *pita* triangles or chips or as a side dish. Makes about 2 cups.

Mushroom Ragout on Toast

2 garlic cloves, minced
1 tablespoon olive oil
1 small onion, chopped fine
1½ tablespoons finely chopped fresh sage leaves
    or 1½ teaspoons dried sage, crumbled
½ pound mushrooms, trimmed and sliced thin
    (about 2¾ cups)

1½ tablespoons soy sauce
3 tablespoons medium-dry Sherry
1 tablespoon red-wine vinegar
2 teaspoons cornstarch dissolved in
    1 cup water
1 tablespoon minced fresh parsley leaves
six ½-inch-thick diagonal slices French or Italian
    bread, toasted

In a 9-inch heavy skillet cook garlic in oil over moderate heat, stirring, until pale golden. Add onion and sage and cook, stirring, until onion is softened.

Add mushrooms and soy sauce and cook, stirring, until liquid mushrooms give off is evaporated and mushrooms begin to brown. Add Sherry and vinegar and boil until liquid is evaporated.

Stir cornstarch mixture and add to mushrooms. Bring liquid to a boil, stirring, and simmer until thickened to desired consistency. Stir in parsley and salt and pepper to taste.

Spoon mushroom ragout over toasts. Serves 2 as a hearty first course or light supper.

Grilled Portobello Mushrooms with Parmesan Crisps

3 tablespoons balsamic vinegar
3 garlic cloves, minced
1½ teaspoons minced fresh thyme leaves or
    ½ teaspoon dried, crumbled
½ cup olive oil
1½ pounds Portobello mushrooms, stems
    discarded
18 to 24 *arugula* leaves, trimmed, washed
    thoroughly, and spun dry
6 Parmesan crisps (recipe follows)

In a small bowl whisk together vinegar, garlic, thyme, and salt and pepper to taste. Whisk in oil in a stream, whisking until dressing is emulsified.

In a large resealable plastic bag drizzle dressing over mushrooms and seal. Marinate mushrooms at room temperature, turning bag once or twice, 1 hour.

Heat a well-seasoned ridged grill pan over moderately high heat until hot and grill mushrooms in batches, covered, 2 to 3 minutes on each side, or until tender. Transfer mushrooms as cooked to a platter and keep warm, covered with foil.

Divide *arugula* among 6 plates. Slice mushrooms thin and serve with *arugula* and Parmesan crisps. Serves 6 as a first course.

PHOTO ON PAGE 32

Parmesan Crisps

¾ cup finely shredded Parmesan cheese
    (preferably Parmigiano-Reggiano)
1½ teaspoons all-purpose flour

Preheat oven to 350° F. and line a lightly greased baking sheet with parchment paper.

In a small bowl stir together Parmesan and flour. On prepared baking sheet spoon level tablespoons of mixture in mounds 4 inches apart and spread mounds gently into 3½-inch-long ovals. Bake crisps in middle of oven until golden, 8 to 10 minutes. Cool crisps completely on baking sheet and remove carefully with a metal spatula. *Crisps may be made 2 days ahead and kept between layers of wax paper in an airtight container at room temperature.* Makes about 9 crisps.

PHOTO ON PAGE 32

Dried-Tomato–Stuffed Mushrooms

6 mushrooms (about 6 ounces),
    stems reserved
2 scallions, chopped fine
1 tablespoon unsalted butter
1 tablespoon minced drained bottled
    dried tomatoes
1 tablespoon fine dry bread crumbs
2 tablespoons freshly grated Parmesan cheese

Preheat oven to 400° F. and lightly grease a baking dish.

Chop reserved mushroom stems fine. In a heavy skillet cook chopped stems and scallions in butter over moderately low heat, stirring, until stems are very tender. Stir in tomatoes, bread crumbs, 1 tablespoon of cheese, and salt and pepper to taste. Divide mixture among mushroom caps, mounding it slightly, and sprinkle with remaining tablespoon cheese.

Arrange mushrooms in prepared baking dish and bake 12 minutes. Serves 2.

Grilled Tortilla and Onion Cake

twelve 7- to 8-inch flour tortillas
1½ pounds red onions, chopped fine
   (about 3 cups)
2 tablespoons olive oil
¾ cup minced fresh parsley leaves
⅓ cup freshly grated Parmesan cheese
¾ cup mayonnaise
1 tablespoon balsamic vinegar
about 3 dozen wooden picks

Prepare grill.

On a rack set 5 inches over glowing coals toast tortillas lightly a few at a time, turning them once, until they begin to puff on each side but are still soft. (Alternatively, tortillas may be toasted on a stove-top griddle over moderately high heat.)

In a large non-stick skillet cook onions in oil over moderately low heat, stirring occasionally, until soft, about 15 minutes. Transfer onions to a bowl and cool. Stir in parsley, Parmesan, ½ cup mayonnaise, and salt and pepper to taste.

Spread onion mixture on 11 tortillas, stacking them, and top the stack with remaining tortilla. Wrap cake well in plastic wrap and chill at least 1 hour and up to 4 hours.

Discard plastic wrap and with large sharp knife cut cake into ¾-inch-wide slices (not wedges). Turn each slice onto its side and secure ends and middle with wooden picks.

In a small bowl stir together vinegar and remaining ¼ cup mayonnaise and brush some of mixture on a cut side of each slice.

Grill slices, mayonnaise sides down, until golden brown, 3 to 4 minutes. Brush tops with remaining mayonnaise mixture, turn slices, and grill until golden brown, 3 to 4 minutes more.

(Alternatively, broil slices on rack of broiler pan about 4 inches from heat, mayonnaise sides up, until golden brown, 3 to 4 minutes. Turn slices and brush tops with remaining mayonnaise. Broil until golden brown, 3 to 4 minutes more.)

Discard wooden picks. Makes about 8 slices.

PHOTO ON PAGE 48

Balsamic-Glazed Pearl Onions

2½ pounds assorted pearl onions such as red,
   white, and/or yellow (about 8 cups)
2 tablespoons olive oil
1 cup balsamic vinegar
½ cup water

In a saucepan of boiling water blanch one third of onions 3 minutes and drain. Blanch remaining onions in batches in same manner. Cool onions and peel.

In a large heavy skillet heat oil over moderately high heat until hot but not smoking and sauté onions until lightly browned, about 5 minutes. Add vinegar and water and simmer, stirring occasionally, until onions are tender, about 15 minutes. Transfer onions with a slotted spoon to a platter, reserving liquid. *Glazed onions may be prepared up to this point 2 days ahead and onions and reserved liquid chilled separately, covered. Reheat onions in reserved liquid, adding a little water if necessary, and transfer with slotted spoon to platter. Simmer reserved liquid until thickened and syrupy and reduced to about ½ cup.*

Spoon sauce over onions and serve warm or at room temperature. Serves 8.

PHOTO ON PAGE 77

Red Onion Sauerkraut

3 tablespoons vegetable oil
5½ cups thinly sliced red onion
    (about 1 pound)
3 whole cloves
5 juniper berries*
4 cups thinly sliced red cabbage (about
    ¼ medium head)
a 1-pound package sauerkraut,
    drained
3 tablespoons firmly packed dark brown sugar
½ cup dry red wine
¼ cup red-wine vinegar
1 bay leaf

*available in spice section of supermarkets

In a large heavy skillet (measuring about 12 inches across and 2½ inches deep) heat oil over moderately high heat until hot but not smoking and sauté onion with cloves and juniper berries, stirring, until browned, about 10 minutes. Add cabbage, sauerkraut, sugar, wine, vinegar, and bay leaf and simmer, stirring occasionally and adding water if mixture becomes dry, until cabbage is tender, about 30 minutes. *Sauerkraut may be made 2 days ahead and chilled, covered.*

Discard bay leaf and serve sauerkraut at room temperature. Serves 6.

PHOTO ON PAGE 70

Buttered Peas

3 cups shelled fresh peas (about 3 pounds
    unshelled)
2 tablespoons unsalted butter, cut into bits

In a saucepan bring 3 cups water to a boil and add peas and salt to taste. Simmer peas until tender, 3 to 8 minutes, and drain. In a bowl toss hot peas with butter and salt and pepper to taste. Serves 4 to 6.

PHOTO ON PAGES 34 AND 35

Sautéed Snow Peas

¾ pound snow peas, trimmed
1 tablespoon vegetable oil

In a saucepan of boiling salted water boil snow peas 30 seconds and drain. Refresh snow peas under cold water and drain. *Snow peas may be prepared up to this point 8 hours ahead and chilled, covered.*

In a heavy skillet sauté snow peas in oil over moderately high heat, stirring, until heated through and season with salt and pepper. Serves 6.

PHOTO ON PAGE 42

Potato and Porcini Gratin

1 ounce dried *porcini* mushrooms* (about 1 cup)
1 cup warm water
5 large russet (baking) potatoes (about 3 pounds)
3 garlic cloves, minced
1 tablespoon unsalted butter
2 cups milk
1 cup heavy cream
2 tablespoons minced fresh chives
1 teaspoon salt

*available at specialty foods shops and some
    supermarkets

In a bowl soak *porcini* in warm water 30 minutes, or until softened. Slowly strain soaking liquid through a fine sieve lined with a coffee filter or a double thickness of rinsed and squeezed cheesecloth into a small saucepan, being careful to leave last tablespoon (containing sediment) in bowl. Boil soaking liquid until reduced to about ½ cup.

Preheat oven to 350° F.

Wash *porcini* under cold water to remove any grit and pat dry. Chop *porcini* coarse. Peel potatoes and slice ⅛ inch thick. In a large (4-quart) saucepan cook *porcini* and garlic in butter over moderate heat, stirring, 2 minutes. Add potatoes, reduced *porcini* liquid, milk, cream, 4 teaspoons chives, and salt and bring liquid to boil, stirring.

Transfer mixture to a buttered 2-quart gratin dish and bake 1 hour, or until potatoes are tender. Sprinkle gratin with remaining 2 teaspoons chives. Serves 8.

PHOTO ON PAGE 82

Anchovy Mashed Potatoes

6 large russet (baking) potatoes (about 3½ pounds)
1 onion, chopped fine
¾ stick (6 tablespoons) unsalted butter
8 flat anchovies, rinsed, patted dry, and minced
¾ cup milk
¼ cup heavy cream
¼ cup thinly sliced fresh chives or scallion greens

Peel potatoes and cut into 1-inch pieces.

In a steamer set over boiling water steam potatoes, covered, until tender, 15 to 20 minutes.

In a large heavy saucepan cook onion in 4 tablespoons butter over moderately low heat, stirring, until softened. Add anchovies and cook, mashing them, until they dissolve, about 1 minute. Stir in milk, cream, and remaining 2 tablespoons butter and heat until hot but not boiling.

Force potatoes through ricer or food mill into pan and stir until smooth. Stir in chives or scallion greens and salt and pepper to taste. Serves 6.

Garlic-Herb Mashed Potatoes

1 pound red potatoes (peeled if desired), cut into
    1-inch pieces
⅓ cup milk
¼ cup garlic- and herb-flavored soft cheese such
    as Boursin

In a saucepan simmer potatoes in water to cover until tender, about 10 minutes. Drain potatoes and return to pan. Mash potatoes with milk, cheese, and salt and pepper to taste over moderate heat until they are smooth and mixture is heated through. Serves 2.

Sage and Garlic Mashed Potatoes

1 large garlic clove, sliced
3 tablespoons olive oil
1 tablespoon fresh sage leaves, minced, or
    1½ teaspoons dried, crumbled
For fried sage leaves
olive oil for frying
12 whole fresh sage leaves
coarse salt for sprinkling

4 russet (baking) potatoes (about 2 pounds)
1 cup plain yogurt
1 tablespoon unsalted butter, softened

In a small saucepan simmer garlic in oil until golden. Stir in sage and remove pan from heat. Let mixture stand 15 minutes and drain oil through a fine sieve into a small bowl, discarding solids.

Make fried sage leaves:

In a small skillet heat ⅛ inch oil over moderately high heat until hot but not smoking and fry sage leaves, 1 at a time, until crisp, about 3 seconds, transferring with a slotted spoon to paper towels to drain. Sprinkle sage leaves with coarse salt.

Peel potatoes and quarter. In a large saucepan cover potatoes by 1 inch with salted cold water and simmer until tender, about 20 minutes. Reserve about ⅓ cup cooking water and drain potatoes.

Preheat oven to 350° F.

While potatoes are still warm force through a ricer or medium disk of a food mill into a bowl and beat in yogurt, butter, seasoned oil, enough reserved cooking water to reach desired consistency, and salt and pepper to taste. Transfer to an ovenproof serving dish. *Mashed potatoes may be made 1 day ahead and chilled, covered.*

Heat potatoes in oven until heated through and top with fried sage leaves. Serves 6 to 8.

Warm Mashed Potato and Swiss Chard Terrine

1 bunch Swiss chard (about 1 pound), rinsed
5 russet (baking) potatoes (about 2½ pounds)
¾ stick (6 tablespoons) unsalted butter, softened
4 large eggs, beaten lightly

Remove coarse chard stems, reserving them for another use. In a saucepan cook chard in water clinging to its leaves, covered, over moderately high heat, stirring once or twice, until wilted and tender, 3 to 5 minutes. Drain chard well in a colander and pat dry between paper towels. In a food processor chop chard fine and season with salt and pepper.

Preheat oven to 350° F. Butter a loaf pan, 9 by 5 by 3 inches, and line bottom with buttered wax paper.

Peel potatoes and quarter. In a kettle cover potatoes by 1 inch with salted cold water and simmer until tender, about 20 minutes. Drain potatoes and while still warm force through a ricer or medium disk of a food mill into a bowl. With an electric mixer beat in butter, eggs, and salt and pepper to taste until smooth.

Transfer half of potato mixture to another bowl and beat in chard until smooth. Spread chard mixture in prepared pan and spread plain potato mixture evenly over it. *Terrine may be prepared up to this point 3 days ahead and chilled, covered.*

Put loaf pan in a baking pan and pour enough hot water into baking pan to reach halfway up sides of loaf pan. Bake terrine in middle of oven 40 minutes, or until a thin knife inserted in center comes out clean, and let stand in loaf pan on a rack 5 minutes. Run knife around edge of terrine and invert onto a plate.

Serve terrine cut into slices. Serves 8 to 10.

Crusty Puffed Potatoes

4 small red potatoes
1 teaspoon olive oil
1 teaspoon coarse salt

Preheat oven to 475° F.

Rinse potatoes and dry well with paper towels. Rub potatoes with oil. Cut each potato in half and sprinkle cut sides with salt. Put potatoes on a baking rack and let stand 10 minutes so salt can draw some water out of potatoes.

Bake potatoes on the baking rack in middle of oven until cooked through, about 20 minutes.

Increase temperature to 500° F. and bake potatoes until puffed and golden, about 5 minutes more. Serves 2.

Roasted Potato Fans with Creamed Leeks

3 pounds leeks
3 large onions, sliced (about 6 cups)
3 tablespoons vegetable oil
2 large garlic cloves, minced
1 tablespoon all-purpose flour
1½ cups chicken broth
1 tablespoon fresh lemon juice
4 russet (baking) potatoes (about 2 pounds)
2 tablespoons unsalted butter, melted
paprika to taste

Trim leeks, discarding dark green part, and halve lengthwise. Cut leeks crosswise into ½-inch-thick slices and in a large bowl of cold water wash well. Drain leeks.

In a 12-inch heavy ovenproof skillet cook leeks and onions in oil over moderate heat, stirring, until softened, about 15 minutes. Add garlic and cook, stirring, 1 minute. Add flour and cook, stirring, 3 minutes. Add broth in a stream, stirring, and simmer, stirring, until thickened, about 3 minutes. Stir in lemon juice and salt and pepper to taste and remove skillet from heat.

Preheat oven to 400° F.

Peel potatoes and halve lengthwise. Arrange each potato flat side down and make crosswise slices about ¼ inch apart, cutting down to about ¼ inch from flat side but not all the way through (a metal skewer inserted lengthwise about ¼ inch from flat side will prevent slicing all the way through). Remove skewer if using.

Arrange potato halves, flat sides down, in leek mixture and bring mixture to a simmer. Brush potatoes with butter and sprinkle with paprika and salt and pepper to taste. Bake mixture in lower third of oven 1 hour and 15 minutes, or until potatoes are tender within and crisp and golden on top. Serves 8.

Roasted Potato Slices with Lime and Chili

two ½-pound russet (baking) potatoes
1 tablespoon extra-virgin olive oil
2 tablespoons mayonnaise
2 teaspoons fresh lime juice
¼ teaspoon chili powder

Preheat oven to 450° F.
Peel russet potatoes and halve lengthwise. Cut potatoes crosswise into ¼-inch-thick slices and on a baking sheet toss with extra-virgin olive oil and salt and pepper to taste. Bake potatoes in one layer in middle of oven, stirring occasionally, 15 minutes, or until golden.
In a bowl stir together mayonnaise, lime juice, and chili powder. Add warm potatoes and combine well. Serves 2.

Scalloped Potatoes

3 tablespoons unsalted butter
¼ cup all-purpose flour
2 cups chicken broth
1½ cups coarsely grated extra-sharp
   Cheddar cheese
2 pounds boiling potatoes
½ cup fresh bread crumbs

Preheat oven to 350° F. and butter a 2-quart shallow baking dish.
In a heavy saucepan melt butter over moderately low heat and whisk in flour. Cook *roux*, whisking, 3 minutes and add broth in a stream, whisking. Bring sauce to a boil, whisking, and simmer, whisking, until thickened, about 2 minutes. Remove pan from heat and whisk in cheese and salt and pepper to taste, whisking until cheese is melted.
Peel potatoes and slice about ⅛ inch thick. In prepared baking dish make 5 layers each of potatoes and sauce, beginning with potatoes and ending with sauce. *Scalloped potatoes may be prepared up to this point 2 hours ahead and kept covered.*
Sprinkle fresh bread crumbs on top and bake, uncovered, in middle of oven 1 hour, or until scalloped potatoes are tender and top is golden brown. Serves 4 to 6.

PHOTO ON PAGES 34 AND 35

Crispy Gruyère Potato Wedges

1 large russet (baking) potato (about ½ pound)
1½ teaspoons olive oil
½ cup coarsely grated Gruyère cheese
   (about 2 ounces)

Peel potato and grate coarse. Press potato between several thicknesses of paper towel to remove any excess moisture.
In an 8-inch non-stick skillet heat oil over moderately high heat until hot but not smoking and add half grated potato, spreading and tamping down with a spatula. Reduce heat to moderate and sprinkle Gruyère over potato. Spread remaining potato on top, tamping down with a spatula, and cook until golden brown and crisp, about 10 minutes on each side. Season potato with salt and pepper and cut into 6 wedges. Serves 2.

Boiled New Potatoes with Garlic Lemon Dressing

3 pounds very small red potatoes
5 large garlic cloves, peeled
1 tablespoon plus 1 teaspoon fresh lemon juice,
   or to taste
4 tablespoons olive oil
3 tablespoons chopped fresh parsley leaves,
   or to taste

Peel a wide strip from around the middle of each potato. In a kettle combine potatoes and garlic with enough salted water to cover by 2 inches and boil until potatoes are just tender, about 15 minutes. Drain mixture. Transfer potatoes to a large bowl and transfer garlic to a blender. Add to blender lemon juice, oil, and salt and pepper to taste and purée dressing. In the bowl toss potatoes with dressing and parsley. *Potatoes may be prepared 4 hours ahead and kept covered.*
Serve potatoes warm or at room temperature. Serves 6.

Chili Sweet Potato Gratin

two 10-ounce cans mild enchilada sauce (2 cups)
1 cup water

2 large garlic cloves, minced and mashed
   to a paste
5 large sweet potatoes (about 3½ pounds)
1⅓ cups coarsely grated Monterey Jack cheese
   (about 6 ounces)

Preheat oven to 375° F.

In a large saucepan simmer enchilada sauce, water, and garlic with salt to taste, stirring occasionally, 5 minutes.

Peel potatoes and cut crosswise into ⅛-inch-thick slices. In a 3-quart gratin or shallow baking dish layer one fourth of potatoes in concentric circles, overlapping slightly, and sprinkle with ⅓ cup cheese. Continue to layer remaining potatoes and cheese in same manner, ending with cheese.

Pour sauce slowly over potatoes, letting it seep between layers, and bake gratin set in a shallow baking pan (it may bubble over) in middle of oven 1 hour, or until potatoes are tender. *Gratin may be made 2 days ahead and chilled, covered. Reheat gratin, covered, in oven.* Serves 6 to 8.

Cinnamon-Sugar Glazed Sweet Potato Slices

4 large sweet potatoes (about 3 pounds)
3 tablespoons vegetable oil
1 tablespoon sugar
1 teaspoon cinnamon

Preheat oven to 425° F.

Peel potatoes and cut crosswise into ⅓-inch-thick slices. In a large bowl toss potatoes with oil to coat and spread in one layer in shallow baking pans. Bake potatoes until just tender, about 20 minutes.

In a bowl stir together sugar and cinnamon and sprinkle evenly over potatoes. Bake potatoes until glazed and tender, about 5 minutes. Serves 4 to 6.

Curried Sweet Potato Squares with Peanut Phyllo Crust

For filling
2 large sweet potatoes (about 1½ pounds)
2 tablespoons fresh orange juice
2 tablespoons Major Grey's chutney, any
   large pieces chopped

2 tablespoons unsalted butter, melted
1 large egg, beaten lightly
1 teaspoon curry powder
½ teaspoon freshly grated orange zest

½ stick (¼ cup) unsalted butter, melted
1 teaspoon curry powder
6 *phyllo* sheets, stacked between 2 sheets wax
   paper and covered with a kitchen towel
⅓ cup peanuts, chopped very fine

Make filling:
Preheat oven to 450° F.

Prick sweet potatoes and bake in middle of oven 1½ hours, or until very soft. Scoop flesh into a bowl and beat in remaining filling ingredients with salt to taste. *Filling may be made 2 days ahead and chilled, covered.*

Reduce oven temperature to 425° F.

In a small bowl stir together butter and curry powder. Put 1 *phyllo* sheet on a work surface with long side facing you. Brush left half of *phyllo* with some curry butter and sprinkle with about 1 teaspoon peanuts. Fold plain half over and fold in each end to make an 8-inch square. Brush top with curry butter and sprinkle with about 1 teaspoon peanuts.

Arrange *phyllo* in an 8-inch square baking pan. Fold, butter, and sprinkle 2 more *phyllo* sheets in same manner, arranging them in the baking pan as prepared.

Spread filling on bottom crust. Fold, butter, and sprinkle remaining 3 *phyllo* sheets in same manner, arranging over filling to form top crust and inverting last sheet so that folded-over *phyllo* is on underside.

Bake sweet potato mixture in middle of oven 20 minutes, or until crust is flaky and golden, and cut into squares. Serves 9.

187

Roasted Curried Sweet Potatoes

1½ tablespoons unsalted butter
½ teaspoon curry powder
¾ pound sweet potatoes, peeled and cut into
    1-inch pieces (about 2 cups)

Preheat oven to 450° F.

In a small saucepan melt butter and stir in curry powder and salt and pepper to taste. In a small baking pan toss potatoes with butter mixture and roast in oven, shaking pan occasionally, until golden and tender, 15 to 20 minutes. Serves 2.

Sweet Potato and Apricot Purée with Pecan Streusel

5 large sweet potatoes (about 3½ pounds)
6 ounces dried apricots (about 1½ cups)
1 tablespoon granulated sugar, or to taste
1 tablespoon all-purpose flour
⅓ cup firmly packed light brown sugar
1 tablespoon unsalted butter, softened
⅔ cup chopped pecans (about 3 ounces),
    toasted lightly

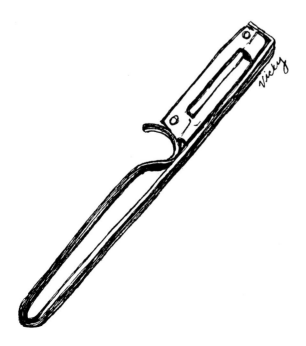

Preheat oven to 450° F.

Prick potatoes and bake in middle of oven 1½ hours, or until very soft. Scoop flesh into a bowl.

In a saucepan cover apricots by 1 inch with cold water and simmer until soft, about 30 minutes. Reserve 2 tablespoons cooking water and drain apricots. In a food processor purée apricots with granulated sugar and reserved cooking water until smooth.

Add purée to potatoes with salt to taste and with an electric mixer beat until smooth. Spread mixture in a buttered 2-quart shallow baking dish. *Purée may be prepared up to this point 1 day ahead and chilled, covered.*

Reduce oven temperature to 400° F.

In a small bowl blend with your fingers flour, brown sugar, butter, pecans, and salt to taste until combined well and crumble over purée. Bake purée in middle of oven until heated through and streusel is bubbling, about 15 minutes. Serves 6 to 8.

Sautéed Spinach

2 tablespoons olive oil
2 pounds fresh spinach (about 3 bunches), coarse
    stems discarded and leaves washed thoroughly
    and spun dry

In a large deep heavy skillet at least 12 inches across top heat oil over moderately high heat until hot but not smoking and add spinach. Cook spinach, covered, stirring occasionally, until wilted, about 3 minutes, and season with salt and pepper. Serves 6.

PHOTO ON PAGE 26

Spicy Butternut Squash with Bacon and Lime

1 small butternut squash, peeled, seeded,
    and cut into ½-inch cubes
3 slices bacon
2 teaspoons fresh lime juice
½ teaspoon Tabasco,
    or to taste

Steam squash on a steamer rack set over boiling water, covered, until tender, about 5 to 8 minutes.

In a skillet cook bacon over moderate heat until crisp, reserving 2 teaspoons bacon fat.

Crumble bacon into a bowl and toss with squash, lime juice, Tabasco, reserved bacon fat, and salt and pepper to taste. Serves 2.

Broiled Tomato, Corn, and Okra

2 medium vine-ripened tomatoes, halved and cut
   into ¼-inch-thick slices
1½ tablespoons olive oil
½ cup fresh corn kernels (cut from 1 ear of corn)
¼ pound okra, trimmed and sliced ½ inch thick
   (about 1 cup)
1 tablespoon shredded fresh basil leaves

Preheat broiler.
Arrange tomatoes on a lightly greased jelly-roll pan and brush with 1 tablespoon oil. Season tomatoes with salt and pepper and broil about 4 inches from heat 5 minutes.
In a bowl toss together corn, okra, remaining ½ tablespoon oil, and salt and pepper to taste.
Spread corn and okra evenly on pan with tomatoes and broil about 4 inches from heat until tender, about 5 minutes. In a bowl toss vegetables gently with basil. Serves 2.

Tomato, Pickled Onion, and Coriander Sandwiches

eight ½-inch-thick slices whole-grain bread,
   toasted lightly if desired
¼ cup mayonnaise
2 large tomatoes, sliced
½ cup pickled onions (recipe follows)
1 cup fresh coriander sprigs

Spread bread with mayonnaise and make 4 sandwiches with tomato slices, pickled onions, and coriander sprigs, pressing together gently. Makes 4 sandwiches.

Pickled Onions

1 medium onion, halved lengthwise and sliced
   crosswise ⅛ inch thick
½ teaspoon mustard seeds, crushed
½ teaspoon freshly ground black pepper
¼ teaspoon ground cumin
¼ teaspoon salt
¼ cup plus 2 tablespoons cider vinegar
1 tablespoon sugar
3 garlic cloves, crushed

In a saucepan of boiling water blanch onion 1 minute and drain. In pan simmer onion and remaining ingredients 3 minutes. Transfer mixture to a small bowl and cool. *Onions may be made 2 weeks ahead and chilled, covered.* Makes about 1 cup.

Vegetables in Salsa Verde

1 large boiling potato
1 carrot
1 zucchini
1 large egg
For sauce
⅓ cup flat-leafed parsley leaves
1 small garlic clove
1 small shallot
2 small pimiento-stuffed green olives
1 tablespoon fresh lemon juice
1 teaspoon drained capers
⅛ teaspoon anchovy paste
3 tablespoons extra-virgin olive oil

Peel potato and cut it, carrot, and zucchini into 3- by ½- by ½-inch sticks. Prick large end of egg with a pin and in a saucepan combine egg, potato, and carrot with cold water to cover by 2 inches. Bring water to a simmer and add salt to taste. Simmer mixture 10 minutes, or until vegetables are just tender, and with a slotted spoon transfer egg and vegetables to a bowl of ice and cold water. Add zucchini to pan and simmer 3 minutes, or until just tender. Remove zucchini with a slotted spoon and add to egg and vegetables.
Make sauce:
In a blender or small food processor purée parsley, garlic, shallot, olives, juice, capers, and anchovy paste until smooth. While motor is running, add oil in a stream, blending until emulsified.
Drain vegetables and egg and pat vegetables dry with paper towels. Peel egg and quarter lengthwise. Divide egg and vegetables between 2 plates and spoon sauce over them. Serves 2 as a first course.

Glazed Baby Turnips and Carrots

1 pound baby turnips (about 2 pounds with
  greens attached) or regular turnips
¾ pound baby carrots (about 2 pounds with
  greens attached)
1½ tablespoons unsalted butter
½ teaspoon sugar

Trim baby turnips and carrots, leaving ½-inch stems if greens were attached, and peel if desired. If using regular turnips, peel and cut into 1-inch pieces. In a steamer set over boiling water steam turnips and carrots separately, covered, until just tender, 6 to 8 minutes. *Vegetables may be prepared up to this point 1 day ahead and chilled, covered.*

In a large heavy skillet cook vegetables in butter with sugar and salt and pepper to taste over moderately low heat, stirring, until heated through and glazed, about 4 minutes. Serves 6.

PHOTO ON PAGE 33

Grilled Open-Faced Vegetable, Pesto, and Mozzarella Sandwiches

1 red bell pepper, quartered
1 yellow bell pepper, quartered
3 small eggplants (about ½ pound total), sliced
  diagonally ¼ inch thick
olive oil for brushing vegetables and bread
a 14-inch-long loaf Italian bread, halved
  horizontally with a serrated knife
½ cup *pesto* (page 214)
1 cup diced mozzarella cheese (about ¼ pound)

Garnish: 3 tablespoons finely shredded
  fresh basil leaves

Prepare grill.

Lightly brush bell peppers and eggplants with oil and grill on an oiled rack set about 4 inches over glowing coals about 4 minutes on each side, or until cooked through. Cut peppers into strips.

Lightly brush cut sides of bread with oil and grill, cut sides down, about 2 minutes, or until golden. Spread each piece of bread with 4 tablespoons *pesto* and divide peppers, eggplants, and mozzarella between them. Grill sandwiches, covered, just until cheese is melted. (Alternatively, vegetables and assembled sandwiches may be broiled.)

Sprinkle each sandwich with basil and cut in half. Makes 4 sandwiches.

Marinated Vegetables with Mustard Dill Dressing

For marinade
⅔ cup white-wine vinegar
⅔ cup water
1½ tablespoons sugar
2 teaspoons dill seed
2 garlic cloves, forced through a garlic press
1 teaspoon salt

2 pounds beets, scrubbed and trimmed, leaving
  about 1 inch of stems attached
2 pounds carrots, cut crosswise into 3 sections and
  each section quartered lengthwise
2 pounds green beans, cut into 1½-inch pieces
For dressing
3 tablespoons Dijon mustard
2 tablespoons white-wine vinegar
1 tablespoon water
1 tablespoon sugar
¾ teaspoon salt
⅓ cup olive oil
3 tablespoons finely chopped fresh dill

Make marinade:

In a small saucepan bring marinade ingredients to a boil, stirring until sugar is dissolved, and cool.

Preheat oven to 400° F.

Wrap beets tightly in foil and roast in middle of oven 1 to 1½ hours, or until tender. In a large saucepan of boiling salted water cook carrots until crisp-tender, 6 to 7 minutes, and transfer with a slotted spoon to a bowl.

Unwrap beets carefully and cool. Slip off skins and slice beets, transferring to another bowl. Divide marinade between beets and carrots, combining well, and marinate, covered and chilled, at least 4 hours.

In the saucepan of boiling cooking water cook beans until crisp-tender, 5 to 6 minutes, and drain in a colander. Rinse beans under cold water and pat dry between paper towels. *Vegetables may be prepared up to this point 1 day ahead and chilled, covered.*

Make dressing:

In a bowl whisk together mustard, vinegar, water, sugar, and salt and add oil in a stream, whisking until dressing is emulsified. Whisk in dill.

Just before serving, toss beans in a large bowl with 2 tablespoons dressing and drain beets and carrots. Arrange vegetables decoratively on a platter and drizzle with remaining dressing. Serves 12.

SALADS

Chicken and Roasted Vegetable Salad

6 small beets (about 1 pound),
  trimmed
⅓ cup plus 4 teaspoons olive oil
6 small red potatoes
  (about ¾ pound)
2 zucchini (about 1 pound)
4 medium carrots
3 tablespoons fresh lemon juice
1 tablespoon minced fresh parsley leaves
2 cups shredded cooked chicken such as
  rotisserie chicken
1 small head *frisée* or other curly endive or
  escarole, quartered

Preheat oven to 400° F.

Peel beets and cut into ¾-inch wedges. In a bowl toss beets with 1 teaspoon oil to coat and in one end of a shallow baking pan spread in one layer.

Cut potatoes into ¼-inch-thick slices. In another bowl toss potatoes with 1 teaspoon oil to coat and at other end of baking pan spread in one layer, making sure that potatoes do not touch beets (beets will bleed).

Cut zucchini diagonally into ½-inch-thick slices and cut slices lengthwise into ½-inch-wide sticks. In a small bowl toss zucchini with 1 teaspoon oil to coat and in one end of another shallow baking pan spread in one layer.

Cut carrots diagonally into ⅓-inch-thick slices. In a bowl toss carrots with 1 teaspoon oil to coat and at the other end of second baking pan spread in one layer.

In a small bowl whisk together lemon juice, parsley, remaining ⅓ cup oil, and salt to taste.

Bake vegetables in oven 5 minutes, or until zucchini is just tender, and transfer zucchini to a shallow bowl. Bake remaining vegetables, testing them every 5 minutes, 10 to 15 minutes more, or until tender, and transfer as cooked to separate shallow bowls.

Stir dressing and spoon about 1 tablespoon over each vegetable, tossing to coat. In a bowl toss chicken with remaining dressing.

Arrange vegetables and salad greens on a platter and mound chicken in middle. Alternatively, vegetables, chicken, and dressing may be tossed together, but beets will bleed. Serve salad at room temperature. Serves 2 or 3.

Crab Salad with Yogurt Mustard Dressing

¼ cup plain yogurt
2 tablespoons sour cream
⅛ teaspoon paprika
2 teaspoons Dijon mustard
fresh lemon juice to taste
1 cup lump crab meat,
  picked over
1 scallion, chopped fine
1 celery rib, chopped fine

Accompaniment: toast points

In a bowl whisk together yogurt, sour cream, paprika, mustard, lemon juice, and salt and pepper to taste. Add crab meat, scallion, and celery and toss salad gently.

Serve salad with toast points. Serves 2.

Lobster, Corn, Zucchini, and Basil Salad

4 zucchini (about 2 pounds)
1½ cups fresh corn (cut from about 3 ears)
12 boiled or steamed 1¼-pound lobsters
½ cup mayonnaise, or to taste
3 to 4 tablespoons white-wine vinegar or
  fresh lemon juice
½ cup finely shredded fresh basil leaves

Garnish: fresh basil sprigs and finely shredded basil leaves

With a small (about ¼-inch) melon-ball cutter scoop outer flesh of zucchini, reserving remaining zucchini for another use if desired. (There should be about 1½ cups zucchini pieces.) In a saucepan of boiling water blanch zucchini and corn 1 minute and drain well. Let zucchini and corn cool and transfer to a large bowl.

Break off claws at body of each lobster. Crack claws and remove meat. Cut claw meat into ½-inch pieces and add to vegetables. Twist tails off lobster bodies, keeping them intact, and discard bodies. With a pair of kitchen shears remove thin hard membrane from each lobster tail by cutting just inside outer edge of shell. Remove meat from tail and reserve tail shells for serving. Cut tail meat into ½-inch pieces and add to claw meat mixture.

In a small bowl whisk together mayonnaise, vinegar or lemon juice, and salt and pepper to taste and add to lobster mixture. Toss salad gently just to combine well. *Salad may be prepared up to this point 8 hours ahead and chilled, covered.*

Just before serving, stir shredded basil into salad. Mound about ½ cup salad into each reserved lobster tail and arrange on a platter. Transfer remaining salad to a serving bowl and garnish platter and bowl with basil. Makes about 12 cups.

PHOTO ON PAGE 64

Warm Salad of Seared Scallops, Haricots Verts, and Bell Peppers in Walnut Vinaigrette

½ pound *haricots verts* (thin French green beans)*, trimmed
1 pound sea scallops
5 tablespoons extra-virgin olive oil
3 yellow bell peppers, cut into 2- by ¼-inch strips
3 orange bell peppers, cut into 2- by ¼-inch strips
2 large shallots, minced
3 tablespoons Sherry vinegar
½ teaspoon sugar
3 tablespoons walnut oil**
4 heads *radicchio*, outer leaves only
⅓ cup walnuts, toasted lightly
and chopped

*available at specialty produce markets
**available at specialty foods shops and some supermarkets

In a saucepan of boiling salted water boil *haricots verts* until crisp-tender, 2 to 3 minutes. Drain beans in a colander and refresh in cold water to stop cooking. Pat beans dry and wrap in a kitchen towel. *Beans may be prepared 1 day ahead and chilled, covered.*

Remove tough muscle from side of each scallop if necessary. Halve scallops horizontally and pat dry. Season scallops with salt and pepper.

In a non-stick skillet large enough to hold scallops in one layer heat 1 tablespoon olive oil over moderately high heat until hot but not smoking and sauté scallops until golden, 2 minutes on each side. Transfer scallops with a slotted spoon to a large bowl.

In skillet heat 1 tablespoon remaining olive oil until hot but not smoking and sauté bell peppers, stirring, until crisp-tender. Transfer bell peppers with slotted spoon to bowl with scallops.

In skillet cook shallots in 1 tablespoon remaining olive oil over moderate heat, stirring, until softened. Add Sherry vinegar, sugar, walnut oil, remaining 2 tablespoons olive oil, and salt to taste and simmer 1 minute. Remove skillet from heat and let vinaigrette cool 5 minutes.

Divide *radicchio* among 8 plates. Add beans and vinaigrette to scallop mixture and toss. Divide salad among plates and sprinkle with walnuts. Serves 8.

PHOTO ON PAGE 82

Shrimp and Rice Salad

½ cup long-grain rice
3 tablespoons olive oil
¾ pound small shrimp (about 35), shelled and
    deveined
1½ tablespoons fresh lime juice
1 large garlic clove,
    minced
¼ cup minced fresh parsley leaves
¼ teaspoon freshly grated lime zest

To a kettle of salted boiling water add rice, stirring, and boil 10 minutes. Drain rice well in a sieve and rinse. Steam rice in sieve over boiling water, covered with a paper towel and a lid, 20 minutes, or until tender.

In a heavy skillet heat 1 tablespoon of oil over moderately high heat until hot but not smoking and stir-fry shrimp until just cooked through, about 1 minute. Remove skillet from heat and stir in lime juice and garlic.

In a bowl stir together rice, shrimp, remaining 2 tablespoons oil, parsley, zest, and salt and pepper to taste. Serves 2.

Herbed Shrimp Salad with
Watercress on Toasted Brioche

1¼ pounds small shrimp (about 60), shelled and
    deveined
¼ cup mayonnaise
½ cup finely diced celery
1 to 2 tablespoons minced fresh chives, tarragon,
    or dill
2 teaspoons fresh lemon juice
1 cup watercress sprigs
eight ½-inch-thick slices brioche or challah,
    toasted lightly

In a large saucepan of salted boiling water cook shrimp 1 minute, or until just cooked through. Drain shrimp well and cool completely.

Chop shrimp and in a bowl toss with mayonnaise, celery, herbs, lemon juice, and salt and pepper to taste. Make 4 sandwiches with shrimp salad, watercress sprigs, and bread, pressing together gently. Makes 4 sandwiches.

SALADS WITH GREENS

Caesar Salad

For croutons
3 cups ½-inch cubes of fresh French or
    Italian bread
2 tablespoons olive oil
For dressing
2 large garlic cloves, chopped
6 flat anchovies, rinsed, patted dry, and chopped
2 tablespoons fresh lemon juice
2 tablespoons mayonnaise
¼ teaspoon salt
⅓ cup olive oil (preferably extra-virgin)
2 tablespoons water

1 head romaine lettuce, trimmed and torn into
    bite-size pieces
⅓ cup freshly grated Parmesan cheese

Make croutons:
Preheat oven to 350° F.

In a bowl toss bread cubes with oil and salt to taste and spread in a jelly-roll pan. Bake croutons in middle of oven until golden, 10 to 15 minutes.

Make dressing:

In a blender blend together at high speed garlic, anchovies, lemon juice, mayonnaise, and salt until smooth. With motor running add oil in a slow stream and blend until emulsified. Add water and blend dressing well.

In a bowl toss romaine with dressing, Parmesan, croutons, and pepper to taste. Serves 6.

Mixed Baby Greens with
Aniseed Vinaigrette and Goat Cheese Crostini

1 shallot, quartered
2 garlic cloves, halved
1 teaspoon freeze-dried green peppercorns
½ teaspoon aniseed
1 tablespoon white-wine vinegar
¼ cup olive oil (preferably extra-virgin)
8 cups mixed baby greens
goat cheese *crostini* (recipe follows)

In a blender chop shallot, garlic, peppercorns, and aniseed. Add vinegar and salt and pepper to taste and blend well. With motor running, add oil in a stream and blend dressing until emulsified. *Vinaigrette may be made 1 week ahead and chilled, covered.* In a bowl toss greens with vinaigrette until coated well.

Divide salad among 4 plates and serve with goat cheese *crostini*. Serves 4.

PHOTO ON PAGE 28

Goat Cheese Crostini

3 ounces soft mild goat cheese, such as
   Montrachet, at room temperature
1 tablespoon snipped fresh chives
four ¾-inch-thick slices French or Italian bread
1 tablespoon freshly grated Parmesan cheese

In a small bowl stir together goat cheese, chives, and salt and pepper to taste until combined well. *Goat cheese mixture may be made 2 days ahead and chilled, covered.*

Preheat oven to 350° F.

Toast bread on a baking sheet in middle of oven until golden, about 10 minutes. *Toasts may be made 2 days ahead. Cool toasts and keep in an airtight container.*

Preheat broiler.

Spread cheese mixture on toasts and sprinkle with Parmesan. Broil *crostini* on the baking sheet 2 inches from heat until cheese is browned in spots, about 2 minutes. Serves 4.

PHOTO ON PAGE 28

Mixed Greens with Walnut Vinaigrette

about 3 cups torn mixed greens such as *frisée* *,
   Lollo rosso* or other red-leaf lettuce, and
   radicchio
1 tablespoon imported walnut oil**
1 teaspoon fresh lemon juice

*available at specialty produce markets and some
   supermarkets
**available at specialty foods shops

In a bowl toss greens with oil, lemon juice, and salt and pepper to taste and divide salad between 2 plates. Serves 2.

PHOTO ON PAGE 17

each slice into cubes and bake croutons on a baking sheet in middle of oven until golden brown, about 10 minutes.

In a saucepan boil salt pork in cold water to cover 2 minutes and drain in a colander. Rinse salt pork under cold water and pat dry with paper towels. Heat remaining 1 tablespoon oil in a skillet over moderate heat and in it cook salt pork, stirring frequently, until browned. Remove salt pork with a slotted spoon and drain on paper towels.

Pour ½ cup fat from skillet into a small bowl and whisk in shallots, white-wine vinegar, tarragon, garlic cloves, and salt and pepper to taste until dressing is combined well.

Fill a wide skillet with 2 inches water and add distilled vinegar. Bring liquid to a rolling boil over high heat and reduce heat to a bare simmer. Poach eggs, 3 at a time, by breaking each one into a saucer and sliding it into the water. As each egg goes in, push white back immediately toward yolk with a large slotted spoon, moving egg gently, and simmer 3 minutes. *Note: In this traditional French salad, the poached egg yolks are served runny. If there is a problem with eggs in your region, cook them longer.* Drain eggs separately in slotted spoon, blot carefully with paper towels, and trim ragged edges of whites.

In a large bowl toss together *frisée*, dressing, salt pork, and croutons. Divide salad among 6 plates and top with poached eggs. Serves 6.

PHOTO ON PAGES 18 AND 19

Frisée Salad with Poached Eggs

4 tablespoons olive oil
ten 1-inch-thick slices French or Italian bread
½ pound salt pork, diced
2 shallots, sliced thin
3 tablespoons white-wine vinegar
1 tablespoon chopped fresh tarragon leaves or
    1 teaspoon dried, crumbled
2 garlic cloves, minced
2 teaspoons distilled white vinegar
6 large eggs
2 heads *frisée**, torn into pieces (about 12 cups)

*available at specialty produce markets and
    some supermarkets

Preheat oven to 350° F.
Spread 3 tablespoons olive oil with a brush on both sides of bread and season with salt and pepper. Cut

Mesclun Salad

1 pound *mesclun* (mixed baby greens)*, rinsed
    and spun dry
¼ cup extra-virgin olive oil
1½ tablespoons Champagne vinegar* or other
    wine vinegar

*available at specialty foods shops and some
    supermarkets

In a large bowl toss *mesclun* with oil and drizzle with vinegar. Season salad with salt and pepper and toss. Serves 12.

PHOTO ON PAGE 65

Red-Leaf Lettuce and Watercress Salad with Buttermilk Dressing

½ cup buttermilk
¼ cup mayonnaise
1 garlic clove, minced and mashed to a paste
    with ¼ teaspoon salt
½ teaspoon English-style dry mustard,
    or to taste
¼ teaspoon dried tarragon, or to taste,
    crumbled
1 large head red-leaf lettuce, rinsed, spun dry,
    and torn into pieces
1 bunch watercress, coarse stems discarded and
    sprigs rinsed and spun dry
½ small red onion, sliced thin

In a small bowl whisk together buttermilk, mayonnaise, garlic paste, mustard, tarragon, and salt and pepper to taste until smooth.

In a large bowl toss lettuce, watercress, and onion with dressing. Serves 4 to 6.

PHOTO ON PAGE 35

Spinach Salad with Bacon, Dates, and Feta Dressing

For feta dressing
⅓ cup crumbled feta cheese (about 2 ounces)
1 tablespoon fresh lemon juice
2½ tablespoons water
1 tablespoon mayonnaise
2 tablespoons olive oil

3 slices bacon, chopped
1 bunch fresh spinach (about ¾ pound), stems
    discarded and leaves washed well, spun dry,
    and torn into bite-size pieces
½ medium red onion, sliced thin
⅓ cup pitted dates, chopped

Make feta dressing:
In a blender blend together feta, lemon juice, water, and mayonnaise until smooth. With motor running add oil and blend until emulsified.

In a small skillet cook bacon over moderate heat, stirring, until crisp and transfer with a slotted spoon to paper towels to drain.

In a large bowl toss together spinach, bacon, onion, and dates with feta dressing. Serves 4.

VEGETABLE SALADS AND SLAWS

Azuki Bean and Vegetable Salad in Pita Bread

½ cup dried *azuki* beans* or lentils, picked over
    and rinsed
3 carrots, cut into ¼-inch dice
3 large broccoli stems, peeled and cut into
    ¼-inch dice
2 ribs celery, cut into ¼-inch dice
1 small red bell pepper, cut into
    ¼-inch dice
⅓ cup minced fresh parsley leaves
2 large garlic cloves,
    minced
1 cup coarsely grated provolone cheese
    (about 2 ounces)
3 tablespoons white-wine vinegar
½ cup extra-virgin olive oil
6 *pita* loaves, halved crosswise

*available at natural foods stores and some
    specialty foods shops

In a small saucepan combine beans with water to cover by 2 inches and simmer until tender, about 45 minutes for *azuki* beans or about 15 minutes for lentils. In a sieve drain beans and rinse. Drain beans well and transfer to a bowl.

In a large saucepan of boiling salted water blanch carrots 1 minute and add broccoli stems. Blanch carrot mixture 2 minutes and drain in sieve. Rinse vegetables under cold water until cool and drain well. Add blanched vegetables to beans with celery, bell pepper, parsley, garlic, and provolone.

In a small bowl whisk together vinegar and salt and pepper to taste. Add oil in a stream, whisking, and whisk until emulsified. Pour dressing over bean mixture and toss well. *Salad may be made 1 day ahead and chilled, covered.*

Serve salad in *pita* halves. Serves 6.

PHOTO ON PAGE 67

Herbed Goat Cheese, Roasted Beet, and Watercress Salad

4 medium beets, scrubbed and trimmed, leaving about 1 inch of stems attached

For vinaigrette
1¼ teaspoons Dijon mustard
2 tablespoons white-wine vinegar
¼ teaspoon dried tarragon, crumbled
¼ teaspoon salt
¼ teaspoon freshly ground black pepper
¼ cup plus 2 tablespoons extra-virgin olive oil

For herbed goat cheese
¾ cup fresh bread crumbs
½ teaspoon dried tarragon, crumbled
¾ teaspoon salt
⅛ teaspoon freshly ground black pepper
8 ounces Montrachet or other soft goat cheese, cut into eight ½-inch rounds and chilled, covered

2 bunches watercress, coarse stems discarded, rinsed and spun dry (about 8 cups)
1 small red onion, sliced thin

Preheat oven to 400° F.

Wrap beets tightly in foil and roast in middle of oven 1 to 1½ hours, or until tender. Unwrap beets carefully and cool until they can be handled. Discard stems and peel beets. *Beets may be prepared up to this point 1 day ahead and chilled, covered.* Cut each beet into 8 wedges and cover.

Make vinaigrette:

In a blender blend together mustard, vinegar, tarragon, salt, and pepper. With motor running add oil in a stream and blend until emulsified. *Vinaigrette may be made 1 day ahead and chilled, covered.*

Make herbed goat cheese:

In a bowl stir together bread crumbs, tarragon, salt, and pepper. Cut each cheese round in half crosswise. Coat each piece of cheese evenly with crumb mixture, pressing gently, and transfer to a baking sheet. *Goat cheese may be prepared up to this point 1 day ahead and chilled, covered loosely. Let cheese come to room temperature before proceeding.*

Preheat broiler.

Broil goat cheese about 2 inches from heat until crumbs are lightly browned, about 2 minutes.

In a bowl toss watercress and onion with half of vinaigrette. Arrange watercress mixture, beets, and goat cheese on 8 salad plates and drizzle remaining vinaigrette over beets. Serves 8.

PHOTO ON PAGES 74 AND 75

Grapefruit, Beet, and Blue Cheese Salad

½ bunch watercress, coarse stems discarded
1 grapefruit, peel and pith cut away with a serrated knife and sections cut free from membranes
1 ounce chilled fine-quality blue cheese, cut into small thin slices
2 peeled cooked beets, grated coarse (about 1 cup)
4 teaspoons extra-virgin olive oil
1 tablespoon balsamic vinegar
coarse salt to taste
coarsely ground pepper to taste

Divide watercress between 2 salad plates and arrange grapefruit sections and cheese decoratively on top. In a small bowl toss together beets, 2 teaspoons oil, and vinegar and divide between salads. Drizzle salads with remaining 2 teaspoons oil and season with coarse salt and pepper. Serves 2.

Carrot and Beet Salad with Gingerroot Vinaigrette

¼ cup minced shallot
2 tablespoons minced peeled fresh gingerroot
1 garlic clove, minced
¼ cup rice vinegar*
1 tablespoon soy sauce
½ teaspoon Asian (toasted) sesame oil
Tabasco to taste
½ cup olive oil
4 cups finely shredded carrots (about 10 carrots)
4 cups finely shredded peeled raw beets

Garnish: spinach leaves, washed thoroughly

*available at Asian markets and some supermarkets

In a blender purée shallot, gingerroot, and garlic with rice vinegar, soy sauce, sesame oil, and Tabasco. With motor running add olive oil in a stream and blend until smooth.

In two separate bowls toss carrots with half of the dressing and beets with remaining half. Divide carrot salad and beet salad among 6 plates and garnish with spinach leaves. Serves 6.

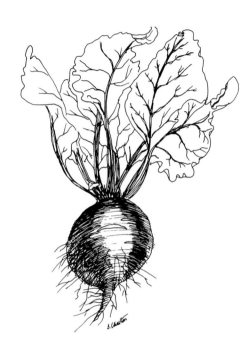

Carrot Walnut Salad

3 large carrots, shredded (about 1½ cups)
1 tablespoon extra-virgin olive oil
2 teaspoons fresh lemon juice, or to taste
¼ teaspoon salt
1½ tablespoons chopped walnuts, toasted lightly

In a bowl toss carrots with oil. Add remaining ingredients and toss well. Serves 2.

Celery Root Rémoulade

¼ cup mayonnaise
2 tablespoons *crème fraîche* or sour cream
2 *cornichons* (sour gherkins), minced, or
   1 tablespoon minced dill pickle
1 tablespoon minced fresh parsley leaves
2 teaspoons fresh lemon juice
½ teaspoon drained bottled capers,
   minced
½ teaspoon Dijon mustard
a pinch dried tarragon,
   crumbled
2 small celery roots (about 1¼ pound total),
   peeled and cut into matchstick pieces or
   shredded coarse

In a small bowl stir together mayonnaise, *crème fraîche* or sour cream, *cornichons* or dill pickle, parsley, lemon juice, capers, mustard, tarragon, and salt and pepper to taste until combined well.

In a large saucepan of boiling salted water cook celery root 2 minutes. Drain celery root in a sieve and refresh under cold water. Dry celery root completely. Add celery root to sauce and stir together. Chill salad until ready to serve. Serves 2.

Viennese Cucumber Salad

2 large seedless cucumbers
   (about 2 pounds)
1 tablespoon salt
⅓ cup white-wine vinegar
¼ cup water
2 teaspoons sugar
1 garlic clove, forced through a garlic press
1 teaspoon dill seed

Score cucumbers lengthwise with a fork and slice thin, preferably with slicing disk of a food processor. In a large bowl toss cucumbers with salt and let stand 1 hour.

In a small saucepan bring vinegar and water to a boil with sugar, garlic, and dill seed, stirring until sugar is dissolved, and let dressing cool.

In a colander drain cucumbers and rinse under cold water. Drain cucumbers well, squeezing out excess liquid. In a bowl combine cucumbers with dressing and marinate, covered and chilled, at least 1 hour and up to 6 hours. (After about 2 hours cucumber skin will discolor, but there will be no effect on flavor.) Makes about 4 cups.

PHOTO ON PAGE 85

Cucumber Carrot Salad

1 garlic clove, minced and mashed to a paste
2 tablespoons fresh lime juice
1½ tablespoons Asian fish sauce (preferably
  naam pla*)
1 tablespoon sugar
1 fresh Thai or serrano chili*, or to taste, seeded
  and minced (wear rubber gloves)
2 seedless cucumbers, quartered lengthwise,
  seeded, and cored
1 carrot, shredded coarse
soft-leafed lettuce for serving

*available at Asian markets, some specialty foods
  shops, and by mail order from Adriana's
  Caravan, Brooklyn, NY, tel. (800) 316-0820
  or (718) 436-8565, or Uwajimaya, 519 Sixth
  Avenue South, Seattle, WA 98104, tel.
  (206) 624-6248

In a bowl stir together garlic, lime juice, fish
sauce, sugar, and chili until sugar is dissolved.
  Thinly slice cucumbers crosswise and add to garlic
mixture with carrot. Toss salad well. *Salad may be
made 4 hours ahead and chilled, covered, but cucumber will wilt and give off liquid.*
  Serve salad in lettuce "cups." Serves 6.

Cucumber, Carrot, and Red Onion Salad

4 cucumbers (about 2 pounds), peeled, leaving
  stripes of skin, and sliced thin (about 6 cups)
1 cup coarsely shredded carrot
1 cup paper-thin slices red onion
⅓ cup white-wine vinegar
3 tablespoons vegetable oil
1½ teaspoons salt, or to taste
1 teaspoon sugar

In a bowl combine vegetables. In a small bowl stir
together vinegar, oil, salt, sugar, and pepper to taste
until salt and sugar are dissolved. Pour dressing over
salad and toss to combine well. Chill salad, covered,
stirring occasionally, at least 1 hour and up to 3
hours. Serves 6.

Coriander Eggplant Salad

6 garlic cloves, unpeeled
1 large eggplant (about 1½ pounds)
¾ teaspoon cuminseed
½ teaspoon fennel seeds
½ teaspoon coriander seeds
2 medium vine-ripened tomatoes, peeled, seeded,
  and chopped (about 1 cup)
3 tablespoons chopped fresh coriander

2 tablespoons fresh lemon juice,
    or to taste
2 tablespoons olive oil
1½ teaspoons minced peeled fresh gingerroot
½ teaspoon paprika
coarse salt to taste
4 tablespoons minced fresh mint leaves

Preheat oven to 400° F.

Wrap garlic cloves in foil. Prick eggplant all over. On a baking sheet roast garlic and eggplant in middle of oven 30 minutes, or until garlic is tender. Transfer garlic to a plate and continue to roast eggplant until blackened and collapsed, about 45 minutes more.

While eggplant is roasting, in a small skillet dry-roast seeds over moderate heat, shaking the skillet, until fragrant, being careful not to burn them, and in a mortar with a pestle, an electric spice grinder, or a cleaned coffee grinder grind fine.

With a large spoon scrape eggplant flesh from skin, discarding skin, and chop coarse. Peel garlic cloves and with flat side of a knife mash to a paste. In a bowl stir together eggplant, garlic paste, spice mixture, tomatoes, fresh coriander, lemon juice, oil, gingerroot, paprika, salt, and 2 tablespoons mint until combined well. *Salad may be made 2 days ahead and chilled, covered.*

Sprinkle salad with remaining 2 tablespoons mint and serve at room temperature. Serves 6 as a first course.

Jicama, Carrot, and Peanut Salad

¼ teaspoon dried hot red pepper flakes,
    or to taste
1½ cups julienne strips of *jicama* or firm pear
1½ cups julienne strips of carrot
¼ cup chopped salted roasted peanuts
3 tablespoons fresh lime juice
2 tablespoons thinly sliced scallion greens
⅛ teaspoon ground cumin

In a small heavy skillet dry-roast red pepper flakes over moderate heat, stirring, until fragrant, about 2 minutes. Transfer pepper flakes to a bowl and toss together with remaining ingredients and salt to taste. Serves 2.

Green Lentil, Sun-Dried Tomato, and Feta Salad

3 tablespoons extra-virgin olive oil
2 tablespoons white-wine vinegar
¼ teaspoon dried thyme, crumbled
¼ cup drained finely chopped sun-dried tomatoes
    packed in oil
1 cup *lentilles du Puy* (French green lentils)*,
    picked over and rinsed
½ cup crumbled feta cheese
    (about 2 ounces)

*available at specialty foods shops and some
    supermarkets

In a large bowl whisk together oil, vinegar, thyme, tomatoes, and salt and pepper to taste.

Add lentils to a large saucepan of salted water and bring water to a boil. Cook lentils at a bare simmer until just tender, about 20 minutes. Drain lentils in a sieve and rinse gently.

Toss lentils well with dressing and gently stir in feta. Serves 4 as a side dish.

Red Onion, Parsley, and Preserved Lemon Salad

3 cups thinly sliced red onions
½ cup coarsely chopped fresh flat-leafed parsley
    leaves
2 tablespoons olive oil
peel of ⅛ preserved lemon*, cut into julienne
    strips, plus ⅓ cup preserved lemon juice or
    fresh lemon juice to taste
1 large garlic clove, minced
¼ teaspoon ground coriander
a pinch cayenne, or to taste
coarse salt to taste

*available by mail order from The Gardener,
    1836 Fourth Street, Berkeley, CA 94710,
    tel. (510) 548-4545, or recipe on page 92

In a bowl cover onions with cold water and soak 30 minutes. Drain onions well and pat dry between layers of paper towels. In a bowl stir together onions with remaining ingredients and let stand, stirring occasionally, 15 minutes. Serves 6 as a first course.

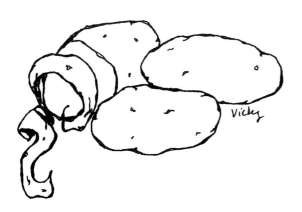

Warm German Potato Salad

3 pounds small red potatoes (about 2 inches in
   diameter), washed well
10 slices bacon, cut crosswise into ¼-inch strips
   (about ½ pound)
1 large onion, chopped (about 1½ cups)
½ teaspoon sugar
3 tablespoons cider vinegar
¾ cup beef broth
2 tablespoons chopped fresh parsley leaves

Garnish: chopped fresh parsley leaves

In a large saucepan combine potatoes with salted
water to cover by 1 inch and simmer until just tender,
about 20 minutes.

While potatoes are cooking, in a large heavy skillet
cook bacon over moderate heat, stirring, until
browned and crisp and transfer with a slotted spoon
to paper towels to drain.

Drain potatoes and let stand until cool enough to
handle. Cut potatoes into eighths and in a bowl combine with bacon. Keep mixture warm, covered.

Pour off all but 3 tablespoons fat from skillet and
sauté onion over moderately high heat, stirring, until
softened, about 3 minutes. Add sugar, 2 tablespoons
vinegar, and broth and simmer 2 minutes. Add onion
mixture to warm potatoes with parsley and remaining
1 tablespoon vinegar, tossing gently, and season with
salt and pepper.

Serve potato salad warm or at room temperature,
garnished with parsley. Serves 6.

PHOTO ON PAGE 70

Potato Salad with Egg, Dill Pickle, and Tarragon

1¼ pounds small new potatoes (1 to 2 inches in
   diameter)
1 hard-cooked large egg, peeled and chopped
3 tablespoons mayonnaise
3 tablespoons sour cream
¼ cup finely chopped dill pickle
1 tablespoon finely chopped shallot
2 tablespoons Dijon mustard
2 teaspoons finely chopped fresh tarragon
   leaves or ½ teaspoon dried, crumbled

In a large saucepan combine potatoes with enough
salted water to cover by 1 inch and simmer until just
tender, about 15 to 20 minutes. Drain potatoes and
cool until they can be handled.

While potatoes are cooling, in a bowl combine remaining ingredients with salt and pepper to taste. Cut
potatoes into ½-inch dice and gently toss with egg
mixture. Serve potato salad chilled or at room temperature. Serves 2.

Potato Salad with Garlic Mayonnaise and Chives

2 pounds small boiling potatoes (1 to 1½ inches
   in diameter)
3 garlic cloves, minced and mashed to a paste
   with 1 teaspoon salt
3½ tablespoons fresh lemon juice plus additional
   to taste if desired
⅓ cup mayonnaise
1 tablespoon hot water
¼ cup chopped fresh chives

In a large saucepan combine potatoes with salted
water to cover by 1 inch and simmer until just tender,
15 to 20 minutes. Drain potatoes and cool until they
can be handled.

While potatoes are cooling, in a large bowl whisk
together garlic paste, 3½ tablespoons lemon juice,
mayonnaise, and hot water.

Peel potatoes and cut in half. Add potatoes and
chives to dressing and toss well. Season salad with
additional lemon juice and salt and pepper to taste.
*Salad may be made 1 day ahead and chilled, covered.
Before serving, toss salad with 1 to 2 tablespoons
water to moisten dressing.*

Serve potato salad at room temperature. Serves 4 generously.

PHOTO ON PAGE 61

Radish and Mushroom Salad with Parsley

2½ tablespoons vegetable oil
2 tablespoons sour cream
2 teaspoons fresh lemon juice
2 tablespoons minced fresh parsley leaves
10 radishes, sliced thin
6 medium white mushrooms, sliced thin
4 Boston lettuce leaves

In a bowl whisk together oil, sour cream, lemon juice, parsley, and salt and pepper to taste until smooth. Add radishes and mushrooms and toss gently to coat with dressing. Nestle 1 lettuce leaf inside another, rib sides down, and arrange on plate to form a cup. Repeat with remaining lettuce and divide salad between lettuce cups. Serves 2.

Orange and Radish Salad

2 tablespoons fresh lemon juice
½ teaspoon orange-flower water*
1 teaspoon sugar
⅛ teaspoon cinnamon, or to taste
⅛ teaspoon cayenne, or to taste
coarse salt to taste
3 navel oranges
2 large radishes, preferably with leaves

Garnish: small radish leaves

*available at specialty foods shops and some
  supermarkets

In a small bowl stir together lemon juice, orange-flower water, sugar, cinnamon, cayenne, and salt until sugar is dissolved.

With a serrated knife cut away orange peels and pith, discarding them, and cut oranges crosswise into ¼-inch-thick slices. Arrange orange slices on a platter and pour lemon juice mixture over them. Let orange slices macerate 30 minutes.

Trim radishes, reserving small leaves for garnish,

and halve lengthwise. Cut radishes into thin half circles and scatter over orange slices. Garnish salad with radish leaves. Serves 6 as a first course.

PHOTO ON PAGE 56

Tomato, Cucumber, and Avocado with Lemon Vinaigrette

¼ teaspoon finely grated fresh lemon zest
¼ cup fresh lemon juice
1 tablespoon white-wine vinegar
1 cup vegetable oil
1½ pounds vine-ripened tomatoes (about 3),
  chopped
2 seedless cucumbers, chopped
3 avocados (preferably California), chopped

In a bowl whisk together zest, lemon juice, vinegar, and salt and pepper to taste and whisk in oil, whisking until dressing is emulsified.

Put tomatoes, cucumbers, and avocados in 3 separate bowls and toss with dressing. *Vegetables may be made 2 hours ahead and chilled, covered.* Serves 12.

PHOTO ON PAGE 53

Sautéed Apple, Carrot, and Onion Slaw with Pecans

2 tablespoons chopped pecans
1½ tablespoons unsalted butter
1 Granny Smith apple
1 carrot
½ red onion, sliced thin lengthwise
2 tablespoons water
1½ teaspoons sugar
¼ teaspoon salt

In a 10- to 12-inch non-stick skillet sauté pecans in butter over moderately high heat, stirring, until golden and transfer with a slotted spoon to a small dish. Using the julienne blade of a hand-held slicing device or food processor cut apple, cored, and carrot into ⅛-inch julienne strips and add with onion to skillet. In the skillet sauté mixture over moderately high heat, stirring, 1 minute and stir in water, sugar, salt, and pepper to taste. Simmer slaw, covered, until carrot is just tender, 1 to 2 minutes. Serves 2.

Two-Cabbage Slaw

1 carrot, shredded fine
1½ cups thinly sliced green cabbage
   (about ¼ head)
1½ cups thinly sliced red cabbage
   (about ¼ head)
1½ tablespoons extra-virgin olive oil
2 teaspoons rice vinegar (not seasoned)
½ teaspoon sugar

In a bowl toss together carrot and cabbages and drizzle with oil, tossing to coat. Add vinegar, sugar, and salt and pepper to taste and toss well. Let slaw stand 10 minutes. Serves 2 or 3.

Napa Cabbage and Caraway Slaw

2 teaspoons white-wine vinegar
2 tablespoons vegetable oil
2 tablespoons finely chopped scallion
½ teaspoon caraway seeds, chopped fine
3 cups thinly sliced Napa cabbage

In a bowl whisk together vinegar, oil, and salt and pepper to taste. Add scallion, caraway, and cabbage and toss well. Serves 2.

Wilted Red Cabbage and Bell Pepper Slaw

½ cup distilled white vinegar
½ cup water
¼ cup sugar
¾ teaspoon salt
½ teaspoon Dijon mustard
3 tablespoons olive oil
1 tablespoon mustard seeds
½ head red cabbage, shredded (about 3 cups)
2 red or yellow bell peppers, cut into 1-inch
   julienne strips

In a saucepan bring vinegar and water to a boil with sugar, salt, and mustard and simmer, stirring occasionally, 3 minutes.

In a heavy skillet heat oil over moderately high heat until hot but not smoking. Add mustard seeds and sauté until they begin to pop. Stir in cabbage and sauté, stirring, 1 minute. Stir in peppers and sauté, stirring, 1 minute. Add vinegar mixture and simmer vegetables 1 minute.

Drain vegetables in a large fine sieve set over a saucepan and transfer them to a bowl. Boil liquid over moderately high heat until reduced to about 3 tablespoons and stir into vegetables. *Chill slaw, covered, at least 1 hour or overnight.* Serves 4.

PHOTO ON PAGE 48

Carrot and Celery Slaw with Yogurt Caraway Dressing

¼ cup plain yogurt
1 tablespoon mayonnaise
¼ teaspoon caraway seeds, chopped fine
1 cup shredded carrot
1 cup paper-thin slices peeled celery

In a bowl whisk together yogurt, mayonnaise, caraway seeds, and salt and pepper to taste and stir in carrot and celery. Serves 2.

Celery Root, Gruyère, and Apple Slaw with Horseradish

½ pound Gruyère cheese
1 medium celery root
1½ Granny Smith apples
2 tablespoons fresh lemon juice
¾ cup mayonnaise
2 tablespoons spicy brown mustard
1 tablespoon honey
1 teaspoon salt
about 3 tablespoons bottled horseradish, drained,
   or grated fresh horseradish to taste

Cut cheese into matchsticks and put in a large bowl. Peel celery root and apples and cut into matchsticks. Add celery root, apples, and lemon juice to cheese, tossing gently.

In a small bowl stir together remaining ingredients and add to slaw, tossing gently. *Slaw may be made 1 day ahead and chilled, covered. Add additional horseradish to taste before serving if necessary.* Season slaw with salt and pepper. Serves 6.

PHOTO ON PAGE 70

Black-Eyed Pea and Cabbage Slaw

1½ cups dried black-eyed peas, picked over
1 bay leaf
2 parsley sprigs plus 1 cup minced parsley leaves
¼ cup white-wine vinegar
3 tablespoons Dijon mustard
⅓ cup drained bottled horseradish
¾ cup vegetable oil
a 2½- to 3-pound cabbage, grated coarse in a food
    processor (about 10 cups)
6 carrots, grated coarse in a food processor
    (about 4 cups)
½ cup minced scallion
2 large garlic cloves, minced

Soak peas in enough water to cover by 2 inches overnight. Drain peas and rinse. In a large saucepan simmer peas, bay leaf, and parsley sprigs in enough water to cover by 2 inches until tender, about 25 minutes. *Peas may be cooked 2 days ahead and chilled, covered.*

Drain peas and discard bay leaf and parsley sprigs. In a large bowl whisk together vinegar, mustard, horseradish, and salt and pepper to taste and add oil in a stream, whisking until dressing is emulsified. Add peas, cabbage, carrots, scallion, garlic, minced parsley, and salt and pepper to taste and toss well. *Slaw may be made 1 day ahead and chilled, covered.* Serves 12.

a 6-ounce jar marinated artichoke hearts, drained
    and chopped
a 6- to 7-ounce can tuna, drained
1 red bell pepper, chopped
½ cup finely chopped red onion
1½ tablespoons minced fresh thyme leaves
⅓ cup Kalamata or other brine-cured black olives
    if desired, chopped
2 cups chopped *arugula*, washed and spun dry

In a large saucepan of salted boiling water cook *orzo* until tender and drain in a colander. Rinse *orzo* well under cold water and drain well. Transfer *orzo* to a large bowl.

In a small saucepan of salted boiling water cook beans until crisp-tender, about 4 to 5 minutes. Drain beans and add to *orzo*.

Make dressing:

In a blender blend together vinegar, lemon juice, anchovies, mustard, and garlic paste. With motor running add oil in a stream and blend until emulsified.

Add dressing to *orzo* mixture with artichokes, tuna, bell pepper, onion, thyme, olives, and salt and pepper to taste and toss well. *Salad may be prepared up to this point 1 day ahead and chilled, covered. Bring salad to room temperature before proceeding.*

Add *arugula* and toss well. Serves 4 to 6 as a main course.

PASTA AND GRAIN SALADS

Niçoise Orzo Salad

1 cup (about ½ pound) *orzo* (rice-shaped pasta)
½ pound green beans, cut diagonally into
    ½-inch pieces
For dressing
2 tablespoons red-wine vinegar
1 tablespoon fresh lemon juice
4 anchovies, chopped
1 tablespoon Dijon mustard
1 garlic clove, minced and mashed to a paste
    with ½ teaspoon salt
¼ to ⅓ cup olive oil (preferably extra-virgin)

Herbed Tricolor Pasta Salad

1½ cups plain yogurt
¾ cup mayonnaise
1½ tablespoons white-wine vinegar,
    or to taste
¾ cup minced fresh parsley leaves
1 large red onion, quartered and sliced thin
¾ cup finely chopped assorted fresh herbs such as
    basil, dill, and chives
1½ pounds tricolor pasta such as *penne* or *fusilli**

*available at specialty foods shops

In a large bowl whisk together yogurt, mayonnaise, vinegar, parsley, onion, and herbs.

In a kettle of boiling salted water boil pasta until tender, about 12 minutes. Drain pasta in a large colander and rinse well under cold water. Drain pasta well and toss with dressing and salt and pepper to taste. *Pasta salad may be made 4 hours ahead and chilled, covered. If pasta absorbs dressing while standing, toss with about 3 tablespoons warm water.* Serves 12.

PHOTO ON PAGE 52

Whole-Wheat Pasta Salad with Grilled Zucchini and Olives

1½ pounds vine-ripened tomatoes, chopped
½ cup red onion, chopped fine
2 garlic cloves, minced and mashed to a paste
    with 1 teaspoon salt
2 tablespoons red-wine vinegar
¼ cup olive oil (preferably extra-virgin) plus
    additional for brushing zucchini
1½ pounds zucchini, cut diagonally into
    ⅓-inch-thick slices
1 pound whole-wheat *penne** or other
    tubular pasta
⅔ cup Kalamata or other brine-cured black olives,
    chopped coarse
6 ounces *ricotta salata* or feta cheese,
    diced
1½ cups whole small or torn large fresh basil
    leaves

*available at specialty foods shops, natural foods stores, and many supermarkets

In a large bowl gently stir together tomatoes, onion, garlic paste, vinegar, and ¼ cup oil.

Brush one side of zucchini slices lightly with additional oil and season with salt and pepper. Heat a well-seasoned ridged grill pan over moderate heat until hot and grill zucchini, oiled sides down, in batches, brushing tops with more oil before turning, 1 to 2 minutes on each side, or until just tender but not soft. Transfer zucchini as grilled to a small bowl.

In a kettle of salted boiling water cook pasta until just tender and drain well. Add hot pasta to tomato mixture and toss well. Cool pasta slightly and stir in zucchini, olives, cheese, basil, and salt and pepper to taste. *Pasta may be made 4 hours ahead and kept covered at room temperature.*

Serve pasta warm or at room temperature. Serves 6 as an entrée or 8 as a side dish.

Bulgur and Lentil Salad with Tarragon and Walnuts

⅓ cup finely chopped shallot
3 tablespoons tarragon white-wine vinegar*
½ cup brown or green lentils, preferably
    lentilles du Puy (French green lentils)*
1½ cups water
1 cup bulgur**, preferably fine
1 teaspoon salt
½ cup finely chopped celery

½ cup finely shredded carrot

3 tablespoons finely chopped fresh tarragon leaves

3 tablespoons olive oil, preferably extra-virgin

½ cup walnuts, toasted lightly and chopped fine

*available at specialty foods shops and some
    supermarkets
**available at natural foods stores

In a small bowl combine shallot and 1 tablespoon vinegar. In a small saucepan simmer lentils in water to cover by 2 inches until just tender but not falling apart, about 15 to 20 minutes, and drain well. Add hot lentils to shallot mixture and season with salt and pepper. Cool mixture, stirring occasionally.

In a small heavy saucepan combine 1½ cups water, bulgur, and salt and simmer, covered, until water is absorbed, 12 to 15 minutes. Transfer bulgur to a large bowl and cool completely, stirring occasionally.

Add lentils to bulgur with celery, carrot, tarragon, remaining 2 tablespoons vinegar, oil, walnuts, and salt and pepper to taste and toss well. *Salad may be made 1 day ahead and chilled, covered. Bring salad to room temperature before serving.* Serves 4 as an entrée or 6 as a side dish.

Couscous Salad with Peppers, Olives, and Pine Nuts

2 cups water

⅓ cup currants or raisins

¾ teaspoon salt

4 tablespoons olive oil (preferably extra-virgin)

1½ cups couscous

2 large garlic cloves, minced

1 small onion, chopped fine

2 tablespoons red-wine vinegar

3 red bell peppers, roasted (page 92) and
    chopped

a 3-ounce jar small pimiento-stuffed green olives
    (½ cup packed), drained and sliced thin

2 tablespoons drained capers

½ cup pine nuts, toasted lightly

½ cup finely chopped fresh parsley leaves
    (preferably flat-leafed)

In a small saucepan bring water to a boil with currants or raisins, salt, and 1 tablespoon oil. Stir in

couscous and let stand, covered, off heat 5 minutes. Fluff couscous with a fork and transfer to a bowl.

In a small skillet cook garlic in 2 tablespoons oil over moderate heat, stirring, until pale golden. Add onion and cook, stirring, until softened. Stir onion mixture into couscous with vinegar, bell peppers, olives, capers, pine nuts, parsley, remaining 1 tablespoon oil, and salt and pepper to taste. *Salad may be made 1 day ahead and chilled, covered.* Bring salad to room temperature before serving. Serves 6 to 8 as a side dish.

Herbed Whole-Oat Salad

1 cup whole oats (also called oat groats)*

½ cup minced onion

1 large shallot if desired, minced

1⅛ teaspoons ground allspice

1 teaspoon salt

2 tablespoons fresh lemon juice,
    or to taste

2 tablespoons olive oil (preferably extra-virgin),
    or to taste

½ cup finely chopped fresh parsley leaves

⅓ cup finely chopped fresh mint leaves

1 cucumber, peeled if desired, seeded, and
    chopped

1 cup vine-ripened cherry tomatoes,
    quartered

*available at natural foods stores

In a large saucepan of salted boiling water cook oats 25 minutes. Drain oats in a colander and rinse under cold water. Set colander over a kettle of boiling water (oats should not touch water) and steam oats, covered with a kitchen towel and lid, until fluffy and dry, 5 to 10 minutes (check water level in kettle occasionally, adding water if necessary).

While oats are cooking, in a large bowl stir together onion, shallot, allspice, and salt. Stir in hot oats and cool. Stir in lemon juice, oil, parsley, mint, and salt and pepper to taste. Add cucumber and tomatoes and toss salad gently. *Salad may be made 1 day ahead and chilled, covered (herbs may discolor slightly). Bring salad to room temperature before serving.* Serves 4 to 6 as a side dish.

Quinoa and Black Bean Salad

1½ cups quinoa (small disk-shaped seeds)*
1½ cups cooked black beans, rinsed if canned
1½ tablespoons red-wine vinegar
1½ cups cooked corn (cut from about 2 large ears)
¾ cup finely chopped green bell pepper
2 pickled *jalapeño* chilies, seeded and minced
    (wear rubber gloves)
¼ cup finely chopped fresh coriander
For dressing
5 tablespoons fresh lime juice, or to taste
1 teaspoon salt
1¼ teaspoons ground cumin, or to taste
⅓ cup olive oil

*available at specialty foods shops and natural
    foods stores

In a bowl wash quinoa in at least 5 changes cold water, rubbing grains and letting them settle before pouring off most of water, until water runs clear and drain in a large fine sieve.

In a saucepan of salted boiling water cook quinoa 10 minutes. Drain quinoa in sieve and rinse under cold water. Set sieve over a saucepan of boiling water (quinoa should not touch water) and steam quinoa, covered with a kitchen towel and lid, until fluffy and dry, about 10 minutes (check water level in kettle occasionally, adding water if necessary).

While quinoa is cooking, in a small bowl toss beans with vinegar and salt and pepper to taste.

Transfer quinoa to a bowl and cool. Add beans, corn, bell pepper, *jalapeños,* and coriander and toss.

Make dressing:

In a small bowl whisk together lime juice, salt, and cumin and add oil in a stream, whisking.

Drizzle dressing over salad and toss with salt and pepper to taste. *Salad may be made 1 day ahead and chilled, covered. Bring salad to room temperature before serving.* Serves 4 as an entrée or 8 as a side dish.

"California Roll" Salad
(Sushi Rice Salad with Avocado, Cucumber, and Scallions)

1½ cups long-grain rice
¼ cup plus 3 tablespoons rice vinegar*
    (not seasoned)

¼ cup sugar
1½ teaspoons salt
1 tablespoon sesame seeds
    (preferably unhulled*)
3 tablespoons vegetable oil
2 tablespoons finely chopped pickled ginger*
4 scallions, cut lengthwise into thin 1-inch strips
    (about ¾ cup)
½ cup finely shredded carrot
1 large seedless cucumber (about 1 pound),
    quartered lengthwise, cored, and chopped
2 sheets *nori* (paper-thin sheets of
    dried seaweed)*
1 avocado (preferably California)
¼ pound *surimi* (mock crab legs) if desired,
    sliced thin
For dressing
2 teaspoons *wasabi* (Japanese green horseradish)
    powder*
1 tablespoon hot water
2 tablespoons cold water
2 tablespoons soy sauce
2 teaspoons ginger juice (squeezed from freshly
    grated gingerroot)

*available at Asian markets, natural foods stores,
    and some supermarkets

Into a large saucepan of salted boiling water stir rice and boil 10 minutes. Drain rice in a colander and rinse. Set colander over a kettle of boiling water (rice should not touch water) and steam rice, covered with a kitchen towel and lid, until fluffy and dry, 10 to 15 minutes (check water level in kettle occasionally, adding water if necessary).

While rice is steaming, in a small saucepan bring ¼ cup vinegar to a boil with sugar and salt, stirring until sugar is dissolved, and remove from heat. In a dry small skillet toast sesame seeds over moderate heat, stirring, until golden and fragrant and transfer to a small bowl.

Transfer rice to a large bowl and stir in vinegar mixture. Cool rice and stir in sesame seeds, remaining 3 tablespoons vinegar, oil, ginger, scallions, carrot, and cucumber. *Salad may be prepared up to this point 1 day ahead and chilled, covered. Bring salad to room temperature before proceeding.*

Dry-roast *nori*, 1 sheet at a time, directly above

moderate heat (gas or electric burner), holding it at opposite corners and moving it back and forth, until it turns bright green, 30 seconds to 1 minute. With scissors cut *nori* into thin 2-inch strips.

Peel and pit avocado. Quarter avocado and cut crosswise into thin slices. Add avocado to rice salad with *surimi* if using and two thirds of *nori* strips and toss well.

Make dressing:

In a small bowl stir *wasabi* powder into hot water and stir in cold water, soy sauce, and ginger juice.

Serve salad sprinkled with remaining *nori* strips and drizzled with dressing. Serves 4 to 6 as an entrée or 8 as a side dish.

SALAD DRESSINGS

Balsamic Vinaigrette

2 tablespoons balsamic vinegar
2 tablespoons white-wine vinegar
2 teaspoons Dijon mustard
1 shallot,
    minced
⅔ cup olive oil

In a bowl whisk together vinegars, mustard, shallot, and salt and pepper to taste. Add oil in a stream, whisking, and whisk vinaigrette until emulsified. Makes about 1 cup.

Basil, Mint, and Orange Vinaigrette

½ cup packed fresh basil leaves
½ cup packed fresh mint leaves
¼ teaspoon freshly grated orange zest
1 tablespoon fresh orange juice
2 teaspoons white-wine vinegar,
    or to taste
1 garlic clove,
    chopped
½ cup vegetable oil

In a blender blend together all ingredients until emulsified. Makes about ⅔ cup.

Chutney Garlic Dressing

¼ cup Major Grey's chutney
½ teaspoon dried hot red pepper flakes
2 tablespoons fresh lemon juice
⅓ cup water
2 large garlic cloves, chopped
½ cup vegetable oil

In a blender blend together chutney, red pepper flakes, lemon juice, water, garlic, and salt to taste until smooth. With motor running, add oil in a stream and blend dressing until emulsified. Makes 1 cup.

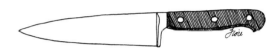

Spicy Ginger Vinaigrette

⅓ cup finely chopped peeled fresh gingerroot
3 garlic cloves, minced
1 shallot, chopped fine (about 2 tablespoons)
1 teaspoon firmly packed brown sugar
1 tablespoon soy sauce
¼ cup seasoned rice vinegar
1 tablespoon fresh lemon juice
¼ teaspoon five-spice powder*
½ teaspoon dried red pepper flakes, or to taste
½ teaspoon salt, or to taste
freshly ground black pepper to taste
1 cup vegetable oil

*available at Asian markets and many specialty
    foods shops and supermarkets

In a blender blend all ingredients except oil until smooth. With motor running, add oil in a stream and blend dressing until emulsified. Transfer vinaigrette to a jar with a tight-fitting lid. *Vinaigrette keeps, covered and chilled, 1 week.* Makes about 2 cups.

Honey Lemon Buttermilk Dressing

¼ teaspoon freshly grated lemon zest
2 teaspoons fresh lemon juice
1 tablespoon plus 1 teaspoon honey
½ cup buttermilk
¼ cup plain yogurt
1 tablespoon vegetable oil
¼ teaspoon vanilla

In a bowl whisk together zest, lemon juice, and honey until combined well and whisk in buttermilk, yogurt, oil, vanilla, and a pinch of salt.

Serve buttermilk dressing with fruit salad. Makes about ¾ cup.

Miso Vinaigrette

2 tablespoons red *miso*
  (fermented bean paste)*
2 teaspoons Dijon mustard
1 tablespoon water
1½ tablespoons fresh lemon juice
¼ cup vegetable oil
1 teaspoon minced peeled fresh gingerroot
1 scallion, minced

*available at Asian markets and natural
  foods stores

In a bowl mash together *miso* and mustard and whisk in water and juice. Add oil in a stream, whisking, and whisk vinaigrette until emulsified. Whisk in gingerroot and scallion. Makes about ½ cup.

Roquefort and Toasted Pecan Dressing

2 tablespoons fresh lemon juice
½ cup plain yogurt
¼ cup olive oil
¼ cup packed fresh parsley leaves
¼ pound Roquefort or blue cheese, crumbled
  (about ¾ cup)
½ cup pecans, toasted lightly and cooled

In a blender blend together all ingredients with salt and pepper to taste until smooth. Makes 1½ cups.

Spiced Tahini Dressing

½ teaspoon whole cuminseed
½ teaspoon whole coriander seeds
¼ cup *tahini* (sesame seed paste)*
¼ cup hot water
2 teaspoons white-wine vinegar, or to taste
½ cup sour cream

*available at natural foods stores and some
  supermarkets

In a dry small heavy skillet toast cuminseed and coriander seeds over moderate heat, shaking skillet, until spices are fragrant, about 2 minutes. Cool spices completely and in a mortar with a pestle or in an electric spice or coffee grinder grind fine.

In a bowl whisk together *tahini* and water until smooth and whisk in spices, vinegar, sour cream, and salt and pepper to taste. Thin dressing with additional water if necessary. Makes about 1 cup.

Salsa Vinaigrette

1 cup chopped peeled seeded vine-ripened tomato
   (about ¾ pound)
3 tablespoons chopped onion
1 small *jalapeño* chili, chopped (wear rubber
   gloves)
2½ tablespoons fresh lime juice
¼ cup vegetable oil
2 tablespoons finely chopped fresh coriander

In a blender blend together tomato, onion, *jalapeño*, lime juice, and salt to taste until smooth. With motor running, add oil in a stream and blend vinaigrette until emulsified. Stir coriander into vinaigrette. Makes about 1¼ cups.

Dried Tomato, Caper, and Olive Dressing

½ cup mayonnaise
1 tablespoon fresh lemon juice
1 tablespoon dried tomatoes packed in oil,
   minced
1 tablespoon drained bottled capers,
   minced
1 tablespoon minced pitted drained Kalamata or
   other brine-cured black olives
2 tablespoons water, or enough to
   thin dressing to desired
   consistency

In a bowl whisk together all ingredients with salt and pepper to taste. Makes about ¾ cup.

SAUCES

Cranberry Quince Chutney

a 12-ounce bag fresh or unthawed frozen
   cranberries, picked over
1 cup quince preserves* or apple jelly
1 red bell pepper, chopped (about 1 cup)
¼ cup firmly packed dark brown sugar
¾ teaspoon ground coriander seeds
1 teaspoon mustard seeds
¾ teaspoon dried hot red pepper flakes
1 teaspoon salt
¼ teaspoon freshly ground black pepper
½ cup raisins
¼ cup cider vinegar
a 4-inch strip fresh lemon zest, removed with
   a vegetable peeler
1 medium onion, sliced (about 1 cup)

*available at specialty foods shops and some
   supermarkets and by mail order from Grace's
   Marketplace, 1237 Third Avenue, New York,
   NY 10021, tel. (212) 737-0600

In a large saucepan combine all ingredients except
onion and simmer, stirring occasionally, 30 minutes.
Add onion and simmer 20 minutes, or until chutney is
thickened. *Chutney may be made 1 week ahead and
chilled, covered.*
   Serve chutney chilled or at room temperature.
Makes about 3½ cups, serving 8.

PHOTO ON PAGE 77

Garlic Rosemary Jelly

1¾ cups dry white wine
¼ cup white-wine vinegar
⅓ cup finely chopped garlic
¼ cup finely chopped fresh rosemary
   leaves
3½ cups sugar
a 3-ounce pouch liquid pectin
four ½-pint Mason-type jars, sterilized
   (procedure follows)

In a kettle stir together well wine, vinegar, garlic,
rosemary, and sugar and bring mixture to a rolling
boil over high heat, stirring constantly. Stir in pectin
quickly and bring mixture back to a full rolling boil.

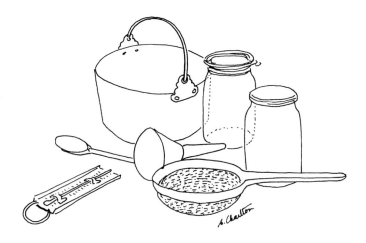

Boil jelly, stirring constantly, 1 minute and remove kettle from heat.

Skim off any foam and ladle jelly immediately into jars, filling to within ⅛ inch of top. Wipe rims with dampened cloth and seal jars with lids.

Put jars in water-bath canner or on a rack set in a large deep kettle. Add enough hot water to cover jars by 2 inches and bring to a boil. Boil jars, covered, 5 minutes and transfer with tongs to a rack. Cool jars completely and store in a cool, dark place. Makes four ½-pint jars.

PHOTO ON PAGE 33

To Sterilize Jars and Glasses for Pickling and Preserving

Wash jars in hot suds and rinse in scalding water. Put jars in a kettle and cover with hot water. Bring water to a boil, covered, and boil jars 15 minutes from the time that steam emerges from the kettle. Turn off heat and let jars stand in hot water. Just before they are to be filled invert jars onto a kitchen towel to dry. (Jars should be filled while still hot.) Sterilize jar lids 5 minutes, or according to manufacturer's instructions.

Gingerroot Shallot Marmalade

10 shallots, sliced thin lengthwise
2 tablespoons julienne strips peeled fresh
   gingerroot
2 tablespoons unsalted butter
1 garlic clove, cut into
   thin strips
½ cup chicken broth
⅓ cup balsamic vinegar
¼ cup honey
¼ teaspoon salt
¼ teaspoon freshly ground black pepper

In a heavy 10-inch skillet (preferably cast-iron) cook shallots and gingerroot in butter over moderate heat, stirring frequently, until pale golden, about 12 minutes. Add garlic and cook, stirring, 1 minute. Increase heat to moderately high and stir in remaining ingredients. Cook mixture, stirring frequently, until syrupy and almost all liquid is absorbed, about 12

minutes. *Marmalade keeps, covered and chilled, up to 2 weeks.*

Serve marmalade with meat, poultry, fish, or vegetables. Makes about 1 cup.

Mustard Sauce

½ cup Dijon mustard
2 tablespoons sugar
¼ cup white-wine vinegar
⅔ cup vegetable oil
3 to 4 tablespoons water

In a bowl whisk together mustard, sugar, and vinegar until sugar is dissolved and whisk in oil until sauce is emulsified. Whisk in water to thin sauce to the desired consistency. *Sauce may be made 1 day ahead and chilled, covered. Serve sauce at room temperature.* Makes about 1½ cups.

PHOTO ON PAGE 23

Gingerroot Pear Sauce

10 small ripe pears (about 3 pounds)
1 cup pear nectar
4 dried pear halves*, chopped
¼ cup sugar, or to taste
2 tablespoons unsalted butter
1 tablespoon julienne strips peeled fresh
   gingerroot
1 tablespoon fresh lemon juice
1 cinnamon stick
1 teaspoon vanilla

*available at health foods stores and specialty
   foods shops

Peel, core, and finely chop fresh pears. In a saucepan simmer fresh pears, nectar, dried pears, sugar, butter, gingerroot, lemon juice, cinnamon stick, and a pinch of salt until pears are tender, about 25 minutes. Remove pan from heat and stir in vanilla. Discard cinnamon stick.

Force pear mixture through a food mill or ricer, or in a food processor purée to desired consistency.

Serve sauce on its own or as an accompaniment to meats. Makes about 4 cups.

Pesto

1 cup packed fresh basil leaves
3 tablespoons pine nuts or chopped walnuts,
    toasted lightly and cooled
1 large garlic clove, chopped
3 tablespoons freshly grated Parmesan cheese
⅓ cup olive oil

In a blender or small food processor blend together all ingredients with salt and pepper to taste until smooth. Pesto *keeps, covered and chilled, 1 week.* Makes about ⅔ cup.

Homemade Tomato Ketchup

4 medium onions, chopped
4 garlic cloves, chopped
four 28-ounce cans whole tomatoes,
    drained
½ cup sugar
1 cup cider vinegar
1 teaspoon whole cloves
1 teaspoon whole allspice berries,
    crushed
1 cinnamon stick
1 teaspoon celery seed
2 teaspoons dry mustard
1 teaspoon paprika
Tabasco to taste

In a heavy kettle cook onions, garlic, and tomatoes, covered, over moderately low heat, stirring occasionally, until onions are very soft, about 40 minutes. Force mixture through a food mill fitted with coarse disk into a bowl.

In cleaned kettle stir together purée, sugar, and vinegar and simmer, uncovered, stirring frequently to prevent scorching, until reduced by half, about 20 minutes.

Tie cloves, allspice, cinnamon, and celery seed in a cheesecloth bag and add to tomato mixture with mustard and paprika. Simmer mixture, stirring, until very thick, about 10 minutes. Discard bag and season mixture with Tabasco and salt. *Ketchup may be made 10 days ahead and chilled, covered.*

Makes about 1½ cups.

PHOTO ON PAGE 52

Winter Salsa with Chipotle and Orange

1 yellow bell pepper, chopped coarse
1 onion, chopped coarse
5 tablespoons olive oil
1 navel orange
1 tablespoon minced canned *chipotle* chilies in
    adobo*, or to taste
a 28-ounce can whole Italian plum tomatoes,
    seeded and drained well
1 small green bell pepper, diced
1 tablespoon chopped fresh coriander
1 tablespoon fresh lime juice

*available at Hispanic markets, some specialty
    foods shops, and by mail order from Los
    Chileros de Nuevo Mexico, P.O. Box 6215,
    Santa Fe, NM 87502, tel. (505) 471-6967, or
    Adriana's Caravan, Brooklyn, NY,
    tel. (800) 316-0820 or (718) 436-8565

In a skillet sauté yellow bell pepper and onion in 1½ tablespoons oil over moderately high heat until vegetables are just tender and beginning to brown.

Grate ½ teaspoon zest from orange and reserve. Squeeze juice from orange. Add orange juice and chilies to onion mixture and cook 1 minute.

Chop tomatoes coarse and in a bowl combine with reserved zest, onion mixture, green bell pepper, coriander, and lime juice. In a blender purée ¼ cup *salsa* and with blender on medium speed add remaining 3½ tablespoons oil gradually to purée in a thin stream. Stir purée into *salsa* and transfer to a jar with a tight-fitting lid. Salsa *keeps, covered and chilled, 1 week.* Makes about 3 cups.

FLAVORED OILS

Chipotle Pepper Oil

2 dried *chipotle* peppers*
½ cup peanut or vegetable oil

*available at Hispanic markets and some specialty
    foods shops

Preheat oven to 300° F.

Wearing rubber gloves, remove seeds from peppers and reserve ¼ teaspoon seeds.

Crumble peppers into a 1-cup metal measure or very small metal bowl and add reserved seeds and oil. Set measuring cup or bowl on a baking sheet and cook in lower third of oven 1 hour. Cool on a rack 30 minutes.

Line a small strainer with several layers of cheesecloth and strain oil into a glass jar. *Flavored oil keeps, covered loosely and refrigerated at all times, 1 month.* Makes about ½ cup.

Curry Oil

4 teaspoons curry powder
½ cup peanut or vegetable oil

Preheat oven to 300° F.

In a 1-cup metal measure or very small metal bowl combine curry powder and oil. Set measuring cup or bowl on a baking sheet and cook in lower third of oven 40 minutes. Cool on a rack 30 minutes.

Line a small strainer with several layers of cheesecloth and strain oil into a glass jar. *Flavored oil keeps, covered loosely and refrigerated at all times, 1 month.* Makes about ½ cup.

Lemon Spice Oil

1 teaspoon freshly grated lemon zest
10 whole cloves
1 bay leaf
½ teaspoon cinnamon
½ teaspoon whole allspice
½ teaspoon whole black peppercorns
1 tablespoon fresh lemon juice
½ cup peanut or vegetable oil

Preheat oven to 300° F.

With a mortar and pestle or a spice grinder grind coarse zest, cloves, bay leaf, cinnamon, allspice, and peppercorns with lemon juice to form a paste.

In a 1-cup metal measure or very small metal bowl stir together paste and oil. Set measuring cup or bowl on a baking sheet and cook in lower third of oven 1 hour. Cool on a rack 30 minutes.

Line a small strainer with several layers of cheesecloth and strain oil into a glass jar. *Flavored oil keeps, covered loosely and refrigerated at all times, 1 month.* Makes about ½ cup.

Dill Caraway Oil

1 teaspoon caraway seeds
½ cup chopped fresh dill
½ cup vegetable oil

Preheat oven to 300° F.

With a mortar and pestle or in a spice grinder grind caraway seeds coarse. In a 1-cup measure or very small metal bowl combine seeds with remaining ingredients. Set measuring cup or bowl on a baking sheet and cook in lower third of oven 1 hour. Cool on a rack 30 minutes.

Line a small strainer with several layers of cheesecloth and strain oil into a glass jar. *Flavored oil keeps, covered loosely and refrigerated at all times, 1 month.* Makes about ½ cup.

Orange Rosemary Oil

1 tablespoon fennel seeds
zest of 1 navel orange, removed with vegetable
    peeler and chopped
1 tablespoon chopped fresh rosemary leaves
½ cup peanut or vegetable oil

Preheat oven to 300° F.

With a mortar and pestle or a spice grinder grind fennel seeds coarse. In a 1-cup metal measure or very small metal bowl combine seeds with other ingredients. Set measuring cup or bowl on a baking sheet and cook in lower third of oven 1 hour and 20 minutes. Cool on a rack 30 minutes.

Line a small strainer with several layers of cheesecloth and strain oil into a glass jar. *Flavored oil keeps, covered loosely and refrigerated at all times, 1 month.* Makes about ½ cup.

Pesto Oil

½ cup packed fresh basil leaves
1 small garlic clove, crushed
½ cup olive or vegetable oil

Preheat oven to 300° F.

In a 1-cup metal measure or very small metal bowl combine all ingredients. Set measuring cup or bowl on a baking sheet and cook in lower third of oven 1 hour. Cool on a rack 30 minutes.

Line a small strainer with several layers of cheesecloth and strain oil into a glass jar. *Flavored oil keeps, covered loosely and refrigerated at all times, 1 month.* Makes about ½ cup.

DESSERT SAUCES

Mexican Chocolate Sauce

8 ounces Mexican chocolate*, chopped
½ cup water
¼ cup heavy cream
1 tablespoon Kahlúa or other coffee-flavored
    liqueur

*available by mail from Kitchen, 218 Eighth
    Avenue, New York, NY 10011,
    tel. (212) 243-4433

In a metal bowl set over a saucepan of barely simmering water combine chocolate and water and stir until chocolate is melted and sauce is somewhat smooth, about 20 minutes. (Most of the water will have evaporated and mixture will have thickened slightly.) Remove bowl from heat and stir in cream and liqueur until combined well. Cool sauce completely and transfer to a jar with a tight-fitting lid. *Sauce keeps, covered and chilled, 1 month.* Serve sauce over ice cream. Makes about 1¼ cups.

Sambuca Chocolate Sauce

½ cup water
⅔ cup sugar
¾ cup unsweetened cocoa powder
    (preferably Dutch process)
½ teaspoon salt
½ cup heavy cream
½ stick (¼ cup) unsalted butter
1 teaspoon vanilla
¼ cup Sambuca, or to taste

In a small heavy saucepan combine water and sugar and boil, stirring, until sugar is dissolved. Remove pan from heat and whisk in cocoa powder, whisking until smooth. Whisk in salt, cream, and butter and return pan to moderately low heat, whisking until butter is melted. Simmer sauce until thickened slightly, about 2 minutes, and stir in vanilla and Sambuca. Cool sauce completely and transfer to a jar with a tight-fitting lid. *Sauce keeps, covered and chilled, 1 month.* Serve sauce warm over ice cream. Makes about 2 cups.

Ginger Crème Anglaise

1¾ cups half-and-half
½ vanilla bean, split lengthwise
3 tablespoons finely chopped crystallized ginger
2 large eggs
¼ cup sugar

In a small heavy saucepan bring half-and-half just to a boil with vanilla bean and ginger and remove pan from heat. Scrape seeds from vanilla bean with a knife into pan, reserving pod for another use.

While half-and-half mixture is heating, in a bowl with an electric mixer whisk together eggs and sugar until light and fluffy. Add hot half-and-half mixture in a stream, beating, and transfer to a saucepan. Cook custard over moderately low heat, stirring constantly with a wooden spoon, until thickened (170° F. on a candy thermometer), but do not let it boil, and strain through a fine sieve into a metal bowl. Set bowl in a bowl of ice and cold water and cool sauce, stirring occasionally. Chill sauce, covered, at least 2 hours, or until very cold. Crème anglaise *may be made 2 days ahead and chilled, covered.* Makes about 2 cups.

Gingerroot Custard Sauce

1 cup heavy cream
1½ tablespoons minced peeled fresh gingerroot
¼ teaspoon freshly grated lemon zest
⅛ teaspoon coriander seeds,
    crushed
3 large egg yolks
3 tablespoons sugar
½ teaspoon vanilla

In a small saucepan bring heavy cream, gingerroot, lemon zest, and coriander seeds just to a boil. Remove saucepan from heat and let mixture stand, covered, 15 minutes.

In a bowl with an electric mixer beat yolks with sugar until mixture is thick and pale and forms a ribbon when beaters are lifted. Whisk yolk mixture into cream and heat mixture over moderately low heat, whisking, until a candy thermometer registers 160° F. Remove pan from heat and stir in vanilla. Strain sauce through a fine sieve into a bowl.

Serve sauce, warm or chilled, with fresh berries, poached fruit, or pound cake. Makes about 2 cups.

DESSERTS

Chocolate Pound Cake

3 cups cake flour (not self-rising)
1 cup unsweetened Dutch-process cocoa powder
1 teaspoon salt
4 sticks (2 cups) unsalted butter, softened
2 cups granulated sugar
1 tablespoon vanilla
8 large eggs
2 tablespoons instant espresso powder dissolved in
    ¼ cup warm water
confectioners' sugar for sifting over cake

Preheat oven to 350° F. and butter and flour a 3-quart bundt pan, knocking out excess flour. (Alternatively, use two 1-quart bundt pans and 2 pint-size loaf pans, 6 by 3 by 2 inches.)
Into a bowl sift together flour, cocoa, and salt.

In a large bowl with an electric mixer beat together butter and granulated sugar until light and fluffy. Beat in vanilla and add eggs, 1 at a time, beating well after each addition. With mixer on low speed, beat in flour mixture gradually until just combined. Beat in espresso mixture and pour batter into prepared pan(s).

Bake cake in 3-quart pan in middle of oven until a tester comes out clean, about 1 hour 20 minutes. (Alternatively, bake cakes in 1-quart pans and loaf pans 40 minutes.) Cool cake in pan(s) on a rack 10 minutes and turn out onto rack to cool completely. *Pound cake keeps, wrapped well in plastic, 1 week.*

Before serving, sift confectioners' sugar over cake.

Chocolate Almond Torte

¾ cup whole blanched almonds (about 4 ounces),
    toasted lightly and cooled
½ cup sugar

1½ sticks (¾ cup) unsalted butter, softened
4 large eggs, separated
½ teaspoon freshly grated orange zest
1 tablespoon kirsch
6 ounces fine-quality bittersweet chocolate (not
    unsweetened), broken into pieces and ground
    fine in a food processor

Garnish: confectioners' sugar
Accompaniments
sweetened whipped cream
sour cherry compote (recipe follows)

Preheat oven to 350° F. Line bottom of a buttered 9- by 2-inch cake or springform pan with a round of wax paper. Butter paper and dust pan with flour, knocking out excess.

In food processor pulse almonds with 1 tablespoon sugar until just ground fine. (Do not grind to point when oil is released.)

In a bowl with an electric mixer cream butter with ¼ cup remaining sugar until light and fluffy. Beat in yolks, 1 at a time, beating well after each addition, and beat in zest and kirsch. Stir almond sugar and chocolate into yolk mixture (mixture will be very thick). In another bowl with cleaned beaters beat whites until foamy and add a pinch of salt and remaining 3 tablespoons sugar in a stream, beating until they just hold stiff peaks. Fold one third whites into yolk mixture to lighten and fold in remaining whites gently but thoroughly. Pour batter into prepared pan and smooth top.

Bake torte in middle of oven 45 to 55 minutes, or until it begins to pull away from side of pan. (Torte will fall slightly and continue to set as it cools.) Cool torte in pan on a rack and remove from pan. *Torte may be made 1 day ahead and chilled, covered. Let torte come to room temperature before serving.*

Sprinkle torte with confectioners' sugar and serve with whipped cream and sour cherry compote.

PHOTO ON PAGE 71

218

Sour Cherry Compote

1 cup dried sour cherries, preferably unsweetened*
   (about 5 ounces)
½ cup kirsch
½ cup water
¾ cup cherry jam or preserves
   (about 7 ounces)
1 cinnamon stick,
   broken in half
a 3-inch strip orange zest

*available at specialty foods shops and by
   mail order from Chukar Cherry Company,
   tel. (800) 624-9544

In a small saucepan simmer all ingredients, covered, 5 minutes. Remove pan from heat and let mixture stand, covered, 10 minutes. Remove cover and cool completely. *Compote may be made 2 days ahead and chilled, covered. Let compote come to room temperature before serving.* Serves 6.

PHOTO ON PAGE 71

Chocolate Almond Sherry Cake

1 cup almonds with skins
½ cup plus 1 tablespoon sugar
2 ounces fine-quality bittersweet chocolate
   (not unsweetened), broken
   into pieces
4 large eggs,
   separated
¼ teaspoon salt
⅓ cup fresh orange juice
¼ cup medium-dry Sherry

Accompaniments
Sherry custard sauce (recipe follows)
caramelized pears (recipe follows)

Preheat oven to 350° F. Line bottom of a buttered 8-inch round cake pan (2 inches deep) with a round of foil and butter foil.

In a food processor grind almonds fine with ¼ cup sugar. Add chocolate and, pulsing motor, chop into ¼-inch pieces.

In a bowl with an electric mixer beat yolks with ¼ cup remaining sugar until thick and pale and stir in almond mixture. (Mixture will be very stiff.)

In a large bowl with cleaned beaters beat whites with salt until they just hold stiff peaks. Stir one third whites into almond mixture to lighten it and fold in remaining whites gently but thoroughly.

Pour batter into pan, smoothing top, and bake in middle of oven until a tester comes out clean, about 45 minutes. Cool cake in pan on a rack about 5 minutes.

In a small bowl stir together orange juice, Sherry, and remaining 1 tablespoon sugar until sugar is dissolved. With a skewer poke holes evenly in top of cake and spoon juice mixture evenly over cake.

Cool cake completely. Run knife around edge of pan and invert cake onto plate (discard foil). *Cake keeps, wrapped and chilled, 5 days.*

Serve cake at room temperature with Sherry custard sauce and caramelized pears.

PHOTO ON PAGE 16

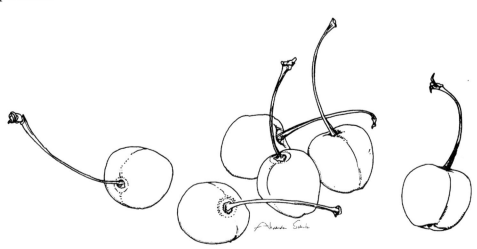

Sherry Custard Sauce

½ cup half-and-half
1 large egg yolk
1 tablespoon sugar
1 tablespoon medium-dry Sherry

In a small saucepan heat half-and-half over moderate heat until it barely simmers. In a small bowl whisk together yolk, sugar, Sherry, and a pinch of salt.

Whisk ¼ cup half-and-half into yolk mixture to temper it and pour yolk mixture into remaining half-and-half, whisking.

Cook sauce over moderate heat, whisking, until thickened (160° F. on a candy thermometer), about 3 minutes, being careful not to let it boil. Transfer sauce to a small pitcher and chill, covered partially, at least 30 minutes. *Sauce keeps, covered and chilled, 2 days.* Makes about ⅔ cup.

PHOTO ON PAGE 16

Caramelized Pears

1 firm-ripe Bosc pear
1 tablespoon unsalted butter
1 tablespoon sugar

Cut pear (unpeeled) into eighths and trim core. In a heavy 8-inch skillet heat butter over moderately high heat until melted and foamy. Add pear wedges and sauté 1 minute on each side. Sprinkle sugar over pear wedges and sauté, turning a few times, until sugar is caramelized and pear is tender, 2 to 4 minutes. Serves 2.

PHOTO ON PAGE 16

Individual Coconut Rum Chocolate Cakes

3 ounces fine-quality bittersweet chocolate
    (not unsweetened), chopped
½ stick (¼ cup) unsalted butter
½ cup sugar
2 large eggs
2 tablespoons dark rum
½ teaspoon vanilla
½ teaspoon salt

⅓ cup all-purpose flour
½ cup sweetened flaked coconut, toasted and
    cooled

Accompaniments
vanilla ice cream or whipped cream
toasted sweetened flaked coconut

Preheat oven to 350° F. and butter and flour six ½-cup muffin tins.

In a metal bowl set over a pan of simmering water melt chocolate with butter, whisking until smooth. Remove bowl from heat and whisk in sugar. Whisk in eggs, 1 at a time, and add remaining ingredients, whisking until combined well. Divide batter among prepared tins and bake in middle of oven until a tester comes out clean, 20 to 25 minutes.

Turn cakes out onto a rack and serve warm or at room temperature with accompaniments. Makes 6 small cakes.

Raspberry Chocolate Meringue Icebox Cake

4 large egg whites
¼ teaspoon cream of tartar
1½ cups sugar
2¾ cups heavy cream
6 ounces fine-quality bittersweet chocolate
    (not unsweetened), chopped

1½ teaspoons unflavored gelatin
3 tablespoons cold water
1½ cups sour cream
1 teaspoon vanilla
3 pints fresh raspberries

Preheat oven to 250° F. Line 2 baking sheets with parchment paper and trace three 8-inch circles onto paper.

In a large bowl with an electric mixer beat whites with cream of tartar and a pinch salt until they just hold soft peaks. Add 1 cup granulated sugar gradually, beating, and beat meringue until it holds stiff peaks. Transfer meringue to a pastry bag fitted with a ¾-inch plain tip and pipe onto circles, filling them in. Smooth meringues with a long metal spatula or knife. (Alternatively, if pastry bag is not used, circles may be made by spreading meringues freehand with spatula.)

Bake meringues 30 minutes and switch position of baking sheets in oven. Bake meringues 30 minutes more, or until pale golden and crisp. (If the weather is humid, cooking time may be longer.) Cool meringues completely and peel off paper. *Meringues may be made 1 day ahead and kept in turned-off oven.*

In a saucepan bring ¼ cup heavy cream just to a boil and remove from heat. Add chocolate and stir mixture until chocolate is melted completely. Divide *ganache* between 2 meringue layers and gently spread evenly, leaving ½-inch borders. Chill *ganache* until hardened, about 10 minutes.

In a small saucepan sprinkle gelatin over water and soften 1 minute. Heat mixture over low heat, stirring until gelatin is dissolved, and keep warm. In a bowl with an electric mixer beat remaining 2½ cups heavy cream with remaining ½ cup sugar until it just holds stiff peaks and beat in sour cream and vanilla. Add gelatin mixture in a stream, beating, and beat until mixture holds stiff peaks.

Arrange 1 *ganache*-topped meringue on a plate and spread it with about 1½ cups cream mixture, mounding it at the edge. Arrange 1 pint raspberries over cream mixture and top with second *ganache*-topped meringue. Repeat procedure with about 1½ cups more cream mixture and another pint raspberries and top with third meringue.

Transfer about 1 cup more cream mixture to pastry bag fitted with a star tip and reserve for decoration.

Frost top and side of cake with remaining cream mixture and decorate with reserved mixture. *Chill cake at least 2 hours and up to 8 hours.* Remove wax paper carefully and scatter remaining pint raspberries on and around cake. Cut cake into 12 wedges with a serrated or electric knife.

Mocha Rum Cake

unsweetened cocoa powder
   for dusting pan
3 cups all-purpose flour
1½ teaspoons baking soda
¾ teaspoon salt
¾ pound fine-quality bittersweet chocolate
   (not unsweetened), chopped
3 sticks (1½ cups) unsalted butter,
   cut into pieces
⅓ cup dark rum
2 cups strong brewed coffee
2¼ cups granulated sugar
3 large eggs, beaten lightly
1½ teaspoons vanilla

Garnish: confectioners' sugar for dusting
Accompaniment: lightly sweetened whipped
   cream

Preheat oven to 300° F. Butter a 4½-inch-deep (12-cup) *Kugelhupf* or bundt pan and dust with cocoa powder, knocking out excess.

In a bowl whisk together flour, baking soda, and salt. In a large metal bowl set over a saucepan of barely simmering water melt chocolate and butter, stirring until smooth. Remove chocolate from heat and stir in rum, coffee, and granulated sugar. With an electric mixer beat in flour mixture, ½ cup at a time, scraping down side, and beat in eggs and vanilla until batter is combined well. Pour batter into prepared pan.

Bake cake in middle of oven until a tester comes out clean, about 1 hour and 50 minutes. Let cake cool completely in pan on a rack and turn it out onto rack. *Mocha rum cake may be made 3 days ahead and chilled, wrapped well .*

Dust cake with confectioners' sugar and serve with whipped cream.

PHOTO ON PAGE 15

Lemon Raspberry Wedding Cake

For each batch of batter

2½ cups cake flour (not self-rising)

2½ teaspoons baking powder

1¼ teaspoons salt

1 stick (½ cup) plus 2 tablespoons unsalted butter, softened

1¼ cups sugar

3 large eggs

1½ teaspoons vanilla

1 cup milk

1½ tablespoons freshly grated lemon zest

Note: 2 separate batches of this batter are required in this recipe (do not double)

For syrup

⅔ cup sugar

1 cup water

zest of 1 large lemon removed in strips with a vegetable peeler

⅓ cup fresh lemon juice

2 tablespoons *eau-de-vie de framboise*

For assembly

two 9-inch cardboard rounds*

two 7-inch cardboard rounds*

two 6-inch cardboard rounds*, trimmed to form 5-inch rounds

lemon meringue buttercream (page 224)

about 5 cups raspberries, picked over

five 8-inch plastic straws

#66 leaf tip*

#70 leaf tip*

#113 leaf tip*

Note: A cake-decorating turntable is extremely helpful for assembling and decorating a wedding cake*

Decoration: crystallized edible flowers and mint leaves**

Accompaniments

crème fraîche ice cream (page 224)

raspberries

*available by mail order from The Chocolate Gallery, 34 West 22nd Street, New York, NY 10010, tel. (212) 675-CAKE

**available by mail order from Meadowsweets, tel. (800) 484-7347, code 4884

Make first batch of batter:

Preheat oven to 350° F. and line a buttered 10-inch round cake pan (at least 2 inches deep) with a round of wax paper. Butter paper and dust pan with flour, knocking out excess.

Into a bowl sift together flour, baking powder, and salt. In another bowl with an electric mixer cream butter with sugar until light and fluffy and beat in eggs, 1 at a time, beating well after each addition, and vanilla. Add flour mixture and milk alternately in batches, beginning and ending with flour mixture and beating until just combined after each addition, and beat in zest (do not overmix).

Pour first batch of batter into prepared pan and bake in middle of oven 35 to 40 minutes, or until a tester comes out clean. Cool cake in pan on a rack 5 minutes and invert onto rack. Peel off paper and cool cake completely.

Make second batch of batter:

Line a buttered 6-inch round cake pan and a buttered 8-inch round cake pan (each at least 2 inches deep) with rounds of wax paper. Butter paper and dust pans with flour, knocking out excess.

Make batter in same manner.

Pour 1¾ cups of second batch of batter into prepared 6-inch pan. Pour remaining batter into prepared 8-inch pan. Bake 6-inch cake in middle of oven 30 to 35 minutes and 8-inch cake 35 to 40 minutes, or until a tester comes out clean. Cool cakes in pans on racks 5 minutes and invert onto racks. Peel off paper and cool cakes completely.

Cake layers may be made 2 weeks ahead, wrapped well in plastic wrap and foil, and frozen. Defrost layers (without unwrapping) at room temperature.

Make syrup:

In a saucepan combine sugar, water, and zest and bring to a boil, stirring until sugar is dissolved. Remove pan from heat and let syrup cool. Discard zest and stir in juice and *framboise*. *Syrup may be made 2 weeks ahead and chilled in an airtight container.*

Assemble cake:

With a long serrated knife halve each layer horizontally. Put each 10-inch layer, cut side up, on a 9-inch cardboard round. Put 8-inch layers similarly on 7-inch rounds and 6-inch layers on 5-inch rounds. Brush cut sides of all 6 layers generously with syrup, dividing it evenly among layers, and let layers stand 15 minutes to absorb syrup.

Spread about 1½ cups lemon meringue buttercream on top half of 10-inch layer, cut side up, and arrange enough raspberries, side by side and open ends down, in concentric circles to cover entire layer. Invert bottom half of 10-inch layer, cut side down, on top of raspberries and gently press layers together to form an even tier. (Discard top cardboard round.) Frost top and sides smoothly with some remaining lemon meringue buttercream and chill while assembling remaining 2 tiers.

Assemble and frost 8-inch tier in same manner (use about 1 cup buttercream between layers) and chill while assembling remaining tier. Assemble and frost 6-inch tier in same manner (use about ⅔ cup buttercream between layers) and chill until buttercream is firm.

Cut 3 straws in half and insert 1 straw piece all the way into center of 10-inch bottom tier. Trim straw level with top of tier and insert remaining 5 straw pieces in same manner in a circle about 1½ inches from center straw. (Straws serve to support tiers.) Carefully put 8-inch middle tier (still on cardboard) in center of bottom tier. Cut remaining 2 straws in half and insert into middle tier in same manner, with 1 straw piece in center and remaining 3 straw pieces in a circle around it. Carefully put 6-inch top tier (still on cardboard) in center of middle tier.

Fill in any gaps between tiers with buttercream and transfer remaining buttercream to a pastry bag fitted with a small (#66) leaf tip. Pipe a decorative border around top edge of top tier. With a medium-sized (#70) leaf tip pipe border in same manner around bottom edges of top and middle tiers. With same tip pipe 5 evenly spaced ribbons from top to bottom of cake. (These ribbons will support cascades of crystallized flowers.)

Transfer cake to a cake stand or other serving plate and with a larger (#113) leaf tip pipe border around bottom edge of cake. With same tip pipe mound of buttercream on top of cake. (This mound will support crystallized flower arrangement.)

Arrange crystallized flowers and mint leaves decoratively on top and sides of cake. *Chill cake at least 6 hours and up to 1 day. Let cake stand at cool room temperature (buttercream is sensitive to warm temperatures) 2 to 4 hours before serving.*

Serve cake with *crème fraîche* ice cream and raspberries. Serves about 50 (including top tier).

Lemon Meringue Buttercream

For lemon curd
5 large egg yolks
½ cup plus 2 tablespoons sugar
½ cup fresh lemon juice
½ stick (¼ cup) unsalted butter,
  softened
For buttercream
2 cups sugar
⅔ cup water
8 large egg whites
¾ teaspoon cream of tartar
10 sticks (5 cups) unsalted butter, cut into pieces
  and softened to cool room temperature
½ teaspoon salt
3 to 4 tablespoons *eau-de-vie de framboise*

Make lemon curd:
In a small heavy saucepan whisk together yolks and sugar and whisk in lemon juice, butter, and a pinch salt. Cook mixture over moderately low heat, whisking, until it just reaches boiling point, 5 to 7 minutes (do not let it boil). Strain curd through a fine sieve into a bowl and cool, its surface covered with plastic wrap. Chill curd, covered, at least 4 hours or overnight.

Make buttercream:
In a heavy saucepan combine sugar and water and bring to a boil, stirring until sugar is dissolved. Boil syrup, undisturbed, until it reaches 248° F. on a candy thermometer. While syrup is boiling, in a standing electric mixer beat whites with a pinch salt until foamy and beat in cream of tartar. Beat whites until they just hold stiff peaks and add hot syrup in a stream, beating. Beat mixture at medium speed until *completely* cool, 15 to 20 minutes. Beat in butter, 1 piece at a time, and beat until thick and smooth. (Buttercream will at first appear very thin but as more butter is beaten in, it will thicken.) Beat in lemon curd and salt, beating until smooth, and drizzle in *eau-de-vie de framboise*, 1 tablespoon at a time, beating. *Buttercream may be made 4 days ahead and chilled in an airtight container or 2 weeks ahead and frozen in an airtight container. Let buttercream come completely to room temperature (this may take several hours if frozen) and beat before using.* Makes about 12 cups.

Crème Fraîche Ice Cream

1 pound (about 2 cups) *crème fraîche**
2 cups buttermilk
⅓ cup fresh lemon juice
1¼ cups sugar

*available at specialty foods shops and some
  supermarkets

In a blender blend together all ingredients, scraping down sides, until very smooth, about 2 minutes. Chill mixture until cold and freeze in an ice-cream maker. Makes about 1 quart, serving 12 as an accompaniment to cake.

Macadamia Coconut Cake

For cake
¾ stick (6 tablespoons) unsalted butter, softened
1 cup sugar
1¼ cups cake flour (not self-rising)
1½ teaspoons baking powder
½ teaspoon salt
½ cup milk
1 teaspoon vanilla
3 large egg whites
For filling
⅓ cup plus 3 tablespoons sugar
¾ cup macadamia nuts
3 large egg yolks
¾ cup milk
2 tablespoons cornstarch
¾ teaspoon vanilla
¼ cup chilled heavy cream
For frosting
1 cup sugar
¼ cup water
2 large egg whites
¼ teaspoon salt

1 cup sweetened flaked coconut for coating cake

Garnish: macadamia nuts brushed with honey

Make cake:
Preheat oven to 350° F. Line bottom of a buttered 9- by 2-inch round cake or springform pan with a

round of wax paper. Butter paper and dust pan with flour, knocking out excess.

In a bowl with an electric mixer cream butter with ⅔ cup sugar until light and fluffy. Onto a sheet of wax paper sift together flour, baking powder, and salt. Stir flour into butter mixture alternately with milk in batches, beginning and ending with flour. Stir in vanilla and blend batter until just combined well.

In another bowl with clean beaters beat egg whites until they hold soft peaks. Beat in remaining ⅓ cup sugar gradually and beat meringue until it holds stiff peaks. Stir one fourth meringue into batter to lighten and fold in remaining meringue gently but thoroughly.

Spread batter evenly in prepared pan and bake in middle of oven 30 to 35 minutes, or until cake begins to pull away from side of pan and a tester comes out clean. Cool cake in pan on a rack 10 minutes. Invert cake onto rack and cool completely. *Cake may be made 1 day ahead and kept at room temperature, tightly wrapped.*

Make filling:

In a dry heavy skillet cook ⅓ cup sugar over moderate heat, undisturbed, until it begins to melt. Cook sugar, stirring with a fork, until melted completely and a light caramel. Add macadamia nuts and cook, stirring, until nuts are coated well and caramel is deep golden. Pour praline onto a sheet of foil and cool completely. Break praline into pieces and in a food processor grind fine. (Do not purée to a paste.)

In a small saucepan whisk together remaining 3 tablespoons sugar, egg yolks, milk, and cornstarch. Bring pastry cream to a boil over moderate heat, whisking, and cook over low heat, whisking constantly, 2 minutes. Whisk in vanilla. Transfer pastry cream to a bowl and chill until cold, its surface covered with plastic wrap. (Pastry cream will be stiff.)

In a bowl beat heavy cream until it just holds stiff peaks. Whisk pastry cream to loosen and whisk in praline. Fold in whipped cream and chill filling while making frosting.

Make frosting:

In a metal bowl set over a pan of simmering water whisk together frosting ingredients until mixture is warm and sugar is dissolved. With a hand-held electric mixer on high beat frosting 6 to 7 minutes, or until thick and fluffy. Remove bowl from heat and beat frosting until cooled slightly.

Assemble cake:

With a long serrated knife cut cake horizontally into 3 layers. Spread filling between layers on a cake plate and spread cake with frosting. Coat cake with coconut. *Cake may be made 6 hours ahead and chilled, covered loosely.*

Garnish cake with macadamia nuts. *(In our photo we garnished this cake with Vanda orchids, an edible flower often used to decorate in Hawaii.)*

PHOTO ON PAGE 43

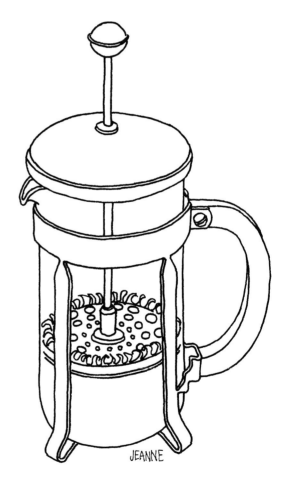

225

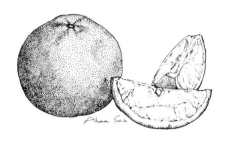

Orange and Sour-Cream Drop Shortcakes
with Assorted Berries

6 cups blackberries, picked over
1 cup granulated sugar
6 cups raspberries, picked over
6 cups blueberries, picked over
For shortcakes
3 cups all-purpose flour
⅓ cup granulated sugar
1 tablespoon baking powder
¾ teaspoon baking soda
¾ teaspoon salt
1½ sticks (¾ cup) cold unsalted butter, cut into bits
1½ teaspoons freshly grated orange zest
1 cup sour cream
1 cup milk

2 cups well-chilled heavy cream
¼ cup confectioners' sugar

In a bowl with a potato masher mash 2 cups black-berries with ⅓ cup granulated sugar and stir in remaining blackberries. In 2 more bowls mash sepa-rately raspberries and blueberries with remaining granulated sugar in same manner. Let berries stand at room temperature 4 hours. *Berry mixtures may be made 1 day ahead and chilled, covered.*

Make shortcakes:
Preheat oven to 425° F. and lightly butter 2 baking sheets.

In a large bowl whisk together flour, granulated sugar, baking powder, baking soda, and salt and blend in butter until mixture resembles coarse meal. In a small bowl whisk together zest, sour cream, and milk and add to flour mixture. Stir mixture until it just forms a soft and sticky dough and drop into 12

mounds at 1-inch intervals onto prepared baking sheets. Pat dough to ½-inch thickness and bake 12 to 15 minutes, or until pale golden. Transfer shortcakes to a rack and cool. *Shortcakes may be made 4 hours ahead and kept in airtight containers.*

In a large bowl beat cream with confectioners' sugar until it holds soft peaks. *Whipped cream may be made 1 hour ahead and chilled in a cheesecloth-lined large sieve set over a bowl, its surface covered with plastic wrap. Whisk cream lightly before serving.*

Split shortcakes horizontally with a fork and serve with berries and whipped cream. Serves 12.

Prune Armagnac Gingerbread

unsweetened cocoa powder for dusting pan
1 cup chopped pitted prunes
½ cup Armagnac or Cognac
1 tablespoon minced peeled fresh gingerroot
3 cups all-purpose flour
2 teaspoons baking soda
2 teaspoons cinnamon
1 teaspoon ground ginger
1 teaspoon ground cloves
⅛ teaspoon cayenne
¾ teaspoon salt
1 cup vegetable shortening at room temperature
1½ cups firmly packed light brown sugar
1 cup unsulfured molasses
½ cup strong brewed coffee
4 large eggs, beaten lightly
1 teaspoon vanilla
½ cup chopped crystallized ginger

Garnish: sliced kumquats
Accompaniment: crème fraîche or sour cream

Preheat oven to 350° F. Butter a 10-inch spring-form pan and dust with cocoa powder, knocking out excess.

In a small skillet cook prunes, Armagnac, and gin-gerroot over moderately high heat, stirring frequently, until almost all liquid is evaporated. Remove pan from heat.

Into a bowl sift flour, baking soda, spices, and salt. In another bowl with an electric mixer cream shorten-ing. Add sugar, beating, and beat mixture until light and fluffy. Add molasses in a stream, beating until combined well. Beat in coffee, flour mixture, eggs, and vanilla until batter is just combined. (It may separate at this point.) Reserve 1 tablespoon crystallized ginger and stir remainder into batter with prune mixture. Turn batter into prepared pan and sprinkle top with reserved ginger.

Bake gingerbread 1 hour and 20 minutes, or until a tester comes out clean, and cool on a rack 1 hour. (The gingerbread will fall slightly in center.)

Garnish gingerbread with kumquats and serve warm or at room temperature with *crème fraîche* or sour cream.

Rhubarb Lemon Cake Roll

For filling
1 pound rhubarb, chopped
  (about 4 cups)
½ cup granulated sugar
1 teaspoon unflavored gelatin
1 tablespoon cold water
For cake
4 large eggs, separated
½ cup granulated sugar
2 teaspoons freshly grated lemon zest
1 teaspoon vanilla
¼ teaspoon salt
¼ cup all-purpose flour
¼ cup cornstarch
confectioners' sugar for dusting
For lemon syrup
2 tablespoons granulated sugar
1 tablespoon fresh lemon juice
1 tablespoon water
For lemon glaze
½ cup confectioners' sugar
1 tablespoon fresh lemon juice

Accompaniment: white chocolate toasted almond
  semifreddo (page 228)

Make filling:
In a heavy saucepan cook rhubarb with sugar over moderate heat, stirring often, 20 to 25 minutes, or until rhubarb is a thick purée (1½ cups). In a small bowl sprinkle gelatin over water and let soften 1

minute. Add gelatin to rhubarb and stir over low heat 1 minute, or until gelatin is dissolved. Transfer filling to a metal bowl set in a bowl of ice and cold water and stir occasionally until cooled and thickened.

Make cake:
Preheat oven to 350° F. Line the bottom of a greased jelly-roll pan, 15½ by 10½ by 1 inch, with foil. Grease foil and dust with flour, knocking out excess.

In a bowl with an electric mixer beat egg yolks, ¼ cup granulated sugar, zest, and vanilla until thick and pale and mixture forms a ribbon when beaters are lifted.

In a large bowl with cleaned beaters beat egg whites with salt until they hold soft peaks. Beat in the remaining ¼ cup granulated sugar gradually and beat whites until they hold stiff peaks.

Stir one third of whites into yolk mixture to lighten it and fold in remaining whites gently but thoroughly. Sift flour and cornstarch over batter and fold in until batter is just combined.

Spread batter evenly in prepared pan and bake in middle of oven 6 to 9 minutes, or until cake is lightly colored and springs back when pressed lightly.

Dust a kitchen towel generously with confectioners' sugar and invert cake onto it. Remove foil carefully from cake. Starting with a long side, roll up cake loosely and gently in kitchen towel and cool 30 minutes.

Make lemon syrup:
In a very small saucepan bring syrup ingredients to a simmer, stirring until sugar is dissolved. Keep lemon syrup warm.

Assemble cake:
Unroll cake carefully and brush with half of warm syrup. Spread cake with filling and reroll cake carefully. Transfer cake to a platter, seam side down, and brush with remaining syrup. Chill roll, covered loosely, at least 2 hours or overnight.

Make lemon glaze:
In a small bowl stir together sugar and lemon juice to make a pourable glaze.

Transfer lemon glaze to a small resealable plastic bag and snip one corner to make a small hole. Trim ends of cake diagonally and squeeze glaze decoratively over cake.

Serve cake, sliced crosswise, with white chocolate toasted almond *semifreddo*.

White Chocolate Toasted Almond Semifreddo

1 scant cup sliced almonds (3½ ounces),
  toasted lightly
¼ teaspoon salt
1 tablespoon unsalted butter
6 ounces fine-quality white chocolate,
  chopped
2 large eggs
⅓ cup sugar
1 teaspoon vanilla
¼ teaspoon almond extract
1½ cups well-chilled heavy cream

Line a metal loaf pan, 8½ by 4½ by 2½ inches, with plastic wrap, leaving a 2-inch overhang on ends, and chill in freezer.

In a skillet cook almonds with salt in butter over moderately low heat, stirring, until almonds are coated well, about 1 minute. Chill almonds until cold.

In a metal bowl set over hot but not simmering water melt chocolate, stirring occasionally, and remove bowl from heat.

In another metal bowl beat eggs with sugar to combine. Set bowl over a pan of simmering water and beat until thick and pale and mixture registers 140° F. on an instant-read thermometer. Continue beating over simmering water 3 minutes (for egg safety) and remove from heat. Beat in chocolate, vanilla, and almond extract.

In another bowl beat cream until it just holds stiff peaks and fold into egg mixture gently but thoroughly. Fold in almonds and pour mixture into prepared pan. Cover pan with plastic wrap and freeze *semifreddo* 8 hours or overnight.

Unmold *semifreddo* onto a platter, discarding plastic wrap, and cut into thick slices. Cut slices crosswise into thirds and serve with rhubarb lemon cake roll. Serves 6 to 8.

COOKIES

Benne Seed Raisin Bars

2 sticks (1 cup) unsalted butter, softened
1 cup firmly packed light brown sugar
⅔ cup *tahini* (sesame seed paste)*
1 large egg
1½ teaspoons vanilla
½ teaspoon salt
2 cups all-purpose flour
1 cup raisins, chopped
½ cup benne (sesame) seeds, toasted lightly
  and cooled

*available at natural foods stores and some
  supermarkets

Preheat oven to 350° F.

In a large bowl with an electric mixer cream butter and sugar until light and fluffy. Add *tahini* and beat until combined well. Beat in egg, vanilla, and salt. Add flour and beat batter until just combined. Beat in raisins and benne seeds. Spread batter evenly in a buttered jelly-roll pan, 15½ by 10½ by 1 inch, and bake in middle of oven until a tester comes out clean, about 16 to 20 minutes. Let cool in pan on a rack and cut into 36 bars. *Bars may be made 3 days ahead and kept in an airtight container.* Makes 36 bars.

PHOTO ON PAGE 15

Coconut Chocolate Chip Cookies

1¼ cups all-purpose flour
1 teaspoon baking soda
1 teaspoon salt
2 sticks (1 cup) unsalted butter, softened
1¼ cups firmly packed light brown sugar
¼ cup granulated sugar
2 large eggs
1 teaspoon vanilla
3 cups sweetened flaked coconut
2 cups (12 ounces) semisweet chocolate chips

Preheat oven to 375° F. and butter baking sheets.

In a bowl whisk together flour, baking soda, and salt. In another bowl with an electric mixer cream butter and sugars until light and fluffy. Beat in eggs, 1 at a time, beating well after each addition, and beat in flour mixture. Beat in vanilla and stir in coconut and chocolate chips.

Drop dough by level tablespoons 2 inches apart onto prepared baking sheets and bake cookies in middle of oven 10 minutes, or until golden. Cool cookies on baking sheets 1 minute and transfer to racks to cool completely. *Cookies keep in airtight containers 5 days.* Makes about 72 cookies.

Chocolate Chip Ginger Crisps

1½ cups all-purpose flour
¾ teaspoon baking powder
½ teaspoon cinnamon, or to taste
⅛ teaspoon ground cloves, or to taste
¼ teaspoon ground cardamom, or to taste

½ teaspoon salt
2 sticks (1 cup) unsalted butter, softened
1 cup firmly packed light brown sugar
1 large egg
⅓ to ½ cup crystallized ginger, chopped fine
1½ cups (9 ounces) semisweet chocolate chips

Preheat oven to 350° F. and butter baking sheets.

In a bowl whisk together flour, baking powder, cinnamon, cloves, cardamom, and salt. In another bowl with an electric mixer cream butter and sugar until light and fluffy and beat in egg. Beat in flour mixture and stir in ginger and chocolate chips.

Drop dough by rounded teaspoons 3 inches apart onto prepared baking sheets and bake cookies in batches in middle of oven 10 to 12 minutes, or until golden. Cool cookies on baking sheets 1 minute and transfer to racks to cool completely. *Cookies keep in airtight containers 5 days.* Makes about 70 cookies.

Chocolate Chip Oatmeal Cookies

2 cups all-purpose flour
1 teaspoon baking soda
½ teaspoon baking powder
1 teaspoon salt
1 cup old-fashioned rolled oats
2 sticks (1 cup) unsalted butter, softened
1¼ cups firmly packed light brown sugar
¼ cup granulated sugar
2 large eggs
1 teaspoon vanilla
2 cups (12 ounces) semisweet chocolate chips

Preheat oven to 350° F. and butter baking sheets.

In a bowl whisk together flour, baking soda, baking powder, salt, and oats. In another bowl with an electric mixer cream butter and sugars until light and fluffy. Beat in eggs, 1 at a time, beating well after each addition, and beat in vanilla. Beat in flour mixture and stir in chocolate chips.

Drop dough by rounded tablespoons 2 inches apart onto prepared baking sheets and bake cookies in batches in middle of oven 12 to 15 minutes, or until golden. Cool cookies on racks. *Cookies keep in airtight containers 5 days.* Makes about 72 cookies.

Double-Peanut Double-Chocolate Chip Cookies

1 cup all-purpose flour
½ cup unsweetened cocoa powder
½ teaspoon baking soda
1 teaspoon baking powder
1½ sticks (¾ cup) unsalted butter, softened
½ cup chunky or creamy peanut butter
1 cup sugar
2 large eggs
1 cup (6 ounces) semisweet chocolate chips
1 cup (6 ounces) peanut-butter chips

Preheat oven to 350° F. and butter baking sheets.

In a bowl whisk together flour, cocoa powder, baking soda, and baking powder. In another bowl with an electric mixer cream butter, peanut butter, and sugar until light and fluffy. Beat in eggs, 1 at a time, beating well after each addition. Beat in flour mixture and stir in chocolate chips and peanut-butter chips.

Drop dough by level tablespoons 2 inches apart onto prepared baking sheets and bake cookies in batches in middle of oven 10 minutes. Cool cookies on racks. *Cookies keep in airtight containers 5 days.* Makes about 60 cookies.

Double Chocolate Walnut Biscotti

2 cups all-purpose flour
½ cup unsweetened cocoa powder
1 teaspoon baking soda
1 teaspoon salt
¾ stick (6 tablespoons) unsalted butter, softened
1 cup granulated sugar
2 large eggs
1 cup walnuts, chopped
¾ cup semisweet chocolate chips
1 tablespoon confectioners' sugar

Preheat oven to 350° F. and butter and flour a large baking sheet.

In a bowl whisk together flour, cocoa powder, baking soda, and salt. In another bowl with an electric mixer beat together butter and granulated sugar until light and fluffy. Add eggs and beat until combined well. Stir in flour mixture to form a stiff dough. Stir in walnuts and chocolate chips.

On prepared baking sheet with floured hands form dough into two slightly flattened logs, each 12 inches long and 2 inches wide, and sprinkle with confectioners' sugar. Bake logs 35 minutes, or until slightly firm to the touch. Cool *biscotti* on baking sheet 5 minutes.

On a cutting board cut *biscotti* diagonally into ¾-inch slices. Arrange *biscotti*, cut sides down, on baking sheet and bake until crisp, about 10 minutes. Cool *biscotti* on a rack. Biscotti *keep in airtight containers 1 week and, frozen, 1 month.* Makes about 30 *biscotti*.

Fudge Bars with Pecan-Graham Crust

For crust
five 5- by 2½-inch graham crackers or
⅔ cup crushed graham crackers
½ cup pecans, toasted lightly
2 tablespoons sugar
¾ stick (6 tablespoons) unsalted butter, melted
¼ teaspoon salt
For fudge layer
4 ounces unsweetened chocolate, chopped
1 stick (½ cup) unsalted butter, cut into pieces
2 large eggs, beaten lightly
¼ teaspoon vanilla
¼ teaspoon salt
2 cups firmly packed light brown sugar
1 cup all-purpose flour

Preheat oven to 350° F.
Make crust:
Into a food processor crumble crackers and grind into crumbs. Add pecans, sugar, butter, and salt and pulse motor until nuts are chopped fine. Press crumb mixture evenly onto bottom of an 11- by 7-inch baking pan and bake in middle of oven 5 minutes. Cool crust in pan on a rack.
Make fudge layer:
In a medium metal bowl set over a saucepan of barely simmering water melt chocolate with butter, stirring. Remove bowl from pan and cool to room temperature. With an electric mixer beat in remaining ingredients, beating until smooth.

Spread fudge layer on top of crust and bake in middle of oven 30 to 35 minutes, or until top is set, edges have begun to pull away from sides of pan, and a tester inserted in center comes out with moist chocolate adhering. While fudge is still hot, score with a sharp knife into 24 small bars and cut into bars, wiping knife blade clean after each cut. Cool bars in pan on a rack. Bars will continue to set as they cool but will remain somewhat soft. *Bars keep in an airtight container 3 days or, covered and chilled, 1 week.* Makes 24 bars.

Granola and Dried Cranberry Chocolate Chip Cookies

1 cup all-purpose flour
½ teaspoon baking soda
¼ teaspoon baking powder
½ teaspoon salt
1 stick (½ cup) unsalted butter,
   softened
¾ cup firmly packed light brown sugar

1 large egg
½ teaspoon vanilla
1½ cups granola
¼ cup dried cranberries,
   chopped
1 cup (6 ounces) semisweet chocolate chips

Preheat oven to 350°F. and butter baking sheets.

In a bowl whisk together flour, baking soda, baking powder, and salt. In another bowl with an electric mixer cream butter and sugar until light and fluffy. Beat in egg, beating until combined well, and beat in vanilla. Beat in flour mixture and stir in remaining ingredients.

Drop dough by rounded tablespoons 2 inches apart onto prepared baking sheets and bake in batches in middle of oven 12 to 15 minutes, or until golden. Cool cookies on racks. *Cookies keep in airtight containers 5 days.* Makes about 36 cookies.

PHOTO ON PAGE 66

Raspberry Cheesecake Brownies

For brownie batter
4 ounces fine-quality bittersweet chocolate,
   chopped
2 ounces unsweetened chocolate, chopped
1 stick (½ cup) unsalted butter
1¼ cups sugar
3 large eggs
1½ teaspoons vanilla
¾ teaspoon salt
¾ cup all-purpose flour
For cheesecake topping
8 ounces cream cheese, softened
⅔ cup sugar
2 teaspoons fresh lemon juice
1 large egg
½ teaspoon vanilla
¼ teaspoon salt
2 tablespoons all-purpose flour

1½ cups raspberries
1 tablespoon sugar

Garnish: confectioners' sugar

Preheat oven to 350° F. and butter and flour a 13-by 9-inch baking pan.
Make brownie batter:
In a metal bowl set over a pan of barely simmering water melt chocolates with butter, stirring, and cool. Whisk in sugar and eggs, 1 at a time, and whisk in vanilla and salt. Whisk in flour until just combined and spread batter evenly in prepared pan.
Make cheesecake topping:
In a bowl with an electric mixer cream together cream cheese and sugar until light and fluffy and beat in lemon juice, egg, vanilla, and salt. Beat in flour and spread mixture evenly over brownie batter.
Scatter raspberries over cheesecake topping and sprinkle with sugar.
Bake brownies in middle of oven 35 to 40 minutes, or until top is puffed and pale golden and a tester comes out with crumbs adhering to it. Cool brownies completely in pan on a rack. *Chill brownies, covered, at least 6 hours or overnight.*
Cut cheesecake brownies into bars and sprinkle with confectioners' sugar.

Serve brownies cold or at room temperature. Makes about 24 brownies.

Mocha Cinnamon Shortbread Squares

1 stick (½ cup) unsalted butter,
   softened
½ cup plus 2 tablespoons confectioners' sugar
1 cup all-purpose flour
1 tablespoon instant espresso powder
1 tablespoon unsweetened cocoa powder
⅛ teaspoon salt
¼ teaspoon ground cinnamon
2 ounces fine-quality bittersweet chocolate
   (not unsweetened), chopped

Preheat oven to 350° F. and butter an 8-inch-square baking pan.
In a bowl with an electric mixer beat butter with sugar until light and fluffy. In another bowl whisk together flour, espresso powder, cocoa powder, salt, and cinnamon. Beat flour mixture into butter mixture until just combined.
On a lightly floured surface knead dough about 5 times, or until it just comes together. Press dough evenly into prepared pan and bake in middle of oven 35 minutes, or until browned lightly and just firm.
Cool shortbread in pan on a rack 10 minutes. While shortbread is still warm, loosen edges from pan with a small knife and carefully invert onto your hand covered with a kitchen towel. Invert shortbread onto a cutting board and cut into 9 squares. Cool shortbread completely on a rack set over a sheet of wax paper.
In a metal bowl set over a pan of barely simmering water melt chocolate, stirring, and cool slightly. Drizzle chocolate decoratively over shortbread and let stand until chocolate is hardened. Makes 9 shortbread squares.

Rosemary Shortbread

¾ stick (6 tablespoons) unsalted butter,
   softened
1 tablespoon honey
¼ cup confectioners' sugar
1 cup all-purpose flour

¼ teaspoon baking powder
½ teaspoon salt
1 tablespoon chopped fresh rosemary leaves or
    1½ teaspoons dried rosemary, crumbled

Garnish: small rosemary sprigs

Preheat oven to 350° F. and butter generously a 9-inch cake pan or coat lightly a 9-inch round shortbread mold with vegetable oil spray.

In a bowl with an electric mixer beat butter and honey with sugar until light and fluffy. In another bowl whisk together flour, baking powder, salt, and rosemary. Beat flour mixture into butter mixture until just combined.

On a lightly floured surface knead dough about 8 times, or until it just comes together. With floured hands press dough evenly into pan or mold. If using cake pan score dough into 8 wedges with floured tines of a fork and with flat sides of tines press edges decoratively. Press small rosemary sprigs on top.

Bake shortbread in middle of oven 20 to 30 minutes, or until pale golden, and let stand in pan for 10 minutes. While shortbread is still warm, loosen edges from pan with a small knife and invert onto your hand covered with a kitchen towel. Invert shortbread onto a cutting board and cut halfway through round along score marks. Cool shortbread on a rack. Makes 8 shortbread cookies.

PIES, TARTS, AND PASTRIES

Apple and Dried-Cherry Lattice Pie

For filling
2 pounds Granny Smith, Braeburn, or other
    tart apples
⅓ cup granulated sugar
½ cup dried sour cherries, dried cranberries,
    or raisins
2 tablespoons fresh lemon juice
½ teaspoon cinnamon
¼ cup all-purpose flour
¾ cup firmly packed brown sugar
½ stick (¼ cup) unsalted butter, softened

For pastry dough
2½ cups all-purpose flour
1¼ teaspoons salt
1 cup chilled vegetable shortening
4 to 6 tablespoons cold water

2 tablespoons milk
1 tablespoon granulated sugar

Make filling:
Peel, halve, and core apples and cut into ¼-inch slices. In a large bowl toss apples slices with granulated sugar, dried sour cherries, dried cranberries, or raisins, lemon juice, cinnamon, and 2 tablespoons flour. In a small bowl blend together with fingertips brown sugar, butter, and remaining 2 tablespoons flour.

Make pastry dough:
In a large bowl stir together flour and salt. With a pastry blender or fingertips blend in shortening, blending until mixture resembles coarse meal. Add cold water, 1 tablespoon at a time, tossing to incorporate until mixture forms a dough. On a work surface smear dough in several forward motions with heel of hand to develop the gluten in flour and make dough easier to work with. Scrape dough together to form a ball and halve, flattening halves to 1-inch-thick disks.

Wrap 1 dough disk in plastic wrap and reserve. Roll other dough disk into an 11-inch round and fit into a 9-inch (1-quart) pie plate, leaving ¾-inch overhang. Spoon apple mixture into pastry and top with brown sugar mixture. Cover pie filling loosely with plastic wrap.

Preheat oven to 350° F.

Halve reserved dough. On a lightly floured surface roll 1 half into a very thin 11-inch round and with a fluted pastry wheel cut round into 1¾-inch-wide strips. Repeat procedure with remaining dough.

Weave dough strips in a closed lattice pattern over pie and trim lattice edges flush with rim of pie plate. Roll overhanging dough from bottom pastry up over edge of lattice top and crimp edge decoratively. Brush lattice top with milk and sprinkle with granulated sugar.

Put sheet of foil on lower rack of oven. Bake pie in middle of oven 1 hour and 15 minutes, or until top is golden and filling is bubbling. Cool pie on a rack and serve warm or at room temperature.

Chocolate Cream Pie

For crust
2 cups vanilla wafer crumbs (about 45 wafers)
¾ stick (6 tablespoons) unsalted butter,
    melted
⅓ cup sugar
For filling
5 ounces fine-quality bittersweet chocolate,
    chopped
4 ounces unsweetened chocolate,
    chopped
1 cup sugar
½ cup cornstarch
¾ teaspoon salt
6 large egg yolks
4½ cups milk
3 tablespoons unsalted butter, cut into bits
    and softened
1½ teaspoons vanilla

1 cup well-chilled heavy cream
1½ tablespoons sugar,
    or to taste

Garnish: grated bittersweet chocolate

Make crust:
Preheat oven to 350° F.

In a bowl stir together well crumbs, butter, and sugar and press onto bottom and up side of a 10-inch (1½-quart) pie plate. Bake crust in middle of oven until crisp and golden, 15 to 20 minutes, and cool on a rack.

Make filling:
In a metal bowl set over barely simmering water melt chocolates, stirring, until smooth and remove bowl from heat. In a heavy saucepan (about 3 quarts) whisk together sugar, cornstarch, salt, and yolks until combined well and add milk in a stream, whisking. Bring milk mixture to a boil over moderate heat, whisking, and simmer, whisking, until thick, about 1 minute. Force custard through a fine sieve into a bowl and whisk in melted chocolate, butter, and vanilla until smooth. Cover surface of filling with plastic wrap and cool completely.

Pour filling into crust. *Chill pie, covered, at least 6 hours or overnight.*

In a bowl with an electric mixer beat cream to soft peaks. Beat in sugar and beat cream just to stiff peaks. Spoon whipped cream decoratively onto pie and sprinkle with grated chocolate.

Pear and Pumpkin Pie

For poached pears
1 tablespoon whole allspice berries
½ vanilla bean, split lengthwise
1 tablespoon freshly grated lemon zest (from
    about 2 lemons)
4 cups dry red wine
2 cups water
1 cup sugar
3 firm-ripe pears such as Bosc

pastry dough for a single-crust 9-inch pie
    (recipe follows)
an egg wash made by beating 1 large egg yolk
    with 1 teaspoon water
For filling
3 large eggs
¾ cup heavy cream
1½ cups canned solid-pack pumpkin
½ cup firmly packed light brown sugar
2 teaspoons cinnamon
1 teaspoon ground ginger
¾ teaspoon salt
1 teaspoon ground allspice
⅛ teaspoon freshly grated nutmeg

¼ cup apricot jam, heated and strained

Accompaniment: ginger *crème anglaise* (page 217)

Make poached pears:
In a 3-quart saucepan combine all poached pear ingredients except pears and boil, stirring, until sugar is dissolved. Peel pears and simmer in wine mixture, covered, turning occasionally, until firm-tender, about 20 minutes. Remove pan from heat and let stand, covered, turning pears occasionally for even color, 30 minutes. Discard poaching mixture and halve pears lengthwise. Remove stems and with a melon-ball cutter or small knife remove core. Cut pears lengthwise into ¼-inch-thick slices.

Roll out dough ⅛ inch thick on a lightly floured surface. Fit dough into a 9-inch (1-quart) pie plate and trim edge, leaving a ½-inch overhang. Cut edge of dough with scissors every ½ inch to form curved points and brush edge lightly with egg wash. Chill shell 30 minutes.

Preheat oven to 375° F.

Make filling:

In a large bowl whisk together filling ingredients until combined well.

Pour filling into shell and bake in middle of oven 35 minutes. Remove pie from oven and arrange pears decoratively on top of filling. Bake pie 15 to 20 minutes more, or until custard is set and pears are tender. Cool pie on a rack and brush pears with jam. *Chill pie, covered loosely, at least 4 hours and up to 2 days.* Serve pie at room temperature with *crème anglaise.*

Pastry Dough

1¼ cups all-purpose flour
¾ stick (6 tablespoons) cold unsalted butter, cut into bits
2 tablespoons cold vegetable shortening
¼ teaspoon salt
2 to 4 tablespoons ice water

In a bowl with a pastry blender or in a food processor blend or pulse together flour, butter, shortening, and salt until mixture resembles meal. Add 2 tablespoons ice water and toss or pulse until water is incorporated. If necessary, add enough of remaining ice water to form a dough and form dough into a disk. Lightly dust dough with flour and chill, wrapped in wax paper, 1 hour. Makes enough dough for a 9-inch single-crust pie.

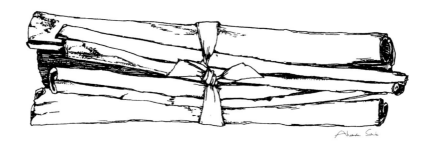

Apple "Flag" Tart

For pastry dough
2 cups all-purpose flour
¼ cup sugar
1 teaspoon salt
1 teaspoon cinnamon
1½ sticks (¾ cup) cold unsalted butter, cut into bits
¼ to ⅓ cup cold water

5 large Golden Delicious, Fuji, or Jonagold apples
1½ cups fresh or unthawed frozen cranberries
1 cup sugar
For glaze
¼ cup red-currant jelly
¼ cup apple jelly

Make pastry dough:

In a bowl stir together flour, sugar, salt, and cinnamon. With a pastry blender or fingertips blend in butter until mixture resembles coarse meal. Add cold water, 1 tablespoon at a time, tossing to incorporate until mixture forms a dough. On a work surface smear dough in several forward motions with heel of hand to develop gluten in flour and make dough easier to work with. Scrape dough together and pat into an 8- by 6-inch rectangle. Chill dough, wrapped in plastic wrap, 30 minutes.

Reserve 1 apple for making stars. Peel, quarter, and core remaining 4 apples and cut lengthwise into scant-¼-inch slices.

For stars, stand reserved apple on its stem end and, starting from the outside, cut scant-¼-inch vertical slices, rotating apple to cut more slices as you reach the core. With a 1¼-inch star-shaped cutter cut out as many whole stars as possible from slices and then cut partial stars from scraps.

In a food processor pulse fresh or frozen cranberries with ¾ cup sugar until chopped fine.

Preheat oven to 400° F.

On a lightly floured surface roll dough into a 17- by 14-inch rectangle and transfer to a large baking sheet. Hand-roll the edges 1 inch toward center to make a raised border and spread cranberry mixture inside. Arrange apple slices lengthwise, overlapping them, in close horizontal rows (apples will shrink slightly during baking) to resemble stripes on an American flag, leaving a space in the upper-left corner for stars. Arrange partial stars in corner and top with whole stars. Brush pastry edge with water and sprinkle remaining ¼ cup sugar over entire tart.

Bake tart 50 minutes, or until apples are tender and pastry is golden. Cool tart on baking sheet on a rack.

Make glaze:

In a small saucepan melt jellies over moderate heat, stirring frequently until smooth.

Brush hot glaze over warm tart. Serve tart warm or at room temperature.

Thyme-Scented Apple Galette

For pastry dough
1½ cups all-purpose flour
¼ cup confectioners' sugar
1 teaspoon salt
1½ sticks (¾ cup) cold unsalted butter, cut into bits
1 large egg yolk
2 tablespoons cold water

4 medium Gala or Empire apples
   (about 2 pounds)
¼ cup white wine
⅓ cup granulated sugar
For glaze
½ cup white wine
½ cup apple jelly
¼ cup loosely packed fresh thyme sprigs

Garnish: fresh thyme sprigs and 1 tablespoon
   fresh thyme leaves

Make pastry dough:

In a bowl stir together flour, sugar, and salt. With a pastry blender or fingertips blend in butter until mixture resembles coarse meal. In a bowl stir together yolk and cold water. Add yolk mixture to flour mixture, 1 tablespoon at a time, tossing to incorporate until mixture forms a dough. On a work surface smear dough in several forward motions with heel of hand to develop gluten in flour and make dough easier to work with. Scrape dough together to form a ball and flatten to a 1-inch-thick disk. Chill dough, wrapped in plastic wrap, 30 minutes.

Halve and core apples (do not peel) and cut crosswise into ¼-inch-thick slices. In a large bowl toss apple slices gently with wine.

Preheat oven to 400° F.

On a lightly floured surface roll out dough to a 15-inch round and transfer to a large baking sheet. Fold in edge 1 inch all around to form a border.

Arrange apple slices on pastry round in overlapping concentric circles. Brush apple slices and pastry border with wine remaining in bowl and sprinkle with sugar.

Bake *galette* 45 minutes, or until apples are tender and pastry border is golden. Cool *galette* on baking sheet on a rack.

Make glaze while galette is cooling:

In a saucepan simmer wine with jelly and thyme until liquid is reduced by half, about 15 minutes.

Remove thyme with a slotted spoon and brush hot glaze generously over apple slices. Garnish *galette* with thyme sprigs and leaves.

Individual Upside-Down Apple Tarts

¾ cup sugar
4 medium Golden Delicious apples
2 tablespoons cold unsalted butter
4 gingersnap cookies
1 sheet frozen puff pastry, thawed

Accompaniment: lightly sweetened whipped
   cream or ice cream

Preheat oven to 450° F.

In a dry heavy saucepan (about 1-quart capacity) cook sugar over moderate heat, undisturbed, until it begins to melt. Continue cooking sugar, stirring with a fork until it is melted and then swirling pan, until it is a deep-golden caramel. Pour caramel into four 6-ounce ramekins (3¼ to 3½ inches in diameter).

Peel and cut 1 apple into 5 wedges and core wedges. Put wedges back together to re-form apple shape and stand upright, stem end down, in a ramekin (wedges will protrude over rim). Repeat procedure with remaining apples.

Cut butter into 4 pieces. Put 1 gingersnap, broken into 4 pieces, in center of each re-formed apple and top with 1 piece of butter. Arrange ramekins in a shallow baking pan and bake apples in middle of oven 45 minutes.

While apples are baking, halve pastry sheet crosswise and then lengthwise to make 4 nearly square pieces and chill, wrapped in plastic wrap. Remove baking sheet with ramekins from oven and drape a piece of puff pastry over each apple (edges of pastry will extend beyond rims). Return pan to oven and reduce oven temperature to 350° F. Bake tarts 20 to 25 minutes, or until pastry is puffed and golden brown.

Remove tarts from oven. Invert heatproof plates over ramekins and invert tarts carefully onto them.

Serve tarts warm with whipped cream or ice cream. Makes 4 individual tarts.

Pink Applesauce Meringue Tart
with Hazelnut Cookie Crust

For applesauce filling
2½ pounds McIntosh apples (about 6)
1 pound purple or red plums (about 4), halved
    and pitted
¾ cup sugar
¼ cup apple juice
2 tablespoons fresh lemon juice
For cookie crust
½ cup hazelnuts, toasted and skinned
    (procedure on page 170)
3 tablespoons sugar
1⅓ cups all-purpose flour
½ teaspoon salt
1 stick (½ cup) unsalted butter, softened
1 large egg yolk beaten lightly with
    2 tablespoons water
For meringue
2 large egg whites
⅓ cup sugar

Make applesauce filling:
Quarter and core apples (do not peel). In a 5-quart saucepan simmer apples, uncovered, with remaining filling ingredients 2 hours, or until mixture is reduced to about 3¾ cups. (Stir mixture frequently during last 30 minutes of cooking to prevent scorching.) Force mixture through a food mill fitted with coarse disk or a medium-mesh sieve into a bowl, discarding solids, and chill. *Applesauce may be made 3 days ahead and chilled, covered.*
Preheat oven to 375° F.
Make cookie crust :
In a food processor grind hazelnuts fine with sugar, flour, and salt. Add butter and pulse mixture well. Add yolk mixture, 1 tablespoon at a time, pulsing after each addition, and pulse mixture until it forms a dough. Press dough onto bottom and up side of a 10-inch tart pan with a removable fluted rim. Bake crust in middle of oven 25 minutes, or until browned lightly, and cool in pan on a rack. *Crust may be made 3 days ahead and kept, covered, in a cool dry place.*
Spread applesauce onto crust.
Preheat oven to 450° F.
Make meringue:
In a bowl with an electric mixer beat whites with a pinch of salt until they hold soft peaks. Add sugar gradually, beating whites until they hold stiff peaks.

Transfer meringue to a pastry bag fitted with a ½-inch star tip and pipe some in a lattice pattern over filling. Pipe remaining meringue onto edge of tart to make a decorative border.

Bake tart in middle of oven 10 minutes, or until meringue is golden, and cool. *Chill tart at least 30 minutes and up to 3 hours.*

Fig and Apple Phyllo Tart

For filling
an 8-ounce package dried Calimyrna figs
    (about 1 cup)
¾ cup apple juice
¼ cup fresh lemon juice
½ cup sugar

¾ stick (6 tablespoons) unsalted butter, melted
8 sheets *phyllo* dough, thawed if frozen
4 medium Empire, Winesap, or Jonagold apples
    (about 2 pounds)
⅓ cup granulated sugar
½ cup vanilla yogurt
1 large egg, beaten lightly
2 tablespoons natural almonds, toasted and
    chopped

Garnish: confectioners' sugar

Make filling:
Remove any stems from figs. In a saucepan combine figs with remaining filling ingredients and simmer, covered, 20 minutes, or until very tender. Transfer mixture to a food processor and blend until smooth.

Brush a 9-inch square or 10-inch round tart pan with a removable fluted rim with some butter. On a work surface arrange 1 sheet *phyllo* with a short side facing you and brush with some butter. On it layer 3 more sheets *phyllo* and more butter in same manner and line pan, pressing *phyllo* into pan with fingertips and leaving short sides overhanging.

Repeat layering procedure with remaining *phyllo* and some of remaining butter and arrange in pan at a 90-degree angle to the first lining, easing to fit. Put pan on a baking sheet and roll overhanging edges under loosely (outside the pan) to form a decorative edge. Brush edge with remaining butter and spread fig mixture evenly on bottom.

Preheat oven to 350° F.

Peel, quarter, and core apples and cut each quarter into 3 or 4 wedges. Arrange apple wedges over fig mixture in a decorative pattern and sprinkle with sugar. Bake tart in middle of oven 40 minutes.

In a small bowl stir together yogurt and egg.

Remove tart from oven and increase oven temperature to 475° F.

Pour yogurt mixture over apples and cover edge of tart with foil. Return tart to oven and bake 15 minutes, or until apples begin to brown. Cool tart in pan on a rack 30 minutes and sprinkle with almonds and confectioners' sugar.

Lemon-Curd Strawberry Tart

For lemon curd
½ cup granulated sugar
5 tablespoons unsalted butter, cut into bits
2 large eggs, beaten lightly
¼ cup fresh lemon juice
2 tablespoons freshly grated lemon zest
For shell
1½ cups all-purpose flour
6 tablespoons confectioners' sugar
1 stick (½ cup) cold unsalted butter,
    cut into bits
3 tablespoons sour cream
1 large egg yolk
⅛ teaspoon vanilla

1½ pints small strawberries (about 18), hulled
¼ cup heavy cream

Make lemon curd:

In a metal bowl set over a saucepan of simmering water cook sugar, butter, eggs, lemon juice, and zest, whisking frequently, until curd is thick enough to hold marks of whisk and the first bubble appears on surface, 12 to 15 minutes. Strain curd through a sieve into a bowl and cool. Chill curd, covered, until ready to use. *Lemon curd may be made 1 week ahead and chilled, covered.*

Make shell:

In a food processor pulse flour, sugar, butter, and a pinch of salt until mixture resembles coarse meal. In a small bowl stir together sour cream, yolk, and vanilla until combined well and add to flour mixture. Process mixture until a ball of dough is formed. Shape dough into a thick disk and chill, wrapped in plastic wrap, at least 30 minutes.

Preheat oven to 375° F.

On a floured surface roll out dough ⅜ inch thick and cut out an 11-inch circle. Transfer dough with 2 spatulas to baking sheet. Crimp edge decoratively and chill dough 20 minutes.

Prick shell all over with a fork and bake in middle of oven until pale golden, 15 to 17 minutes. Cool shell completely on baking sheet on a rack.

Assemble tart:

Spread lemon curd evenly on pastry shell, leaving a 1-inch border, and arrange strawberries on it. *Tart may be assembled up to this point 3 hours ahead and kept covered.*

Beat cream until it holds stiff peaks and spoon into a pastry bag fitted with a large star tip. Pipe rosettes of cream between strawberries and transfer tart to a platter.

Praline Pecan Tarts

2 recipes pastry dough (page 235), or
    enough for 2 single-crust 9-inch pies
¾ cup light corn syrup
3 large eggs
¼ teaspoon salt
2 teaspoons dark rum or vanilla
1 tablespoon unsalted butter,
    melted
1 cup finely chopped Louisiana pralines* (about 6
    ounces) or homemade pralines (recipe follows)
2 cups pecan halves (about 6 ounces)

*available by mail from The Praline Connection,
    New Orleans, LA, tel. (800) 392-0362

Roll out each disk of dough ⅛ inch thick on a lightly floured surface and cut out six 7-inch rounds. Fit rounds into tart pans with removable bottoms measuring 4 inches across top and ¾ inch deep and roll a rolling pin over pan edges to trim excess dough. *Pastry shells may be prepared 5 days ahead and kept covered and frozen on a baking sheet. Let shells stand at room temperature 10 minutes before proceeding with recipe.*

Preheat oven to 375° F. with a baking sheet on middle rack.

In a bowl whisk together syrup, eggs, salt, rum or vanilla, and butter. Divide pralines among shells and pour in syrup mixture. Arrange pecan halves on praline mixture and press pecans to coat with mixture. Bake tarts on preheated baking sheet 20 to 25 minutes, or until tops are golden brown. Makes 6 tarts.

PHOTO ON PAGE 39

Pralines

2 cups firmly packed light brown sugar
    (a 1-pound box)
1 cup granulated sugar
1 cup heavy cream
½ teaspoon salt
¼ teaspoon cream of tartar
½ stick (¼ cup) unsalted butter,
    cut into bits
1½ teaspoons vanilla
2½ cups pecan halves

Oil 3 baking sheets lightly.

In a 2-quart heavy saucepan combine sugars, cream, salt, and cream of tartar and cook mixture over moderate heat, stirring and washing down any sugar crystals clinging to side with a brush dipped in cold water, until sugar is dissolved.

Boil mixture, undisturbed, over moderately high heat until a candy thermometer registers 238° F. Remove pan from heat and cool mixture, undisturbed, until thermometer registers 220° F. Stir in butter and vanilla. Beat mixture until creamy and stir in pecan halves. Drop tablespoons of mixture quickly onto prepared baking sheets and let harden.

Pralines keep, wrapped individually in wax paper, in an airtight container in a cool place 2 weeks. Makes 2 pounds, about 36 pralines.

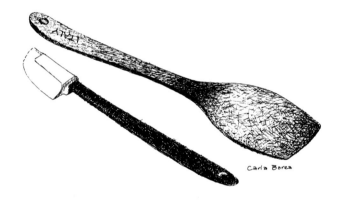

Carla Borea

Chocolate Praline Croquembouche

For cream puffs
1 recipe *pâte à chou* (page 242)
For filling
about 1 cup chocolate pastry cream (page 242)
½ cup heavy cream
½ cup praline powder (page 242)
For caramel
2 cups sugar
½ cup water
For assembly
large pastry bag
½-inch plain tip

¼-inch plain tip

Note: a cake-decorating turntable* is helpful for assembling a croquembouche

*available by mail order from The Chocolate Gallery, 34 West 22nd Street, New York, NY 10010, tel. (212) 675-CAKE; or Sweet Celebrations, Edina, MN, tel. (800) 480-2505

Make cream puffs:

Preheat oven to 425° F. and butter and flour 2 baking sheets.

Spoon *pâte à chou* into a large pastry bag fitted with a ½-inch plain tip and pipe about 55 mounds onto baking sheets, each about 1½ inches in diameter, leaving 1½ inches between mounds. With a finger dipped in water gently smooth pointed tip of each mound to round puffs. Bake puffs in upper third of oven 10 minutes, switching position of sheets in oven halfway through baking if necessary. Reduce temperature to 400° F. and bake puffs 20 minutes more, or until puffed and golden. Let puffs stand in turned-off oven 30 minutes. Transfer puffs to racks to cool. With a skewer poke a ¼-inch hole in bottom of each puff. *Puffs may be made 2 days ahead and kept in an airtight container. Recrisp puffs in 400° F. oven 5 minutes and cool before filling.*

Make filling:

In bowl of a standing electric mixer beat pastry cream until just smooth and soft enough to fold in heavy cream (do not overbeat). In a chilled bowl with cleaned beaters beat heavy cream until it holds soft peaks and fold in praline powder. Fold whipped cream mixture into pastry cream. Chill filling, covered, about 1 hour, or until cold.

Fill cream puffs:

Transfer filling to a large pastry bag fitted with a ¼-inch plain tip and barely fill each puff (do not overfill), putting filled puffs in a shallow baking pan.

Make caramel:

In a heavy saucepan stir together sugar and water and bring to a boil over moderately low heat, stirring and washing down sides of pan with a brush dipped in cold water to dissolve any sugar crystals until sugar is dissolved. Boil syrup over moderately high heat, without stirring, until it begins to turn pale caramel. Still without stirring, gently swirl syrup in pan (so that it colors evenly) until it begins to turn golden caramel and remove from heat. Caramel will continue to color slightly off heat and will thicken as it cools. As caramel begins to reach thickness of corn syrup, return pan to a burner at lowest possible heat, using a flame-tamer if necessary, and keep warm (do not simmer).

Assemble croquembouche:

Line a tray with wax paper. Working quickly with 1 cream puff at a time, impale bottom of each puff on tip of a small serrated knife and carefully dip top in caramel, leaving bottom ⅓ inch uncoated (to facilitate handling) and letting excess drip off. (Be extremely careful when working with hot caramel.) Set puff, coated side up, on prepared tray. When all puffs are coated, center 3, touching to form a triangle, on a cake-decorating turntable. Form a ring of 9 puffs around triangle and, working with 1 of the 9 puffs at a time, carefully dip 1 edge into caramel, letting excess drip off, and affix puffs to one another in a tight ring around first 3 puffs. Dip bottom of a puff in caramel and center it over middle of first 3 puffs. Working with 1 puff at a time, carefully dip 1 edge of each puff into caramel, letting excess drip off, and build a second, slightly smaller ring on top of the first using 8 puffs (if necessary adding an additional puff in center to stabilize ring), making sure each puff is glued with caramel to the one before it.

Build on top of first 2 rows 4 more rings of 5 puffs each in same manner, always building from inside out with an additional puff in center as support.

For top of *croquembouche* build 1 layer of 3 puffs and top with 1 puff. Let caramel harden 5 minutes and loosen *croquembouche* from turntable with a spatula. Transfer *croquembouche* with hands to a platter.

Slip 5-inch-wide bands of wax paper under edges of *croquembouche* to protect from caramel drips. Remove caramel from heat and cool to thickness of molasses, 2 to 3 minutes. Dip tip of a small spoon in caramel and drizzle caramel decoratively over *croquembouche*. (Alternately, all puffs may be dipped in initial caramel and put in a shallow serving bowl without being molded into a cone shape.) Let caramel harden and remove wax paper. Croquembouche *is best served as soon as possible but may be made up to 12 hours ahead and chilled but not covered.*

To serve *croquembouche*, shatter caramel cage with back of a knife and dismantle, 1 puff at a time.

Pâte à Chou
(Cream Puff Pastry)

1¼ cups water
1½ sticks (¾ cup) unsalted butter, cut into pieces
½ teaspoon salt
1½ cups unbleached flour
4 to 6 large eggs

In a heavy saucepan bring water to a boil with butter and salt over high heat. Reduce heat to moderate. Add flour all at once and beat with a wooden spoon until mixture pulls away from sides of pan, forming a dough.

Transfer dough to bowl of a standing electric mixer and, beat in 4 eggs, 1 at a time, on high speed, beating well after each addition. Batter should be stiff enough to just hold soft peaks and fall softly from a spoon. If batter is too stiff, in a small bowl beat remaining 2 eggs lightly, 1 at a time, and add to batter, a little at a time, beating on high speed, until batter is desired consistency.

Chocolate Pastry Cream

4 large egg yolks
¼ cup sugar
3 tablespoons cornstarch
3 tablespoons unsweetened cocoa powder
¼ teaspoon salt
1 cup milk
a 3-ounce bar fine-quality bittersweet chocolate
   (not unsweetened), broken into pieces
2 tablespoons unsalted butter, cut into bits
   and softened

In a heatproof bowl whisk together yolks, sugar, cornstarch, cocoa powder, and salt (mixture will be very stiff). In a heavy saucepan bring milk just to a boil over moderate heat and in a stream add ¼ cup to egg mixture, whisking until smooth, and whisk in remaining ¾ cup milk. Transfer egg mixture to pan and bring to a boil, whisking (mixture will look curdled but will become smooth as whisked). Boil pastry cream, whisking vigorously, 1 minute and remove from heat. Stir in chocolate and butter, stirring until melted and combined well. Transfer hot pastry cream to a heatproof bowl and chill, surface covered with

plastic wrap, until cold, about 2 hours. *Pastry cream may be made 2 days ahead and chilled, covered.* Makes about 1 cup.

Praline Powder

½ cup sugar
½ cup blanched whole almonds

Grease a small baking pan.

In a small heavy saucepan heat sugar over moderate heat, stirring, until melted. Cook melted sugar, swirling pan occasionally, until deep golden. Immediately stir in almonds and pour praline into prepared baking pan.

Cool praline until hardened completely and break into large pieces. *Praline may be made 1 day ahead and kept in an airtight container.*

In a food processor grind praline to a fine powder. *Praline powder may be made 2 days ahead and chilled in an airtight container.* Makes 1⅓ cups.

Glazed Jelly Crêpes

⅓ cup all-purpose flour
3 tablespoons milk
2 tablespoons water
1 large egg
1 tablespoon unsalted butter, melted and cooled,
   plus additional for brushing the pan and crêpes
1½ ounces cream cheese, cut into thin slices
⅓ cup jelly
1 teaspoon sugar

In a blender or small food processor blend flour, milk, water, egg, 1 tablespoon of butter, and a pinch of salt 5 seconds. Turn off motor and scrape down sides of container. Blend batter 20 seconds more. Transfer batter to a bowl and let stand, covered, 15 minutes.

Heat a 6- to 7-inch crêpe pan (preferably cast iron) over moderate heat until hot. Brush pan lightly with additional butter and heat until hot but not smoking. Remove pan from heat. Stir batter and half-fill a ¼-cup measure with it. Pour batter into pan, tilting and rotating pan quickly to cover bottom with a thin layer of batter, and return any excess to bowl. Return pan to heat and loosen edge of crêpe with a spatula.

Cook crêpe until underside is browned lightly. Turn crêpe and brown other side lightly. Transfer crêpe to a plate. Make more crêpes with remaining batter in same manner, brushing pan with additional butter.

Preheat broiler.

Divide cream cheese and jelly among crêpes. Fold each crêpe into quarters and arrange, overlapping slightly, in a buttered shallow flameproof dish. Brush crêpes lightly with additional butter and sprinkle with sugar. Broil crêpes under broiler about 4 inches from heat 1 minute, or until bubbling and golden. Serves 2.

FROZEN DESSERTS

Baked Alaska Peanut S'mores

1½ cups graham cracker crumbs (about ⅓ pound)
¾ stick (6 tablespoons) unsalted butter, melted
2 tablespoons plus ⅓ cup sugar
1½ pints premium chocolate ice cream, softened slightly
½ cup salted roasted peanuts, chopped
2 large egg whites

Preheat oven to 350° F.

In a bowl stir together crumbs, butter, and 2 tablespoons sugar and reserve about one-fourth mixture. Press remaining mixture onto bottom of flameproof 8-inch-square baking pan. Bake crust 12 minutes, or until golden, and cool in pan on a rack.

In bowl stir together ice cream and peanuts and spread on crust. Sprinkle reserved crumb mixture evenly on top, pressing lightly. Freeze ice-cream mixture, covered with foil, overnight.

Preheat broiler.

In a metal bowl combine whites and remaining ⅓ cup sugar and set over a pan of simmering water. Stir mixture just until sugar is dissolved. Remove bowl from heat and with an electric mixer beat meringue until it holds stiff glossy peaks.

Spread meringue over ice cream and broil under preheated broiler about 4 inches from heat until golden, about 30 seconds. *Freeze dessert, uncovered, 30 minutes to harden meringue and if desired freeze, covered, overnight.*

Cut dessert into 4 squares and halve each square diagonally into triangles. Serves 8.

PHOTO ON PAGE 49

Pavlovas with Kir Royale Sorbet and Kiwis

4 large egg whites
¼ teaspoon salt
⅛ teaspoon cream of tartar
1 cup sugar
1 tablespoon distilled white vinegar
1 tablespoon cornstarch
1 teaspoon vanilla
Kir Royale *sorbet* (page 244)
whipped cream, sweetened lightly if desired
1 cup baby kiwis*, halved, peeled and chopped

*available at specialty foods shops

Preheat oven to 250° F. and line a baking sheet with parchment or foil.

In a bowl with an electric mixer beat egg whites with salt and cream of tartar to soft peaks. Add sugar gradually, beating, and beat meringue to stiff peaks. Beat in vinegar, cornstarch, and vanilla.

Onto prepared baking sheet spread meringue with the back of a spoon into 3½- to 4-inch rounds, making them slightly higher around the edges to form shells. Bake meringues in lower third of oven 1 hour, or until crisp on outside but soft in middle.

Peel parchment carefully from meringues and cool meringues on rack. *Meringues keep in an airtight container 1 day.*

Serve meringues topped with *sorbet*, whipped cream, and kiwis. Serves 6.

PHOTO ON PAGE 27

Kir Royale Sorbet

⅔ cup sugar
⅔ cup water
2½ cups raspberries
1 cup Champagne
¼ cup *crème de cassis*
1½ tablespoons fresh lemon juice

In a small heavy saucepan combine sugar and water and bring to a boil, stirring until sugar is dissolved. Remove pan from heat.

In a blender or food processor purée raspberries with Champagne, *crème de cassis*, and sugar syrup until smooth. Force purée through a fine sieve set over a bowl, pressing hard on solids, and stir in juice.

Chill mixture until cold and freeze in an ice-cream maker. Makes about 1 quart.

PHOTO ON PAGE 27

Date Walnut Yogurt Ice Cream

½ cup sugar
1 tablespoon cornstarch
⅛ teaspoon salt
2 large eggs
2½ cups milk
1½ teaspoons vanilla
1 cup pitted dates, chopped fine
1½ cups plain yogurt
⅔ cup walnuts, toasted lightly and chopped fine

In a bowl whisk together sugar, cornstarch, salt, and eggs. In a heavy saucepan heat milk just to boiling and add to egg mixture in a stream, whisking. In pan cook custard over moderate heat, stirring constantly, until it comes to a simmer and simmer, stirring constantly, 2 minutes. Stir in vanilla and dates and chill custard until cold.

Stir in yogurt and freeze ice cream in an ice-cream maker. Stir in walnuts. *Ice cream may be made 3 days ahead.* Makes about 6 cups.

Kahlúa, Toasted Coconut, and Ice-Cream Parfaits

¼ cup sweetened flaked coconut,
    toasted lightly

3 tablespoons Kahlúa or other coffee-flavored
    liqueur
¾ pint premium vanilla ice cream, softened
    slightly

Put 3 layers each coconut, liqueur, and ice cream in each of 2 wineglasses or parfait glasses, reserving about 1 tablespoon coconut and 2 teaspoons liqueur. Top parfaits with reserved coconut and liqueur and freeze, covered, 20 minutes. Serves 2.

Vanilla Ice Cream with Kiwi and Banana in Lime Rum Syrup

1 cup water
¼ cup sugar
1 tablespoon dark rum
¼ teaspoon freshly grated lime zest
1 kiwi, peeled, quartered lengthwise, and cut
    into ¼-inch-thick pieces
1 small banana
vanilla ice cream

In a small saucepan simmer water with sugar, rum, and zest 5 minutes. Add kiwi and simmer 2 minutes. Cut banana into ¼-inch slices and simmer in syrup 30 seconds. Transfer fruit with a slotted spoon to a small bowl. Boil syrup until reduced to about ½ cup and stir in fruit.

Serve fruit and syrup over ice cream. Serves 2.

Watermelon Sorbet with Chocolate Seeds

a 3½- to 4-pound piece of watermelon (about a
    quarter of a large watermelon that has been
    halved lengthwise and crosswise)
1½ ounces fine-quality bittersweet chocolate
    (not unsweetened), chopped
1 cup sugar
¼ cup fresh lime juice
2 tablespoons Sambuca or other anise-flavored
    liqueur if desired

Cut watermelon into 1-inch-thick semicircular slices and chop flesh coarse, reserving rind.

Arrange reserved watermelon rind slices on their sides on foil-lined baking sheets and cover tightly with plastic wrap. Freeze rinds until frozen hard, about 2 hours.

Line another baking sheet or a tray with parchment or wax paper. In a small bowl set over a small saucepan of barely simmering water melt chocolate and remove bowl from heat. Transfer chocolate to a small resealable bag and seal bag. Snip off tip of one corner of bag to form a tiny hole and onto prepared baking sheet or tray pipe and spread chocolate into ⅓- to ½-inch ovals to resemble watermelon seeds. Freeze chocolate "seeds" on baking sheet until very firm, about 30 minutes. Working quickly, peel "seeds" from paper into another small bowl and keep frozen.

Discard real seeds from watermelon flesh and in a blender purée enough flesh to yield 5 cups. In a saucepan heat 1 cup purée with sugar over moderate heat, stirring, until sugar is dissolved and stir into remaining purée with lime juice and liqueur. Chill mixture, covered, until cold.

Freeze *sorbet* in an ice-cream maker. When *sorbet* is frozen to a thick slush add three fourths of chocolate "seeds" and continue to freeze until frozen.

Working quickly, fill frozen watermelon rinds with *sorbet,* smoothing it with a rubber spatula. Arrange remaining chocolate "seeds" realistically on slices and smooth *sorbet* again. Cover *sorbet* with plastic wrap and freeze until very firm, about 6 hours. *Watermelon* sorbet *slices may be made 3 days ahead and frozen, wrapped tightly.* Makes about 4 to 6 slices, serving 4 generously.

PHOTO ON PAGE 60

FRUIT FINALES

Baked Bananas with Chocolate

2 small bananas, peeled and sliced thin crosswise
2 ounces fine-quality bittersweet chocolate
(not unsweetened), chopped fine
¼ cup heavy cream
⅛ teaspoon vanilla

Preheat oven to 425° F.
Divide half of the banana slices between two 1-cup ramekins and sprinkle half of chocolate over them.

Arrange remaining banana slices over chocolate and top with remaining chocolate.

In a bowl stir together cream and vanilla and pour over mixtures. Bake desserts in middle of oven 10 minutes. Serves 2.

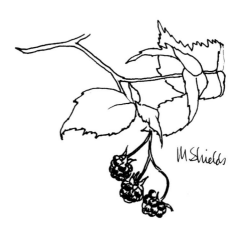

Blackberry and Nectarine Cobbler

⅓ cup sugar
1 teaspoon cornstarch
1 large nectarine, cut into½-inch pieces
(about 1 cup)
1 cup blackberries, picked over
½ cup all-purpose flour
½ teaspoon baking powder
¼ teaspoon salt
2½ tablespoons cold unsalted butter, cut into bits
¼ cup milk
2 tablespoons sliced almonds

Preheat oven to 400° F. and butter an 8-inch square baking dish.

In a bowl stir together sugar and cornstarch. Add fruit and combine well.

In another bowl whisk together flour, baking powder, and salt and add butter. Blend mixture until it resembles coarse meal and stir in milk, stirring until dough is just combined.

In a prepared baking dish spread fruit mixture and drop dough onto it in 4 mounds.

Sprinkle almonds over cobbler and bake in middle of oven 20 minutes, or until top is golden. Serves 2.

Red-Wine-Poached Figs with Vanilla Ice Cream

1½ cups dry red wine
2 tablespoons honey
1 tablespoon sugar
1 cinnamon stick
2 whole cloves
6 dried Calimyrna figs (about ¼ pound),
   halved lengthwise

Accompaniment: vanilla ice cream

In a 1½-quart saucepan combine all ingredients and bring to a boil, stirring occasionally. Simmer figs, covered, until tender, about 30 minutes.

Transfer figs with a slotted spoon to a bowl and boil syrup until reduced to about ¼ cup. Strain syrup through a fine sieve into another bowl. Add syrup to figs and cool to warm.

Serve fig mixture spooned over ice cream. Serves 2.

Honeydew with Mint, Basil, and Lime

3 cups 1-inch cubes honeydew melon
   (about ½ melon)
2 tablespoons fresh lime juice
1 tablespoon fresh opal basil leaves or
   chopped fresh basil leaves
1 tablespoon chopped fresh mint leaves
sugar to taste if desired

In a bowl combine all ingredients and chill, covered. Serves 2.

Poached Pears

2 small firm-ripe Bosc or Bartlett pears
   (about 6 ounces each)
2 cups cranberry-raspberry juice cocktail
½ cup sugar
2 bay leaves
2 whole cloves
1 teaspoon julienne orange zest

Core pears from blossom ends with melon-ball scoop and peel, leaving stems intact.

In a 2-quart saucepan simmer pears in cranberry-raspberry juice with remaining ingredients, uncovered, turning occasionally, 10 to 15 minutes, or until pears are tender but still hold their shape. Transfer pears to a plate with a slotted spoon, reserving poaching liquid, and chill in freezer 15 minutes.

While pears are chilling, boil reserved liquid until reduced to about 1 cup. Pour liquid into a bowl and put bowl in a larger bowl of ice and cold water. Stir liquid until cooled slightly.

Serve pears in shallow bowls with some poaching liquid and garnished with bay leaves. (Do not eat bay leaves.) Serves 2.

Caramelized Pear Charlottes with Persimmon

2 firm-ripe Bosc pears
½ stick (¼ cup) unsalted butter
1 tablespoon sugar plus additional to taste
7 slices homemade-type white bread
3 very ripe Hachiya persimmons*
   (not Fuyu)
fresh lemon juice to taste

*available at specialty produce markets

Peel and core pears and cut into sixths. In a small non-stick skillet melt 1 tablespoon butter over moderately high heat until foam begins to subside and sauté pears, turning occasionally, until golden, about 10 minutes. Sprinkle 1 tablespoon sugar over pears and cook, stirring once or twice, until golden brown and caramelized, about 1 minute.

In a food processor or blender purée pears until smooth and transfer to a bowl. *Pear purée may be made 1 day ahead and chilled, covered.*

Preheat oven to 400° F.

In a small saucepan melt remaining 3 tablespoons butter. Cut 2 bread slices into rounds the same size as bottoms of two ½-cup charlotte molds, ramekins, or custard cups and cut 2 bread slices into rounds the same size as tops of molds, reserving trimmings.

In a small food processor grind trimmings fine and stir into pear purée.

Brush smaller rounds on both sides with some melted butter and with them line bottoms of molds. Cut remaining 3 bread slices into 1-inch squares and discard crusts. Brush squares on both sides with some remaining butter and line sides of molds with them, overlapping slightly and pressing gently against side of molds.

Divide enough pear purée between lined molds to fill them to within ⅛ inch of top. Brush remaining 2 bread rounds on both sides with remaining butter and top molds with them, pressing down gently but firmly to cover pear purée completely. *Charlottes may be prepared up to this point 3 hours ahead and chilled, covered.*

Bake charlottes 20 minutes, or until bread is golden brown.

While charlottes are baking, peel and core 2 persimmons and in food processor purée with lemon juice and additional sugar.

Divide persimmon purée between 2 dessert plates and carefully invert charlottes onto it. Cut remaining persimmon into wedges and arrange around charlottes. Serves 2.

PHOTO ON PAGE 72

CONFECTIONS

Chocolate-Covered Almond Brittle

½ cup water
2 cups sugar
6 tablespoons light corn syrup
4 teaspoons baking soda
¾ teaspoon salt
2 cups whole natural almonds, chopped
    coarse and toasted
    until golden
6 ounces fine-quality bittersweet chocolate
    (not unsweetened), chopped coarse

Butter a large baking sheet and a metal spatula.

In a heavy 5- to 6-quart saucepan combine water, sugar, and corn syrup and bring to a boil over moderately high heat, stirring until sugar is dissolved. Boil syrup, without stirring, until it registers 310° F. on a candy thermometer.

Remove pan from heat (syrup will be very hot). Carefully add baking soda and salt and, working quickly, stir until syrup foams and thickens. Stir in almonds and pour mixture onto prepared baking sheet, spreading with prepared spatula.

Cool brittle 5 minutes and sprinkle chocolate evenly over it. Let chocolate melt, about 5 minutes, and spread it with a clean spatula. Chill brittle on baking sheet until chocolate hardens. Loosen brittle with a clean spatula from baking sheet and, holding brittle underneath with palms of hands to avoid smearing chocolate, drop from height of a few inches onto work surface to break into pieces. Transfer brittle, separating it with layers of wax paper, to airtight container. *Brittle keeps, covered and chilled, 2 weeks.* Makes about 1½ pounds.

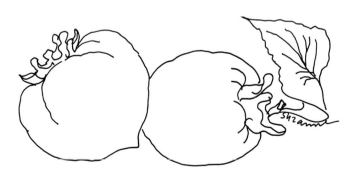

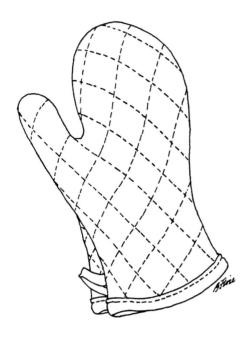

Chocolate Caramel Truffles

1 cup sugar
⅔ cup heavy cream
9 ounces fine-quality bittersweet chocolate
    (not unsweetened), chopped
¼ teaspoon salt
1 teaspoon vanilla
For coating
¼ to ½ cup unsweetened cocoa powder, sifted,
    and/or ½ to 1 cup pecans, ground fine

In a dry heavy saucepan (about 3½ quarts) cook sugar over moderate heat, stirring with a fork until melted, and swirl pan until sugar is a golden caramel. Remove pan from heat and add cream carefully (mixture will bubble up). Return pan to heat and simmer, stirring, until caramel is dissolved.

Remove pan from heat and add chocolate, salt, and vanilla. Let mixture stand 5 minutes and stir until chocolate is melted. Transfer mixture to a bowl and cool, uncovered. Chill mixture, covered, 2 hours, or until firm.

Coat truffles:
Scoop out truffle mixture with a spoon and form into 1-inch balls. Roll truffles in ½ cup cocoa powder or coat with 1 cup pecans, pressing nuts slightly to adhere. (Alternatively, roll half of truffles in ¼ cup cocoa powder and coat remaining truffles with ½ cup pecans.) Chill truffles on a tray lined with wax paper until firm, about 1 hour. *Truffles keep in an airtight container, chilled, 2 weeks.* Makes about 40 truffles.

Chocolate Pistachio Log

½ cup golden raisins
10 ounces (about 1¾ cups) semisweet chocolate
    chips
½ stick (¼ cup) unsalted butter,
    cut into bits
4 tablespoons superfine sugar
¾ cup finely ground gingersnaps
    (about 14 cookies)
2 large egg yolks, beaten lightly
½ cup shelled natural pistachios
½ cup dried sour cherries*, chopped coarse

*available at specialty foods shops and by
    mail order from American Spoon Foods,
    tel. (800) 222-5886

In a bowl soak raisins in warm water to cover 15 minutes and drain.

In a metal bowl set over a saucepan of barely simmering water melt chocolate chips with butter, stirring occasionally. Stir in raisins, sugar, gingersnaps, and egg yolks and cook mixture, stirring constantly, 8 minutes. Remove bowl from pan and stir in pistachios and cherries. Cool mixture completely and on a sheet of wax paper roll into a 2-inch-diameter log, using wax paper as a guide. Chill log, wrapped in wax paper, overnight. *Log may be made 1 week ahead and chilled, covered.* Cut log into thin slices. Makes about 48 slices, serving 16 to 20.

Honey Nut Candies

½ pound blanched whole almonds (about
    1½ cups), toasted, cooled, and ground fine
    (use a food processor)

1 cup golden raisins, half chopped fine and
    half chopped coarse
⅓ cup honey
3 tablespoons unsalted butter
2 tablespoons minced crystallized ginger
8 whole allspice berries, ground fine
⅛ teaspoon ground mace
⅛ teaspoon freshly ground nutmeg
⅛ teaspoon fennel seeds,
    ground fine
⅛ teaspoon cinnamon
a pinch of cayenne
a pinch of saffron threads,
    crumbled
⅓ cup sesame seeds

In a small heavy saucepan stir together all ingredients except sesame seeds and cook over very low heat, stirring occasionally, 20 minutes. Cook, stirring frequently so mixture does not burn, 40 minutes more, or until very thick.

Remove pan from heat and let mixture cool slightly. Form tablespoons of warm mixture into 1-inch balls and roll in sesame seeds to coat. *Candies maybe made 1 week ahead and kept in an airtight container in a cool dark place.* Makes about 35 candies.

PHOTO ON PAGE 59

SWEET TERRINE, PUDDINGS, AND OTHER DESSERTS

Chocolate, Orange, and Chestnut Pavé

For chocolate orange filling
1 stick (½ cup) unsalted butter, cut into pieces
1½ pounds fine-quality bittersweet chocolate
    (not unsweetened)
2 teaspoons freshly grated orange zest (from
    about 1½ navel oranges)
1¾ cups well-chilled heavy cream
For chestnut rum filling
6 ounces fine-quality white chocolate
¼ cup chopped vacuum-packed chestnuts*
    (about 1 ounce)

3 teaspoons dark rum
¼ cup well-chilled heavy cream

Garnish: chestnuts in dark and light syrup**,
    sliced, *"paté"* pears*, and candied orange
    halves**, sliced
Accompaniment: ginger *crème anglaise*
    (page 217)

*available at specialty foods shops and by mail
    order from Balducci's, New York, NY,
    (800) 572-7041
**available at some specialty foods shops and
    by mail order from Maison Glass Delicacies,
    111 East 58th Street, New York, NY 10022,
    tel. (212) 755-3316

Make chocolate orange filling:
In a large metal bowl set over a pan of barely simmering water melt butter and chocolate, stirring occasionally, until smooth and remove bowl from heat. Stir in zest and cool completely. In a bowl with an electric mixer beat cream until it just holds stiff peaks. Whisk about one fourth of cream into chocolate mixture to lighten and fold in remaining cream gently but thoroughly.

Line an oiled terrine or loaf pan, 10 by 4½ by 3 inches (7-cup capacity), with plastic wrap. Pour in half of chocolate orange filling, smoothing top, and freeze 5 minutes.

Make chestnut rum filling:
In a small metal bowl set over a pan of barely simmering water melt white chocolate, stirring occasionally, until smooth and remove bowl from heat. Stir in chestnuts and rum gently and cool completely. In a bowl with an electric mixer beat cream until it just holds stiff peaks. Fold cream into white chocolate mixture.

Pour chestnut rum filling over chocolate orange layer, smoothing top, and freeze 5 minutes. Pour in remaining chocolate orange filling, smoothing top. *Chill* pavé, *covered with plastic wrap, at least 8 hours and up to 2 days.*

Discard plastic from top and invert *pavé* onto a plate. Discard remaining plastic. Garnish *pavé* with chestnut slices, *"paté"* pears, and candied orange.

Pour some ginger *crème anglaise* onto 8 plates and top with a ½-inch-thick slices of *pavé*. Serves 8.

Danish Applesauce Bread Crumb Pudding

¾ stick (6 tablespoons) unsalted butter
12 slices homemade-type white bread, ground fine
   in a food processor (about 2½ cups)
4 cups homemade chunky applesauce (recipe
   follows) or bottled chunky applesauce
1 cup lingonberry preserves* or raspberry
   preserves

Garnish: lightly sweetened whipped cream and
   lingonberry or raspberry preserves
Accompaniment: lightly sweetened whipped cream

*available at specialty foods shops, some
   supermarkets, and by mail order from
   Old Denmark Scandinavian Food Specialties,
   133 East 65th Street, New York, NY 10021,
   tel. (212) 744-2533

Preheat oven to 325° F.

In a large heavy skillet melt butter over moderate heat and stir in bread crumbs. Cook bread crumbs, stirring constantly and breaking up lumps, until golden, about 5 minutes.

In a 1½-quart soufflé dish layer 1 cup crumbs, 2 cups applesauce, and ½ cup preserves and repeat. Sprinkle remaining ½ cup crumbs on top and bake pudding in middle of oven 25 minutes, or until top is golden brown. *Pudding may be made 1 day ahead and chilled, covered. Reheat pudding in a 325° F. oven.*

Garnish pudding with whipped cream and preserves and serve warm with sweetened whipped cream. Serves 6.

Chunky Applesauce

3 pounds McIntosh apples
   (about 8 large)
⅔ cup water
½ cup sugar

Peel and core apples and cut into ¾-inch pieces. In a large heavy saucepan bring water, apples, and sugar to a boil and simmer, stirring occasionally, until apples are soft and starting to fall apart, about 25 minutes. *Applesauce may be made 3 days ahead and chilled, covered.* Makes about 5 cups.

Butterscotch Bread Puddings

1 cup ½-inch cubes white bread
1¼ cups half-and-half
1 tablespoon unsalted butter
½ teaspoon salt
½ teaspoon vanilla
¼ cup firmly packed dark brown sugar
1 large egg
1 large egg yolk

Accompaniment: vanilla ice cream

Preheat oven to 350° F.

Butter two 1¼-cup ramekins and divide bread cubes between them.

In a saucepan heat half-and-half, butter, salt, and vanilla over moderate heat until hot. In a bowl whisk together sugar, egg, and yolk and add half-and-half mixture in a stream, whisking. Pour mixture over bread cubes and bake puddings in middle of oven until puffed and golden, about 25 minutes.

Serve puddings warm with ice cream. Serves 2.

Orange Currant Noodle Kugel

½ cup currants
1⅓ cups sour cream
1⅓ cups cottage cheese
3 large eggs
½ cup sugar
5 tablespoons unsalted butter, melted
1 tablespoon freshly grated orange zest
1 teaspoon vanilla
½ teaspoon cinnamon
¼ teaspoon salt
½ pound wide egg noodles
1 large Granny Smith apple
⅓ cup sliced blanched almonds

In a small bowl soak currants in hot water to cover 5 minutes and drain well.

In a blender blend together sour cream, cottage cheese, eggs, ¼ cup plus 2 tablespoons sugar, 3 tablespoons butter, zest, vanilla, ¼ teaspoon cinnamon, and salt until smooth.

Preheat oven to 350° F. and butter a 2-quart gratin dish or other shallow baking dish.

In a kettle of salted boiling water cook noodles until just tender, about 5 minutes, and drain well. Peel apple and grate coarse into a bowl. Add noodles and toss with sour cream mixture and currants. Transfer mixture to prepared dish.

In a small bowl stir together remaining 2 table-spoons sugar, remaining ¼ teaspoon cinnamon, and almonds and sprinkle evenly over kugel. Drizzle top with remaining 2 tablespoons melted butter. *Kugel may be made up to this point 6 hours ahead and chilled, covered. Bring to room temperature before baking.*

Bake kugel in middle of oven 40 to 45 minutes, or until cooked through and golden. Serves 6 to 8 as a side dish or dessert.

Austrian Sweet Cheese Crêpes Baked in Custard

For filling
½ cup dried currants
1 cup boiling-hot water
two 8-ounce packages cream cheese, softened
½ cup apricot jam
2 large eggs, separated
1 teaspoon freshly grated lemon zest
1 teaspoon vanilla
¼ cup granulated sugar

about 25 Austrian crêpes (page 252)
2 large eggs
3 tablespoons granulated sugar
1 cup milk
confectioners' sugar for dusting

Accompaniment: apricot caramel sauce (page 252)

Make filling:
In a small heatproof bowl plump currants in boil-ing-hot water 15 minutes and drain. Pat currants dry between paper towels. In a food processor or in a bowl with an electric mixer blend together well cream cheese, jam, yolks, zest, and vanilla. In a bowl with an electric mixer (beaters cleaned if necessary) beat whites with a pinch of salt until they hold soft peaks. Add sugar to whites and beat meringue until it holds stiff peaks. Fold cheese mixture into meringue gently but thoroughly and fold in currants.

Preheat oven to 400° F. and lightly butter a 14-inch-long oval gratin dish or other 2½-quart shallow baking dish.

Working with 1 crêpe at a time, spread 2 generous tablespoons filling on each crêpe, leaving a ½-inch border all around, and roll up crêpes jelly-roll fash-ion. With a sharp knife cut crêpes on a diagonal in half and arrange, overlapping slightly, in layers in baking dish. *Crêpes may be prepared up to this point 4 hours ahead and chilled, covered. Bring crêpes to room temperature before proceeding.*

In a small bowl whisk together eggs, granulated sugar, and milk and pour over crêpes, letting custard seep between layers. Bake crêpes in middle of oven 30 to 35 minutes, or until puffed and custard is set, and cool to warm.

Dust crêpes with confectioners' sugar and serve with apricot caramel sauce. Serves 12.

Austrian Crêpes

2 cups all-purpose flour
2½ tablespoons sugar
¾ teaspoon salt
4 large eggs
1⅓ cups milk
1½ cups club soda or seltzer (from a new bottle)
½ stick (¼ cup) unsalted butter, melted

In a bowl whisk together flour, sugar, and salt. In another bowl whisk together eggs, milk, and club soda or seltzer and add to flour mixture in a stream, whisking. Whisk batter until smooth and chill, covered, 1 hour.

Stir batter well. Heat a non-stick skillet measuring 8 inches across bottom over moderate heat until hot. Brush skillet lightly with melted butter. Remove skillet from heat. Fill a ¼-cup measure three-fourths full with batter and pour into skillet, tilting and rotating skillet quickly to cover bottom of pan.

Return skillet to heat and cook crêpe until underside is golden and top appears almost dry, 30 seconds to 1 minute. Turn crêpe and cook until underside is golden, 15 to 30 seconds. Slide crêpe onto a kitchen towel to cool. Make more crêpes in same manner with remaining batter, brushing skillet lightly with butter for each and stacking cooked crêpes on another kitchen towel as they cool. *Crêpes may be made 3 days ahead and chilled, stacked and wrapped well in plastic wrap.* Makes about 25 crêpes.

Apricot Caramel Sauce

1 cup sugar
4 cups water
1 cup firmly packed dried apricots
   (about 6 ounces)
2 teaspoons vanilla

In a dry heavy saucepan (about 3-quart capacity) cook sugar over moderate heat, stirring with a fork until melted and then swirling pan, until sugar is a golden caramel. Remove pan from heat and carefully add 3 cups water down side of pan (it will bubble up and steam). Return pan to heat and simmer, stirring, until caramel is dissolved.

Add apricots and simmer, covered, until soft, about 10 minutes. Cool mixture 10 minutes and in a blender purée with remaining 1 cup water and vanilla until very smooth. *Sauce may be made 3 days ahead and chilled, covered.* Serve sauce warm. Makes about 5 cups.

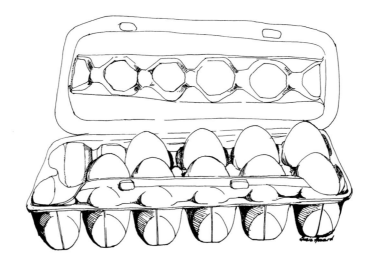

Sticky Rice with Mango

1½ cups glutinous (sweet) rice*
1⅓ cups well-stirred canned unsweetened coconut
   milk*
⅓ cup plus 3 tablespoons sugar
¼ teaspoon salt
1 tablespoon sesame seeds, toasted lightly
1 large mango, peeled, pitted, and cut into thin
   slices (at least 24)

*available at Asian markets, some specialty foods
   shops, and by mail order from Adriana's
   Caravan, Brooklyn, NY, tel. (800) 316-0820
   or (718) 436-8565, or Uwajimaya, 519 Sixth
   Avenue South, Seattle, WA 98104,
   tel. (206) 624-6248

In a bowl wash rice well in several changes of cold
water until water is clear. Soak rice in cold water to
cover overnight.

Drain rice well in a sieve. Set sieve over a large
deep saucepan of simmering water (sieve should not
touch water) and steam rice, covered with a kitchen
towel and a lid, 30 to 40 minutes, or until tender
(check water level in pan periodically, adding more
water if necessary).

While rice is cooking, in a small saucepan bring 1
cup coconut milk to a boil with ⅓ cup sugar and salt,
stirring until sugar is dissolved, and remove from
heat. Keep mixture warm.

Transfer cooked rice to a bowl and stir in coconut-
milk mixture. Let rice stand, covered, 30 minutes, or
until coconut-milk mixture is absorbed. *Rice may be
prepared up to this point 2 hours ahead and kept covered at room temperature.*

While rice is standing, in cleaned small pan slowly
boil remaining ⅓ cup coconut milk with remaining 3
tablespoons sugar, stirring occasionally, 1 minute.
Transfer sauce to a small bowl and chill until cool
and thickened slightly.

Mold ¼ cup servings of sticky rice on 6 dessert
plates. Drizzle desserts with sauce and sprinkle with
sesame seeds. Divide mango slices among plates.
Serves 6.

PHOTO ON PAGE 47

BEVERAGES

Banana Rum Fizzes

1 cup softened vanilla ice cream
½ cup chopped banana
1 ounce (2 tablespoons) *crème de cacao*,
   or to taste
1 ounce (2 tablespoons) dark rum,
   or to taste
¾ cup chilled club soda

Garnish: banana slices

In a blender blend ice cream and chopped banana until smooth but still thick and pour into 2 chilled stemmed glasses. Add *crème de cacao*, rum, and club soda and garnish with banana slices. Makes 2 drinks.

Brandy Alexander Shakes

1½ cups softened vanilla ice cream
2 ounces (¼ cup) brandy, or to taste
2 ounces (¼ cup) *crème de cacao*, or to taste

Garnish: freshly grated nutmeg

In a blender blend ice cream, brandy, and *crème de cacao* until smooth but still thick. Pour mixture into 2 chilled stemmed glasses and garnish with nutmeg. Makes 2 drinks.

Cappuccino Rum Shakes

1 pint (2 cups) softened coffee ice cream
3 ounces (6 tablespoons) dark rum,
   or to taste
¼ teaspoon ground cinnamon
½ cup whipped cream

Garnish: unsweetened cocoa powder and
   cinnamon sticks

In a blender blend ice cream, rum, and cinnamon until smooth but still thick and pour into 2 chilled stemmed glasses. Top drinks with cream and garnish with cocoa powder and cinnamon sticks. Makes 2 drinks.

Espresso Sambuca Ice-Cream Sodas

1 cup coffee ice cream
1 teaspoon instant espresso powder dissolved
   in 2 tablespoons hot water and cooled
2 ounces (¼ cup) Sambuca,
   or to taste
¾ cup chilled club soda

Garnish: 2 tablespoons finely chopped chocolate-
   covered espresso beans

With a small ice-cream scoop or spoon divide ice cream between 2 chilled stemmed glasses. Add espresso mixture, Sambuca, and club soda and top with espresso beans. Makes 2 drinks.

Grand Marnier Smoothies

½ cup softened vanilla ice cream
1½ cups fresh orange juice
1 ounce (2 tablespoons) Grand Marnier,
   or to taste
½ teaspoon freshly grated orange zest

Garnish: navel orange slices

In a blender blend ice cream, orange juice, Grand Marnier, and zest until smooth but still thick. Pour mixture into 2 chilled stemmed glasses and garnish with orange slices. Makes 2 drinks.

Lime Southside Cocktails

10 cups water
2¼ cups sugar, or to taste
3 cups fresh lime juice (from about 24 limes)
1 lime, sliced very thin
18 ounces gin, vodka, or rum

Garnish: fresh mint sprigs

In a saucepan cook 3 cups of water with sugar over moderate heat, stirring, until sugar is dissolved. Remove pan from heat and cool syrup.

In a large pitcher stir together syrup, remaining 7 cups water, lime juice, and lime slices.

To serve, add 1½ ounces (1 jigger) gin, vodka, or rum to each of 12 large goblets or tall glasses filled with ice cubes and add lime mixture to taste. Garnish cocktails with mint. Serves 12.

Orange Rum Rickey

1½ ounces (3 tablespoons) light rum
½ ounce (1 tablespoon) Cointreau or triple sec
1½ tablespoons fresh lime juice
superfine sugar to taste
    if desired
chilled club soda or seltzer

Garnish: lime wedge and a strip of fresh
    orange zest

In a tall glass filled with ice combine light rum, Cointreau or triple sec, lime juice, and sugar and top off with soda or seltzer. Stir drink well and garnish with lime wedge and orange zest. Makes 1 drink.

PHOTO ON PAGE 55

Peach Schnapps Fizzes

1½ cups softened vanilla ice cream
½ cup sliced peaches
2 ounces (¼ cup) peach schnapps,
    or to taste
¼ cup plus 2 tablespoons chilled club soda

Garnish: sliced peaches

In a blender blend ice cream and peaches until smooth but still thick and pour into 2 chilled stemmed glasses. Add schnapps and club soda and garnish with peach slices. Makes 2 drinks.

Nose-Warmer Punch
(Mulled Red Wine)

3 bottles dry red wine
1½ cups brandy
1½ cups sugar
3 cinnamon sticks
8 whole cloves
3 small lemons, zest scored lengthwise if desired
    with a channel knife and fruit sliced thin
    crosswise

In a large saucepan bring wine and brandy to a simmer with sugar, cinnamon, and cloves, stirring, and cook at a bare simmer 2 minutes. Stir in lemon slices and ladle into heatproof cups. Makes about 12½ cups, serving 12.

PHOTO ON PAGE 84

Rusty Nail Shakes

1 pint (2 cups) softened vanilla ice cream
1 ounce (2 tablespoons) Scotch, or to taste
1 ounce (2 tablespoons) Drambuie, or to taste

Garnish: chopped toasted pecans

In a blender blend vanilla ice cream, Scotch, and Drambuie until smooth but still thick and pour into 2 chilled stemmed glasses. Garnish drinks with pecans. Makes 2 drinks.

Strawberry Margarita Fizzes

sugar for coating rims of glasses
1½ cups softened strawberry ice cream
½ cup chopped strawberries
1 ounce (2 tablespoons) Tequila, or to taste

½ teaspoon fresh lime juice
⅓ cup chilled club soda

Garnish: whole strawberries and lime slices

Rub rims of 2 chilled stemmed glasses with water and dip in sugar to coat them.
In a blender blend ice cream, chopped strawberries, Tequila, and lime juice until smooth but still thick and pour into glasses. Add club soda and garnish with strawberries and lime slices. Makes 2 drinks.

Tropical Rum Shakes

1 pint (2 cups) softened vanilla ice cream
1 ounce (2 tablespoons) light rum, or to taste
½ ounce (1 tablespoon) *crème de cacao*, or to taste
1 tablespoon chopped crystallized ginger

In a blender blend all ingredients until smooth but still thick and pour into 2 chilled stemmed glasses. Makes 2 drinks.

Vodka Coolers

¾ cup grape juice, or to taste
1-liter bottle ginger ale
1½ cups vodka, or to taste
lemon slices

In a pitcher stir together all ingredients and add ice. Makes 8 drinks.

PHOTO ON PAGE 55

White Russian Shakes

1 pint (2 cups) softened vanilla ice cream
2 ounces (¼ cup) vodka, or to taste
2 ounces (¼ cup) Kahlúa, or to taste

Garnish: grated fine-quality bittersweet chocolate

In a blender blend ice cream, vodka, and Kahlúa until smooth but still thick and pour into 2 chilled stemmed glasses. Garnish drinks with chocolate. Makes 2 drinks.

Gingerroot Tea

½ cup thinly sliced fresh gingerroot
6 cups water
2 tablespoons honey or
    brown sugar

Garnish: lemon wedges

In a saucepan simmer gingerroot and water 20 minutes, or more for stronger tea. Add honey or brown sugar and strain tea through a sieve set over a teapot. Serve tea garnished with lemon wedges. Makes about 4 cups.

Moroccan Mint Tea

2 cups loosely packed fresh mint leaves
⅓ cup sugar
2 tablespoons gunpowder green tea*
6 cups boiling water

Garnish: fresh mint sprigs

*available at specialty tea shops and by mail
    order from Kalustyan's, 123 Lexington Avenue,
    New York, NY 10016, tel. (212) 685-3451

In a teapot combine mint, sugar, and tea and add boiling water. Let tea steep 5 to 10 minutes. Strain tea through a fine sieve into teacups and garnish with mint. Makes 6 cups.

PHOTO ON PAGE 59

THE FLAVORS OF

MEXICO

Mexico is a land of captivating contrasts. In the Yucatán, imposing ancient Mayan ruins dominate the peninsula; a short distance away, modern Caribbean resorts with pristine white sand beaches and turquoise waters are flooded with sun worshipers from around the globe. Amidst the crowded skyscrapers of bustling Mexico City, business people enjoy their midday meal at fashionable restaurants; in the Oaxacan countryside under a blistering sun, Huave women patiently grind dried corn for fresh tortillas. In the northernmost regions of the country, *vaqueros* drive cattle across dry, vast mountain ranges surrounding barren deserts and deep gorges; while in the high, fertile plateaus to the southwest, plodding oxen plow fields of corn, garlic, and onions. Farther west still, coconuts, mangoes, and pineapples flourish among palm trees on the lush, tropical Pacific coast.

Like the land and culture it springs from, Mexican cuisine is a hybrid that is at once ancient and modern, simple and complex, primitive and sophisticated. With roots dating back to the ancient Indians, it is one of the oldest indigenous cuisines in the world. The highly developed dishes that are enjoyed in Mexico today have evolved from the marriage of Indian and Spanish cooking in the sixteenth century. The food is rich in texture, flavor, and aroma, and there is an ongoing effort to create new combinations with the vegetables, seafood, fruits, and spices available. Specialties differ around the country: seafood is enjoyed in fishing villages along the Pacific coast, where abundant shrimp, scallops, and oysters are found; in the fertile plateau area around Guadalajara, simple, rustic dishes made from an extensive variety of vegetables are favored; and beef, dairy products, and flour tortillas are featured in the northern ranch country, where livestock and wheat fields abound.

In the often rudimentary Mexican kitchen, the preparation and enjoyment of food are a priority of the day. Modern conveniences are available in the cities, but in many rural sections the same implements used by ancient ancestors are still utilized. Hours are spent simmering beans in the *olla* (large-necked clay pot with two handles), preparing complex sauces with dozens of ingredients, making fresh *masa* (corn dough for tortillas), and baking breads. Only the freshest regional ingredients are used, and they are all diligently prepared. It is not unusual to find cooks chopping countless vegetables and grinding spices with a *molcajete* and *tejolote* (mortar and pestle) and *cacao* beans, dried corn, and chilies with a *metate y mano* (flat lava stone and cylindrical "pin").

Countryside outside Pátzcuaro in Michoacán

The ancient peoples of Mexico believed that food was a gift from the gods, and, consequently, it played an important role in their spiritual life. They worshiped deities of corn, earth, flowers, rain, salt, fire, cactus, sea snails, and the sun and cultivated fields of *maíz* (corn), squash, and beans to sustain their mainly vegetarian diet. From A.D. 900, the agriculturally advanced Mayans, famous for their massive pyramids and temples, were dominant in the southern state of Chiapas and the Yucatán peninsula. Corn was used to make tortillas, the principal form of bread. Pheasants, partridges, quail, ducks, and rabbits were abundant, and turkey and deer were domesticated. Centuries later, in 1325, the Aztecs settled in central Mexico and began to build a strong empire. Food was their passion, and the emperor, Moctezuma II, held legendary banquets. Chiefs, warriors, women, and priests arrayed in gold and pearl jewelry and ornaments with bright blue and green feathers gathered at the palace, where over thirty elaborate dishes — such as pink salmon with finely ground onions, tamales wrapped in corn husks, wild turkey smothered in chili sauce, and foaming hot chocolate spiced with cinnamon — were presented.

The fate of the Aztecs, and all of Mexico, was changed forever by the arrival of the Spanish conquistadors in the early sixteenth century. In search of spice routes to India, the explorers landed in Cuba, and they eventually found themselves in a race to conquer and occupy the New World. In 1521 Hernán Cortés defeated Moctezuma II and the Aztecs, and the new settlers were amazed by the abundance and diversity of goods they had never seen. In awe they witnessed the incredible Aztec marketplace, where thousands of Indians came every day to buy or sell multi-colored beans, corn, chilies, onions, sweet potatoes, squash, tomatoes, avocados, coconuts, papayas, pineapples. . . . New World foods were transported to Europe and beyond, and many cuisines changed forever — the Italians were introduced to tomatoes, the Irish to potatoes, the French to turkey, and the Asians to countless chilies.

In turn, the Spanish settlers brought their homeland foods — pork, beef, chicken, wheat, rice, garlic, nuts, and sugar cane — to Mexico. They also introduced soups and desserts. The Indians adapted these new ingredients and began cooking with pork lard, preparing *sopas secas* (dry soups) with rice, and discovering different ways to prepare chicken. At the same time, the Spanish learned how to grind pumpkin seeds, chilies, *cacao* beans, and corn with the *metate y mano* and how to cook with turkey, cactus leaves, guavas, and dozens of other New World foods. The union of these two cuisines is epitomized in the wonderful *mole* sauces developed in Mexico by the Spanish nuns, who combined New World chilies, tomatoes, and squash seeds with Old World meats, nuts, spices, and sesame seeds.

The Spaniards held power until 1821, when they were defeated in the Mexican War of Independence. Mexico's freedom was short-lived, however, and between 1864 to 1867 the French controlled the country with Maximilian of Vienna as emperor. Carlotta, the new empress, brought Austro-Hungarian chefs to Mexico, and breads and sweets assumed an important role in the meals of the ruling classes. Eventually French-style breads became widespread throughout the country.

Both Indian and European culinary traditions are seen in Mexican life today. Bustling farmers' markets, reminiscent of the Aztec bazaar, still take place in the *zócalo* (main plaza) of cities and towns, where pyramids of brightly-colored fruits and vegetables, bouquets of squash blossoms, mounds of beans, dried spices, herbs, and steaming stacks of fresh tortillas are all displayed. Beef, pork loin, sausage, eggs, snapper, catfish, and mackerel are all ready to be purchased. Food stands serve fresh *antojitos* (snacks) of grilled corn, *aguas frescas* (blended fruit drinks), hot *bolillos* (crusty rolls), and tortilla treats such as quesadillas, tacos, tostadas, and enchiladas.

European influence is most obvious in the manner in which Mexicans enjoy daily meals. Habits of city dwellers and country residents vary, but in most of the land breakfast is followed by the main meal of the day, and then a light dinner is enjoyed in the evening. In the early mornings students and business people stop in at a *cafetería* or *fonda* (small inn offering home-style cooking) for some hot, dark coffee with fresh *bolillos;* others have a more substantial breakfast, or *almuerzo,* which might include *huevos rancheros* (eggs with tomato chile sauce), *frijoles refritos* (well-fried beans), or *chorizo mexicano* (spicy sausage). When the sweltering sun becomes unbearable for any kind of labor, the *comida* begins. This family meal starts around 2 P.M. and is leisurely enjoyed for about two hours. It generally comprises five courses: a light broth soup; a *sopa seca* (dry soup), which is either rice, pasta, or stale tortillas mixed with diced vegetables or fried eggs; the entrée, a stewed fowl or meat in a sauce, served with tortillas and vegetables; beans; and dessert, usually sliced or stewed fruit in the provinces, and pastries or puddings in the cities. The evening meal is often enjoyed with friends and is kept simple, consisting of snacks such as enchiladas, tamales, and tacos.

On the following pages we offer a primer on the essentials of Mexican cuisine. We begin with a discussion of Mexico's basic ingredients — corn, beans, and chilies — and offer practical information on each. Next we address the topic of Mexican sauces, from the simplest to the most complex, and unlock the mysteries of Mexican spices and seasonings. And, finally, we offer information and tips on making Mexican breads, including tortillas, sweet breads, and crusty rolls. Three diverse menus follow that will give you a helpful overview of the cuisine. When creating these menus, we took a few liberties to accommodate American tastes and eating habits. For example, many of the tortilla dishes that are considered snack dishes in Mexico, such as enchiladas, are eaten as entrées in the United States.

Hearty breakfasts are a delightful surprise to first-time travelers to Mexico, and our Almuerzo menu includes typical dishes enjoyed on weekends. Eggs, beef, tomatoes, and chilies are combined in our flavorful Machacado con Huevos. We've replaced the hard-to-find traditional *machacado* (sun-cured salted beef of Mexico's northern states) with seasoned shredded roast beef. Also common is Baked Chilaquiles with Tomato Chile Sauce — corn tortillas coated with a robust sauce. Pineapple, oranges, and bananas are favorite fruits in Mexico, and our light, tropical salad with a zesty lime dressing refreshes the palate. Naturally, we have also included delicious sweet and savory breads — Bolillos sprayed with a saltwater mist for a crispy crust and Pan Dulce, soft buns sprinkled with a cinnamon-sugar topping. The classic breakfast beverages are frothy hot chocolate, made with cinnamon-flavored Mexican chocolate, and *café con leche*, a blend of strong coffee and hot milk. Use dark-roast coffee beans so your brew will be strong enough to hold up to the hot milk, and try proportions of about 3 parts milk to 1 part coffee.

Our Oaxacan Dinner celebrates the region of south-central Mexico known as the home of the seven *moles*. To start, shrimp, abundant in the salt waters of the coast, is accompanied by a fragrant spicy pumpkin-seed sauce. Our succulent entrée of tender pork loin smothered in a rich *mole coloradito* follows. In traditional style, this brownish-red sauce is slow-cooked and infused with cinnamon, *guajillo* chilies, allspice berries, cloves, and sesame seeds. Inviting and simple Mango Ice Cream and crispy Buñuelos, Mexican treats usually eaten at Christmastime, make a light dessert.

Finally, our Mexican Buffet serves as a showcase for some of the country's most enticing foods. We begin with *tostadas* featuring *frijoles negros* (black beans) and lively pickled red onions. A selection of favorites follows, including lime-marinated slivered beef with onions accompanied by flour tortillas, both very popular in the north; red snapper, a specialty of the coastal regions that is cooked and then marinated in a spiced escabeche; and chicken enchiladas coated with a light tomatillo sauce. Our flan, a glorious dessert originally imported by the Spanish, is enhanced with coconut, the main ingredient of sweets on the Pacific coast.

Let *The Flavors of Mexico* take you south-of-the-border, where you will discover how much more there is to Mexican food than tacos, burritos, and salsa. Our information, photographs, and menus will introduce you to a world where tradition is revered, innovation is encouraged, and there is always time to enjoy well-prepared fare.

CORN, BEANS, AND CHILIES

Although Mexican dishes can be complex, with sophisticated sauces, only a few foods — corn, beans, and chilies — form the foundation of the cuisine. These prolific crops, grown and harvested for centuries, are still an integral part of the Mexican diet.

CORN, considered the staff of life in Mexico, is a tall, graceful plant that grows in all parts of the country regardless of temperature, type of soil, or amount of rainfall. Many varieties exist, offering kernels of pure ivory to purple-black, red, or speckled. Unlike American sweet corn, this is a substantial, chewy field corn that is harvested at maturity for full flavor.

For three thousand years, corn (*maíz*) has been a central element of the cuisine of Mexico, and life there revolves around its growing cycle. Hieroglyphics found by archaeologists prove that from prehistoric

times it was considered a gift from the gods, and, as such, it was consumed to celebrate oneness with them. Even today, corn is used in religious rituals celebrated among rural peoples.

Corn appears daily throughout most of Mexico in the form of the corn tortilla (unleavened corn dough cooked on a griddle), made from either fresh *masa*, prepared dried corn that is ground to a paste, or *masa harina*, fresh *masa* that is dried and powdered and then mixed with water. In Sonora and northern Sinaloa, however, where wheat is grown, flour tortillas are preferred. (For more information on both types of tortillas, see our Tortillas and Breads section, page 271.)

For many Mexicans, particularly those in rural areas, where coffee is too costly to drink throughout the day, corn is also enjoyed in hot *atole*, a breakfast or dinner drink made from corn gruel sweetened with raw sugar and flavored with crushed fruits or chilies. It is usually paired with *pan dulce* (sweet bread) or tamales. *Champurrado* is another *atole,* made from ground corn and water or from milk with chocolate, cinnamon, and sugar.

Naturally, fresh corn kernels are enjoyed in many traditional soups and vegetable dishes; hominy, lime-treated dried corn kernels, is also used in *pozole* (a favorite soup). But perhaps the most revered corn dish is the tamale, a dough of *masa,* water, and lard stuffed with various fillings such as pork, shrimp,

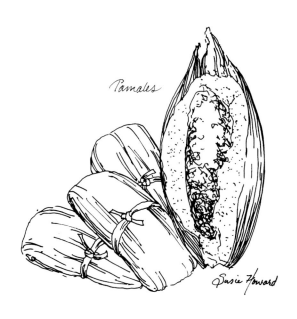

Tamales

Susie Howard

fish, and pumpkin, and wrapped in corn husks and steamed. This traditional gift to the gods is reserved for fiestas and Sunday suppers in restaurants, although it is also sold at some early-morning markets.

BEANS, plentiful in every region, grow alongside fields of corn. At the marketplace, regional dried beans (*frijoles*) are piled high, and the variety available is astonishing. Black beans (nicknamed *veracruzanos*) are found throughout the country, while speckled pinto beans are the most popular in the north. Reddish-brown kidney beans, purple *flor de*

mayo, deep yellow *canarios,* brownish *bayos,* white *aluvias,* and big green-and-white *habas* are also common in various parts of the country. Each is enjoyed for its special flavor and texture.

There is a bean dish present at almost every Mexican meal. Traditionally, Mexicans breakfast on beans that have been cooked slowly in an earthenware pot in water with a little onion, lard, and salt and a good sprig of the herb *epazote* to complement their flavor. Today, modern Mexicans, with less time to spend in the kitchen, use a pressure cooker or metal pot to cook their beans. Our Frijoles Negros (Black Beans, page 280) are simply cooked without lard in a saucepan with garlic and onion. These beans are also enjoyed after the main course of the midday meal, served in their broth and scooped up with a tortilla. A kind of cream cheese is sometimes melted in the hot broth of the beans, or *serrano* or *jalapeño* chilies can be added.

For the best-flavored beans, do not soak them overnight to soften them. Simply cook dried beans gently, remembering that older ones are tough and take longer to cook. Also, wait until the beans are soft before salting them or the skins will harden. Beans are best eaten a day or so after they are cooked. Once they are cool, simply refrigerate them, covered, and reheat them when needed.

Frijoles refritos ("well-fried" beans — not "refried," as is generally assumed) are another favorite that appear in many forms, often with breakfast eggs or as dinnertime snacks. Cooked beans are lightly fried to a loose paste and served with a variety of toppings, depending on regional preference. In Michoacán, for example, beans are simply cooked in their own broth and served with a bit of sour cream, while in Veracruz they are fried along with chopped onions and a dried red chili. In Yucatán the beans are sieved to a paste and then fried with onion and a whole *habanero* chili for an even hotter dish. In our Black Bean Tostadas (page 296) cooked beans are fried with pork fat (or vegetable oil, if preferred), onion, and garlic. This mixture is spread on tortillas, topped with pickled red onions and another tortilla, and fried again.

CHILIES, the beautiful and lively members of the *Capsicum* family, grow in nearly 100 different varieties in Mexico, where they pervade the cuisine. It is believed that the first chilies were actually wild berries that grew on vines in the Amazon jungle in South America thousands of years ago. These plants flourished, and, with the help of birds spreading the seeds, as well as trade among the peoples of South America and Mesoamerica, chilies spread northward. In Mexico, the Mayans cultivated at least 30 varieties, and the Aztecs used them in almost every dish.

Most chilies grow easily in various soils, but the type of soil helps determine a chili's level of heat. *Jalapeños* grown in the United States are usually milder than Mexican varieties, but you should never assume that you know how bland or *picante* a particular chili might be. (If you consume an extremely hot one, it is good to know that you can put out the fire with milk, yogurt, or ice cream!) The heat of a chili comes from *capsaicin*, a chemical that is concentrated in its veins (internal ribs) and seeds, and the more *capsaicin* in a chili, the hotter it is. Because smaller chilies have proportionately more seeds and veins, they are more piquant than larger ones. To avoid the full heat of any chili, simply cut out the ribs and discard them along with the seeds. Always wear rubber gloves and take care not to touch your eyes or skin. In addition to adding flavor, chilies aid digestion and stimulate the appetite.

Many chilies are used in various stages of ripeness, ranging from green to red. The riper (redder) it is, the sweeter and fruitier it becomes. Regarding heat, the broader the shoulders of a chili, the milder it is. Dried chilies, while not necessarily hotter than fresh, are more intense in flavor.

When selecting fresh chilies, choose those that are dry, firm, and heavy for their size. The skin should be unblemished, shiny, and smooth and have a fresh smell. Wash the chilies in water and dry them thoroughly. To store, wrap them in paper towels and keep them in the crisper section of your refrigerator for two or three weeks. Do not leave them uncovered or stored in plastic bags.

When buying dried chilies, look for a uniform deep or brilliant color and some flexibility. Avoid faded or dusty chilies or those that have white spots, indicating improper drying or disease. Never purchase broken chilies, as they will be void of essential oils that give them their unique flavors. They should have a nice aroma. You can store dried chilies and chili powder in an airtight container in a cool, dry, dark place for up to six months.

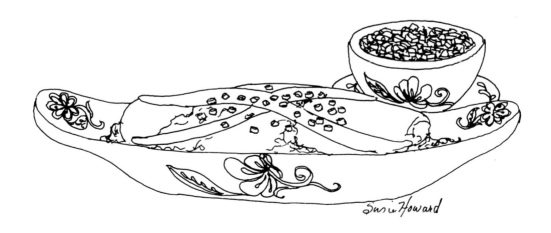

With so many types of chilies available, confusion abounds. And in both Mexican and American markets, chilies often are mislabeled. Below is a list of chilies used in our Mexican menus. They are generally arranged from mild to piquant:

FRESH CHILIES

Anaheim (green or red): Mild heat. Includes a green-colored chili also known as the California or long green chili and a red-colored chili also known as *chile colorado*. About 6 inches long and 1 to 1½ inches in diameter. Originally grown around Anaheim, California, and now available in California and the southwestern United States. Closely related to the New Mexico chili.

New Mexico (green or red): Mild to medium heat. Green-colored chili also known as long green chili. Tapered, 6 to 9 inches long; about 1½ inches in diameter. Hotter and clearer taste than the Anaheim. Grown in the Rio Grande Valley, New Mexico, where it is available fresh nearly year-round. When red chili is dried, it is called *chile pasado*.

Poblano (green or red): Medium to hot heat. One of the most popular chilies in Mexico. From the Puebla region, the central valley of Mexico, and California. The green-colored *poblano* is dark green with a purple-black tinge; the red *poblano* is a deep red-brown color. Wide shoulders tapering down to a point. About 4 to 5 inches long and 2½ to 3 inches in diameter; thick-fleshed. When the red *poblano* is dried it is known as the *ancho* chili or the *mulato* chili.

Jalapeño (green or red): Medium to hot heat. Measures 2 to 3 inches long and ¾ to 1 inch in diameter with tapered to rounded end. Thick-fleshed. When *jalapeños* are dried by smoking them, usually over mesquite wood, they are known as *chipotle* chilies. *Jalapeños* are grown in Veracruz, Oaxaca, and Chihuahua and in Texas and other parts of the southwestern United States.

Guero: Medium to hot heat. Yellow chili (meaning light-skinned or blond), such as the Hungarian wax or banana chili, or the Santa Fe grande. Size varies from 3 to 5 inches long and 1 to 1½ inches in diameter. Medium-fleshed. Grown in northern Mexico and the southwestern United States.

DRIED CHILIES

Serrano (green or red): Hottest chili commonly available in the United States. Bright dark green to scarlet when ripe. Cylindrical with tapered, rounded end; measures 1 to 2 inches long and ½ to ¾ inches in diameter. Thick-fleshed. Green and red *serranos* can be used interchangeably, although red is somewhat sweeter. Grown in Mexico and in the southwestern United States.

Habanero (dark green, orange, orange-red, to red when ripe): Among hottest of chilies grown in the world. Lantern shape, measuring about 1½ inches long and 1¼ to 1¾ inches in diameter. Can be found in dried form. Grown and used extensively in Yucatán and the Caribbean.

Ancho: Mild to medium heat. (Means "wide" in Spanish.) This is the dried *poblano* chili, the most commonly used dried chili in Mexico. (Frequently mislabeled as *pasilla* chili.) Brick red to dark mahogany, with an orange-red cordovan tint. Wrinkled, with broad shoulders. Medium-thick-fleshed. Sold in three grades in Mexico. At best, it is flexible and aromatic. From the Puebla region and central valley in Mexico and from California.

Pasilla: Mild to medium heat. Also known as *chile negro*, it is the dried *chilaca* chili. Dark raisin brown, wrinkled, elongated, and tapering. Measures about 5 to 6 inches long and ¾ to 1½ inches across. Thin-fleshed. Found in Guanajuato, Jalisco, and Zacatecas. Sold in three grades in Mexico.

Guajillo: Mild to medium heat. Shiny, deep orange-red with brown tones. Elongated, tapering to a point. Measures 4 to 6 inches long and 1 to 1½ inches across. Thin-fleshed. Grown in north and central Mexico.

SAUCES

Every cuisine of the world uses a particular combination of flavors that distinguishes it from the rest. In Mexico, it is the myriad sauces that provide such distinction. Cooking with fresh, local ingredients is a passion in this country, and its sauces reflect the variety of crops available, as well as an eclectic mix of favorite regional recipes.

Chilies (page 265) provide the most characteristic flavoring of Mexican dishes. They are prized for their *picante* nature and are combined with tomatoes, onions, and garlic to form the foundation of all *salsas* (sauces). All vegetables must be absolutely fresh, and tomatoes should be vine-ripened. When tomatoes are out of season, however, canned Italian plum tomatoes are acceptable. And be sure to use only white onions — they are closer in flavor to the Mexican *cebolla*.

Perhaps the most universal sauce of Mexico is *salsa cruda* — known in the United States simply as

salsa — an uncooked combination of tomatoes, onion, chilies, coriander, salt, and water. This refreshing sauce has a permanent place in every kitchen and is used to complement breakfast eggs, lunchtime roasted or broiled meats, evening tacos, and the ubiquitous *frijoles de olla* (beans cooked in a pot) and tortillas. Depending on the type of chilies used, it can be a gentle tomato sauce as it is in Sonora or quite fiery as in Yucatán, where *habanero* chilies are preferred. Other regional variations include the Sinaloa version, where scallions and lime juice replace the onion and water.

Another Mexican favorite is *guacamole* (Aztec, meaning avocado mixture), an uncooked sauce of avocado, onion, *serrano* chili, tomato, cilantro, lime juice, and salt that is usually served as a condiment with tacos or *botanas* (before-meal snacks). (Our milder *guacamole* recipe (page 298) omits the chili and adds garlic.) In Mexico, it is often made with a

268

molcajete and *tejolote* (mortar and pestle), although it can be made with a fork and bowl. Just remember that it is important to mash the avocado without pulverizing the other ingredients, so avoid using a blender or food processor. Avocados can be ripened in a paper bag at room temperature, then stored in the refrigerator. In the United States look for California avocados, preferably Hass or Fuerte varieties.

Salsa verde (tomatillo sauce) is yet another sauce that appears on Mexican tables as a condiment, but it also appears in various dishes. Usually the *tomatillo* (also known as *tomate verde* — "green tomato") is dehusked and cooked with chilies, then blended with onion and coriander. The *tomatillo* is a lime-green fruit that is actually not a true tomato, although it is a member of the nightshade family. It is enclosed in a papery husk and has a tart taste that melds with other ingredients once it is cooked. Since *tomatillos* are grown in the southwestern United States, they are available, fresh or canned, at Hispanic markets and by mail order. Use canned *tomatillos* only if the fresh are not available, and be sure to drain them first, because the canning liquid is quite strong. Fresh *tomatillos* will keep in the refrigerator for two weeks.

On Sundays and festive days the Mexicans enjoy a sauce that takes the better part of a day to prepare and cook. It is called *mole* (from the Aztec, meaning "chili mixture") and contains as many as 27 ingredients, including various chilies and spices. The Spanish conquistadors first tasted intricate chili sauces at the table of Moctezuma II in the sixteenth century, but it was the Christian nuns who further developed these sauces by combining Indian and Spanish flavorings. *Mole poblano*, now a Mexican national treasure, was created in the convent kitchen of Santa Rosa in Puebla by the sister superior in charge of the food preparations for the visiting archbishop and Spanish viceroy. This is a chocolate *mole* traditionally served with turkey.

Neighboring Oaxaca is also known for various *mole* sauces. *Mole coloradito*, another typical *mole*, is a brownish-red sauce that we have paired with roast pork (page 288) in our Oaxacan dinner menu. Here the pork, a Spanish offering, is complemented with the flavors of the Indians — tomatoes, *guajillo* chilies, plantain, and a host of seasonings — for a sumptuous entrée. As with most Mexican cooked sauces using dried, soaked, and blended chilies, the fat is heated, the onion is sautéed, and then the chili mixture is "fried" into the hot fat to combine and bond the flavors. It is a messy process, as the chili mixture spatters! Broth is added after the "frying," and then the sauce is cooked over low heat until it thickens. Preparing any *mole* is time-consuming; luckily, ours can be prepared up to three days before your guests arrive.

Another very popular sauce is *pepián* or *pipián* (from *pepitas*, meaning "squash seeds"), which uses ground seeds or nuts for flavoring and as a thickening agent. This rich, multiflavored sauce is a direct descendant of Aztec pumpkin-seed mixtures that the Spanish conquerors enjoyed and adapted. Our Oaxacan butterflied shrimp starter (page 286) is complemented by a golden-colored, spicy pumpkin-seed sauce that combines puréed *pasilla* and *ancho* chilies with dry-roasted and husked pumpkin seeds.

Below is a listing of seasonings that are essential in cooking Mexican sauces and various other dishes (see menus for mail order sources):

- *Achiote* paste: A mixture of *achiote* (dark red seeds of the annatto tree), garlic, cumin, Mexican oregano, and other spices that lends reddish color and earthy flavor to dishes of Yucatán.
- *Cacahuate* (Aztec for "peanut"): Ground peanuts used for thickening and flavoring sauces.
- *Canela* (cinnamon): The light brown bark of the true cinnamon tree, native to Sri Lanka and the Spice Islands. In the United States we more often find a darker, harder bark from Vietnam.
- *Coriander* (also known as cilantro or Chinese parsley): An herb with a unique pungent flavor that adds freshness to any dish and tones down spicy ones. Store in refrigerator with roots in water, covered with a plastic bag or wrap.
- *Epazote*: Pungent annual herb with anise flavor, indigenous to Mexico. Used in tamales, omelets, sauces, and medicinal teas, and with beans.
- *Lime*: The common lime in Mexico is closer to the small Key lime than it is to the larger, sweeter Persian lime we see in our markets. The lemon is seldom found in Mexico.
- *Oregano*: Mexican oregano is a stronger version than that used in the United States.

- *Parsley*: Italian parsley, with its flat leaves, is used for fuller flavor than the curly-leaved type.
- *Recados*: Seasoning pastes used in Central America and Yucatán. The best-known contains *achiote* and other herbs and spices. These pastes can be found in Latin American markets or can be made at home.
- *Vinegar*: In Mexico, made from sugar cane, pineapples, apples, or bananas. It is blander than those varieties found in the United States.

Other important Mexican tastes and flavorings:

- *Adobo*: A vinegar, salt, herb, garlic, spice, chili (and sometimes tomato) mixture used in canned *chipotle* chilies; as a marinade for meats, fish, or seafood; or in enchiladas.
- *Chorizo*: Spicy pork sausage that is used with potatoes (page 300), scrambled eggs, or cheese.
- *Escabeche*: Sauce or marinade (page 298) made with vinegar, garlic, onions, whole peppercorns, bay leaves, marjoram, and thyme. It preserves meat, poultry, fish, and seafood.
- *Lard*: Rendered pork fat. Used in traditional Mexican cooking and essential in some dishes. Lard has half the cholesterol of butter. Try to use real lard instead of the processed, hydrogenated kind sold in supermarkets.

TORTILLAS AND BREADS

Over a thousand years ago a creative Indian took dried *maíz* (corn), ground it into a smooth paste, formed thin, unleavened rounds, and cooked them over a fire. The tortilla was born, and Mexican cuisine has never been the same since. This unleavened corn bread became an integral part of Mexican cooking, and it now appears in countless forms and shapes: in tacos, enchiladas, tostadas, and quesadillas; as croutons for soups; layered between meats, vegetables, and cheese in *sopas secas* — the list goes on and on. But the tortilla was just the beginning of the country's love affair with breads. Centuries later, in the 1500s, the Spanish brought wheat to the New World, and the natives immediately acquired the newcomers' fondness for yeast breads. They learned how to make hearty loaves, as well as soft, light rolls and wonderful sweet breads. During the short French occupation of Mexico in the 1860s, French-style loaves and sweet breads were introduced and yeast breads became even more widespread. Now they are consumed every day.

Corn tortillas are a mainstay throughout Mexico. Although they are still often made at home, they are also purchased in *tortillerías* and at the popular food stands that sell snacks. Tortillas are made from fresh *masa* (corn dough) or *masa harina* (literally "dough flour") and water and do not vary much from region to region. Fresh *masa* is made with dried corn kernels that are simmered and soaked in water that has been treated with powdered limestone. Most of the skin of the kernels is then rubbed off, and the remaining corn is ground to a paste. In the United States fresh *masa* is sold at tortilla factories, often still hot, tied tightly in plastic bags. It is also available by mail order from Maria and Ricardo's Tortilla Factory in Jamaica Plain, Massachusetts, (617) 524-6107. Be sure to use fresh *masa* within a day or two, as it will taste sour if left too long. Unused portions should be formed into flat cakes and stored in the freezer. *Masa harina* is fresh *masa* that has been dried and powdered, and since it keeps indefinitely, it is a good alternative. (We use *masa harina* for our corn tortillas, page 288.) Tortillas made with this dried corn flour have a toasted flavor and slight graininess. Never substitute all-purpose flour or cornmeal. In the United States *masa harina* is widely available in supermarkets under the Quaker brand.

Once *masa harina* is mixed with water, the tortilla dough is prepared just like *masa* — it is rolled into balls and each ball is flattened into a "pancake." In some rural areas of Mexico, the dough is still artfully patted between the hands as it was centuries ago, but in most regions a tortilla press is used. (They are fairly inexpensive. If you buy one, keep in mind that a heavy press is better than one made of a lightweight alloy.) Throughout Mexico, tortillas are made in different sizes or thicknesses according to preference: in Oaxaca *banditas*, white, smooth, very thin tortillas, are popular; in Tabasco, thick tortillas the size of salad plates are enjoyed. When the dough rounds are all flattened and stacked, the cooking begins. Traditionally, a *comal* (round, unglazed earthenware or metal plate) is set over an open flame, but a griddle or skillet works just as well. The pressed tortillas are carefully placed on the hot griddle and cooked until slightly speckled but still soft. Tortillas should be stacked and wrapped in a kitchen towel as they are cooked to keep them from drying out.

The versatile corn tortilla appropriately appears in all three of our menus. In our Chilaquiles (literally "pieces of broken up old sombrero," page 278), stale tortillas are cut up and baked with a tomato chili sauce and cheese for a warming brunch dish. You will find tortillas again as part of a starter in our Butterflied Shrimp with Pumpkin Seed Sauce and Cheese Quesadillas (page 286), where they are stuffed with a simple mild cheese and coriander filling, folded over to make a "turnover," and then lightly fried until golden. And, finally, in our buffet they appear twice: In our Black Bean Tostadas (page 296), cut tortilla wedges are spread with black beans and pickled onions, and in our Chicken Enchiladas with Tomatillo Sauce (page 297) tortillas are filled with a chicken mixture, rolled, and dipped in a zesty sauce.

In northern regions of the country, where wheat is grown, flour tortillas are popular. These soft white tortillas are made from an all-purpose flour, shortening, salt, and water dough. It is important to combine the shortening and the flour completely so no particles remain visible or the tortillas will have an irregular texture. The dough is rolled into balls and must stand for at least 30 minutes. Then each ball is rolled out (no tortilla press is used) and cooked in the same manner as corn tortillas. Flour tortillas are generally used to wrap sliced meat, another northern favorite, as in our Slivered Beef with Onions (page 298).

Corn and flour tortillas are *not* interchangeable. Store-bought frozen tortillas are adequate for many dishes and can be ordered by mail from Maria and Ricardo's Tortilla Factory (see page 271).

Tortilla Press

Susie Howard

Although tortillas are the preferred bread for everyday fare, French-style yeast breads are also very common, especially for breakfast and *almuerzo* (brunch). *Bolillos* (split-topped, crispy rolls) can be found today in restaurants throughout most of the country. They are often enjoyed lightly toasted as an accompaniment to *huevos rancheros* (eggs with tomato chili sauce). (Our recipe for *bolillos*, page 280, gives you the option of spraying the rolls with a saltwater mist before baking, to give them an even crisper crust.) *Pan dulce* (sweet bread), from the local *panadería* (bakery), is usually savored with a cup of foaming hot chocolate for a typical early-morning meal. It is made in various shapes with different sweet toppings (see page 281 for our plump, cinnamon-sugar-topped buns).

Another sweet treat are *buñuelos*, paper-thin fritters, sometimes sprinkled with cinnamon sugar or dipped in vanilla-flavored syrup. These delightful morsels are direct descendants of the Spanish *churros* and were originally made for festive occasions, such as saints' days and Christmas Eve. Today they are enjoyed in the morning or as a snack. People gather in the *zócalo* (city plaza) in the evenings and eat *buñuelos acaremlizados* (still crisp) or *piloncillo* (cooked in syrup until soft). The simple dough for our *buñuelos* (page 291) is flavored with a hint of aniseed and cinnamon for a slightly spiced taste.

ALMUERZO

(A MEXICAN BRUNCH)

Ensalada de Naranja, Piña, y Platano con Salsa de Lima Agria
(Orange, Pineapple, and Banana Salad with Lime Dressing)

Chilaquiles al Horno con Salsa de Chiles y Tomates
(Baked Chilaquiles with Tomato Chili Sauce)

Machacado con Huevos
(Shredded Beef with Eggs)

Frijoles Negros
(Black Beans)

Bolillos
(Crusty Mexican Rolls)

Pan Dulce
(Mexican Sweet Buns)

•

Chocolate Mexicano
(Mexican Hot Chocolate)

Café con Leche
(Coffee with Milk)

•

Serves 6

Chilaquiles al Horno con
Salsa de Chiles y Tomates;
Frijoles Negros; Bolillos;
Machacado con Huevos

Café con Leche;
Chocolate Mexicano;
Pan Dulce

Ensalada de Naranja, Piña, y Platano con Salsa de Lima Agria

276

*Ensalada de Naranja, Piña, y Platano con
Salsa de Lima Agria*
(Orange, Pineapple, and Banana Salad with
Lime Dressing)

For dressing
4 tablespoons fresh lime juice
2 teaspoons sugar
¼ teaspoon salt
the zest of 1 lime, removed with a vegetable peeler
    and cut into ½-inch-long fine shreds
1 tablespoon vegetable oil

1 pineapple
4 navel oranges
3 bananas

Make dressing:
In a small bowl whisk together lime juice, sugar,
and salt, whisking until sugar is dissolved, and whisk
in zest and oil.

With a serrated knife peel pineapple, leaving flesh
in one piece, and cut into ¼-inch-thick rounds. Halve
pineapple rounds and cut out and discard core. With
serrated knife cut away orange peel and pith and section oranges, discarding membranes. Cut bananas
into ¼-inch-thick rounds. Arrange fruit decoratively
on a platter and spoon dressing over it. *Fruit salad
may be made 30 minutes ahead and chilled, covered.*
Serves 6.

Chilaquiles al Horno con Salsa de Chiles y Tomates
(Baked Chilaquiles with Tomato Chili Sauce)

For tomato chili sauce
2 fresh green or red Anaheim or New Mexico
    chilies* (about ¼ pound)
1 medium onion, chopped
2 tablespoons vegetable oil or lard
1 large garlic clove, minced
2 fresh green or red *serrano** or *jalapeño* chilies,
    seeded and minced (wear rubber gloves)
1½ pounds fresh plum tomatoes (about
    10 medium), peeled and chopped, or a 28-ounce
    can whole plum tomatoes, drained and chopped
½ cup chicken broth

⅓ cup vegetable oil
8 stale 6-inch corn tortillas, cut into eighths

½ cup chicken broth
¾ cup grated Monterey Jack cheese
½ cup sour cream
3 tablespoons milk
2 tablespoons finely chopped red onion

*available at Hispanic markets, specialty produce
    markets, some supermarkets, and by mail
    order from Kitchen, New York, NY,
    tel. (212) 243-4433

Make tomato chili sauce:
Using a long-handled fork char Anaheim or New
Mexico chilies over an open flame, turning until
skins are charred and blackened, 2 to 3 minutes.
(Alternatively, broil chilies on rack of a broiler pan
under a preheated broiler about 2 inches from heat,
turning every 5 minutes, until skins are blistered and
charred, about 15 minutes.) Transfer charred chilies
to a bowl and let steam, covered, until cool enough to
handle. Wearing rubber gloves peel charred chilies
and discard seeds and ribs. Chop peeled chilies
coarse. In a heavy saucepan cook onion in oil or lard
over moderate heat, stirring, until golden. Add garlic
and *serrano* or *jalapeño* chilies and cook, stirring,
until garlic is fragrant, about 30 seconds. Stir in tomatoes, chopped peeled chilies, and broth and cook over
moderately high heat, stirring frequently, until
reduced to about 2½ cups, about 10 minutes for fresh
tomatoes and 5 minutes for canned. Season sauce
with salt. *Sauce may be made 3 days ahead and
chilled, covered. Reheat sauce over moderate heat.*

In a heavy skillet heat oil over moderate heat until
hot but not smoking and fry tortillas in 5 batches until
browned lightly and slightly crisp, about 1 minute,
transferring tortillas as fried with a slotted spoon to
paper towels to drain.

Preheat oven to 350° F.

In a large bowl combine tortillas gently with sauce
and broth, coating well, and transfer to a 2½- to 3-
quart shallow baking dish. Sprinkle cheese over tortillas and bake *chilaquiles* in middle of oven 20 minutes, or until bubbling and cheese is melted. While
chilaquiles are baking, in a small bowl stir together
sour cream and milk. Transfer *chilaquiles* to a rack.
Drizzle some sour cream mixture over *chilaquiles*
and sprinkle with onion.

Serve remaining sour cream mixture separately.
Serves 6.

Machacado con Huevos
(Shredded Beef with Eggs)

For shredded beef
a 2¾- to 3-pound bottom round roast
1 tablespoon vegetable oil
2 bay leaves
2 garlic cloves, smashed
2 tablespoons fresh lime juice
1 cup water

¼ cup vegetable oil or lard
1 large onion, chopped fine
2 large garlic cloves, minced
5 plum tomatoes, chopped fine
    (about ¾ pound)
4 fresh green or red *serrano** or 3 small
    green or red *jalapeño* chilies, minced
    (wear rubber gloves)
8 large eggs, beaten lightly

Garnish: fresh coriander leaves

* available at Hispanic markets, specialty produce
    markets, some supermarkets, and by mail order
    from Kitchen, New York, NY,
    tel. (212) 243-4433

Make shredded beef:
Pat roast dry. In a heavy kettle heat oil over moderately high heat until hot but not smoking and brown roast on all sides. Add remaining shredded beef ingredients and simmer, covered, until meat is very tender, about 2½ hours. Cool roast, uncovered, in liquid and chill, covered, overnight.

Preheat oven to 350° F.

Cut two-thirds of roast with the grain into ¼-inch-thick slices, reserving remaining meat and cooking liquid for another use and discarding bay leaves, and arrange on an ungreased baking sheet. Bake until almost completely dried out, about 15 minutes, and cool completely. Tear meat into strips and in a blender pulse in 4 batches until chopped into fluffy threads. *Shredded beef may be made 3 days ahead and chilled, covered.*

In a 12-inch heavy skillet heat oil or lard over moderately high heat until hot but not smoking and sauté onion and shredded beef, stirring, until beef is browned. Stir in garlic, tomatoes, and chilies and sauté, stirring, 1 minute. Reduce heat to moderately low. Add eggs and salt to taste and cook, stirring occasionally, until eggs are cooked through.

Garnish *machacado con huevos* with coriander leaves. Serves 6.

Susi Howard

Frijoles Negros
(Black Beans)

1½ cups dried black beans, picked over and rinsed
1 garlic clove, chopped
1 small onion, chopped
3 scallions, sliced thin

In a large saucepan combine beans, garlic, onion, and cold water to cover by 2 inches. Bring water to a boil and simmer, covered partially, stirring occasionally, until beans are tender, about 1 to 1½ hours. Season beans with salt and serve sprinkled with scallions. Serves 6.

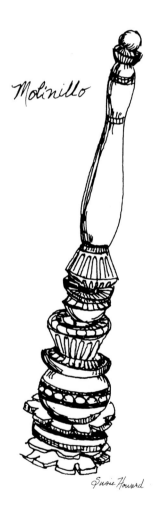

Molinillo

Susie Howard

Bolillos
(Crusty Mexican Rolls)

For sponge
1 tablespoon sugar
2½ cups warm water (110° to 115° F.)
1 tablespoon active dry yeast
   (one and one-half ¼-ounce packages)
1 cup bread flour (preferably unbleached*)
1 cup all-purpose flour

1 tablespoon salt
2 tablespoons unsalted butter, softened
3 cups bread flour (preferably unbleached*)
2 to 2½ cups all-purpose flour
a spray bottle filled with salted water if desired

*available at specialty foods shops and some
   natural food stores

Make sponge:
In bowl of a standing electric mixer dissolve sugar in water. Sprinkle yeast over water and let stand until foamy, about 5 minutes. Add flours and beat sponge with paddle attachment until combined well (sponge will not be smooth). Let sponge stand, covered with plastic wrap, in a warm place 1 hour.

To sponge add salt, butter, bread flour, and 2 cups all-purpose flour and beat with dough hook, scraping down side and adding enough of remaining ½ cup all-purpose flour if necessary to form a soft and slightly sticky dough. Knead dough with dough hook 5 minutes or by hand 10 minutes. Form dough into a ball and transfer to a large buttered bowl. Turn dough to coat and let rise, covered with plastic wrap, until double in bulk, about 1 hour.

Lightly grease 2 heavy baking sheets.

Punch down dough and divide into 12 pieces. Form each piece into a 4½-inch-long oblong shape and transfer to prepared baking sheets. Let rolls rise, uncovered, in a warm place until double in bulk, about 30 minutes.

Preheat oven to 400° F.

Cut a shallow lengthwise slash in each roll with a single-edged razor blade or very sharp knife and, if a harder crust is desired, with spray bottle mist lightly with salted water. Bake rolls in middle of oven 10 minutes. Reduce oven temperature to 375° F. and bake rolls until very pale golden and sound hollow when tapped on bottom, about 15 minutes more. Transfer rolls to racks to cool. Bolillos *may be made 2 weeks ahead and frozen, wrapped in foil. To recrisp bake frozen* bolillos, *unwrapped, on baking sheet in a preheated 350° F. oven about 8 minutes.* Makes 12 bolillos.

Pan Dulce
(Mexican Sweet Buns)

½ cup plus 1 teaspoon sugar
2 tablespoons warm water (110° to 115° F.)
a ¼-ounce package active dry yeast
⅓ cup milk, heated to warm
1½ teaspoon vanilla
4 large eggs
2 large egg yolks
4½ to 5 cups all-purpose flour
1 teaspoon salt
¾ stick (6 tablespoons) unsalted butter, cut into
    6 pieces and softened
For topping
¼ cup all-purpose flour
⅓ cup sugar
1 teaspoon cinnamon
3 tablespoons cold unsalted butter,
    cut into bits

an egg wash made by beating 1 yolk with 1
    tablespoon water

In bowl of a standing electric mixer fitted with paddle attachment dissolve 1 teaspoon sugar in the water. Sprinkle yeast over water and let stand until foamy, about 5 minutes. Add milk, vanilla, and remaining ½ cup sugar and beat until combined well. Beat in eggs and yolks, 1 at a time, and beat in 1 cup flour, salt, and butter, beating until combined well. Beat in 3½ cups flour, adding enough of remaining ½ cup to form a soft and sticky dough (dough should not be too sticky to knead). Using a pastry scraper to facilitate kneading turn dough out onto work surface and knead until smooth and elastic and loses its stickiness, about 10 minutes. Form dough into a ball and transfer to a large buttered bowl. Turn dough to coat and let rise, covered with plastic wrap, in a warm place until double in bulk, about 1½ hours.

Make topping:

In a small bowl combine well flour, sugar, and cinnamon and blend in butter until mixture resembles coarse meal. Chill topping, covered.

Butter 2 heavy baking sheets.

Punch down dough and divide into 12 pieces. Form each piece into a ball and flatten into a 3½-inch bun, transferring as formed to prepared baking sheets. Brush tops of buns lightly with egg wash and sprinkle evenly with topping. Let buns rise, covered loosely with kitchen towels, in a warm place 30 minutes.

Preheat oven to 375° F.

Bake buns in 2 batches in middle of oven 12 minutes, or until bottom edges are golden. (Topping will not turn golden.) Transfer buns to racks to cool. Pan dulce *may be made 1 day ahead and kept in airtight containers, but topping will lose its crispness.* Makes 12 buns.

Chocolate Mexicano
(Mexican Hot Chocolate)

three 3.3-ounce tablets Mexican chocolate*,
    chopped
6 cups milk
3 cups water

*available at some specialty foods shops and
    by mail order from Kitchen, New York, NY,
    tel. (212) 243-4433

In a blender in batches or with a hand grater grind chocolate fine. In a heavy saucepan heat milk, water, and chocolate over moderate heat, stirring occasionally, until smooth and just comes to a boil. Pour hot chocolate into a heatproof pitcher and with a *molinillo* (Mexican chocolate beater), whisk, or hand-held electric mixer beat until frothy. (Alternatively, hot chocolate may be beaten in batches in a blender, covered loosely, until frothy.) Serve hot chocolate immediately. Makes about 9 cups.

COMIDA DE OAXACA
(OAXACAN DINNER)

Maní de Chiles
(Chili-Dusted Peanuts)

Lime Refresher

•

Camarones con Salsa de Calabaza y Quesadillas
(Butterflied Shrimp with Pumpkin Seed Sauce and Cheese Quesadillas)

Murphy-Goode Alexander Valley Reserve Fumé, Barrel-Fermented Sauvignon Blanc 1992

•

Loma de Cerdo Asado con Mole Coloradito
(Roast Pork Loin with Coloradito Mole)

Calabacitas Salteadas con Menta
(Sautéed Zucchini with Mint)

Arroz Blanco con Fajas de Chile Poblano en Escabeche
(White Rice with Marinated Poblano Chili Strips)

Fess Parker Santa Barbara County Syrah 1992

•

Helado de Mango   *Buñuelos*
(Mango Ice Cream)   *(Oaxacan Sweet Fritters)*

•

Serves 6

Camarones con Salsa de Calabaza y Quesadillas

Loma de Cerdo Asado con Mole Coloradito;
Calabacitas Salteadas con Menta;
Arroz Blanco con Fajas de Chile Poblano en Escabeche

Refresco de Lima Agria
(Lime Refresher)

6 cups water
1 cup sugar
¼ cup freshly grated lime zest (from about
    12 dark green limes)
½ cup fresh lime juice

Garnish: lime wedges

In a large saucepan bring water to a boil with sugar and simmer, stirring, until sugar is dissolved. Cool sugar syrup to room temperature. Add zest and lime juice and chill at least 4 hours or overnight.

Serve drink over ice and garnish with lime wedges. Makes about 7½ cups.

Maní de Chiles
(Chili-Dusted Peanuts)

1½ tablespoons vegetable oil
1½ teaspoons chili powder (preferably New
    Mexican*), or to taste
¾ pound unsalted peanuts (about 2 cups)
¾ teaspoon salt, or to taste
4 large garlic cloves, chopped

*available at some specialty foods shops and
    by mail order from Kitchen, New York, NY,
    tel. (212) 243-4433

In a large heavy skillet heat oil over moderate heat until hot but not smoking. Stir in remaining ingredients and cook, stirring, until peanuts darken slightly, about 5 minutes (peanuts will become crisp as they cool). Spread peanuts in one layer in a shallow baking pan to cool and season with salt to taste. *Peanuts may be made 1 week ahead and kept in an airtight container.* Makes about 2 cups.

Camarones con Salsa de Calabaza y Quesadillas
(Butterflied Shrimp with Pumpkin Seed Sauce and Cheese Quesadillas)

½ pound raw unhulled pumpkin seeds*
1 *pasilla* chili**, stems, seeds, and ribs discarded
    (wear rubber gloves)
1 *ancho* chili**, stems, seeds, and ribs discarded
    (wear rubber gloves)
4 garlic cloves
4 cups water
1 teaspoon cuminseed
2 tablespoons vegetable oil
1 small white onion, diced fine
1½ pounds medium shrimp (about 45), shelled,
    leaving tail intact, and deveined

Garnish: 2 tablespoons fresh coriander leaves,
    chopped
Accompaniment: cheese *quesadillas*
    (recipe follows)

*available at some natural foods stores,
    and by mail order from Sultan's Delight,
    tel. (800) 852-5046
**available at Hispanic markets, and by mail
    order from Kitchen, New York, NY,
    tel. (212) 243-4433

In a large heavy skillet dry-roast pumpkin seeds over moderate heat, stirring, until darkened slightly, being careful not to burn, 5 to 7 minutes (seeds will crack and pop). Spread seeds in one layer in a shallow baking pan to cool.

In a small saucepan simmer chilies, in water to cover by ½ inch, 10 minutes. Remove pan from heat and let chilies stand 10 minutes. Drain chilies, discarding liquid, and in a blender purée with 3 garlic cloves and 1 cup water until smooth.

In a clean coffee mill or electric spice grinder grind cooled pumpkin seeds in batches with cumin-seed until ground fine but not pulverized and in a large bowl stir together with remaining 3 cups water until combined well. Let sit 15 minutes.

Force pumpkin seed mixture in batches through a fine disk of food mill into a large bowl (discard seed husks in food mill before adding each batch).

In large deep heavy skillet (preferably non-stick) heat 1 tablespoon oil over moderate heat until hot but not smoking. Add chili mixture and simmer, stirring, until thickened, about 2 to 3 minutes. Stir in pumpkin seed mixture and onion and bring to a boil. Reduce heat and simmer sauce slowly, stirring and scraping down sides of pan, until thickened and oil starts to appear on surface, about 20 minutes. If a smoother consistency is desired strain sauce through a coarse sieve into a bowl. *Sauce may be made 3 days ahead and chilled, covered. Reheat sauce over low heat, adding water if necessary to thin sauce, and season with salt.*

Chop remaining garlic clove. In another large heavy skillet heat remaining tablespoon oil over moderately high heat until hot but not smoking and cook shrimp with garlic, stirring, until just cooked through, about 3 minutes.

Divide sauce among 6 plates and top with shrimp. Garnish shrimp with coriander and serve with *quesadillas.* Serves 6.

Cheese Quesadillas

six 6-inch corn tortillas
   (page 288 or store-bought)
36 fresh coriander leaves,
   rinsed and patted dry
1½ cups grated fresh mozzarella cheese or
   münster cheese (about 6 ounces)
1 tablespoon vegetable oil plus additional
   for frying

Preheat oven to 300° F.

Stack tortillas and wrap in foil. Heat tortillas in middle of oven until warm, about 10 minutes.

Spread tortillas in one layer. In middle of a tortilla arrange 3 coriander leaves in one layer and top with ¼ cup cheese. Top cheese with 3 more coriander leaves and fold tortilla over to form a half circle, pressing down gently. Repeat with remaining tortillas, coriander, and cheese.

In a large heavy skillet heat 1 tablespoon oil over moderately high heat until hot but not smoking and cook 2 tortillas, pressing down with a spatula until cheese is melted and turning until browned on both sides. Transfer *quesadillas* to paper towels to drain and cook remaining tortillas in same manner, adding additional oil if necessary.

Cut each *quesadilla* into 3 wedges. Makes 18 wedges.

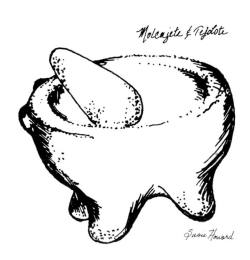

Molcajete & Tejolote

Susie Howard

Susie Howard

Corn Tortillas

3 cups *masa harina**
1¾ to 2 cups water

*available in some supermarkets and by mail order from Maria and Ricardo's Tortilla Factory, Jamaica Plain, MA, tel. (617) 524-6107

In a bowl combine *masa harina* with enough water to form a smooth dough. Divide dough into 18 pieces. Form each piece into a ball and cover balls with plastic wrap.

Cut wax paper into thirty-six 7-inch squares. Put 1 square of wax paper on bottom half of a tortilla press and arrange a dough ball on it, slightly off center toward edge opposite handle. Flatten ball slightly and cover with another square of wax paper. Lower top of press and press down firmly on lever. Remove tortilla, keeping it between wax paper squares. Make more tortillas in same manner with remaining dough and wax paper.

Heat a griddle or cast-iron skillet over high heat until hot. Carefully peel off top wax paper square from a tortilla and invert tortilla onto griddle. After 5 seconds, peel off remaining wax paper and cook tortilla, turning, until dry and flecked with golden brown spots, 1 to 2 minutes. Wrap tortilla in a kitchen towel and cook remaining tortillas in same manner, stacking and enclosing them in towel as they are cooked. If not using tortillas immediately, wrap cooled tortillas in plastic wrap and chill. *Tortillas keep in a plastic bag, chilled 1 day or frozen 1 month. To reheat see page 298.* Makes eighteen 6-inch tortillas.

Loma de Cerdo Asado con Mole Coloradito
(Roast Pork Loin with Coloradito Mole)

For mole
2 pounds vine-ripened tomatoes
9 tablespoons vegetable oil
6 garlic cloves, unpeeled
10 *guajillo* chilies*, stems and seeds discarded
    (wear rubber gloves)
½ large ripe plantain**
    (about 6 ounces)
1 large onion, chopped
    (about 1½ cups)
one 3-inch cinnamon stick (preferably Mexican*),
    halved
4 whole allspice berries
2 whole cloves
4 whole black peppercorns
½ cup sesame seeds
    (about 2½ ounces)
2 teaspoons dried oregano (preferably Mexican*),
    crumbled
2 slices homemade-type white bread,
    toasted
4 cups pork broth (recipe follows)
    or chicken broth

a 2½-pound boned and trimmed pork loin, tied
    (if making pork broth reserve bones and trim
    mings, and, if necessary, purchase pork
    spareribs to bring total weight to 2 pounds)
1 teaspoon dried oregano (preferably Mexican*),
    crumbled
2 tablespoons vegetable oil

*available at Hispanic markets and by mail
    order from Kitchen, New York, NY,
    tel. (212) 243-4433
**available at Hispanic markets and specialty
    produce markets

Make mole:
Preheat oven to 400° F.
Cut tomatoes into ¼-inch-thick slices and arrange in one layer in a shallow baking pan. Brush tomatoes with 1 tablespoon oil. Wrap garlic tightly in foil and add to baking pan. Roast tomatoes and garlic in middle of oven until garlic is tender and tomatoes are lightly browned, about 30 minutes. Peel garlic and

transfer with half of tomatoes to a blender. Heat a dry large heavy skillet (preferably cast-iron) over moderately high heat until hot and toast chilies, 2 at a time, turning and pressing down, about 10 seconds (do not let them burn), until flesh darkens slightly. Rinse chilies under cold water. In a bowl soak chilies in hot water to cover 20 minutes, or until softened. Remove chilies, reserving ½ cup liquid, and add half of chilies to blender. Peel plantain and cut into ½-inch cubes. In same skillet heat 1 tablespoon oil over moderately high heat until hot but not smoking and cook onion, stirring, until softened and transfer with a slotted spoon to blender. In same skillet sauté plantain in 1 tablespoon oil with cinnamon, allspice, cloves, and peppercorns until plantain is fragrant and tender, about 3 minutes, and add to blender. In skillet cook sesame seeds in 4 tablespoons oil over moderate heat, stirring, until seeds are darkened, about 5 minutes. Strain mixture through a fine sieve into a heatproof bowl and discard oil. Add half of sesame seeds to blender. Add 1 teaspoon oregano, 1 bread slice, and ¼ cup reserved chili liquid to blender and purée until smooth, adding some broth if necessary to thin it slightly (purée should be somewhat thick). Pour purée into a large bowl. In blender purée remaining tomatoes, chilies, reserved chili liquid, sesame seeds, oregano, bread slice, and some broth until smooth and pour into same bowl. In a large heavy saucepan or kettle heat remaining 2 tablespoons oil over moderate heat and cook purée, stirring, about 20 minutes. Add remaining broth and salt to taste and cook 30 minutes, or until thickened. If a smoother sauce is desired strain sauce through a coarse sieve into a bowl. Mole *will improve in flavor if made at least 1 day ahead and up to 3 days and chilled, covered. Reheat* mole *over low heat, adding water if necessary to thin sauce and season with salt.*

Let pork loin stand at room temperature 30 minutes and pat dry. Rub pork with salt and oregano.

Preheat oven to 425° F.

In a large heavy skillet heat oil over moderately high heat until hot but not smoking and brown pork on all sides, about 10 minutes. Transfer pork to a roasting pan and roast in middle of oven 40 minutes, or until meat thermometer registers 155° F. for slightly pink meat. Transfer pork to a cutting board and let stand 15 minutes, loosely covered with foil.

Slice pork and serve with *mole.* Serves 6.

Pork Broth

2 pounds pork bones and trimmings
    (if necessary, purchase spareribs to
    bring total weight to 2 pounds)
1 onion, quartered
1 large carrot, sliced
6½ cups water
10 whole black peppercorns
1 sprig fresh thyme or ⅛ teaspoon dried,
    crumbled

Preheat oven to 450° F.

Arrange bones, trimmings, and spareribs in a shallow flameproof baking pan in one layer and roast in middle of oven 30 minutes. Stir in onion and carrot and roast 30 minutes, stirring occasionally.

Transfer bones, trimmings, spareribs, and vegetables with tongs to a kettle, reserving pan juices. Discard fat from baking pan. Deglaze pan with 1 cup water, scraping up browned bits, and add mixture to kettle with remaining 5½ cups water, peppercorns, and thyme. Simmer mixture, skimming froth occasionally, 1 hour. Strain broth through a sieve into a heatproof bowl and cool, uncovered. Season broth with salt. *Broth keeps, chilled, covered, 3 days or frozen 1 month. Bring broth to a boil before using.* Makes about 4 cups.

Piñata

289

Calabacitas Salteadas con Menta
(Sautéed Zucchini with Mint)

2 tablespoons vegetable oil
6 medium zucchini, halved lengthwise and cut
  crosswise into ¼-inch-thick slices
3 tablespoons finely shredded mint leaves

Garnish: squash blossoms (available at specialty
  produce markets)

In a large heavy skillet heat oil over moderately
high heat until hot but not smoking and cook zucchini, stirring, until tender, about 10 minutes. Toss zucchini with mint and season with salt and pepper.
Garnish zucchini with squash blossoms. Serves 6.

Arroz Blanco con Fajas de Chile Poblano
en Escabeche
(White Rice with Marinated Poblano Chili Strips)

2 fresh green or red *poblano* chilies*
3 tablespoons fresh lime juice
¼ teaspoon salt
1 medium onion, chopped (about 1 cup)
1 large garlic clove
2½ tablespoons vegetable oil
2¼ cups low-salt chicken broth or water
1½ cups long- or medium-grain rice
1 large carrot, cut into ¼-inch dice (about ½ cup)

*available at Hispanic markets and by mail
  order from Kitchen, New York, NY,
  tel. (212) 243-4433

Preheat broiler.
On a baking sheet broil chilies 4 inches from heat,
turning with tongs, until blackened on all sides.
Transfer chilies to a heatproof bowl and cover bowl
with plastic wrap. When chilies are cool enough to
handle remove and discard skin and seeds (wear rubber gloves). Cut chilies into thin strips and in a small
bowl combine with lime juice and salt. *Marinate
chilies at least 2 hours and up to 3 days, covered and
chilled.*

In a blender purée onion, garlic, and oil until
almost smooth. In a small saucepan bring broth or
water to a simmer and keep warm. In a 2-quart

saucepan cook onion mixture with rice over moderate
heat, stirring constantly, 7 minutes and stir in hot
broth or water and carrot. Cover pan and reduce heat
to low. Cook rice 15 minutes, covered, and remove
pan from heat. Let rice stand 10 minutes, covered, or
until liquid is absorbed, and season with salt and pepper. Fluff rice with a fork to separate grains and serve
topped with marinated chili strips. Makes about 7
cups, serving 6.

Buñuelos

Susie Howard

Helado de Mango
(Mango Ice Cream)

2 firm ripe mangoes, peeled and cut into
  ¼-inch dice
2 pints premium vanilla ice cream, softened

Garnish: mango slices

In a bowl gently fold mango into ice cream until
combined well and freeze, covered, until firm, about
8 hours or overnight. *Ice cream may be made 1 week
ahead and frozen.*
Garnish ice cream with mango slices. Serves 6.

PHOTO ON FRONT JACKET

Buñuelos
(Oaxacan Sweet Fritters)

½ cup water
1 teaspoon aniseed
two 3-inch cinnamon sticks (preferably Mexican*),
    broken into pieces
1 tablespoon sugar
1 large egg, beaten lightly
1½ to 1¾ cups all-purpose flour
1 teaspoon baking powder
¼ teaspoon cream of tartar
¼ teaspoon salt
¼ cup chilled vegetable shortening
For cinnamon sugar
½ cup sugar
1 tablespoon ground cinnamon

vegetable oil for frying

*available by mail order from Kitchen,
    New York, NY, tel. (212) 243-4433

In a small saucepan bring water to a boil with aniseed, cinnamon sticks, and sugar and remove pan from heat. Let mixture stand 15 minutes. Strain mixture through sieve into a heatproof bowl and cool. Whisk in egg.

In a large bowl whisk together 1½ cups flour, baking powder, cream of tartar, and salt and with fingers rub in shortening until mixture resembles coarse meal. Make a well in center and add egg mixture, stirring mixture until combined well and begins to form a dough (if dough is too wet add up to ¼ cup additional flour). On a lightly floured surface knead dough 5 minutes, vigorously slapping dough on surface, until smooth.

Divide dough into 16 balls and cover with a damp kitchen towel. Let dough rest 30 minutes.

Make cinnamon sugar:
In a small bowl whisk together sugar and ground cinnamon.

On a lightly floured surface roll out 1 ball of dough into a very thin 5- to 6-inch circle, keeping remaining dough covered. Repeat with remaining dough and stack rounds between sheets of wax paper.

In a deep heavy kettle heat 3 inches oil over moderately high heat to 375° F. on a deep-fat thermometer. Gently drop 1 dough round into oil (dough will fall to bottom and then float up) and fry fritter, (dough will puff up in spots) turning once after 30 seconds, until golden brown on both sides, about 1 minute. Transfer fritter with a slotted spoon to paper towels to drain and sprinkle immediately on both sides with some cinnamon sugar. Fry remaining dough in same manner, making sure oil returns to 375° F. before adding each fritter. Buñuelos *may be made 1 day ahead and cooled completely before keeping in an airtight container at room temperature.* Makes 16 fritters.

PHOTO ON FRONT JACKET

A MEXICAN BUFFET

Tostadas de Frijoles Negros
(Black Bean Tostadas)

Enchiladas de Pollo con Salsa Verde
(Chicken Enchiladas with Tomatillo Sauce)

Rebanada de Carne de Res con Cebollas
(Slivered Beef with Onions)

Guacamole   *Tortillas de Harina*
(Avocado Salad)   *(Flour Tortillas)*

Pezugo en Escabeche
(Marinated Snapper)

Papas y Chorizo
(Potatoes and Chorizo)

Ensalada de Jícama
(Jícama Salad)

Joseph Phelps' Vin du Mistral California Granache Rosé 1993

Flan de Coco
(Coconut Flan)

Serves 12

Marta Morales dolls from Uruapan

Clockwise from upper left: Tortillas de Harina;
Rebanada de Carne de Res con Cebollas;
Ensalada de Jícama; Papas y Chorizo;
Enchiladas de Pollo con Salsa Verde; Guacamole;
Pezugo en Escabeche

Traditionally, refried beans are cooked with pork fat, but you can simmer the beans without it and substitute 1 tablespoon vegetable oil when cooking the onions.

Tostadas de Frijoles Negros
(Black Bean Tostadas)

1 cup dried black beans
two 1-ounce pieces pork fat or fat back
   (about 4 by 1 by ¼ inches each)
5 cups water
1 large onion, chopped
1 garlic clove, minced
sixteen 6-inch corn tortillas (page 288) or thawed
   frozen corn tortillas
½ cup pickled red onions (recipe follows),
   drained and chopped
vegetable oil for frying *tostadas*

Garnish: ½ cup shredded romaine and
   ½ cup pickled red onions, drained

In a saucepan simmer beans, 1 piece of pork fat or fat back, water, and half of chopped onion, covered, 1½ hours, or until beans are tender. Uncover mixture and simmer until reduced to about 3 cups and discard solid fat from bean mixture.

Chop remaining piece of fat and cook in a heavy skillet over moderately high heat until rendered (discard solids). Add remaining onion and cook, stirring occasionally, until tender, about 10 minutes. Add garlic and cook, stirring, 1 minute. Add half of bean mixture, stirring and mashing beans with a potato masher until mashed coarse and most of liquid is absorbed. Add remaining bean mixture, mashing in same manner, and salt to taste.

Spread ¼ cup bean mixture on a tortilla and sprinkle with 1 tablespoon chopped pickled red onions. Top *tostada* with another tortilla, pressing gently, and make more *tostadas* with remaining tortillas, bean mixture, and chopped pickled red onions in same manner. Tostadas *may be prepared up to this point 1 day ahead, stacked with a sheet of plastic wrap or wax paper between each, wrapped, and chilled.*

Preheat oven to 200° F.

In a heavy skillet heat 1 tablespoon oil over moderately high heat until hot but not smoking and cook *tostadas* one at a time until lightly brown and heated through, about 1½ minutes on each side, adding more oil as needed. Cut *tostadas* into quarters as they are cooked and transfer to a heatproof platter in oven.

Garnish *tostadas* with shredded romaine and pickled red onions. Serves 12.

Pickled Red Onions

¼ teaspoon cuminseed
¼ teaspoon whole black peppercorns
5 whole cloves
5 whole allspice berries
1 large red onion (about ¾ pound)
1 teaspoon dried oregano (preferably Mexican*),
   crumbled
1 large garlic clove, quartered
1 cup cider vinegar
1 teaspoon salt

*available at Hispanic markets and by mail
   order from Kitchen, New York, NY,
   tel. (212) 243-4433

With a mortar and pestle crush cuminseed, peppercorns, cloves, and allspice. Cut onion into ½-inch wedges. In a saucepan combine spice mixture and onion with remaining ingredients and water to cover and simmer 3 minutes. Remove pan from heat and cool. *Pickled onions keep in a jar with a tight-fitting lid, chilled, 1 month.* Makes about 4 cups.

Traditionally, enchiladas are arranged in a single layer in a baking dish, covered with tomatillo sauce, and then baked, uncovered.

Enchiladas de Pollo con Salsa Verde
(Chicken Enchiladas with Tomatillo Sauce)

a 3½-pound chicken, cut in half
2 carrots, sliced thin
1 small onion, sliced thin
1 teaspoon dried marjoram, crumbled
½ teaspoon dried oregano (preferably Mexican*), crumbled
2 bay leaves
1 teaspoon salt

For tomatillo sauce
1½ pounds fresh *tomatillos**
1 green or red *jalapeño* chili, or to taste, stem discarded (wear rubber gloves)
⅓ cup chicken broth reserved from poached chicken
½ medium onion, chopped
2 tablespoons coarsely chopped fresh coriander
1 tablespoon vegetable oil

½ cup sour cream
1 scallion, minced
2 tablespoons vegetable oil
twelve 6-inch corn tortillas (page 288) or thawed frozen corn tortillas

Garnish: fresh coriander sprigs

*available at Hispanic markets and by mail order from Kitchen, New York, NY, tel. (212) 243-4433

In a large saucepan or kettle combine chicken, carrots, onion, herbs, salt, and enough water to cover and simmer 30 minutes, or until chicken is cooked through. Cool chicken in broth. Remove chicken with a slotted spoon, reserving broth for *tomatillo* sauce. Discard skin and bones and shred meat.

Make tomatillo sauce:

In a saucepan simmer *tomatillos* and *jalapeño* with water to cover until *tomatillos* are tender, about 10 minutes. With a slotted spoon transfer *tomatillos* and

jalapeño to a blender and blend with remaining sauce ingredients except oil until *tomatillos* are chopped well but not completely smooth. In a heavy skillet heat oil until very hot but not smoking and add purée carefully all at once (sauce may splatter). Cook sauce, stirring, 1 minute and reduce heat to low to keep sauce warm. Tomatillo *sauce may be made 1 day ahead and chilled, covered. Reheat* tomatillo *sauce over low heat.*

In another saucepan reheat chicken with 2 tablespoons reserved broth and stir in sour cream and scallion. Keep chicken mixture warm.

In a heavy skillet heat oil over moderate heat until hot. Cook tortillas, 1 at a time, until softened, about 15 seconds and wrap in kitchen towel, stacking and enclosing them in towel as they are cooked. Top each tortilla with about ¼ cup warm chicken mixture and roll it up. *Enchiladas may be prepared up to this point 1 day ahead and chilled in one layer in a baking pan, covered with plastic wrap. Reheat enchiladas, covered with foil, in preheated 450° F. oven 30 minutes.*

With a slotted spatula dip enchiladas, 1 at a time, into *tomatillo* sauce to coat. Arrange enchiladas on a heated large serving dish and spoon remaining sauce over them. (Alternatively, *tomatillo* sauce may be poured evenly over enchiladas arranged in a single layer in baking dish and baked, uncovered, in a 350° F. oven until heated through.) Garnish enchiladas with coriander sprigs. Serves 12.

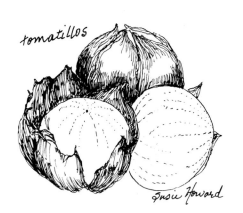

tomatillos

Susie Howard

Rebanada de Carne de Res con Cebollas
(Slivered Beef with Onions)

1½ pounds flank steak
3 tablespoons fresh lime juice
1 large onion (about ¾ pound)
1 tablespoon vegetable oil

Garnish: 1 fresh green or red serrano chili* or
     1 fresh habañero chili*, seeds and ribs
     discarded, minced (wear rubber gloves)
Accompaniments
guacamole (recipe follows)
twelve 8-inch flour tortillas (recipe follows)

*available at Hispanic markets and some specialty
     produce markets

In a baking dish just large enough to hold steak, combine steak, juice, and salt to taste. Marinate steak, covered and chilled, turning occasionally, 2 hours.

Cut onion into ½-inch wedges. In a large heavy skillet heat oil over moderately high heat until hot but not smoking and cook steak 3 to 4 minutes on each side for medium-rare meat. Transfer steak to a cutting board and in fat remaining in skillet cook onion with salt to taste over moderate heat until softened and golden, about 10 minutes. Cut steak across grain into thin slices and toss with onions in skillet.

Garnish beef and onion mixture with chili and serve with guacamole and tortillas. Serves 12.

Guacamole
(Avocado Salad)

3 ripe avocados (preferably California, 1½ pounds)
1 medium vine-ripened tomato, diced
½ small onion, minced
2 tablespoons chopped fresh coriander
1½ tablespoons fresh lime juice
1 small garlic clove, minced and mashed to a paste
     with ½ teaspoon salt

Halve avocados and with a large spoon scoop flesh into a bowl. Mash avocado with a fork until smooth and add remaining ingredients, stirring until combined well. Season with salt and pepper. Makes about 2½ cups.

Tortillas de Harina
(Flour Tortillas)

2 cups all-purpose flour
¼ cup cold vegetable shortening,
     cut into pieces
1 teaspoon salt
⅔ cup warm water

In a bowl blend flour and shortening until mixture resembles fine meal. In a small bowl stir together salt and water. Add salted water to flour mixture and toss until liquid is incorporated. Form dough into a ball and knead on a lightly floured surface until smooth, 2 to 3 minutes. Divide dough into 12 pieces and form each piece into a ball. Let dough stand, covered with plastic wrap, at least 30 minutes and up to 1 hour.

Heat a griddle or cast iron skillet over moderately high heat until hot. On a lightly floured surface roll 1 ball of dough into a 7-inch round and on griddle cook tortilla, turning once, until puffy and golden on both sides, 1 to 1½ minutes. Wrap tortilla in kitchen towel and make more tortillas with remaining dough in same manner, stacking and enclosing them in towel as they are cooked. Tortillas may be made 1 day ahead and chilled in a plastic bag or frozen 1 month. Makes twelve 7-inch tortillas.

To Warm Tortillas

Preheat oven to 325° F.

Stack 6 tortillas at a time and wrap each stack in foil. Heat tortillas in middle of oven 15 minutes. (If tortillas are very dry pat each tortilla between dampened hands before stacking.)

Pezugo en Escabeche
(Marinated Snapper)

For escabeche
2 carrots, cut into ¼-inch dice
1 onion, cut into ¼-inch dice
3 tablespoons olive or vegetable oil
3 garlic cloves, minced
a 1-inch cinnamon stick
10 whole allspice berries
8 whole cloves
½ teaspoon cuminseed

2 cups fish stock (recipe follows or
 frozen store-bought, thawed*)
½ cup cider vinegar
1 tablespoon fresh lime juice
2 roasted fresh *guero* chilies** or red or green
 jalapeño chilies, peeled, seeded, and diced
 (wear rubber gloves)
2 bay leaves

4 red snapper fillets (about ½ pound each)
⅓ cup all-purpose flour seasoned with salt
 to taste
3 tablespoons olive or vegetable oil

Garnish: fresh coriander sprigs plus 1 tablespoon
 chopped fresh coriander and 1 lime, sliced thin

*available at fish markets and some specialty
 foods shops
**available at some Hispanic markets

Make escabeche:

In a saucepan cook carrots and onion in oil over
moderate heat, stirring occasionally, until tender but
not browned, about 10 minutes. Add garlic and cook,
stirring, 1 minute. With a mortar and pestle or in an
electric spice grinder crush cinnamon stick, allspice,
cloves, and cuminseed. To vegetables add spice mixture, fish stock, vinegar, lime juice, chilies, and bay
leaves and simmer 5 minutes.

Cut each snapper fillet into 3 pieces and dredge in
seasoned flour. In a large skillet heat 2 tablespoons
oil over moderately high heat until hot but not smoking and cook fish in 2 batches, turning and adding
remaining tablespoon oil if necessary, until browned
and cooked, about 5 minutes. Transfer fish as cooked
to a baking dish large enough to hold it in one layer.

Pour warm *escabeche* over snapper and cool to
room temperature. Marinate snapper, covered and
chilled, at least 4 hours. *Snapper may be prepared up
to this point 2 days ahead and chilled, covered.*

Serve snapper chilled or at room temperature garnished with coriander and lime slices. Serves 12.

Fish Stock

1 pound bones and trimmings of any white fish
 such as sole, flounder, or whiting, chopped
1 cup sliced onion
12 long parsley sprigs
2 tablespoons fresh lemon juice
½ teaspoon salt
3½ cups cold water
½ cup dry white wine

In a well-buttered heavy saucepan steam fish bones
and trimmings with onion, parsley, lemon juice, and
salt, covered, over moderate heat 5 minutes.

Add water and wine and bring to a boil, skimming
froth. Simmer stock 20 minutes and strain through a
fine sieve into a bowl. Cool stock to warm and chill,
covered. *Stock keeps, frozen, 3 months.* Makes 3 cups.

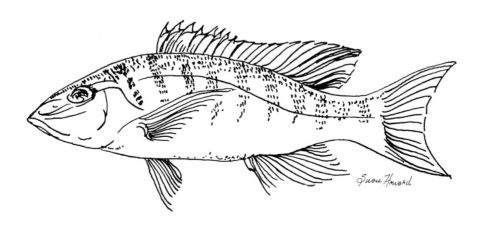

Papas y Chorizo
(Potatoes and Chorizo)

For chorizo
2 *ancho* chilies* and 1 *pasilla* chili*, or
   3 tablespoons freshly ground chili powder
   (preferably New Mexican*)
2 garlic cloves, sliced
1 teaspoon dried oregano (preferably Mexican*),
   crumbled
a ¾-inch cinnamon stick
½ teaspoon coriander seeds
¼ teaspoon whole black peppercorns
2 whole cloves
¾ pound pork shoulder, cut into chunks
¼ pound pork fat or fat back,
   cut into chunks
¼ cup cider vinegar

2 pounds boiling potatoes

* available at Hispanic markets, specialty
   foods shops, some supermarkets, and by mail
   order from Kitchen, New York, NY,
   tel. (212) 243-4433

Make chorizo:
If using whole chilies, tear into large pieces and discard seeds and stems (wear rubber gloves). In a heavy skillet dry-roast chilies over moderate heat until completely dehydrated, about 1 minute on each side (chilies should be crisp when cool). With a mortar and pestle or in an electric spice grinder grind chilies to a powder and transfer to a bowl. With a mortar and pestle coarsely grind garlic and spices. In a food processor pulse pork shoulder and fat until chopped fine but not smooth. Transfer pork mixture to a bowl and knead in chili powder, spice mixture, vinegar, and salt to taste. Chill *chorizo*, covered, 6 hours or overnight. Chorizo *may be made 3 days ahead and chilled, covered.*

Peel potatoes and cut into quarters. In a kettle simmer potatoes in water to cover until almost tender, about 10 minutes, and drain.

In a 12-inch heavy skillet cook *chorizo* over moderately high heat, stirring occasionally, until almost browned and add potatoes with salt to taste. Cook mixture until potatoes are tender and lightly browned and serve warm or at room temperature. Serves 12.

Jícama, cucumber, and watercress may be prepared up to 6 hours ahead and kept separately, covered and chilled.

Ensalada de Jícama
(Jícama Salad)

2 tablespoons fresh lime juice
1½ tablespoons olive or vegetable oil
1½ teaspoons freshly ground chili powder
½ teaspoon sugar
3 navel oranges
1 medium *jícama* (about 2½ pounds), peeled and
   cut into 2½- by ¼-inch matchsticks
1 cucumber, halved lengthwise, seeded, and cut
   crosswise into ¼-inch-thick slices
1 bunch watercress (about 6 cups loosely packed),
   tough stems discarded, chopped coarse

In a large bowl stir together lime juice, oil, chili powder, and sugar. With a serrated knife cut away peel and pith from oranges and holding oranges over bowl to catch any juice cut sections free from membranes, adding them to dressing. Add remaining ingredients and salt to taste and toss to coat vegetables with dressing. Serves 12.

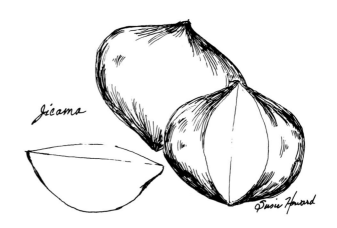

Jícama

Susie Howard

Flan de Coco
(Coconut Flan)

½ cup sugar
4 cups milk
1 cup sweetened shredded coconut
a 15-ounce can cream of coconut
1¼ to 1½ cups half-and-half
6 large eggs plus 6 large yolks

Garnish: shaved fresh coconut

In a dry small heavy saucepan cook sugar over moderate heat, undisturbed, until it begins to melt and continue cooking, swirling pan, until it is a deep-golden caramel. Pour caramelized sugar into a loaf pan, 12- by 3½- by 2½-inches or 9- by 5- by 3-inches.

In a heavy saucepan simmer milk and shredded coconut until reduced to 2½ cups, about 30 minutes.

Preheat oven to 350° F.

In a large bowl stir together milk mixture and cream of coconut and add enough half-and-half for mixture to measure 4⅓ cups. In a large bowl beat together whole eggs and additional yolks and stir in coconut mixture. Pour egg mixture over caramelized sugar in loaf pan.

Put loaf pan in a large baking pan and pour enough hot water into baking pan to reach about halfway up sides of loaf pan. Bake flan in lower third of oven 50 minutes, or until a knife inserted in center comes out clean (flan will still shake in center). Cool flan completely in loaf pan on a rack and chill, covered, about 6 hours.

Run a thin knife around edges of flan and invert a platter over flan. Invert flan onto platter, shaking gently until it releases from pan, and garnish with fresh coconut. Serves 12.

Laura Maestro

A GOURMET ADDENDUM

QUICK AND EASY HORS D'OEUVRES, SNACKS, AND BEVERAGES

Nowadays, everyone has less time to spend in the kitchen, so casual gatherings with simple fare are more popular than ever. Here you will find an assortment of easy, innovative finger foods and drinks that you can use for *any* informal occasion — before the theater, after the game, at an open house — even when friends drop in unexpectedly. All the recipes are quick to prepare, many can be made ahead of time, and most call for ingredients found in any well-stocked pantry and bar.

However, even the simplest gathering requires a little bit of planning and a few decisions. Which hors d'oeuvres should be served and how much food should be prepared? Your hors d'oeuvre and snack selection should reflect the size and length of your get-together. Naturally, a pre-dinner snack for only a few people requires only one or two different choices, while a large, lengthy affair, such as an open-house, should offer more variety and greater quantity. The more different types of hors d'oeuvres you offer, the fewer you need of each. For an "hors d'oeuvres only" party, plan on approximately six appetizers per guest. And be sure to consider the season of the year — people tend to eat more in the colder months and less in warmer weather.

As you peruse our recipe collection to create your own menu of small treats, keep complementary tastes in mind. Ideally, a balance of hot and cold appetizers with contrasting flavors and textures should be offered: spicy and mild, crunchy and smooth, rich and light. For example, since horseradish gives our Beef and Scallion Tortilla Roll-Ups a tangy bite, the mellow flavor of our Spinach and Fontina Quiche would be a nice match. Likewise, our crisp, oven-baked Rosemary Potato Chips could be paired with our creamy-textured Mushrooms Stuffed with Roasted Red Pepper and Cheese.

If you are making an assortment of hors d'oeuvres, plan your time so that all can be accomplished without a lot of fuss. Realize that hot dishes always require last-minute attention, so choose only one or two of them. Also, you will want to take advantage of recipes that provide make-ahead preparation information. For example, our Roasted Tamari Pumpkin Seeds and Almonds can be made as early as three days ahead, and our Cheddar and Jalapeño Corn Biscuits can be baked three hours in advance and then reheated. Cold dishes, such as our Yogurt-Cheese Dip with Crudités, are always an ideal choice, since they can stay refrigerated while you are attending to other matters. Time-consuming tasks, such as slicing bread and chopping vegetables, should be completed before the guests arrive; keep these ingredients wrapped and chilled, if necessary.

After the food has been chosen, a mix of beverages should be selected. It is best to present both alcoholic and non-alcoholic options to accommodate your guests' preferences. We've included drinks from the traditional, such as Frozen Margaritas, to the innovative, such as Minted Orange Iced Tea. All our beverage recipes can be easily prepared with a fully stocked bar, which should include vodka, Scotch, gin, rum, Tequila, triple sec, Champagne, brandy, red and white wine, beer, sparkling water, tonic, and other sodas. Never skimp on quality. Over time you should sample various brands and choose your favorites. Fruit garnishes, such as lemons and limes, and plenty of ice are also essential.

If you're having a larger party, take a few moments to plan the presentation with a nice selection of plates, platters, baskets, trays, and bowls. It is more attractive to use serving dishes of different heights for your buffet of finger foods. Have fun and be innovative by using various objects to create pedestals to elevate plates and platters. Hot trays and chafing dishes are handy to maintain the proper temperature of hot hors d'oeuvres. If they are not available, use casserole dishes that hold heat for a relatively long time. Keep in mind that several smaller plates can be easily refilled and are more convenient and appealing than larger trays standing half-empty. Also, when arranging your food, never crowd it on a plate or tray — guests should be able to remove one item without touching another. Open-faced snacks are best arranged in one layer, while others can be artfully stacked. Room-temperature and cold hors d'oeuvres can be set out just before guests arrive, and, at your convenience, hot foods can be served at various intervals throughout the party. Make sure the food is heated but not too hot to handle.

Let this collection serve as your cache of just-the-right little foods and beverages for a quick snack or a small gathering, or as a starting point for a larger party. With these easy recipes precious time saved in the kitchen can be spent leisurely with family and friends and your delicious new treats. Now there is no excuse not to entertain.

Smoked Salmon Roll-Ups

⅔ cup cream cheese, softened
¼ cup finely chopped fresh chives, minced
    scallion greens, or minced fresh dill
1 tablespoon sour cream
1 teaspoon Dijon mustard
1 teaspoon freshly grated lemon zest
½ pound thinly sliced smoked salmon, cut into
    7- to 8-inch lengths

In a bowl stir together cream cheese, herbs, sour cream, mustard, zest, and salt and pepper to taste. Spread cream cheese mixture over salmon slices and starting with a long side roll up to enclose filling. Arrange rolls on a plate, seam sides down, and cover with plastic wrap. Freeze rolls 20 minutes to facilitate slicing (do not freeze completely) and cut crosswise into ½-inch-thick slices. *Salmon roll-ups may be made 1 day ahead and kept chilled, covered.* Makes 24 hors d'oeuvres.

Roasted Tomato and Mozzarella Crostini

twelve ⅓-inch-thick slices Italian bread
¼ cup olive oil
6 firm vine-ripened plum tomatoes, cored, halved
    lengthwise, and seeded
2 garlic cloves, minced fine
2 teaspoons fresh thyme leaves or 1 teaspoon
    dried, crumbled
½ pound mozzarella cheese,
    cut into 12 slices
2 tablespoons minced fresh basil leaves

Preheat oven to 450° F. and oil a baking sheet.
On prepared baking sheet arrange bread and brush both sides with some oil. Arrange tomatoes, skin sides down, on same sheet and sprinkle with garlic, thyme, and salt and pepper. Drizzle tomatoes with remaining oil and bake bread and tomatoes until bread is browned around edges, about 8 minutes. Turn bread and top with cheese. Bake until cheese is melted, about 6 to 8 minutes more.
Top cheese with tomatoes and sprinkle with basil. Makes 12 hors d'oeuvres.

Spinach and Fontina Quiche

pastry dough (page 235)
raw beans for weighting the shell
1 cup thawed frozen leaf spinach (half a
    10-ounce package)
3 large eggs
1 cup half-and-half
1 cup coarsely grated Italian Fontina cheese
1½ teaspoons Dijon mustard

Preheat oven to 400° F.
Line a 9-inch square baking pan with dough so that it comes 1 inch up sides of pan, trimming and patching if necessary. Prick bottom of shell with a fork and line shell with wax paper. Weight shell with beans and bake until golden, about 15 minutes. Remove paper and beans and cool shell in pan on a rack.
Reduce oven temperature to 375° F.
Squeeze dry spinach and chop. In a bowl whisk together eggs, half-and-half, cheese, mustard, and salt and pepper and stir in spinach. Pour custard into shell and bake 35 minutes, or until puffed and golden. Cool quiche 10 minutes on rack and cut into 16 squares. Makes 16 hors d'oeuvres.

L. maesTro

Shrimp with Chipotle Mayonnaise

For chipotle mayonnaise
1 cup mayonnaise
½ cup sour cream
2 teaspoons Dijon mustard, or to taste
2 canned *chipotle* chilies in *adobo* sauce*, or to
   taste, minced, with 1 tablespoon of the sauce
   (wear rubber gloves)

1 pound large shrimp, shelled and deveined,
   leaving tail intact
2 tablespoons minced fresh coriander

*available at Hispanic markets, some specialty
   foods shops, and some supermarkets or by mail
   order from Adriana's Caravan, Brooklyn, NY,
   tel. (800) 316-0820 or (718) 436-8565

Make chipotle mayonnaise:
In a bowl stir together *chipotle* mayonnaise ingredients and salt and pepper to taste.

To a large saucepan of boiling salted water add shrimp and return water to a boil. Simmer shrimp, stirring, until just firm and opaque and drain in a colander. Refresh shrimp under cold water and pat dry.

Arrange shrimp on a serving plate and sprinkle with coriander.

Serve shrimp with *chipotle* mayonnaise. Serves 6 as an hors d'oeuvre.

Turkey Meatballs with Cucumber Yogurt Sauce

For sauce
1 cucumber, peeled, seeded, and grated coarse
1 small onion, grated coarse
1 cup plain yogurt, drained
½ cup sour cream
fresh lemon juice to taste
2 tablespoons minced fresh coriander
For meatballs
1 pound ground turkey
1 large egg, lightly beaten
1 small onion, grated coarse
1 garlic clove, minced fine
2 teaspoons finely grated peeled fresh gingerroot
1 teaspoon ground cumin
1 teaspoon ground coriander
3 tablespoons minced fresh coriander

3 tablespoons vegetable oil

Make sauce:
In a bowl stir together sauce ingredients and salt and pepper to taste and chill mixture, covered.
Make meatballs:
In a bowl stir together meatball ingredients and salt and pepper to taste and form into 1-inch meatballs.

In a large non-stick skillet heat oil over moderate heat and cook meatballs, turning frequently, 10 to 12 minutes, or until cooked through.

Transfer meatballs to a platter and serve with sauce. Makes about 24 meatballs.

Beef and Scallion Tortilla Roll-Ups

3 ounces cream cheese, softened
¼ cup drained bottled horseradish
six 8-inch flour tortillas
1 pound thinly sliced rare roast beef
6 thin scallions, cut into lengths the diameter of
   tortillas

Preheat oven to 350° F.
In a small bowl stir together cream cheese and horseradish. Heat tortillas in oven, wrapped in foil, until warm and soft, about 5 minutes. Working with 1 tortilla at a time and keeping remaining tortillas wrapped in foil, spread some cream cheese mixture

on one side of each tortilla, leaving a ½-inch border, and cover with several slices of roast beef. Arrange a scallion at one end of tortilla and beginning with scallion end, roll up tortilla, enclosing beef and scallion. Cut each roll diagonally into thirds and transfer to a serving platter, keeping cut rolls covered. Makes 18 hors d'oeuvres.

Prosciutto-Wrapped Fruit

18 thin slices prosciutto, halved crosswise
six 1-inch wedges of pineapple
six 1-inch wedges of melon, such as honeydew or
    cantaloupe
2 peaches, quartered
2 nectarines, quartered
2 pears, quartered

Wrap a prosciutto slice around each piece of fruit and chill, covered, 30 minutes or up to 3 hours. Makes 36 hors d'oeuvres.

Mushrooms Stuffed with Roasted Red Pepper and Cheese

For filling
a 7-ounce jar roasted red peppers,
    drained
an 8-ounce package cream cheese,
    softened
¼ cup freshly grated Parmesan cheese
1 garlic clove, chopped
cayenne to taste
1 tablespoon drained capers, chopped fine

36 medium white mushrooms,
    stems discarded
⅓ cup chopped toasted walnuts

Make filling:
In a food processor blend together all filling ingredients except capers and add salt to taste until just combined. Transfer mixture to a bowl and stir in capers. *Filling may be made 1 day ahead and kept chilled, covered.*
Stuff each mushroom with a heaping teaspoon of filling and sprinkle with toasted walnuts. Makes 36 hors d'oeuvres.

Black Bean Nachos

a 16-ounce can black beans, drained,
    reserving liquid
½ teaspoon ground cumin
½ teaspoon chili powder,
    or to taste
1 garlic clove, minced and mashed to a
    paste with ¼ teaspoon olive oil and
    a pinch of salt
24 large corn tortilla chips
2 cups grated Cheddar cheese
24 slices pickled *jalapeño* chilies, drained
    (wear rubber gloves)

In a food processor blend beans, cumin, chili powder, garlic paste, and salt and pepper to taste until puréed coarse, adding some reserved bean liquid if mixture becomes too thick.
Preheat broiler.
Spread bean mixture on tortilla chips. Sprinkle chips with cheese and top with *jalapeños*. Arrange *nachos* on a baking sheet and broil about 4 inches from heat until cheese melts, about 1 minute. Makes 24 *nachos*.

Grilled Reuben Triangles

3 tablespoons Dijon mustard
8 slices rye bread
½ pound sliced Swiss cheese
1 pound sliced corned beef
⅓ cup drained prepared sauerkraut,
    or to taste
½ stick (¼ cup) unsalted butter,
    softened

On a work surface spread mustard on one side of each bread slice. Divide half of cheese among 4 bread slices. Top cheese with corned beef, sauerkraut, and remaining cheese. Arrange remaining bread slices, mustard sides down, on top and brush top and bottom of each sandwich with butter.
Heat a griddle or large non-stick skillet until hot and grill sandwiches, weighted with a plate, until golden brown, about 2 to 3 minutes on each side.
Quarter sandwiches diagonally. Makes 16 triangles.

Rosemary Potato Chips

two 8-ounce russet (baking) potatoes, unpeeled,
    cut into 1/16-inch-thick slices and patted dry
1/4 cup olive or vegetable oil
2 tablespoons minced fresh rosemary leaves or
    2 teaspoons dried, crumbled

Preheat oven to 450° F. and grease non-stick baking sheets.

On prepared baking sheets arrange potato slices in one layer and brush both sides with oil. Sprinkle potato slices with rosemary and salt and pepper to taste and bake, turning once, until golden brown, about 15 to 18 minutes. Cool potato chips on baking sheets and transfer to a serving dish. *Potato chips may be made 3 hours ahead and kept at room temperature.* Makes about 3 cups.

Cheddar and Jalapeño Corn Biscuits

1½ cups all-purpose flour
½ cup cornmeal
1 tablespoon baking powder
½ teaspoon salt
½ stick (¼ cup) cold unsalted butter, cut
    into bits
½ cup grated Cheddar cheese
1 *jalapeño* chili, seeded and minced (wear rubber
    gloves), or to taste
¾ to 1 cup milk

Preheat oven to 425° F. and grease a baking sheet.

Into a bowl sift together flour, cornmeal, baking powder, and salt. Add butter and with a pastry blender blend until mixture resembles coarse meal. Stir in cheese, *jalapeño*, and ¾ cup milk and form into a ball, adding more milk if necessary. On a floured surface knead dough lightly once or twice and pat out ½-inch-thick.

Cut out rounds with a 1½-inch cookie cutter and transfer to prepared baking sheet. Bake biscuits in middle of oven 12 to 15 minutes. *Biscuits may be made 3 hours ahead and kept chilled, covered. To reheat: warm biscuits in a 350° F. oven until heated through, about 5 minutes.* Makes about 30 biscuits.

Roasted Tamari Pumpkin Seeds and Almonds

1 cup blanched whole almonds
1 cup unsalted pumpkin seeds
1 tablespoon vegetable oil
2 tablespoons *tamari**
    (wheat-free soy sauce)
1 teaspoon honey

*available at many natural foods stores and
    Japanese markets

Preheat oven to 350° F.

In a baking pan combine almonds and pumpkin seeds. In a small bowl combine remaining ingredients and add to almonds and seeds, tossing to coat. Bake mixture 20 minutes, stirring occasionally, and cool in pan on a rack. *Roasted pumpkin seeds and almonds may be made 3 days ahead and kept covered.* Makes 2 cups.

*Goat Cheese, Garlic, and Rosemary Spread
with Herbed Toasted Pita*

For spread
2 garlic cloves, minced
3 tablespoons extra-virgin olive oil
½ teaspoons minced fresh rosemary leaves
½ pound mild goat cheese such as Montrachet

3 to 4 tablespoons unsalted butter, softened,
    or to taste
1 teaspoon minced fresh rosemary leaves
three 6-inch *pita* loaves, halved horizontally and
    each round cut into 4 wedges

Preheat oven to 400° F.
Make spread:

In a small skillet cook garlic in oil with rosemary over moderately low heat, stirring, until garlic is softened. In a food processor purée garlic mixture, goat cheese, and salt and pepper to taste, scraping down bowl of processor, until smooth.

In a bowl combine butter, rosemary, and salt and pepper to taste. Brush butter mixture onto rough sides of pita wedges and on a baking sheet bake bread until light golden and crisp, about 8 to 10 minutes.

Serve spread with toasted *pita*. Makes about 1 cup.

For a sweet variation of our Yogurt-Cheese Dip with Crudités *recipe below—drizzle plain yogurt cheese with honey and sprinkle it with cinnamon to taste. Or, substitute fresh ricotta cheese (drained for 15 minutes) for the plain yogurt and drizzle it with honey. Serve the cheese with fresh strawberries, blueberries, raspberries, orange segments, or sliced melon.*

Yogurt-Cheese Dip with Crudités

a 16-ounce container plain yogurt
¼ cup *olivada, tapenade,* or other black olive paste*, or to taste
1 small garlic clove, minced and mashed to a paste with ¼ teaspoon olive oil and a pinch of salt
assorted *crudités,* such as carrot sticks, celery sticks, scallions, trimmed radishes, endive leaves, and blanched broccoli flowerets

*available at specialty foods shops and some supermarkets

In a fine sieve set over a large bowl drain yogurt, covered and chilled, 3 hours or overnight. Discard whey. *Yogurt-cheese may be made 1 week ahead and kept chilled, covered.*

Stir together 1½ cups yogurt-cheese with olive paste and garlic paste and transfer to a serving bowl. Arrange *crudités* on a platter and serve with dip. Makes about 1½ cups dip.

Apricot, Raisin, and Pecan Squares

1 cup plus 2 tablespoons all-purpose flour
½ cup firmly packed light brown sugar
¾ stick (6 tablespoons) unsalted butter, softened
⅓ cup raisins
1 tablespoon orange juice

½ cup granulated sugar
2 large eggs
1 teaspoon vanilla
½ teaspoon baking powder
2 teaspoons freshly grated orange zest
⅔ cup chopped dried apricots
⅔ cup chopped toasted pecans
sifted confectioners' sugar for dusting the squares

Preheat oven to 350° F. and butter an 8-inch square baking pan.

In a food processor blend 1 cup flour, ¼ cup brown sugar, and butter until just combined. Press mixture onto bottom of prepared pan and bake crust until golden, about 15 minutes.

In a small bowl plump raisins in orange juice.

In a bowl stir together remaining 2 tablespoons flour, remaining ¼ cup brown sugar, granulated sugar, eggs, vanilla, baking powder, zest, apricots, raisin mixture, and pecans and pour over crust. Bake mixture 30 minutes and cool completely in pan on a rack. Cut snack into 16 squares and dust with confectioners' sugar. Makes 16 squares.

L. Maestro

Seaside Bloody Marys

1 quart chilled Clamato juice
⅓ cup vodka, or to taste
2 tablespoons drained bottled horseradish
Tabasco to taste

Garnish: freshly ground black pepper to taste and
    lemon wedges

In a pitcher filled with ice cubes stir together all
ingredients and pour into 4 chilled glasses. Garnish
drinks with pepper and lemon wedges. Makes 4
drinks.

Dubonnet Cooler

½ cup red Dubonnet
½ cup chilled seltzer or club soda
1 lemon wedge

In a 12-ounce glass filled with ice cubes combine
all ingredients. (Alternatively, if serving 2 or more,
simply double, triple, etc. ingredients and combine in
a pitcher.) Serve cooler immediately. Makes 1 drink.

Pineapple Champagne Cocktails

1 cup chilled unsweetened pineapple juice
a dash of Angostura bitters, or to taste
4 cups chilled Champagne

Garnish: fresh pineapple slices and maraschino
    cherries

In a chilled pitcher stir together pineapple juice
and bitters and add Champagne. Pour mixture into 4
chilled glasses and garnish with pineapple slices and
cherries. Makes 4 drinks.

Rum Punch

2 cups chilled fresh orange juice
2 cups chilled unsweetened pineapple juice
1 cup white rum, or to taste

Garnish: orange slices

In a large pitcher stir together juices and rum. Pour
punch into six 12-ounce glasses filled with ice cubes
and garnish with orange slices. Makes 6 drinks.

White-Wine Sangría

1 bottle of chilled dry white wine
2 cups chilled seltzer or club soda
2 tablespoons fresh lemon juice
1 jigger brandy
1 small orange, sliced thin

In a pitcher filled with ice cubes stir together all
ingredients. Makes 6 drinks.

Frozen Margaritas

1 cup fresh lime juice
1 cup Tequila
½ cup triple sec
½ cup water
½ lime
coarse salt for rims of glasses

Garnish: lime slices

In a pitcher combine lime juice, Tequila, triple sec, and water. Transfer mixture to 2 ice cube trays and freeze for at least 4 hours, or until almost frozen. *Margaritas may be prepared up to this point 1 day ahead.* Transfer frozen mixture to a food processor or blender and blend until slushy.

Moisten rims of 4 stemmed glasses with cut lime and dip in salt. Pour Tequila mixture into prepared glasses and garnish with lime slices. Makes 4 drinks.

Limeade

3 cups water
⅔ cup sugar, or to taste
zest of 1 lime, removed with a vegetable peeler
    and cut into thin julienne strips
1 cup fresh lime juice

Garnish: fresh lime slices and fresh mint leaves

In a saucepan bring water to a boil with sugar and zest, stirring. Simmer mixture 2 minutes and cool to room temperature. Stir in lime juice and strain through a fine sieve into a pitcher. Pour limeade into four 12-ounce glasses filled with ice cubes and garnish with lime slices and mint leaves. Makes 4 drinks.

Minted Orange Iced Tea

5 cups water
8 strips orange zest removed with a vegetable
    peeler
6 strips lemon zest removed with a vegetable
    peeler
1 cinnamon stick, broken into pieces
6 whole cloves
5 Earl Grey tea bags
honey to taste

Garnish: fresh mint leaves

In a saucepan bring water to a boil with zests, cinnamon, and cloves and simmer, covered, 8 minutes. Remove pan from heat and add tea bags. Cover mixture and steep 10 minutes. Strain tea into a pitcher and cool. Pour tea into 4 tall glasses filled with ice. Sweeten iced tea with honey and garnish with mint leaves. Makes 4 drinks.

GUIDES TO THE TEXT

GENERAL INDEX

Page numbers in *italics* indicate color photographs

ALCOHOLIC BEVERAGES, 254–256, 310–311

ALMOND(S)

Asparagus Amandine, 171

Brittle, Chocolate-Covered, 247

Chocolate Sherry Cake, *16*, 219

Chocolate Torte, *71*, 218

Pies, and Chicken, Moroccan, *57*, 141

and Pumpkin Seeds, Tamari Roasted, 308

Smoked, with Chicken Salad Tea Sandwiches, 97

Toasted, Semifreddo, White Chocolate, 228

ANCHOVY

Mashed Potatoes, 184

Pita Pizzas, Potato, Jarlsberg and, 108

Puffs, 88

Sauce, Olive, with Spaghetti, 163

Vegetable Spread, Provençal (Anchoïade), 99

APPLE

Carrot, and Onion Slaw, Sautéed, with Pecans, 203

Celery Root, and Gruyère Slaw with Horseradish, *70*, 204

Galette, Thyme-Scented, 237

Pie, and Dried-Cherry, Lattice, 233

Stuffing, Potato and Prune, *76*, *77*, 147

Tart, "Flag", 236

Tart, Phyllo, Fig and, 238

Tarts, Maple-Glazed, Breakfast, 153

Tarts, Upside-Down, Individual, 237

APPLE CIDER Sauce, Honeyed, 154

APPLESAUCE

Bread Crumb Pudding, Danish, 250

Chunky, 250

Pink, Meringue Tart with Hazelnut Cookie Crust, 238

APRICOT

Caramel Sauce, 252

Raisin, and Pecan Squares, 309

and Sweet Potato Purée, with Pecan Streusel, 188

Vanilla Sauce, 154

ARMAGNAC, Prune Gingerbread, 226

ARTICHOKES. *See also* Jerusalem Artichoke

Stuffed, with Red Pepper Vinaigrette, 172

ARUGULA

Cherry Tomatoes, and Roasted Garlic Vinaigrette, with Fillet of Beef, *64*, *65*, 127

with Hamburgers, Herbed, 132

and Prosciutto Tortilla Pizzas, 109

ASPARAGUS

Amandine, 171

Pencil-Thin, Scallions and, *29*, 171

Roasted, with Balsamic Vinegar, 171

AVOCADO

Guacamole, *294*, *295*, 298

Sushi Rice Salad, with Cucumber, Scallions and, 208

Tomato, and Cucumber, with Lemon Vinaigrette, *53*, 203

BACON

Butternut Squash with Lime and, Spicy, 188

Gruyère, and Scallion Muffins, 103

Phyllo Pizza, Butternut Squash, Rosemary and, 108

Spinach Salad with Dates, Feta Dressing and, 197

Swiss Chard, and Ricotta Ravioli with Tomato Sauce, 162

and Tomato Salad in Bibb Lettuce Cups, *55*, 95

BAGUETTES, Antipasto-Stuffed, 88

BAKED ALASKA Peanut S'mores, *49*, 243

BALSAMIC VINEGAR

Pearl Onions, -Glazed, *77*, 182

with Roasted Asparagus, 171

Sirloin Steak, -Glazed, 129

Vinaigrette, 209

BANANA(S)

with Chocolate, Baked, 245

and Kiwi in Lime Rum Syrup, with Vanilla Ice Cream, 244

Orange, and Pineapple Salad with Lime Dressing, *276*, 278

Peach, and Strawberry Bruschetta, 152

Rum Fizzes, 254

BARLEY Mushroom Soup, 117

BASIL

Honeydew with Mint, Lime and, 246

Lobster, Corn, and Zucchini Salad, *64*, 192

Mint, and Orange Vinaigrette, 209

Pasta with Roasted Eggplant, Ricotta and, 162
Pesto, 214
Pesto Oil, 216
BEAN(S). *See also* Black Bean(s); Chick-Pea(s); Green Beans; White Bean
    Azuki and Vegetable Salad in Pita Bread, *67*, 197
    Boston Baked, Gratin, 172
    dried, quick-soaking, 110
    Lima, Purée, Potato and Garlic, with Potato Crisps, *26*, 174
    Pinto Soup, Southwestern, 110
BEEF. *See also* Steak(s)
    Fillet of, with Arugula, Cherry Tomatoes, and Roasted Garlic Vinaigrette, *64*, *65*, 127
    Goulash Soup, Hearty, *84*, *85*, 114
    Gratin of Sliced, and Mustard Gravy (Deviled Miroton), 130
    Hamburgers, Herbed, with Arugula, 132
    Meat Loaf, Old-Fashioned, *34*, *35*, 131
    Noodle Soup, Chinese, 111
    Orange-Flavored, and Snow Pea Stir-Fry with Noodles, 131
    Prime Ribs of, Roast, with Pink and Green Peppercorn Crust and Red-Wine Pan Sauce, *82*, *83*, 128
    Rump Roast with Vegetables, 130
    Shredded, with Eggs, *277*, 279
    Slivered, with Onions, *295*, 298
    Tortilla Roll-Ups, Scallion and, 306
BEET
    and Carrot Salad with Gingerroot Vinaigrette, 198
    Grapefruit, and Blue Cheese Salad, 198
    Roasted, Herbed Goat Cheese, and Watercress Salad, *74*, *75*, 198
    Soup, Celery and, Cold, 111
    Soup, Fennel and, *68*, *69*, 112
BELL PEPPER(S). *See also* Red Pepper(s); Yellow Pepper(s)
    Couscous Salad, with Olives, Pine Nuts and, 207
    and Red Cabbage Slaw, Wilted, *48*, 204
    roasting, 92
    Scallops, Seared, and Haricots Verts, Warm Salad of, in Walnut Vinaigrette, *82*, 193
BENNE SEED Raisin Bars, *15*, 228
BERRY(IES). *See also* names of berries
    Assorted, with Orange and Sour-Cream Drop Shortcakes, 226
    Syrup, Three-, 154
BEVERAGES, 254–257, 310–311
BIBB Lettuce Cups, Tomato and Bacon Salad in, *55*, 95

BISCUITS
    Corn, Cheddar and Jalapeño, 308
    Scallion, 102
BLACK BEAN(S), *277*, 280
    Nachos, 307
    Salad, Quinoa and, 208
    Tostadas, 296
BLACKBERRY and Nectarine Cobbler, 245
BLACK-EYED PEA and Cabbage Slaw, 205
BLOODY MARYS, Seaside, 310
BLUE CHEESE, Grapefruit, and Beet Salad, 198
BOURSIN and Fennel Seed Risotto, 169
BOW TIES
    Four-Cheese Baked, 156
    with Peas, Lemon, and Mint, 156
BRANDY Alexander Shakes, 254
BREAD(S) *See also* Biscuits; Muffins; Pizza(s); Rolls
    Baguettes, Antipasto-Stuffed, 88
    Bolillos (Crusty Mexican Rolls), *277*, 280
    Breadsticks, Pumpernickel and Rye, *68*, *69*, 105
    Corn, Caraway, 140
    Corn Sticks, Thyme, *13*, 105
    Focaccia, Grape and Rosemary, *78*, 101
    Irish Soda, Brown, *2*, 102
    Irish Soda, Golden-Raisin, *2*, 102
    Popovers, Rosemary, *82*, *83*, 105
    Sweet Buns, Mexican, *276*, 281
BREAD PUDDING(S)
    Applesauce Bread Crumb, Danish, 250
    Butterscotch, 250
BREAKFAST DISHES, 152–153
BREAKFAST SAUCES, 154
BRITTLE, Almond, Chocolate-Covered, 247
BROCCOLI and Cauliflower with Horseradish Bread Crumbs, *83*, 174
BROCCOLI RABE
    Cavatelli with Italian Sausage and, 158
    and Chick-Pea Pita Pizzas, 108
    with Sherry Vinegar, *73*, 175
BROTH, Pork, 289
BROWNIES, Raspberry Cheesecake, 232
BROWN SUGAR Pecan Sauce, 154
BRUSCHETTA
    Chicken Liver, Peppered, Sage, and Fried Onion, 96
    Mozzarella, Greens, and Garlic, 96
    Peach, Strawberry, and Banana, 152
    toasts, making, 96
    Tomato and Ricotta Salata, 97

BULGUR
and Lentil Salad with Tarragon and Walnuts, 206
Pine Nut, and Red Pepper Pilaf, *69*, 167
BUNS, Sweet, Mexican, *276*, 281
BURGERS. *See also* Hamburgers
Lentil, with Yogurt Mint Sauce, 179
Turkey, Grilled, *52*, *53*, 148
Turkey, with Mushroom Gravy, 149
BUTTERMILK
Dressing with Red-Leaf Lettuce and Watercress Salad, *35*, 197
Yellow Pepper and Scallion Soup, Chilled, *67*, 118
BUTTERNUT SQUASH
Phyllo Pizza, Bacon, Rosemary and, 108
Spicy, with Bacon and Lime, 188
BUTTERSCOTCH Bread Puddings, 250

CABBAGE. *See* Slaw(s)
CAESAR SALAD, 194
CAKE(S)
Chocolate, Coconut Rum, Individual, 220
Chocolate Almond Sherry, *16*, 219
Chocolate Almond Torte, *71*, 218
Gingerbread, Prune Armagnac, 226
Icebox, Raspberry Chocolate Meringue, 220
Macadamia Coconut, *43*, 224
Mocha Rum, *15*, 221
Pound, Chocolate, 218
Roll, Rhubarb Lemon, 227
Semifreddo, White Chocolate, Toasted Almond, 228
Shortcakes, Drop, Orange and Sour-Cream, with Assorted Berries, 226
Wedding, Lemon Raspberry, 222
CANAPÉS, 95–97
CANDIES, Honey Nut, *59*, 248
CANNELLONI, Spinach, Ricotta, and Prosciutto, 156
CAPPUCCINO Rum Shakes, 254
CARAMEL
Apricot Sauce, 252
Chocolate Truffles, 248
CARAWAY
Corn Bread, 140
Dill Oil, 215
and Napa Cabbage Slaw, 204
Yogurt Dressing, with Carrot and Celery Slaw, 204
CARROT(S)
Apple, and Onion Slaw with Pecans, Sautéed, 203
and Beet Salad, with Gingerroot Vinaigrette, 198

and Celery Slaw with Yogurt Caraway Dressing, 204
Chipotle Mayonnaise Dip with, *51*, 98
and Coconut Milk Soup, Cold Curried, 112
Cucumber, and Red Onion Salad, 200
Cucumber Salad, 200
Jícama and Peanut Salad, 201
and Parsnips, Roasted, *76*, *77*, 175
and Turnips, Baby Glazed, 190
Walnut Salad, 199
CASHEW Dipping Sauce, 94
CAULIFLOWER
and Broccoli with Horseradish Bread Crumbs, *83*, 174
Crispy, with Olives, Capers, and Parsley, 175
CAVATELLI with Italian Sausage and Broccoli Rabe, 158
CAVIAR, Salmon Torte, *62*, 93
CAYENNE, Eggs, Hard-Cooked, with Cumin, Coarse Salt and, 90
CELERY
and Beet Soup, Cold, 111
and Carrot Slaw with Yogurt Caraway Dressing, 204
CELERY ROOT
Gruyère, and Apple Slaw with Horseradish, *70*, 204
Rémoulade, 199
CHEDDAR
Corn Biscuits, Jalapeño and, 308
Tea Sandwiches, Chutney, 97
CHEESE. *See also* names of cheeses
Bow Ties, Baked, -Four, 156
Empanadas, Leek, Prosciutto and, *17*, 179
Macaroni and, 160
Mushrooms Stuffed with Roasted Red Pepper and, 307
Quesadillas, *284*, 288
Straws, Spicy Cumin, *55*, 88
Sweet Crêpes, Baked in Custard, Austrian, 251
Yogurt-, Dip with Crudités, 309
CHEESECAKE Brownies, Raspberry, 232
CHERRY
Dried, and Apple Lattice Pie, 233
and Pecan Cream Cheese Spread, 100
Salsa, with Pork Tenderloin, Peppered, 132
Sour, Compote, *71*, 219
CHERRY TOMATO(ES)
Arugula, and Roasted Garlic Vinaigrette, with Fillet of Beef, *64*, *65*, 127
Pepper-Vodka-Soaked, with Seasoned Sea Salt, 95
CHICKEN
and Almond Pies, Moroccan, *57*, 141
Barbecue, 140

Breasts, with Horseradish-Scallion Crust, 138

Breasts, Spiced, Grilled, *38*, 138

Breast and Vegetables, with Prunes, Roasted, 139

Cobb Salad Pitas, 142

and Dumplings, *20*, 138

Enchiladas with Tomatillo Sauce, *295*, 297

Roast, with Mashed-Potato Stuffing and Root Vegetables, *21*, 137

Salad, Roasted Vegetable and, 192

Salad Tea Sandwiches with Smoked Almonds, 97

Smoked, with Mango and Mint, *63*, 89

CHICKEN LIVER, Peppered, Sage, and Fried Onion Bruschetta, 96

CHICK-PEA(S)

Hummus, 176

Pita Pizzas, Brocolli Rabe and, 108

Sautéed, with Cinnamon and Fresh Coriander, 176

CHILAQUILES, with Tomato Chili Sauce, Baked, *277*, 278

CHILI, CHILIES. *See also* Chipotle; Jalapeño

Harissa, with Black Olives, *57*, 91

Mole, Coloradito, with Pork Loin, Roast, *285*, 288

Peanuts, -Dusted, 286

Poblano Strips, Marinated, with White Rice, 290

Potato Slices, Roasted, with Lime and, 186

roasting, 92

Sauce, Sweet, *46*, 143

Sweet Potato Gratin, 186

Tomato Sauce, with Chilaquiles, Baked, *277*, 278

CHIPOTLE

Mayonnaise Dip with Carrots, *51*, 98

Mayonnaise, with Shrimp, 306

Oil, 214

Salsa, with Orange and, Winter, 214

CHOCOLATE

Almond Brittle, -Covered, 247

with Bananas, Baked, 245

Biscotti, Double, Walnut, 230

Brownies, Raspberry Cheesecake, 232

Cake, Almond Sherry, *16*, 219

Cake, Pound, 218

Cake, Raspberry Meringue Icebox, 220

Cakes, Coconut Rum, Individual, 220

Chip Cookies, Coconut, 229

Chip Cookies, -Double, Double-Peanut, 230

Chip Cookies, Granola and Dried Cranberry, *66*, 231

Chip Cookies, Oatmeal, 229

Chip Crisps, Ginger, 229

Cream Pie, 234

Croquembouche, Praline, 240

Fudge Bars with Pecan-Graham Crust, 230

Hot, Mexican, *276*, 281

Maple Syrup, 155

Orange, and Chestnut Pavé, 249

Pastry Cream, 242

Pistachio Log, 248

Sauce, Mexican, 216

Sauce, Sambuca, 216

Seeds, with Watermelon Sorbet, *60*, 244

Torte, Almond, *71*, 218

Truffles, Caramel, 248

White, Semifreddo, Toasted Almond, 228

CHORIZO and Potatoes, *295*, 300

CHOWDER

Corn, Cumin, 112

Fish, Smoked, 113

CHUTNEY

Cheddar Tea Sandwiches, 97

Cranberry Quince, *77*, 212

Garlic Dressing, 209

CIOPPINO (San Francisco-Style Seafood Soup), 118

COBBLER, Blackberry and Nectarine, 245

COBB SALAD Pitas, 142

COCONUT

Chocolate Chip Cookies, 229

Flan, 301

Gingerroot Rice, 168

Macadamia Cake, *43*, 224

Milk Soup, Carrot and, Cold Curried, 112

Rum Chocolate Cakes, Individual, 220

Toasted, Kahlúa and Ice-Cream Parfaits, 244

COFFEE. *See also* Mocha

Cappuccino Rum Shakes, 254

Espresso Sambuca Ice-Cream Sodas, 254

Syrup, 155

CONDIMENTS, 212–214

CONFECTIONS, 247–249

COOKIES AND BARS

Apricot, Raisin, and Pecan Squares, 309

Benne Seed Raisin Bars, *15*, 228

Biscotti, Double Chocolate, Walnut, 230

Brownies, Raspberry Cheesecake, 232

Chocolate Chip, Coconut, 229

Chocolate Chip, -Double, Double-Peanut, 230

Chocolate Chip Ginger Crisps, 229

Chocolate Chip, Granola and Dried Cranberry, *66*, 231

Chocolate Chip Oatmeal, 229

Crust, Hazlenut, with Pink Applesauce Meringue Tart, 238

Fudge Bars with Pecan-Graham Crust, 230

Pralines, 240

Shortbread, Rosemary, 232

Shortbread Squares, Mocha Cinnamon, 232

CORIANDER

Eggplant Salad, 200

Fresh, Chick-Peas, Sautéed, with Cinnamon and, 176

Tomato, and Pickled Onion Sandwiches, 189

CORN

Boats with Zucchini and Pepper Jack Cheese, *61*, 177

Chowder, Cumin, 112

on the Cob, Cumin, *52*, *53*, 177

Lobster, Zucchini, and Basil Salad, *64*, 192

and Scallop Pot Stickers, with Sesame Vinaigrette, *40*, *41*, 124

Tomato, and Okra, Broiled, 189

CORN BISCUITS, Cheddar and Jalapeño, 308

CORN BREAD, Caraway, 140

CORNISH HENS, Marinated Roast, *46*, 142

CORN MUFFINS

Anadama, Pecan, 104

Feta, 103

Spicy, Roasted Red Pepper, 104

CORN STICKS, Thyme, *13*, 105

CORN TORTILLAS, 288

COUSCOUS Salad with Peppers, Olives, and Pine Nuts, 207

CRAB(-MEAT)

Canapés, Parmesan, *13*, 95

Salad with Yogurt Mustard Dressing, 192

CRACKERS. *See also* Bruschetta; Toasts

Pepper Jack, 90

CRANBERRY

Dried, Chocolate Chip Cookies, Granola and, *66*, 231

French Toast, -Stuffed, 152

Quince Chutney, *77*, 212

CRAWFISH, Rémoulade, Fried, *37*, 124

CREAM CHEESE, Spread, Cherry and Pecan, 100

CRÈME ANGLAISE, Ginger, 217

CRÈME FRAÎCHE Ice Cream, 224

CRÊPES

Austrian, 252

Austrian, Sweet Cheese, Baked in Custard, 251

Jelly Glazed, 242

CROSTINI

Goat Cheese, *28*, 195

Tomato and Mozzarella, Roasted, 305

CRUDITÉS

Green and White, with Herbed Anise Dip, 98

with Yogurt-Cheese Dip, 309

CUCUMBER

Mint Soup, Cold, 113

Relish, with Rib-Eye Steaks, Grilled, 128

Salad, Carrot, 200

Salad, Carrot, and Red Onion, 200

Salad, Viennese, *85*, 199

with Sesame Noodles, Cold Chinese-Style, 165

Sushi Rice Salad with Avocado, Scallions and, 208

Tomato, and Avocado with Lemon Vinaigrette, *53*, 203

Yogurt Sauce, with Turkey Meatballs, 306

CURRANT(S)

Noodle Kugel, Orange, 250

Pear Maple Syrup, with Gingerbread Pancakes, 152

Rice, and Lentils, with Fried Onions, 168

Rice, Saffron Minted, with Pine Nuts and, *33*, 168

CURRY(IED)

Carrot and Coconut Milk Soup, Cold, 112

Herring on Pumpernickel, *22*, 96

Oil, 215

Party Mix, Hot, 91

Shrimp, Crisp, 126

Sweet Potatoes, Roasted, 188

Sweet Potato Squares, with Peanut Phyllo Crust, 187

CUSTARD

Gingerroot Sauce, 217

Sherry Sauce, *16*, 220

Sweet Cheese Crêpes, Baked in, Austrian, 251

DANISH Applesauce Bread Crumb Pudding, 250

DATE(S)

Spinach Salad, with Bacon, Feta Dressing and, 197

Walnut Yogurt Ice Cream, 244

DESSERT SAUCES, 216–217

DILL(ED)

Caraway Oil, 215

Feta Ricotta Spread, 100

Lemon Orzo, Baked, with Gruyère, 160

Mustard Dressing, with Vegetables, Marinated, 190

Mustard Sauce, 121

DIPS AND SPREADS, 98–100, 308–309

DOUGH

Cream Puff (Pâte à Chou), 242

Pastry, 235

Pizza, 106

DUBONNET Cooler, 310

DUCK
Breasts, Crispy, with Pear and Green Peppercorn Sauce, 144
Confit and Mashed Potato Ravioli with White Truffle Sauce, 160
Legs, Red-Wine-Braised, with Roasted Pears and Onions, *78, 79*, 145
and Sausage Gumbo, *14*, 143
DUMPLINGS and Chicken, *20*, 138

EGG(S)
Frittata, Lentil and Red Pepper, 151
Hard-Cooked, with Cumin, Coarse Salt, and Cayenne, 90
Poached, with Frisée Salad, *18, 19*, 196
Potato Salad with Dill Pickle, Tarragon and, 202
Salad Sandwiches, Herbed, 151
with Shredded Beef (Machacado con Huevos), *277*, 279
Stuffed, with Vinegar Sauce on Toast, 151
EGGPLANT
Coriander Salad, 200
and Red Snapper, with Red Bell Pepper Sauce, 122
Roasted, Pasta with Ricotta, Basil and, 162
and Roasted Red Pepper Dip, with Pita Wedges, 99
Rounds, Minted, *46*, 178
Rounds, Parmigiana, 178
EMPANADAS, Leek, Prosciutto, and Cheese, *17*, 179
ENCHILADAS, Chicken, with Tomatillo Sauce, *295*, 297
ENTRÉE SALADS, 192–194
ESCAROLE, White Bean, and Wheat Berry Soup, 110
ESPRESSO Sambuca Ice-Cream Sodas, 254

FENNEL
and Beet Soup, *68, 69*, 112
Lemon Shrimp, with Tarragon, *54*, 94
Seed Risotto, Boursin and, 169
Tuna Melts, Olive and, 123
FETA
Corn Muffins, 103
Dressing, Spinach Salad with Bacon, Dates and, 197
Lentil, Green, and Sun-Dried Tomato Salad, 201
Phyllo Pizza, Parsley Pesto and, 107
Ricotta Spread, Dilled, 100
with Rosemary Pepper Honey, 150
Sautéed, with Tomato Sauce, 150
FIG(S)
and Apple Phyllo Tart, 238
Red-Wine-Poached, with Vanilla Ice Cream, 246

FISH. *See also* Anchovy; Flounder; Halibut; Herring; Red Snapper; Salmon; Shellfish; Sole; Tuna
Chowder, Smoked, 113
with Moroccan Seasoning (Chermoula), *58*, 122
Stock, 299
FLAN, Coconut, 301
FLAVORED OILS, 214–216
FLOUNDER with Bread Crumb Topping, Broiled, 120
FOCACCIA, Grape and Rosemary, *78*, 101
FONTINA and Spinach Quiche, 305
FRENCH TOAST, Cranberry-Stuffed, 152
FRISÉE Salad with Poached Eggs, *18, 19*, 196
FRITTATA, Lentil and Red Pepper, 151
FRITTERS, Sweet Oaxacan, *283*, 291
FROZEN DESSERTS, 243–245
FRUIT. *See also* names of fruits
Prosciutto-Wrapped, 307
FRUIT FINALES, 245–247
FUDGE Bars with Pecan-Graham Crust, 230

GALETTE, Apple, Thyme-Scented, 237
GARLIC
Bread Crumbs, and Cracklings, with Sautéed Kale, *78, 79*, 178
Chutney Dressing, 209
Goat Cheese, and Rosemary Spread with Herbed Toasted Pita, 308
Lemon Dressing, with Boiled New Potatoes, 186
Lima Bean, and Potato Purée, with Potato Crisps, *26*, 174
Mashed Potatoes, -Herb, 184
Mashed Potatoes, Sage and, 184
Mayonnaise, Potato Salad with Chives and, *61*, 202
Mozzarella, and Greens Bruschetta, 96
Orange Pork Chops, 134
and Parmesan Croutons, with Minestrone, 116
Rice Noodles with Herbs and, *46*, 164
Roasted, Vinaigrette, Fillet of Beef with Arugula, Cherry Tomatoes and, *64, 65*, 127
Rosemary Jelly, *33*, 212
Rosemary Shrimp, *48*, 126
GAZPACHO, Spicy, 113
GINGER
Chocolate Chip Crisps, 229
Crème Anglaise, 217
Vinaigrette, Spicy, 209
GINGERBREAD
Pancakes with Currant Pear Maple Syrup, 152
Prune Armagnac, 226

GINGERROOT
  Coconut Rice, 168
  Custard Sauce, 217
  Pear Sauce, 213
  Shallot Marmalade, 213
  Tea, 257
  Vinaigrette, with Carrot and Beet Salad, 198
GOAT CHEESE
  Crostini, *28*, 195
  Herbed, Roasted Beet, and Watercress Salad, *74*, *75*, 198
  Spread, Garlic and Rosemary, with Herbed Toasted Pita, 308
GRAINS, 167–170
GRAIN SALADS, 206–209
GRAND MARNIER Smoothies, 254
GRAPE and Rosemary Focaccia, *78*, 101
GRAPEFRUIT, Beet, and Blue Cheese Salad, 198
GRATIN
  of Beef, Sliced, and Mustard Gravy (Deviled Miroton), 130
  Boston Baked Bean, 172
  Chili Sweet Potato, 186
  Jerusalem Artichoke and Sage, *76*, 172
  Porcini and Potato, *82*, 183
GRAVY
  Mushroom, with Turkey Burgers, 149
  Mustard, and Sliced Beef, Gratin of (Deviled Miroton), 130
  Port, and Roast Turkey, with Potato, Apple, and Prune Stuffing, *76*, *77*, 146
GREEN BEANS, *23*, 173. *See also* Haricots Verts
  and Persimmons, Sautéed, with Chives, *77*, 173
  Stewed, 173
GREEN PEPPERCORN. *See* PEPPERCORN
GREENS. *See also* names of greens
  Baby, Mixed with Aniseed Vinaigrette and Goat Cheese Crostini, *28*, 194
  Bitter, with Lentils, 180
  Mesclun Salad, *65*, 196
  Mixed with Walnut Vinaigrette, *17*, 195
  Mozzarella, and Garlic Bruschetta, 96
GRITS, Tasso Batons, *38*, 167
GRUYÈRE
  Bacon, and Scallion Muffins, 103
  Celery Root, and Apple Slaw with Horseradish, *70*, 204
  with Orzo, Lemon Dill Baked, 160
  Potato Wedges, Crispy, 186

GUACAMOLE, *294*, *295*, 298
GUMBO, Duck and Sausage, *14*, 143

HALIBUT, Baked, with Sherry Onion Vinaigrette, Warm, *26*, 120
HAM, and Lentil Soup, Hearty, 114
HAMBURGERS. *See also* Burgers
  Herbed, with Arugula, 132
HARISSA, Black Olives with, *57*, 91
HERB(S). *See* names of herbs
HERRING, Curried, on Pumpernickel, *22*, 96
HONEY(ED)
  Apple Cider Sauce, 154
  Lemon Buttermilk Dressing, 210
  Nut Candies, *59*, 248
  Rosemary Pepper, with Feta, 150
HONEYDEW with Mint, Basil, and Lime, 246
HORS D'OEUVRES, 88–95, 305–307
HORSERADISH
  Bread Crumbs, with Broccoli and Cauliflower, *83*, 174
  with Celery Root, Gruyère, and Apple Slaw, *70*, 204
  Mustard Vinaigrette, with Seared Salmon, 121
  -Scallion Crust, with Chicken Breasts, 138
HUMMUS, 176
  and Vegetable Lahvash Sandwiches, 176

ICE CREAM
  Baked Alaska Peanut S'mores, *49*, 243
  Crème Fraîche, 224
  Date Walnut Yogurt, 244
  with Figs, Red-Wine-Poached, Vanilla, 246
  with Kiwi and Banana in Lime Rum Syrup, Vanilla, 244
  Mango, *283*, 290
  Parfaits, Kahlúa and Toasted Coconut, 244
  Shakes, Cappuccino Rum, 254
  Shakes, Rum, Tropical, 256
  Shakes, Rusty Nail, 256
  Shakes, White Russian, 256
  Smoothies, Grand Marnier, 254
  Sodas, Espresso Sambuca, 254

JALAPEÑO
  Corn Biscuits, Cheddar and, 308
  Pesto, Sunflower Seed, 166
JELLY
  Crêpes, Glazed, 242
  Garlic Rosemary, *33*, 212
JERUSALEM ARTICHOKE and Sage Gratin, *76*, 172

Jícama
  Carrot, and Peanut Salad, 201
  Salad, *294*, 300

Kahlúa, Toasted Coconut, and Ice-Cream Parfaits, 244
Kale
  Lentil, and Sausage Soup, 115
  Sautéed, with Cracklings and Garlic Bread Crumbs,
    78, *79*, 178
Ketchup, Tomato, Homemade, *52*, 214
Kir Royale Sorbet, *27*, 244
Kiwi(s)
  and Banana in Lime Rum Syrup, with Vanilla Ice Cream,
    244
  Pavlovas with Kir Royale Sorbet and, *27*, 243
Kugel, Noodle, Orange Currant, 250

Lamb
  Chops, Marinated, *28*, *29*, 136
  Crown Roast of, *33*, 135
  Medallions with White-Bean Potato Purée and Red-Wine
    Sauce, 136
  Stew, Sweet Potato and, 136
Lasagne
  Golden Onion and Zucchini, 158
  Sausage and Wild Mushroom, with Red Pepper Tomato
    Sauce, 159
Leek(s)
  Creamed, with Roasted Potato Fans, 185
  Prosciutto, and Cheese Empanadas, *17*, 179
  Soba with Pea Shoots, Shiitake Mushrooms and,
    166
  Vinaigrette, Warm, 178
Lemon(s)
  Bow Ties with Peas, Mint and, 156
  -Curd Strawberry Tart, 239
  Dill Orzo, Baked, with Gruyère, 160
  Fennel Shrimp with Tarragon, *54*, 94
  Garlic Dressing, with Boiled New Potatoes, 186
  Honey Buttermilk Dressing, 210
  Mayonnaise, with Radish Minted Tea Sandwiches, 98
  Meringue Buttercream, 224
  Preserved, Green Olives, Cracked, with Herbs and, 92
  Preserved, Red Onion, and Parsley Salad, 201
  Preserved, Seven-Day, Paula Wolfert's, 92
  Raspberry Wedding Cake, 222
  Rhubarb Cake Roll, 227
  Rosemary Orzo Pilaf, 160

Spice Oil, 215
Vinaigrette, with Tomato, Cucumber, and Avocado,
  53, 203
Zucchini Vichyssoise, 114
Lentil(s)
  with Bitter Greens, 180
  and Bulgur Salad with Tarragon and Walnuts, 206
  Burgers with Yogurt Mint Sauce, 179
  Frittata, Red Pepper and, 151
  Green, Sun-Dried Tomato and Feta Salad, 201
  Red, Refried, 180
  and Rice, Curried, with Fried Onions, 168
  Rotini with Spinach and, 163
  Soup, Ham and, Hearty, 114
  Soup, Kale and Sausage, 115
Lettuce. *See also* Greens; names of lettuces
  and Pea Soup, 115
Lima Bean, Potato, and Garlic Purée, with Potato Crisps,
  26, 174
Lime
  Butternut Squash with Bacon and, Spicy, 188
  Cocktails, Southside, 255
  Dressing, with Orange, Pineapple, and Banana Salad,
    276, 278
  Honeydew with Mint, Basil and, 246
  Potato Slices, Roasted, with Chili and, 186
  Refresher, 286
  Rum Syrup, Vanilla Ice Cream with Kiwi and Banana in,
    244
Limeade, 311
Lobster
  Bisque, Shrimp and, *24*, *25*, 116
  Salad, Corn, Zucchini, and Basil, *64*, 192

Macadamia Coconut Cake, *43*, 224
Macaroni and Cheese, 160
Mango
  Chicken, Smoked, with Mint and, *63*, 89
  Ice Cream, *283*, 290
  with Sticky Rice, *47*, 253
Maple Syrup
  Chocolate, 155
  Currant Pear, with Gingerbread Pancakes, 152
  Glazed-, Apple Tarts, Breakfast, 153
  Rum Raisin, Spiced, 155
Margarita(s)
  Frozen, 310
  Strawberry Fizzes, 310

MARMALADE
Gingerroot Shallot, 213
Onion, with Pork Loin Chops, Boneless, 133
MEATBALL(S), Turkey
with Baked Ziti, 164
with Cucumber Yogurt Sauce, 306
Stroganov, 148
MEAT LOAF, Old-Fashioned, *34, 35*, 131
MEAT(S). *See* Beef; Lamb; Pork
MERINGUE
Lemon Buttercream, 224
Pavlovas with Kir Royale Sorbet and Kiwis, *27*, 243
Pink Applesauce Tart, with Hazlenut Cookie Crust, 238
Raspberry Chocolate Icebox Cake, 220
MESCLUN SALAD, *65*, 196
MINESTRONE with Garlic and Parmesan Croutons, 116
MINT(ED)
Basil, and Orange Vinaigrette, 209
Bow Ties with Peas, Lemon and, 156
Chicken, Smoked with Mango and, *63*, 89
Cucumber Soup, Cold, 113
Eggplant Rounds, *46*, 178
Honeydew with Basil, Lime and, 246
Iced Tea, Orange, 311
Rice, Saffron, with Currants and Pine Nuts, *33*, 168
Tea, Moroccan, *59*, 257
Tea Sandwiches, Radish, with Lemon Mayonnaise, 98
Yogurt Sauce, with Lentil Burgers, 179
with Zucchini, Sautéed, 290
MOCHA
Cinnamon Shortbread Squares, 232
Rum Cake, *15*, 221
MOZZARELLA
Greens, and Garlic Bruschetta, 96
Smoked, and Shrimp Creole Pizzas, 106
and Tomato Crostini, Roasted, 305
Vegetable, and Pesto Sandwiches, Grilled Open-Faced, 190
MUFFINS. *See also* Corn Muffins
Bacon, Gruyère, and Scallion, 103
Limpa, 104
Pecan Anadama, 104
MUSHROOM(S). *See also* Shiitake Mushrooms
Gravy, with Turkey Burgers, 149
Porcini and Potato Gratin, *82*, 183
Portobello, Grilled, with Parmesan Crisps, *32*, 181
and Radish Salad with Parsley, 203
Ragout on Toast, 180

Soup, Barley, 117
Stuffed, Dried-Tomato-, 181
Stuffed, with Roasted Red Pepper and Cheese, 307
Wild, and Sausage Lasagne, with Red Pepper Tomato Sauce, 159
MUSTARD
Dressing, Dill, with Vegetables, Marinated, 190
Dressing, Yogurt, 192
Gravy, and Sliced Beef, Gratin of (Deviled Miroton), 130
Sauce, *23*, 213
Sauce, Dill, 121
Vinaigrette, Horseradish, 121

NACHOS, Black Bean, 307
NAPA Cabbage and Caraway Slaw, 204
NECTARINE and Blackberry Cobbler, 245
NOODLE(S)
Bean-Thread, with Shiitake Mushrooms and Vegetables, *42*, 164
with Beef, Orange-Flavored, and Snow Pea Stir-Fry, 131
Beef Soup, Chinese, 111
Kugel, Orange Currant, 250
Rice, with Garlic and Herbs, *46*, 164
Sesame, Cold Chinese-Style, with Cucumber, 165
Soba with Pea Shoots, Shiitake Mushrooms, and Leeks, 166
NUT(S). *See also* names of nuts
Candies, Honey, *59*, 248
Crisp Spiced, *84*, 90
Party Mix, Hot Curried, 91
Sweet-and-Spicy, 91

OAT, Whole-, Herbed Salad, 207
OATMEAL Chocolate Chip Cookies, 229
OIL
Chipotle Pepper, 214
Curry, 215
Dill Caraway, 215
Lemon Spice, 215
Orange Rosemary, 216
Pesto, 216
OKRA, Tomato, and Corn, Broiled, 189
OLIVE(S)
Anchovy Sauce, with Spaghetti, 163
Black, with Harissa, *57*, 91
Cauliflower, Crispy, with Capers, Parsley and, 175
Couscous Salad, with Peppers, Pine Nuts and, 207
Cracked Green, with Herbs and Preserved Lemon, 92

Dried Tomato and Caper Dressing, 211

Herbed, 92

Pasta Salad, Whole-Wheat, with Grilled Zucchini and, 206

Swiss Chard with Raisins and, 176

Tuna Melts, Fennel and, 123

Vinaigrette, with Sea Scallops and Tomatoes, Grilled, 125

ONION(S). *See also* Red Onion

Apple, and Carrot Slaw with Pecans, Sautéed, 203

with Beef, Slivered, *295*, 298

Browned, Spaghetti with Pepperoni, Peas and, 163

Caramelized, Split-Pea Soup with Cuminseed and, 117

Fried, with Lentils and Curried Rice, 168

Fried, Sage, and Peppered Chicken Liver Bruschetta, 96

Golden, and Zucchini Lasagne, 158

Marmalade, with Pork Loin Chops, Boneless, 133

Pearl, Balsamic-Glazed, *77*, 182

and Pears, Roasted, with Duck Legs, Red- Wine-Braised, *78*, *79*, 145

Pickled, 189

Pickled, Sandwiches, Tomato and Coriander, 189

Sherry Vinaigrette, Warm, with Baked Halibut, *26*, 120

and Tortilla Cake, Grilled, *48*, 182

ORANGE

Basil, and Mint Vinaigrette, 209

Beef, Flavored-, and Snow Pea Stir-Fry, with Noodles, 131

and Chipotle, with Salsa, Winter, 214

Chocolate, and Chestnut Pavé, 249

Garlic Pork Chops, 134

Iced Tea, Minted, 311

Noodle Kugel, Currant, 250

Pineapple, and Banana Salad with Lime Dressing, *276*, 278

and Radish Salad, *56*, 203

Rosemary Oil, 216

Rum Rickey, *55*, 255

and Sour-Cream Drop Shortcakes, with Assorted Berries, 226

ORZO

Lemon Dill, Baked, with Gruyère, 160

Pilaf, Rosemary Lemon, 160

Salad, Niçoise, 205

and Wild Rice, with Toasted Walnuts, *64*, 170

OYSTER, Fried, Po' Boys, 124

PANCAKES. *See also* Crêpes

Gingerbread, with Currant Pear Maple Syrup, 152

PAPAYA Relish, Pineapple, *42*, 135

PARMESAN

Crab-Meat Canapés, *13*, 95

Crisps, *32*, 181

Croutons, Garlic and, 116

PARSNIPS and Carrots, Roasted, *76*, *77*, 175

PARTY MIX, Hot Curried, 91

PASTA. *See also* Bow Ties; Cannelloni; Cavatelli; Lasagne; Macaroni; Noodle(s); Orzo; Ravioli; Rotini; Spaghetti; Ziti

with Eggplant, Roasted, Ricotta, and Basil, 162

Salad, Tricolor, Herbed, *52*, 206

Shellfish, Paella-Style, 126

Whole-Wheat, with Grilled Zucchini and Olives, 206

PASTRY(IES). *See also* Pie(s); Tart(s)

Cream, Chocolate, 242

Cream Puff (Pâte à Chou), 242

Croquembouche, Chocolate Praline, 240

Dough, 235

Galette, Apple, Thyme-Scented, 237

Shortbread Bites, Spicy, 93

PÂTE À CHOU, 242

PAVLOVAS with Kir Royale Sorbet and Kiwis, *27*, 243

PEA(S). *See also* Snow Pea(s)

Black-Eyed, and Cabbage Slaw, 205

Bow Ties with Lemon, Mint and, 156

Buttered, *34*, *35*, 183

Shoots, Soba with Shiitake Mushrooms, Leeks and, 166

Soup, Lettuce and, 115

Soup, -Split, with Caramelized Onions and Cuminseed, 117

Soup, Yellow, *23*, 118

Spaghetti with Pepperoni, Browned Onions and, 163

PEACH

Schnapps Fizzes, 255

Strawberry, and Banana Bruschetta, 152

PEANUT(S)

Chili-Dusted, 286

Double-Chocolate Chip Cookies, -Double, 230

Jícama, and Carrot Salad, 201

Phyllo Crust, with Sweet Potato Squares, Curried, 187

Sauce, Spicy Sichuan, 167

S'mores, Baked Alaska, *49*, 243

PEAR(S)

Caramelized, *16*, 220

Caramelized, Charlottes with Persimmon, *72*, 246

Currant Maple Syrup, with Gingerbread Pancakes, 152

Duck Breasts, Crispy, with Green Peppercorn Sauce and, 144

and Onions, Roasted, with Duck Legs, Red- Wine-Braised, *78*, *79*, 145

Poached, 246

and Pumpkin Pie, 234

Sauce, Gingerroot, 213

PECAN(S)

Anadama Muffins, 104

with Apple, Carrot, and Onion Slaw, Sautéed, 203

Apricot, and Raisin Squares, 309

Brown Sugar Sauce, 154

and Cherry Cream Cheese Spread, 100

Crust, Graham-, Fudge Bars with, 230

Praline Tarts, 39, 240

Streusel, with Apricot and Sweet Potato Purée, 188

Toasted, and Roquefort Dressing, 210

PEPPER(S). See Bell Pepper(s); Chili, Chilies; Red Pepper(s);
Yellow Pepper(s)

PEPPERCORN

Crust, Pink and Green, Roast Prime Ribs of Beef with Red-
Wine Pan Sauce and, 82, 83, 128

Sauce, Green, Duck Breasts, Crispy, with Pear and, 144

PEPPER JACK

Corn Boats, with Zucchini and, 61, 177

Crackers, 90

Tomatillo and Tortilla Pizzas, 109

PEPPERONI, Spaghetti with Peas, Browned Onions and, 163

PERSIMMON(S)

Caramelized Pear Charlottes with, 72, 246

and Green Beans, Sautéed, with Chives, 77, 173

PESTO, 214

Jalapeño Sunflower Seed, 166

Oil, 216

Parsley, and Feta Phyllo Pizza, 107

Tomato, with Steak Sandwiches, 132

Vegetable, and Mozzarella Sandwiches, Grilled Open-
Faced, 190

PHYLLO

Almond Pies, and Chicken, Moroccan, 57, 141

Crust, Peanut, with Sweet Potato Squares, Curried, 187

Pizza, Butternut Squash, Bacon, and Rosemary, 108

Pizza, Parsley Pesto and Feta, 107

Tart, Fig and Apple, 238

PICKLED

Onion, Sandwiches, Tomato and Coriander, 189

Onions, 189

Red Onions, 296

PICKLING, sterilizing jars and glasses, 213

PIE(S). See also Pizza(s); Tart(s)

Almond, and Chicken, Moroccan, 57, 141

Apple and Dried-Cherry Lattice, 233

Chocolate Cream, 234

Dough, Pastry, 235

Pear and Pumpkin, 234

PILAF

Bulgur, Pine Nut, and Red Pepper, 69, 167

Orzo, Rosemary Lemon, 160

PINEAPPLE

Champagne Cocktails, 310

Orange, and Banana Salad with Lime Dressing, 276, 278

Relish, Papaya, 42, 135

PINE NUT(S)

Bulgur, and Red Pepper Pilaf, 69, 167

Couscous Salad with Peppers, Olives and, 207

Rice, Saffron Minted, with Currants and, 33, 168

Sole, Fillet of, with Chives and, 123

PINTO BEAN Soup, Southwestern, 110

PISTACHIO Chocolate Log, 248

PITA(S)

Azuki Bean and Vegetable Salad in, 67, 197

Cobb Salad, 142

Herbed Toasted, with Goat Cheese, Garlic, and Rosemary
Spread, 308

Pizzas, Brocolli Rabe and Chick-Pea, 108

Pizzas, Potato, Anchovy, and Jarlsberg, 108

Wedges, with Eggplant and Roasted Red Pepper Dip, 99

PIZZA(S)

Dough, 106

Phyllo, Butternut Squash, Bacon, and Rosemary, 108

Phyllo, Parsley Pesto and Feta, 107

Pita, Broccoli Rabe and Chick-Pea, 108

Pita, Potato, Anchovy, and Jarlsberg, 108

Sausage and Tomato, Deep-Dish, 106

Shrimp Creole and Smoked Mozzarella, 106

Tortilla, Arugula and Prosciutto, 109

Tortilla, Tomatillo and Pepper Jack, 109

POBLANO CHILI Strips, Marinated, with White Rice, 290

POPOVERS, Rosemary, 82, 83, 105

PORK. See also Bacon; Ham; Sausage(s)

Broth, 289

Chops, Boneless Loin, with Onion Marmalade, 133

Chops, Garlic Orange, 134

Chops, Smoked Glazed, 133

Chops, Teriyaki Grilled, with Pineapple Papaya Relish, 42,
134

Loin Roast, with Beer Sauce, 70, 132

Loin Roast, with Coloradito Mole, 285, 288

Tasso Grits Batons, 38, 167

Tenderloin, Peppered, with Cherry Salsa, 132

PORT
    Gravy, and Roast Turkey, with Potato, Apple, and Prune
        Stuffing, *76*, *77*, 146
    Sauce, Shiitake, with Sautéed Quail, *73*, 146
POTATO(ES)
    Chips, Oven-Fried, with Thyme, 93
    Chips, Rosemary, 308
    and Chorizo, *295*, 300
    Crisps, *26*, 174
    Crusty Puffed, 185
    Fans, Roasted, with Creamed Leeks, 185
    Gratin, Porcini and, *82*, 183
    Mashed, Anchovy, 184
    Mashed, Garlic-Herb, 184
    Mashed, Ravioli, and Duck Confit, with White Truffle
        Sauce, 160
    Mashed, Sage and Garlic, 184
    Mashed, Stuffing-, Roast Chicken, with Root Vegetables
        and, *21*, 137
    Mashed, and Swiss Chard Terrine, Warm, 185
    New, Boiled, with Garlic Lemon Dressing, 186
    Pita Pizzas, Anchovy, Jarlsberg and, 108
    Purée, Lima Bean, and Garlic, with Potato Crisps, *26*, 174
    Purée, White-Bean, Lamb Medallions with Red-Wine
        Sauce and, 136
    Salad, with Egg, Dill Pickle, and Tarragon, 202
    Salad, with Garlic Mayonnaise and Chives, *61*, 202
    Salad, German, Warm, *70*, 202
    Scalloped, *34*, *35*, 186
    Slices, Roasted, with Lime and Chili, 186
    Stuffing, Apple, and Prune, *76*, *77*, 147
    Wedges, Gruyère, Crispy, 186
POULTRY. *See* Chicken; Cornish Hens; Duck; Quail; Turkey
POUND CAKE, Chocolate, 218
PRALINE(S), 240
    Croquembouche, Chocolate, 240
    Pecan Tarts, *39*, 240
    Powder, 242
PRESERVING, sterilizing jars and glasses, 213
PROCEDURES
    beans, dried, quick-soaking, 110
    hazlenuts, toasting and skinning, 274
    peppers, roasting, 92
    pickling and preserving, sterilizing jars and glasses, 213
    toasts, making, 96
    tortillas, warming, 298
PROSCIUTTO
    Fruit, -Wrapped, 307

Leek, and Cheese Empanadas, *17*, 179
    Spinach, and Ricotta Cannelloni, 156
    Tortilla Pizzas, Arugula and, 109
PRUNE(S)
    with Chicken Breast and Vegetables, Roasted, 139
    Gingerbread, Armagnac, 226
    Stuffing, Potato, and Apple, *76*, *77*, 147
PUDDING(S)
    Applesauce Bread Crumb, Danish, 250
    Butterscotch Bread, 250
PUMPKIN
    and Pear Pie, 234
    Seeds and Almonds, Tamari Roasted, 308
    Seed Sauce, Shrimp, Butterflied, with Cheese
        Quesadillas and, *284*, 286
PUNCH
    Nose-Warmer (Mulled Red Wine), *84*, 255
    Rum, 310

QUAIL, Sautéed, with Shiitake Port Sauce, *73*, 146
QUESADILLAS, Cheese, *284*, 288
QUICHE, Spinach and Fontina, 305
QUICK BREADS, 102–105
QUINCE Cranberry Chutney, 212
QUINOA and Black Bean Salad, 208

RADISH
    and Mushroom Salad with Parsley, 203
    and Orange Salad, *56*, 203
    Tea Sandwiches, Minted, with Lemon Mayonnaise, 98
RAISIN(S)
    Apricot, and Pecan Squares, 309
    Benne Seed Bars, *15*, 228
    Irish Soda Bread, -Golden, 102
    Rum Maple Syrup, Spiced, 155
    Swiss Chard with Olives and, 176
RASPBERRY
    Cheesecake Brownies, 232
    Chocolate Meringue Icebox Cake, 220
    Lemon Wedding Cake, 222
RAVIOLI
    Duck Confit and Mashed Potato, with White Truffle
        Sauce, 160
    Swiss Chard, Bacon, and Ricotta, with Tomato Sauce,
        162
RED CABBAGE and Bell Pepper Slaw, Wilted, *48*, 204
RED-LEAF LETTUCE and Watercress Salad with Buttermilk
    Dressing, *35*, 197

RED ONION(S)
    Cucumber, and Carrot Salad, 200
    Parsley, and Preserved Lemon Salad, 201
    Pickled, 296
    Sauerkraut, *70*, 183
RED PEPPER(S). *See also* Bell Pepper(s)
    Bulgur, and Pine Nut Pilaf, *69*, 167
    Frittata, Lentil and, 151
    Harissa, with Black Olives, *57*, 91
    Roasted, Corn Muffins, Spicy, 104
    Roasted, and Eggplant Dip, with Pita Wedges, 99
    Roasted, Mushrooms Stuffed with Cheese and, 307
    Sauce, with Red Snapper and Eggplant, 122
    Sauce, Tomato, 159
    Vinaigrette, with Stuffed Artichokes (M), 172
RED SNAPPER
    with Browned Butter and Capers, 123
    and Eggplant, with Red Bell Pepper Sauce, 122
    Marinated, *295*, 298
RED WINE
    Duck Legs, -Braised, with Roasted Pears and Onions, *78*, *79*, 145
    Figs -Poached, with Vanilla Ice Cream, 246
    Mulled, *84*, 255
    -Pan Sauce, Prime Ribs of Beef, Roast, with Pink and Green Peppercorn Crust and, *82*, *83*, 128
    -Sauce, Lamb Medallions with White-Bean Potato Purée and, 136
RELISH
    Cucumber, with Rib-Eye Steaks, Grilled, 128
    Pineapple Papaya, *42*, 135
RÉMOULADE
    Celery Root, 199
    Crawfish, Fried, *37*, 124
REUBEN Triangles, Grilled, 307
RHUBARB Lemon Cake Roll, 227
RICE. *See also* Risotto; Wild Rice
    Brown and White, 144
    Coconut Gingerroot, 168
    Curried, and Lentils, with Fried Onions, 168
    Saffron Minted, with Currants and Pine Nuts, *33*, 168
    Salad, Shrimp and, 194
    Salad, Sushi, with Avocado, Cucumber, and Scallions ("California Roll" Salad), 208
    Sticky, with Mango, *47*, 253
    White, with Poblano Chili Strips, Marinated, *285*, 290
RICE NOODLES with Garlic and Herbs, *46*, 164

RICOTTA
    Cannelloni, Spinach and Prosciutto, 156
    Pasta with Roasted Eggplant, Basil and, 162
    Salata and Tomato Bruschetta, 97
    Spread, Dilled Feta, 100
RISOTTO
    Boursin and Fennel Seed, 169
    Yellow Pepper, *29*, 169
ROLLS
    Cloverleaf Miniature, *64*, *65*, 101
    Mexican, Crusty, *277*, 280
ROQUEFORT and Toasted Pecan Dressing, 210
ROSEMARY
    Garlic Jelly, *33*, 212
    Garlic Shrimp, *48*, 126
    Goat Cheese, and Garlic Spread with Herbed Toasted Pita, 308
    and Grape Focaccia, *78*, 101
    Lemon Orzo Pilaf, 160
    Orange Oil, 216
    Pepper Honey, with Feta, 150
    Phyllo Pizza, Butternut Squash, Bacon and, 108
    Popovers, *82*, *83*, 105
    Potato Chips, 308
    Shortbread, 232
ROTINI with Lentils and Spinach, 163
RUM
    Coconut Chocolate Cakes, Individual, 220
    Fizzes, Banana, 254
    Lime Syrup, Vanilla Ice Cream with Kiwi and Banana in, 244
    Mocha Cake, *15*, 221
    Punch, 310
    Raisin Maple Syrup, Spiced, 155
    Rickey, Orange, *55*, 255
    Shakes, Cappuccino, 254
    Shakes, Tropical, 256

SAFFRON Rice, with Currants and Pine Nuts, Minted, *33*, 168
SAGE
    Chicken Liver, Peppered, and Fried Onion Bruschetta, 96
    and Garlic Mashed Potatoes, 184
    and Jerusalem Artichoke Gratin, *76*, 172
SALAD DRESSINGS, 209–211. *See also* Vinaigrette
SALADS, 192–209. *See also* Slaw(s); specific ingredients
SALADS WITH GREENS, 194–197
SALMON
    Caviar Torte, *62*, 93

Fillet, Broiled, with Mustard Dill Sauce, 121

Rillettes, 100

Seared, with Horseradish Vinaigrette, 121

Smoked, Roll-Ups, 305

SALSA

Cherry, with Pork Tenderloin, Peppered, 132

with Chipotle and Orange, Winter, 214

Tomatillo and Yellow Tomato, *51*, 99

Verde, Vegetables in, 189

Vinaigrette, 211

SAMBUCA

Chocolate Sauce, 216

Ice-Cream Sodas, Espresso, 254

SANDWICHES

Cobb Salad Pitas, 142

Egg Salad, Herbed, 151

Hamburgers, Herbed, with Arugula, 132

Lahvash, Hummus and Vegetable, 176

Po' Boys, Fried Oyster, 124

Reuben Triangles, Grilled, 307

Shrimp Salad, Herbed, with Watercress on Toasted
    Brioche, 194

Steak, with Tomato Pesto, 132

Tea, Cheddar Chutney, 97

Tea, Chicken Salad, with Smoked Almonds, 97

Tea, Radish, Minted, with Lemon Mayonnaise, 98

Tomato, Pickled Onion, and Coriander, 189

Tuna Melts, Olive and Fennel, 123

Turkey Watercress Club, 149

Vegetable, Pesto, and Mozzarella, Grilled Open-Faced,
    190

SANGRÍA, White-Wine, 310

SAUCE(S). *See also* Breakfast Sauce(s); Dessert Sauce(s);
    Gravy; Pesto; Salsa; Tomato Sauce

Chili, Sweet, *46*, 143

Dipping, Cashew, 94

Gingerroot Pear, 213

Mustard, *23*, 213

Mustard Dill, 121

Peanut, Spicy Sichuan, 167

Red Pepper Tomato, 159

Shiitake Port, *73*, 146

SAUERKRAUT, Red Onion, *70*, 183

SAUSAGE(S)

Chorizo and Potatoes, *295*, 300

and Duck Gumbo, *14*, 143

Grilled, *52*, *53*, 135

Italian, Cavatelli with Broccoli Rabe and, 158

Lentil, and Kale Soup, 115

and Tomato Pizza, Deep-Dish, 106

and Wild Mushroom Lasagne with Red Pepper Tomato
    Sauce, 159

SCALLION(S)

and Asparagus, Pencil-Thin, *29*, 171

Bacon, and Gruyère Muffins, 103

and Beef Tortilla Roll-Ups, 306

Biscuits, 102

-Horseradish Crust, with Chicken Breasts, 138

Sushi Rice Salad with Avocado, Cucumber and, 208

and Yellow Pepper Buttermilk Soup, Chilled, *67*, 118

SCALLOP(S)

and Corn Pot Stickers, with Sesame Vinaigrette,
    40, *41*, 124

Sea, and Tomatoes, Grilled, with Olive Vinaigrette, 125

Seared, Haricots Verts, and Bell Peppers, Warm Salad
    of, in Walnut Vinaigrette, *82*, 193

SCALLOPED Potatoes, *34*, *35*, 186

SEEDS. *See* names of seeds

SEMIFREDDO, White Chocolate, Toasted Almond, 228

SHALLOT Gingerroot Marmalade, 213

SHELLFISH *See also* Crab(-Meat); Crawfish; Lobster; Oyster;
    Scallop(s); Shrimp

Pasta, Paella-Style, 126

Soup, Seafood, San Francisco-Style (Cioppino), 118

SHERRY

Chocolate Almond Cake, *16*, 219

Custard Sauce, *16*, 220

SHERRY VINEGAR

with Broccoli Rabe, *73*, 175

Onion Vinaigrette, Warm, with Baked Halibut, *26*, 120

SHORTBREAD

Bites, Spicy, 93

Rosemary, 232

Squares, Mocha Cinnamon, 232

SHORTCAKES, Drop, Orange and Sour-Cream, with Assorted
    Berries, 226

SHRIMP

Bisque, Lobster and, *24*, *25*, 116

Butterflied, with Pumpkin Seed Sauce and Cheese
    Quesadillas, *284*, 286

with Chipotle Mayonnaise, 306

Creole and Smoked Mozzarella Pizzas, 106

Crisp Curried, 126

Lemon Fennel, with Tarragon, *54*, 94

Rosemary Garlic, Grilled, *48*, 126

Salad, Herbed, with Watercress on Toasted Brioche, 194

Salad, Rice and, 194

Soup, Spiced, *45*, 119

and Vegetable Spring Rolls, Cold, with Cashew Dipping
Sauce, *62*, 94

SLAW(S)

Apple, Carrot, and Onion, with Pecans, Sautéed, 203

Black-Eyed Pea and Cabbage, 205

Cabbage, Two-, 204

Carrot and Celery, with Yogurt Caraway Dressing, 204

Celery Root, Gruyère, and Apple, with Horseradish,
70, 204

Napa Cabbage and Caraway, 204

Red Cabbage and Bell Pepper, Wilted, *48*, 204

SMOKED SALMON Roll-Ups, 305

SNACKS, 307–309

SNOW PEA(S)

and Orange-Flavored Beef Stir-Fry, with Noodles, 131

Sautéed, *42*, 183

SODAS, Ice-Cream, Espresso Sambuca, 254

SOLE, Fillet of, with Pine Nuts and Chives, 123

SORBET

Kir Royale, *27*, 244

Watermelon, with Chocolate Seeds, *60*, 244

SOUP(S). *See also* Chowder; Stock

Bean, Pinto, Southwestern, 110

Bean, White, Wheat Berry, and Escarole, 110

Beef Noodle, Chinese, 111

Beet and Celery, Cold, 111

Beet and Fennel, *68*, *69*, 112

Bisque, Lobster and Shrimp, *24*, *25*, 116

Buttermilk, Yellow Pepper and Scallion, Chilled, *67*, 118

Carrot and Coconut Milk, Curried Cold, 112

Cucumber Mint, Cold, 113

Gazpacho, Spicy, 113

Goulash, Hearty, *84*, *85*, 114

Gumbo, Duck and Sausage, *14*, 143

Lentil and Ham, Hearty, 114

Lentil, Kale, and Sausage, 115

Lettuce and Pea, 115

Minestrone with Garlic and Parmesan Croutons, 116

Mushroom Barley, 117

Pea, -Split, with Caramelized Onions and Cuminseed,
117

Pea, Yellow, *23*, 118

Seafood, San Francisco-Style (Cioppino), 118

Shrimp, Spiced, *45*, 119

Squash, Yellow, and Bell Pepper, 119

Vichyssoise, Lemon Zucchini, 114

SOUR CREAM and Orange Drop Shortcakes, with Assorted
Berries, 226

SPAGHETTI

with Anchovy Olive Sauce, 163

with Pepperoni, Peas, and Browned Onions, 163

SPICE(S). *See also* names of spices

Blend, Moroccan (Ras el Hanout), 142

SPINACH

Cannelloni, Ricotta and Prosciutto, 156

Quiche, Fontina and, 305

Rotini with Lentils and, 163

Salad with Bacon, Dates, and Feta Dressing, 197

Sautéed, *26*, 188

SPREADS AND DIPS, 98–100, 308–309

SPRING ROLLS, Vegetable, and Shrimp, Cold, with Cashew
Dipping Sauce, *62*, 94

SQUASH. *See also* Butternut Squash

Yellow, and Bell Pepper Soup, 119

STEAK(S)

Rib-Eye, Grilled, with Béarnaise Butter, *61*, 127

Rib-Eye, Grilled, with Cucumber Relish, 128

Sandwiches, with Tomato Pesto, 132

Sirloin, Balsamic-Glazed, 129

Skirt, Spicy Grilled, 128

STOCK

Fish, 299

Pork Broth, 289

Turkey Giblet, 147

STRAWBERRY

Lemon-Curd Tart, 239

Margarita Fizzes, 256

Peach, and Banana Bruschetta, 152

STREUSEL, Pecan, with Apricot and Sweet Potato Purée, 188

STUFFING

Mashed-Potato, Chicken, Roast, with Root Vegetables and,
21, 137

Potato, Apple, and Prune, *76*, *77*, 147

SUN-DRIED TOMATO

Caper, and Olive Dressing, 211

Lentil, Green, and Feta Salad, 201

Mushrooms, -Stuffed, 181

SWEET POTATO(ES)

and Apricot Purée with Pecan Streusel, 188

Cinnamon-Sugar Glazed, Slices, 187

Curried Squares, with Peanut Phyllo Crust, 187

Gratin, Chili, 186

and Lamb Stew, 136

Roasted Curried, 188

SWISS CHARD
Bacon, and Ricotta Ravioli with Tomato Sauce, 162
and Mashed Potato Terrine, Warm, 185
with Olives and Raisins, 176
SYRUP. *See also* Maple Syrup
Berry, -Three, 154
Coffee, 155
Lime Rum, Vanilla Ice Cream with Kiwi and Banana in, 244

TAHINI Dressing, Spiced, 210
TAMARI Pumpkin Seeds and Almonds, Roasted, 308
TART(S). *See also* Pie(s)
Apple "Flag", 236
Apple, Maple-Glazed Breakfast, 153
Applesauce, Pink, Meringue, with Hazlenut Cookie Crust, 238
Apple Upside-Down, Individual, 237
Fig and Apple Phyllo, 238
Lemon-Curd Strawbery, 239
Praline Pecan, *39*, 240
TARTAR SAUCE, Po' Boys, Fried Oyster, 124
TASSO Grits Batons, *38*, 167
TEA
Gingerroot, 257
Iced, Minted Orange, 311
Mint, Moroccan, *59*, 257
TEA SANDWICHES, 97–98
TERIYAKI Pork Chops, Grilled, with Pineapple Papaya Relish, *42*, 134
TERRINE
Mashed Potato and Swiss Chard, Warm, 185
Pavé, Chocolate, Orange, and Chestnut, 249
THYME
Apple Galette, -Scented, 237
Corn Sticks, *13*, 105
Potato Chips, Oven-Fried with, 93
TOAST(S). *See also* Bruschetta; Crostini; Croutons
French, Cranberry-Stuffed, 152
making, 96
Mushroom Ragout on, 180
Stuffed Eggs with Vinegar Sauce on, 151
TOMATILLO
Sauce, with Chicken Enchiladas, *295*, 297
Tortilla Pizzas, Pepper Jack and, 109
and Yellow Tomato Salsa, with Tortilla Chips, *51*, 99
TOMATO(ES). *See also* Cherry Tomato(es); Sun-Dried Tomato
Corn, and Okra, Broiled, 189

Cucumber, and Avocado with Lemon Vinaigrette, *53*, 203
Gazpacho, Spicy, 113
Ketchup, Homemade, *52*, 214
Mole, Coloradito, with Pork Loin, Roast, *285*, 288
and Mozzarella Crostini, Roasted, 305
Pesto, with Steak Sandwiches, 132
Pizza, Sausage and, Deep-Dish, 106
and Ricotta Salata Bruschetta, 97
Salad, Bacon and, in Bibb Lettuce Cups, *55*, 95
Salsa, Yellow, Tomatillo and, with Tortilla Chips, *51*, 99
Sandwiches, Pickled Onion and Coriander, 189
and Sea Scallops, Grilled, with Olive Vinaigrette, 125
TOMATO SAUCE
Chili, with Chilaquiles, Baked, *277*, 278
with Feta, Sautéed, 150
with Ravioli, Swiss Chard, Bacon, and Ricotta, 162
Red Pepper, 159
Winter, 157
TORTE
Chocolate Almond, *71*, 218
Salmon Caviar, *62*, 93
TORTILLA(S)
Chilaquiles, Baked, with Tomato Chili Sauce, *277*, 278
Chips, with Salsa, Tomatillo and Yellow Tomato, *51*, 99
Corn, 288
Flour, *294*, 298
and Onion Cake, Grilled, *48*, 182
Pizzas, Arugula and Prosciutto, 109
Pizzas, Tomatillo and Pepper Jack, 109
Quesadillas, Cheese, *284*, 288
Roll-Ups, Beef and Scallion, 306
Tostadas, Black Bean, 296
warming, 298
TRUFFLES, Chocolate Caramel, 248
TRUFFLE, White, Sauce, with Duck Confit and Mashed Potato Ravioli, 160
TUNA, Melts, Olive and Fennel, 123
TURKEY. *See also* Meatballs, Turkey
Burgers, Grilled, *52*, *53*, 148
Burgers, with Mushroom Gravy, 149
Cutlets Milanese with Watercress Salad, 148
Roast, with Potato, Apple, and Prune Stuffing and Port Gravy, *76*, *77*, 146
Sandwiches, Watercress Club, 149
Stock, Giblet, 147
TURNIPS and Carrots, Baby Glazed, *33*, 190

VANILLA Apricot Sauce, 154

VEGETABLE(S). *See also* names of vegetables
    Marinated, with Mustard Dill Dressing, 190
    in Salsa Verde, 189
VEGETABLE SALADS AND SLAWS, 197–205
VINAIGRETTE
    Aniseed, Greens, Mixed Baby, with Goat Cheese Crostini
        and, *28*, 194
    Balsamic, 209
    Basil, Mint, and Orange, 209
    Garlic, Fillet of Beef with Roasted, Arugula, Cherry
        Tomatoes and, *64*, *65*, 127
    Ginger, Spicy, 209
    Gingerroot, with Carrot and Beet Salad, 198
    Horseradish Mustard, with Seared Salmon, 121
    Leeks, Warm, 178
    Lemon, with Tomato, Cucumber, and Avocado, *53*, 203
    Miso, 210
    Olive, with Sea Scallops and Tomatoes, Grilled, 125
    Red Pepper, with Stuffed Artichokes, 172
    Salsa, 211
    Sesame, with Scallop and Corn Pot Stickers, *40*, *41*, 124
    Sherry Onion, Warm, with Baked Halibut, *26*, 120
    Walnut, with Mixed Greens, *17*, 195
    Walnut, Salad of Seared Scallops, Haricots Verts, and Bell
        Peppers in, Warm, *82*, 193
VINEGAR. *See also* Balsamic Vinegar; Sherry Vinegar
    Sauce on Toast, with Stuffed Eggs, 151
VODKA
    Bloody Marys, Seaside, 310
    Coolers, *55*, 256
    -Pepper, Cherry Tomatoes, -Soaked, with Seasoned Sea
        Salt, 95

WALNUT(S)
    Biscotti, Double Chocolate, 230
    Bulgur and Lentil Salad with Tarragon and, 206
    Carrot Salad, 199
    Date Yogurt Ice Cream, 244
    Toasted, with Wild Rice and Orzo, *64*, 170
    Vinaigrette, with Mixed Greens, *17*, 195
    Vinaigrette, Salad of Seared Scallops, Haricots Verts, and
        Bell Peppers in, Warm, *82*, 193

WATERCRESS
    Herbed Goat Cheese and Roasted Beet Salad, *74*, *75*, 198
    and Red-Leaf Lettuce Salad, with Buttermilk Dressing, *35*,
        197
    Salad, with Turkey Cutlets Milanese, 148
    Shrimp Salad, Herbed on Toasted Brioche with, 194
    Turkey Club Sandwiches, 149
WATERMELON Sorbet with Chocolate Seeds, *60*, 244
WEDDING CAKE, Lemon Raspberry, 222
WHEAT BERRY, White Bean, and Escarole Soup, 110
WHITE BEAN
    Potato Purée, Lamb Medallions with Red- Wine Sauce
        and, 136
    Soup, Wheat Berry, Escarole and, 110
WHITE RUSSIAN Shakes, 256
WILD RICE
    Harvest, *78*, *79*, 170
    and Orzo with Toasted Walnuts, *64*, 170

YEAST BREADS, 101
YELLOW PEPPER(S). *See also* Bell Pepper(s)
    Creole Sauce with, *38*, 139
    Risotto, *29*, 169
    and Scallion Buttermilk Soup, Chilled, *67*, 118
    and Yellow Squash Soup, 119
YOGURT
    Caraway Dressing, with Carrot and Celery Slaw, 204
    -Cheese Dip with Crudités, 309
    Cucumber Sauce, with Turkey Meatballs, 306
    Ice Cream, Date Walnut, 244
    Mint Sauce, with Lentil Burgers, 179
    Mustard Dressing, with Crab Salad, 192

ZITI, Baked, with Turkey Meatballs, 164
ZUCCHINI
    Corn Boats, with Pepper Jack Cheese and, *61*, 177
    Grilled, Pasta Salad, Whole-Wheat, with Olives and,
        206
    Lasagne, Golden Onion and, 158
    Lobster, Corn, and Basil Salad, *64*, 192
    Sautéed, with Mint, *285*, 290
    Vichyssoise, Lemon, 114

INDEX OF 45-MINUTE RECIPES

* Starred entries can be prepared in 45 minutes or less but require additional unattended time

Page numbers in *italics* indicate color photographs

Anchovy Vegetable Spread, Provençal (Anchoïade), 99

*Antipasto-Stuffed Baguettes, 88

Apple, Carrot, and Onion Slaw, Sautéed, with Pecans, 203

Apple Cider Sauce, Honeyed, 154

Applesauce, Chunky, 250

Apricot Caramel Sauce, 252

Artichokes, Stuffed, with Red Pepper Vinaigrette, 172

Arugula and Prosciutto Tortilla Pizzas, 109

Asparagus Amandine, 171

Asparagus, Roasted, with Balsamic Vinegar, 171

Asparagus and Scallions, Pencil-Thin, *29*, 171

Balsamic Vinaigrette, 209

Banana Rum Fizzes, 254

Bananas with Chocolate, Baked, 245

Basil, Mint, and Orange Vinaigrette, 209

Beef, Orange-Flavored, and Snow Pea Stir- Fry with Noodles, 131

Beef and Scallion Tortilla Roll-Ups, 306

Berry, -Three, Syrup, 154

Biscuits, Corn, Cheddar and Jalapeño, 308

Biscuits, Scallion, 102

Black Bean Nachos, 307

Blackberry and Nectarine Cobbler, 245

Bloody Marys, Seaside, 310

Boston Baked Bean Gratin, 172

Boursin and Fennel Seed Risotto, 169

Bow Ties with Peas, Lemon, and Mint, 156

Brandy Alexander Shakes, 254

Broccoli and Cauliflower with Horseradish Bread Crumbs, *83*, 174

Broccoli Rabe and Chick-Pea Pita Pizzas, 108

Broccoli Rabe with Sherry Vinegar, *73*, 175

Brown Sugar Pecan Sauce, 154

Bruschetta, Chicken Liver, Peppered, Sage, and Fried Onion, 96

Bruschetta, Mozzarella, Greens and Garlic, 96

Bruschetta, Peach, Strawberry, and Banana, 152

Bruschetta, Tomato and Ricotta Salata, 97

Bulgur, Pine Nut, and Red Pepper Pilaf, *69*, 167

Butternut Squash, Spicy, with Bacon and Lime, 188

Butterscotch Bread Puddings, 250

Cabbage, Napa, and Caraway Slaw, 204

Cabbage, Red, and Bell Pepper Slaw, Wilted, *48*, 204

Cabbage Slaw, -Two, 204

Caesar Salad, 194

Cappuccino Rum Shakes, 254

Carrot and Beet Salad with Gingerroot Vinaigrette, 198

Carrot and Celery Slaw with Yogurt Caraway Dressing, 204

Carrot and Coconut Milk Soup, Cold Curried, 112

Carrot Walnut Salad, 199

Cashew Dipping Sauce, 94

Cauliflower, Crispy, with Olives, Capers, and Parsley, 175

Cavatelli with Italian Sausage and Broccoli Rabe, 158

Celery Root Rémoulade, 199

Cheese Straws, Spicy Cumin, *55*, 88

Cherry and Pecan Cream Cheese Spread, 100

*Cherry Tomatoes, Pepper-Vodka-Soaked, with Seasoned Sea Salt, *64, 65*, 127

Chicken Barbecue, 140

Chicken Breasts with Horseradish-Scallion Crust, 138

Chicken Breasts, Spiced, Grilled, *38*, 138

Chicken Breast and Vegetables with Prunes, Roasted, 139

Chick-Peas, Sautéed, with Cinnamon and Fresh Coriander, 176

Chipotle Mayonnaise Dip with Carrots, *51*, 98

Chocolate-Covered Almond Brittle, 247

Chocolate, Hot, Mexican, *276*, 281

Chocolate Maple Syrup, 155

Chocolate Sauce, Mexican, 216

Cocktails, Lime Southside, 255

Cocktails, Pineapple Champagne, 310

Coconut Rum Chocolate Cakes, Individual, 220

Coffee Syrup, 155

Compote, Sour Cherry, *71*, 219

Corn Bread, Caraway, 140

Corn Chowder, Cumin, 112

Corn on the Cob, Cumin, *52*, *53*, 177
Corn Sticks, Thyme, *13*, 105
Crab-Meat Parmesan Canapés, *13*, 95
Crab Salad with Yogurt Mustard Dressing, 192
Creole Sauce with Yellow Peppers, *38*, 139
Crêpes, Jelly, Glazed, 242
Crostini, Tomato, Roasted, and Mozzarella, 305
Crostini, Goat Cheese, *28*, 195
*Cucumber, Carrot, and Red Onion Salad, 200
Cucumber Carrot Salad, 200
*Cucumber Mint Soup, Cold, 113

Dubonnet Cooler, 310

Eggplant Minted Rounds, *46*, 178
Eggplant Parmigiana Rounds, 178
Eggs, Hard Cooked, with Cumin, Coarse Salt, and Cayenne, 90
Eggs, Stuffed, with Vinegar Sauce on Toast, 151

Feta Ricotta Spread, Dilled, 100
Feta with Rosemary Pepper Honey, 150
Figs, Red-Wine-Poached, with Vanilla Ice Cream, 246
Flounder with Bread Crumb Topping, Broiled, 120
French Toast, Cranberry-Stuffed, 152
Frisée Salad with Poached Eggs, *18*, *19*, 196
Fruit, Prosciutto-Wrapped, 307

*Gazpacho, Spicy, 113
Gingerroot Custard Sauce, 217
Gingerroot Shallot Marmalade, 213
Ginger Vinaigrette, Spicy, 209
Goat Cheese, Garlic, and Rosemary Spread with Herbed Toasted Pita, 308
Grand Marnier Smoothies, 254
Grapefruit, Beet, and Blue Cheese Salad, 198
Green Beans, Stewed, 173
Green Beans (with Mustard Sauce), *23*, 173
Greens, Mixed Baby, with Aniseed Vinaigrette and Goat Cheese Crostini, *28*, 194
Greens, Mixed, with Walnut Vinaigrette, *17*, 195
Guacamole, *294*, *295*, 296

Hamburgers, Herbed, with Arugula, 132
Haricots Verts, *38*, 174
Herring, Curried, on Pumpernickel, *22*, 96
Honeydew with Mint, Basil, and Lime, 246
Hummus, 176

Ice Cream, Mango, *283*, 290
Ice-Cream Parfaits, Kahlúa, Toasted Coconut, 244
Ice-Cream Sodas, Espresso Sambuca, 254
Ice Cream, Vanilla, with Kiwi and Bananas in Lime Rum Syrup, 244

Jalapeño Sunflower Seed Pesto, 166
Jícama, Carrot, and Peanut Salad, 201
Jícama Salad, *294*, 300

Lamb Chops, Marinated, *28*, *29*, 136
Lamb Medallions with White-Bean Potato Purée and Red-Wine Sauce, 136
Lamb and Sweet Potato Stew, 136
Leeks Vinaigrette, Warm, 178
*Lemon Zucchini Vichyssoise, 114
Lentil, Green, Sun-Dried Tomato, and Feta Salad, 201
Lentil, Kale, and Sausage Soup, 115
Lentils with Bitter Greens, 180
Lentils, Red, Refried, 180
Lettuce and Pea Soup, 115
Limeade, 311

Mesclun Salad, *65*, 196
Minestrone with Garlic and Parmesan Croutons, 116
Miso Vinaigrette, 210
Muffins, Bacon, Gruyère, and Scallion, 103
Muffins, Corn, Feta, 103
Muffins, Corn, Spicy, Red Pepper, Roasted, 104
Muffins, Pecan Anadama, 104
Mushroom Ragout on Toast, 180
Mushrooms, Dried-Tomato-Stuffed, 181
Mushrooms Stuffed with Red Pepper, Roasted, and Cheese, 307
Mustard Dill Sauce, 121
Mustard Sauce, *23*, 213

Noodles, Bean-Thread, with Shiitake and Vegetables, *42*, 164
Noodles, Sesame, Cold Chinese-Style, with Cucumber, 165
Nuts, Sweet-and-Spicy, 91

*Olives, Herbed, 92
*Onions, Pickled, 189
Orange, Pineapple, and Banana Salad with Lime Dressing, *276*, 278
Orange Rum Rickey, *55*, 255
Orzo Pilaf, Rosemary Lemon, 160
Orzo Salad, Niçoise, 205

Oyster, Fried, Po' Boys, 124

Pancakes, Gingerbread, with Currant Pear Maple Syrup, 152
Parmesan Crisps, *32*, 181
Pasta Salad, Tricolor, Herbed, *52*, 206
*Pastry Dough, 235
Peach Schnapps Fizzes, 255
Peanut Sauce, Spicy Sichuan, 167
Peanuts, Chili-Dusted, 286
Pears, Caramelized, *16*, 220
Pears, Poached, 246
Peas, Buttered, 183, *34. 35*
Pea Soup, -Split, with Caramelized Onions and Cuminseed, 117
Pesto, 214
*Pineapple Papaya Relish, *42*, 135
Pork Chops, Garlic Orange, 134
Pork Loin Chops, Boneless, with Onion Marmalade, 133
Pork Tenderloin, Peppered, with Cherry Salsa, 132
Potato Chips, Oven-Fried, with Thyme, 93
Potato Chips, Rosemary, 308
Potato Crisps, *26*, 174
Potatoes, Anchovy Mashed, 184
Potatoes, Crusty Puffed, 185
Potatoes, Mashed, Garlic-Herb, 184
Potatoes, New, Boiled, with Garlic Lemon Dressing, 186
Potato Salad with Egg, Dill Pickle, and Tarragon, 202
Potato Slices, Roasted, with Lime and Chili, 186
Potato Wedges, Gruyère, Crispy, 186
Praline Powder, 242
Pumpkin Seeds and Almonds, Tamari, Roasted, 308

Quesadillas, Cheese, *284*, 288
Quiche, Spinach and Fontina, 305

Radish and Mushroom Salad with Parsley, 203
Red-Leaf Lettuce and Watercress Salad with Buttermilk Dressing, *35*, 197
Red Onions, Pickled, 296
Red Snapper and Eggplant with Red Bell Pepper Sauce, 122
Red Wine, Mulled (Nose-Warmer Punch), *84*, 255
Rice, Coconut Gingerroot, 168
Rice, Saffron, with Currants and Pine Nuts, Minted, *33*, 168
Roquefort and Toasted Pecan Dressing, 210
Rum Punch, 310
Rum Raisin Maple Syrup, Spiced, 155
Rum Shakes, Tropical, 256
Rusty Nail Shakes, 256

Salmon Fillet, Broiled, with Mustard Dill Sauce, 121
Salmon Rillettes, 100
Salmon, Seared, with Horseradish Mustard Vinaigrette, 121
Salmon, Smoked, Roll-Ups, 305
Salsa with Chipotle and Orange, Winter, 214
Salsa Vinaigrette, 211
Sandwiches, Egg Salad, Herbed, 151
Sandwiches, Reuben Triangles, Grilled, 307
Sandwiches, Steak, with Tomato Pesto, 132
Sandwiches, Tea, Cheddar Chutney, 97
Sandwiches, Tea, Chicken Salad, with Smoked Almonds, 97
Sandwiches, Tea, Radish Minted, with Lemon Mayonnaise, 98
Sandwiches, Turkey Watercress Club, 149
Sangría, White-Wine, 310
Sausages, Grilled, *52*, *53*, 135
Scallops, Seared, Haricots Verts, and Bell Peppers, Warm Salad of, in Walnut Vinaigrette, *82*, 193
Scallops, Sea, and Tomatoes, Grilled, with Olive Vinaigrette, 125
Sherry Custard Sauce, *16*, 220
Shrimp with Chipotle Mayonnaise, 306
*Shrimp, Lemon Fennel, with Tarragon, *54*, 94
Shrimp and Rice Salad, 194
Shrimp Salad, Herbed, with Watercress on Toasted Brioche, 194
Snapper with Browned Butter and Capers, 123
Snow Peas, Sautéed, *42*, 183
Soba with Pea Shoots, Shiitake Mushrooms, and Leeks, 166
Sole, Fillet of, with Pine Nuts and Chives, 123
*Sorbet, Kir Royale, *27*, 244
Spaghetti with Anchovy Olive Sauce, 163
Spaghetti with Pepperoni, Peas, and Browned Onions, 163
Spice Blend, Moroccan (Ras El Hanout), 142
Spinach Salad with Bacon, Dates, and Feta Dressing, 197
Spinach, Sautéed, *26*, 188
Squash, Yellow, and Bell Pepper Soup, 119
Steak, Sirloin, Balsamic-Glazed, 129
Steak, Skirt, Grilled Spicy, 128
Steaks, Rib-Eye, Grilled, with Béarnaise Butter, *61*, 127
Steaks, Rib-Eye, Grilled, with Cucumber Relish, 128
Strawberry Margarita Fizzes, 256
Sweet Potatoes, Roasted Curried, 188
Swiss Chard, Bacon, and Ricotta Ravioli with Tomato Sauce, 162
Swiss Chard with Olives and Raisins, 176

Tahini Dressing, Spiced, 210
Tea, Gingerroot, 257

Tea, Iced, Minted Orange, 311
Tea, Mint, Moroccan, *59*, 257
Tomatillo and Pepper Jack Tortilla Pizzas, 109
*Tomatillo and Yellow Tomato Salsa with Tortilla Chips, *51*, 99
Tomato and Bacon Salad in Bibb Lettuce Cups, *55*, 95
Tomato, Corn, and Okra, Broiled, 189
Tomato, Cucumber, and Avocado with Lemon Vinaigrette, *53*, 203
Tomato, Dried, Caper, and Olive Dressing, 211
Tuna Melts, Olive and Fennel, 123
Turkey Burgers, Grilled, *52*, *53*, 148
Turkey Burgers with Mushroom Gravy, 149

Turkey Cutlets Milanese with Watercress Salad, 148
Turkey Meatballs with Cucumber Yogurt Sauce, 306
Turkey Meatball Stroganov, 148

Vanilla Apricot Sauce, 154
Vegetables in Salsa Verde, 189
Vodka Coolers, *55*, 256

White Russian Shakes, 256

Yellow Pepper and Scallion Buttermilk Soup, Chilled, *67*, 118

Zucchini with Mint, Sautéed, *285*, 290

INDEX OF RECIPE TITLES

Page numbers in *italics* indicate color photographs

Anchoïade (Provençal Anchovy Vegetable Spread), 99
Anchovy Mashed Potatoes, 184
Anchovy Puffs, 88
Antipasto-Stuffed Baguettes, 88
Apple and Dried-Cherry Lattice Pie, 233
Apple "Flag" Tart, 236
Apricot Caramel Sauce, 252
Apricot, Raisin, and Pecan Squares, 309
Arugula and Prosciutto Tortilla Pizzas, 109
Asparagus Amandine, 171
Austrian Crêpes, 252
Austrian Sweet Cheese Crêpes Baked in Custard, 251
Avocado Salad, 298
Azuki Bean and Vegetable Salad in Pita Bread, *67*, 197

Bacon, Gruyère, and Scallion Muffins, 103
Baked Alaska Peanut S'mores, *49*, 243
Baked Bananas with Chocolate, 245
Baked Chilaquiles with Tomato Chili Sauce, *277*, 278
Baked Halibut with Warm Sherry Onion Vinaigrette, *26*, 120
Baked Ziti with Turkey Meatballs, 164
Balsamic-Glazed Pearl Onions, *77*, 182
Balsamic-Glazed Sirloin Steak, 129
Balsamic Vinaigrette, 209
Banana Rum Fizzes, 254
Basil, Mint, and Orange Vinaigrette, 209
Bean-Thread Noodles with Shiitake Mushrooms and
    Vegetables, *42*, 164
Beef and Scallion Tortilla Roll-Ups, 306
Beet and Fennel Soup, *68*, *69*, 112
Benne Seed Raisin Bars, *15*, 228
Black Bean Nachos, 307
Black Beans, *277*, 280
Black Bean Tostadas, 296
Blackberry and Nectarine Cobbler, 245
Black-Eyed Pea and Cabbage Slaw, 205
Black Olives with Harissa, *57*, 91
Boiled New Potatoes with Garlic Lemon Dressing, 186
Boneless Pork Loin Chops with Onion Marmalade, 133

Boston Baked Bean Gratin, 172
Boursin and Fennel Seed Risotto, 169
Bow Ties with Peas, Lemon, and Mint, 156
Brandy Alexander Shakes, 254
Broccoli and Cauliflower with Horseradish Bread Crumbs,
    83, 174
Broccoli Rabe and Chick-Pea Pita Pizzas, 108
Broccoli Rabe with Sherry Vinegar, *73*, 175
Broiled Flounder with Bread Crumb Topping, 120
Broiled Salmon Fillet with Mustard Dill Sauce, 121
Broiled Tomato, Corn, and Okra, 189
Brown Sugar Pecan Sauce, 154
Brown and White Rice, 144
Bulgur and Lentil Salad with Tarragon and Walnuts, 206
Bulgur, Pine Nut, and Red Pepper Pilaf, *69*, 167
Buttered Peas, *34*, *35*, 183
Butterflied Shrimp with Pumpkin Seed Sauce and Cheese
    Quesadillas, *284*, 286
Butternut Squash, Bacon, and Rosemary Phyllo Pizza, 108
Butterscotch Bread Puddings, 250

Caesar Salad, 194
"California Roll" Salad (Sushi Rice Salad with Avocado,
    Cucumber, and Scallions), 208
Cappuccino Rum Shakes, 254
Caramelized Pear Charlottes with Persimmon, *72*, 246
Caramelized Pears, *16*, 220
Caraway Corn Bread, 140
Carrot and Beet Salad with Gingerroot Vinaigrette, 198
Carrot and Celery Slaw with Yogurt Caraway Dressing, 204
Carrot Walnut Salad, 199
Cashew Dipping Sauce, 94
Cavatelli with Italian Sausage and Broccoli Rabe, 158
Celery Root, Gruyère, and Apple Slaw with Horseradish,
    70, 204
Celery Root Rémoulade, 199
Cheddar Chutney Tea Sandwiches, 97
Cheddar and Jalapeño Corn Biscuits, 308
Cheese Quesadillas, *284*, 287

Cherry and Pecan Cream Cheese Spread, 100

Chicken Barbecue, 140

Chicken Breasts with Horseradish-Scallion Crust, 138

Chicken and Dumplings, *20*, 138

Chicken Enchiladas with Tomatillo Sauce, *295*, 297

Chicken and Roasted Vegetable Salad, 192

Chicken Salad Tea Sandwiches with Smoked Almonds, 97

Chili-Dusted Peanuts, 286

Chili Sweet Potato Gratin, 186

Chilled Yellow Pepper and Scallion Buttermilk Soup, *67*, 118

Chinese Beef Noodle Soup, 111

Chipotle Mayonnaise Dip with Carrots, *51*, 98

Chipotle Pepper Oil, 214

Chocolate Almond Sherry Cake, *16*, 219

Chocolate Almond Torte, *71*, 218

Chocolate Caramel Truffles, 248

Chocolate Chip Ginger Crisps, 229

Chocolate Chip Oatmeal Cookies, 229

Chocolate-Covered Almond Brittle, 247

Chocolate Cream Pie, 234

Chocolate Maple Syrup, 155

Chocolate, Orange, and Chestnut Pavé, 249

Chocolate Pastry Cream, 242

Chocolate Pistachio Log, 248

Chocolate Pound Cake, 218

Chocolate Praline Croquembouche, 240

Chunky Applesauce, 250

Chutney Garlic Dressing, 209

Cinnamon-Sugar Glazed Sweet Potato Slices, 187

Cioppino (San Francisco-Style Seafood Soup), 118

Cobb Salad Pitas, 142

Coconut Chocolate Chip Cookies, 229

Coconut Flan, 301

Coconut Gingerroot Rice, 168

Coffee Syrup, 155

Cold Beet and Celery Soup, 111

Cold Chinese-Style Sesame Noodles with Cucumber, 165

Cold Cucumber Mint Soup, 113

Cold Curried Carrot and Coconut Milk Soup, 112

Cold Shrimp and Vegetable Spring Rolls with Cashew Dipping Sauce, *62*, 94

Coriander Eggplant Salad, 200

Corn Boats with Zucchini and Pepper Jack Cheese, *61*, 177

Corn Tortillas, 288

Couscous Salad with Peppers, Olives, and Pine Nuts, 207

Crab-Meat Parmesan Canapés, *13*, 95

Crab Salad with Yogurt Mustard Dressing, 192

Cracked Green Olives with Herbs and Preserved Lemon, 92

Cranberry Quince Chutney, *77*, 212

Cranberry-Stuffed French Toast, 152

Crème Fraîche Ice Cream, 224

Creole Sauce with Yellow Peppers, *38*, 139

Crisp Curried Shrimp, 126

Crisp Spiced Nuts, *84*, 90

Crispy Cauliflower with Olives, Capers, and Parsley, 175

Crispy Duck Breasts with Pear and Green Peppercorn Sauce, 144

Crispy Gruyère Potato Wedges, 186

Crown Roast of Lamb, *33*, 135

Crusty Mexican Rolls, *277*, 280

Crusty Puffed Potatoes, 185

Cucumber, Carrot, and Red Onion Salad, 200

Cucumber Carrot Salad, 200

Cumin Corn Chowder, 112

Cumin Corn on the Cob, *52*, *53*, 177

Curried Herring on Pumpernickel, *22*, 96

Curried Sweet Potato Squares with Peanut Phyllo Crust, 187

Curry Oil, 215

Danish Applesauce Bread Crumb Pudding, 250

Date Walnut Yogurt Ice Cream, 244

Deep-Dish Sausage and Tomato Pizza, 106

Deviled Miroton (Gratin of Sliced Beef and Mustard Gravy), 130

Dill Caraway Oil, 215

Dilled Feta Ricotta Spread, 100

Double Chocolate Walnut Biscotti, 230

Double-Peanut Double-Chocolate Chip Cookies, 230

Dried Tomato, Caper, and Olive Dressing, 211

Dried-Tomato-Stuffed Mushrooms, 181

Dubonnet Cooler, 310

Duck Confit and Mashed Potato Ravioli with White Truffle Sauce, 160

Duck and Sausage Gumbo, *14*, 143

Eggplant Parmigiana Rounds, 178

Espresso Sambuca Ice-Cream Sodas, 254

Feta Corn Muffins, 103

Feta with Rosemary Pepper Honey, 150

Fig and Apple Phyllo Tart, 238

Fillet of Beef with Arugula, Cherry Tomatoes, and Roasted Garlic Vinaigrette, *64*, *65*, 127

Fillet of Sole with Pine Nuts and Chives, 123

Fish Chermoula (Fish with Moroccan Seasoning), *58*, 122

Fish Stock, 299

Flour Tortillas, *294, 298*

Four-Cheese Baked Bow Ties, 156

Fried Crawfish Rémoulade, 124

Fried Oyster Po' Boys, 124

Frisée Salad with Poached Eggs, *18, 19,* 196

Frozen Margaritas, 310

Fudge Bars with Pecan-Graham Crust, 230

Garlic-Herb Mashed Potatoes, 184

Garlic Orange Pork Chops, 134

Garlic Rosemary Jelly, *33,* 212

Gingerbread Pancakes with Currant Pear Maple Syrup, 152

Ginger Crème Anglaise, 217

Gingerroot Custard Sauce, 217

Gingerroot Pear Sauce, 213

Gingerroot Shallot Marmalade, 213

Gingerroot Tea, 257

Glazed Baby Turnips and Carrots, *33,* 190

Glazed Jelly Crêpes, 242

Glazed Smoked Pork Chops, 133

Goat Cheese, Garlic, and Rosemary Spread with Herbed
    Toasted Pita, 308

Goat Cheese Crostini, *28,* 195

Golden Onion and Zucchini Lasagne, 158

Golden-Raisin Irish Soda Bread, *2,* 102

Grand Marnier Smoothies, 254

Granola and Dried Cranberry Chocolate Chip Cookies,
    66, 231

Grapefruit, Beet, and Blue Cheese Salad, 198

Grape and Rosemary Focaccia, *78,* 101

Green Beans, *23,* 173

Green Lentil, Sun-Dried Tomato, and Feta Salad, 201

Green and White Crudités with Herbed Anise Dip, 98

Grilled Open-Faced Vegetable, Pesto, and Mozzarella
    Sandwiches, 190

Grilled Portobello Mushrooms with Parmesan Crisps, *32,* 181

Grilled Reuben Triangles, 307

Grilled Rib-Eye Steaks with Béarnaise Butter, *61,* 127

Grilled Rib-Eye Steaks with Cucumber Relish, 128

Grilled Rosemary Garlic Shrimp, *48,* 126

Grilled Sausages, *52, 53,* 135

Grilled Sea Scallops and Tomatoes with Olive Vinaigrette,
    125

Grilled Spiced Chicken Breasts, *38,* 138

Grilled Spicy Skirt Steak, 128

Grilled Teriyaki Pork Chops with Pineapple Papaya Relish,
    42, 134

Grilled Tortilla and Onion Cake, 182

Grilled Turkey Burgers, *52, 53,* 148

Guacamole, *294, 295, 298*

Hard-Cooked Eggs with Cumin, Coarse Salt, and Cayenne, 90

Haricots Verts, *38,* 174

Harvest Wild Rice, *78, 79,* 170

Hearty Goulash Soup, *84, 85,* 114

Hearty Lentil and Ham Soup, 114

Herbed Egg Salad Sandwiches, 151

Herbed Goat Cheese, Roasted Beet, and Watercress Salad,
    74, 75, 198

Herbed Hamburgers with Arugula, 132

Herbed Olives, 92

Herbed Shrimp Salad with Watercress on Toasted Brioche,
    194

Herbed Tricolor Pasta Salad, *52,* 206

Herbed Whole-Oat Salad, 207

Homemade Tomato Ketchup, *52,* 214

Honeydew with Mint, Basil, and Lime, 246

Honeyed Apple Cider Sauce, 154

Honey Lemon Buttermilk Dressing, 210

Honey Nut Candies, *59,* 248

Hot Curried Party Mix, 91

Hummus, 176

Hummus and Vegetable Lahvash Sandwiches, 176

Individual Coconut Rum Chocolate Cakes, 220

Individual Upside-Down Apple Tarts, 237

Irish Brown Soda Bread, *2,* 102

Jalapeño Sunflower Seed Pesto, 166

Jerusalem Artichoke and Sage Gratin, *76,* 172

Jícama, Carrot, and Peanut Salad, 201

Jícama Salad, *294, 300*

Kahlúa, Toasted Coconut, and Ice-Cream Parfaits, 244

Kir Royale Sorbet, *27,* 244

Lamb Medallions with White-Bean Potato Purée and Red-
    Wine Sauce, 136

Lamb and Sweet Potato Stew, 136

Leek, Prosciutto, and Cheese Empanadas, *17,* 179

Lemon-Curd Strawberry Tart, 239

Lemon Dill Baked Orzo with Gruyère, 160

Lemon Fennel Shrimp with Tarragon, *54,* 94

Lemon Meringue Buttercream, 224

Lemon Raspberry Wedding Cake, 222

Lemon Spice Oil, 215

Lemon Zucchini Vichyssoise, 114
Lentil Burgers with Yogurt Mint Sauce, 179
Lentil, Kale, and Sausage Soup, 115
Lentil and Red Pepper Frittata, 151
Lentils with Bitter Greens, 180
Lentils and Curried Rice with Fried Onions, 168
Lettuce and Pea Soup, 115
Lima Bean, Potato, and Garlic Purée with Potato Crisps, *26*, 174
Limeade, 311
Lime Refresher, 286
Lime Southside Cocktails, 255
Limpa Muffins, 104
Lobster, Corn, Zucchini, and Basil Salad, *64*, 192
Lobster and Shrimp Bisque, *24, 25*, 116

Macadamia Coconut Cake, *43*, 224
Macaroni and Cheese, 160
Mango Ice Cream, *283*, 290
Maple-Glazed Breakfast Apple Tarts, 153
Marinated Lamb Chops, *28, 29*, 136
Marinated Snapper, *295*, 298
Marinated Vegetables with Mustard Dill Dressing, 190
Mesclun Salad, *65*, 196
Mexican Chocolate Sauce, 216
Mexican Hot Chocolate, *276*, 281
Mexican Sweet Buns, *276*, 281
Minestrone with Garlic and Parmesan Croutons, 116
Miniature Cloverleaf Rolls, *64, 65*, 101
Minted Eggplant Rounds, *46*, 178
Minted Orange Iced Tea, 311
Minted Radish Tea Sandwiches with Lemon Mayonnaise, 98
Minted Saffron Rice with Currants and Pine Nuts, *33*, 168
Miso Vinaigrette, 210
Mixed Baby Greens with Aniseed Vinaigrette and Goat Cheese Crostini, *28*, 194
Mixed Greens with Walnut Vinaigrette, *17*, 195
Mocha Cinnamon Shortbread Squares, 232
Mocha Rum Cake, *15*, 221
Moroccan Chicken and Almond Pies, *57*, 141
Moroccan Mint Tea, *59*, 257
Mozzarella, Greens, and Garlic Bruschetta, 96
Mushroom Barley Soup, 117
Mushroom Ragout on Toast, 180
Mushrooms Stuffed with Roasted Red Pepper and Cheese, 307
Mustard Dill Sauce, 121
Mustard Sauce, *23*, 213

Napa Cabbage and Caraway Slaw, 204
Niçoise Orzo Salad, 205
Nose-Warmer Punch (Mulled Red Wine), *84*, 255

Oaxacan Sweet Fritters, *283*, 291
Old-Fashioned Meat Loaf, *34, 35*, 131
Olive and Fennel Tuna Melts, 123
Orange Currant Noodle Kugel, 250
Orange-Flavored Beef and Snow Pea Stir-Fry with Noodles, 131
Orange, Pineapple, and Banana Salad with Lime Dressing, *276*, 278
Orange and Radish Salad, *56*, 203
Orange Rosemary Oil, 216
Orange Rum Rickey, *55*, 255
Orange and Sour-Cream Drop Shortcakes with Assorted Berries, 226
Oven-Fried Potato Chips with Thyme, 93

Paella-Style Shellfish Pasta, 126
Parmesan Crisps, *32*, 181
Parsley, Pesto and Feta Phyllo Pizza, 107
Pasta with Roasted Eggplant, Ricotta, and Basil, 162
Pastry Dough, 235
Pâte à Chou (Cream Puff Pastry), 242
Paula Wolfert's Seven-Day Preserved Lemons, 92
Pavlovas with Kir Royale Sorbet and Kiwis, *27*, 243
Peach Schnapps Fizzes, 255
Peach, Strawberry, and Banana Bruschetta, 152
Pear and Pumpkin Pie, 234
Pecan Anadama Muffins, 104
Pencil-Thin Asparagus and Scallions, *29*, 171
Peppered Chicken Liver, Sage, and Fried Onion Bruschetta, 96
Peppered Pork Tenderloin with Cherry Salsa, 132
Pepper Jack Crackers, 90
Pepper-Vodka-Soaked Cherry Tomatoes with Seasoned Sea Salt, 95
Pesto, 214
Pesto Oil, 216
Pickled Onions, 189
Pickled Red Onions, 296
Pineapple Champagne Cocktails, 310
Pineapple Papaya Relish, *42*, 135
Pink Applesauce Meringue Tart with Hazlenut Cookie Crust, 238
Pizza Dough, 106
Poached Pears, 246
Pork Broth, 289

Potato, Anchovy, and Jarlsberg Pita Pizzas, 108
Potato, Apple, and Prune Stuffing, *76, 77,* 147
Potato Crisps, *26,* 174
Potatoes and Chorizo, *295,* 300
Potato and Porcini Gratin, *82,* 183
Potato Salad with Egg, Dill Pickle, and Tarragon, 202
Potato Salad with Garlic Mayonnaise and Chives, *61,* 202
Praline Pecan Tarts, *39,* 240
Praline Powder, 242
Pralines, 240
Prosciutto-Wrapped Fruit, 307
Prune Armagnac Gingerbread, 226
Pumpernickel and Rye Breadsticks, *68, 69,* 105

Quinoa and Black Bean Salad, 208

Radish and Mushroom Salad with Parsley, 203
Ras el Hanout (Moroccan Spice Blend), 142
Raspberry Cheesecake Brownies, 232
Raspberry Chocolate Meringue Icebox Cake, 220
Red-Leaf Lettuce and Watercress Salad with Buttermilk
    Dressing, *35,* 197
Red Onion, Parsley, and Preserved Lemon Salad, 201
Red Onion Sauerkraut, *70,* 183
Red Snapper and Eggplant with Red Bell Pepper Sauce, 122
Red-Wine-Braised Duck Legs with Roasted Pears and Onions,
    78, 79, 145
Red-Wine Poached Figs with Vanilla Ice Cream, 246
Refried Red Lentils, 180
Rhubarb Lemon Cake Roll, 227
Rice Noodles with Garlic and Herbs, *46,* 164
Roast Chicken with Mashed-Potato Stuffing and Root
    Vegetables, *21,* 137
Roasted Asparagus with Balsamic Vinegar, 171
Roasted Carrots and Parsnips, *76, 77,* 175
Roasted Chicken Breast and Vegetables with Prunes, 139
Roasted Curried Sweet Potatoes, 188
Roasted Marinated Cornish Hens, *46*
Roasted Potato Fans with Creamed Leeks, 185
Roasted Potato Slices with Lime and Chili, 186
Roasted Red Pepper and Eggplant Dip with Pita Wedges,
    99
Roasted Tamari Pumpkin Seeds and Almonds, 308
Roasted Tomato and Mozzarella Crostini, 305
Roast Pork Loin with Beer Sauce, *70,* 132
Roast Pork Loin with Coloradito Mole, *285,* 288
Roast Prime Ribs of Beef with Pink and Green Peppercorn
    Crust and Red-Wine Pan Sauce, *82, 83,* 128

Roast Turkey with Potato, Apple, and Prune Stuffing and Port
    Gravy, *76, 77,* 146
Roquefort and Toasted Pecan Dressing, 210
Rosemary Lemon Orzo Pilaf, 160
Rosemary Popovers, *82, 83,* 105
Rosemary Potato Chips, 308
Rosemary Shortbread, 232
Rotini with Lentils and Spinach, 163
Rump Roast with Vegetables, 130
Rum Punch, 310
Rusty Nail Shakes, 256

Sage and Garlic Mashed Potatoes, 184
Salmon Caviar Torte, *62,* 93
Salmon Rillettes, 100
Salsa Vinaigrette, 211
Sambuca Chocolate Sauce, 216
Sausage and Wild Mushroom Lasagne with Red Pepper
    Tomato Sauce, 159
Sautéed Apple, Carrot, and Onion Slaw with Pecans, 203
Sautéed Chick-Peas with Cinnamon and Fresh Coriander, 176
Sautéed Feta with Tomato Sauce, 150
Sautéed Kale with Cracklings and Garlic Bread Crumbs, *78,*
    79, 178
Sautéed Persimmons and Green Beans with Chives, *77,* 173
Sautéed Quail with Shiitake Port Sauce, *73,* 146
Sautéed Snow Peas, *42,* 183
Sautéed Spinach, 188
Sautéed Zucchini with Mint, 290
Scallion Biscuits, 102
Scallop and Corn Pot Stickers with Sesame Vinaigrette, *40,*
    41, 124
Scalloped Potatoes, *34, 35,* 186
Seared Salmon with Horseradish Mustard Vinaigrette, 121
Seaside Bloody Marys, 310
Sherry Custard Sauce, *16,* 220
Shredded Beef with Eggs, *277,* 279
Shrimp with Chipotle Mayonnaise, 306
Shrimp Creole and Smoked Mozzarella Pizzas, 106
Shrimp and Rice Salad, 194
Slivered Beef with Onions, *295,* 298
Smoked Chicken with Mango and Mint, *63,* 89
Smoked Fish Chowder, 113
Smoked Salmon Roll-Ups, 305
Snapper with Browned Butter and Capers, 123
Soba with Pea Shoots, Shiitake Mushrooms, and Leeks, 166
Sour Cherry Compote, *71,* 219
Southwestern Pinto Bean Soup, 110

Spaghetti with Anchovy Olive Sauce, 163
Spaghetti with Pepperoni, Peas, and Browned Onions, 163
Spiced Rum Raisin Maple Syrup, 155
Spiced Shrimp Soup, *45*, 119
Spiced Tahini Dressing, 210
Spicy Butternut Squash with Bacon and Lime, 188
Spicy Cumin Cheese Straws, *55*, 88
Spicy Gazpacho, 113
Spicy Ginger Vinaigrette, 209
Spicy Roasted Red Pepper Corn Muffins, 104
Spicy Shortbread Bites, 93
Spicy Sichuan Peanut Sauce, 167
Spinach and Fontina Quiche, 305
Spinach, Ricotta, and Prosciutto Cannelloni, 156
Spinach Salad with Bacon, Dates, and Feta Dressing, 197
Split-Pea Soup with Caramelized Onions and Cuminseed, 117
Steak Sandwiches with Tomato Pesto, 132
Stewed Green Beans, 173
Sticky Rice with Mango, *47*, 253
Strawberry Margarita Fizzes, 256
Stuffed Artichokes with Red Pepper Vinaigrette, 172
Stuffed Eggs with Vinegar Sauce on Toast, 151
Sweet-and-Spicy Nuts, 91
Sweet Chili Sauce, *46*, 143
Sweet Potato and Apricot Purée with Pecan Streusel, 188
Swiss Chard, Bacon, and Ricotta Ravioli with Tomato Sauce, 162
Swiss Chard with Olives and Raisins, 176

Tasso Grits Batons, *38*, 167
Three-Berry Syrup, 154
Thyme Corn Sticks, *13*, 105
Thyme-Scented Apple Galette, 237
Tomatillo and Pepper Jack Tortilla Pizzas, 109
Tomatillo and Yellow Tomato Salsa with Tortilla Chips, *51*, 99
Tomato and Bacon Salad in Bibb Lettuce Cups, *55*, 95
Tomato, Cucumber, and Avocado with Lemon Vinaigrette, *53*, 203
Tomato, Pickled Onion, and Coriander Sandwiches, 189

Tomato and Ricotta Salata Bruschetta, 97
Tropical Rum Shakes, 256
Turkey Burgers with Mushroom Gravy, 149
Turkey Cutlets Milanese with Watercress Salad, 148
Turkey Giblet Stock, 147
Turkey Meatballs with Cucumber Yogurt Sauce, 306
Turkey Meatball Stroganov, 148
Turkey Watercress Club Sandwiches, 149
Two-Cabbage Slaw, 204

Vanilla Apricot Sauce, 154
Vanilla Ice Cream with Kiwi and Banana in Lime Rum Syrup, 244
Vegetables in Salsa Verde, 189
Viennese Cucumber Salad, *85*, 199
Vodka Coolers, *55*, 256

Warm German Potato Salad, *70*, 202
Warm Leeks Vinaigrette, 178
Warm Mashed Potato and Swiss Chard Terrine, 185
Warm Salad of Seared Scallops, Haricots Verts, and Bell Peppers in Walnut Vinaigrette, *82*, 193
Watermelon Sorbet with Chocolate Seeds, *60*, 244
White Bean, Wheat Berry, and Escarole Soup, 110
White Chocolate Toasted Almond Semifreddo, 228
White Rice with Marinated Poblano Chili Strips, 290
White Russian Shakes, 256
White-Wine Sangría, 310
Whole-Wheat Pasta Salad with Grilled Zucchini and Olives, 206
Wild Rice and Orzo with Toasted Walnuts, *64*, 170
Wilted Red Cabbage and Bell Pepper Slaw, *48*, 204
Winter Salsa with Chipotle and Orange, 214
Winter Tomato Sauce, 157

Yellow Pea Soup, *23*, 118
Yellow Pepper Risotto, *29*, 169
Yellow Squash and Bell Pepper Soup, 119
Yogurt-Cheese Dip with Crudités, 309

TABLE SETTING ACKNOWLEDGMENTS

To avoid duplication below of table setting information within the same menu, the editors have listed all such credits for silverware, plates, linen, and the like in its most complete form under "Table Setting."

Any items in the photograph not credited are privately owned.
All addresses are in New York City unless otherwise indicated.

Jacket
Mango Ice Cream; Buñuelos (front): Hand-blown cobalt bowl and blue decorative Mexican dinner plate—Pan American Phoenix, 153 East 53rd Street. Terra-cotta tiles—Elon Inc., 5 Skyline Drive, Hawthorne, NY 10532, tel. (914) 347-7800.
Supper on the Porch (back): See Table Setting credits for Supper on the Porch below.

Frontispiece
Golden-Raisin Irish Soda Bread; Irish Brown Soda Bread (page 2): All items in the photograph are privately owned.

Table of Contents
Tea Sandwiches (page 5): Grape leaf plates (on cake stand); wrought-iron cake stand; croquet set, circa 1900; French galvanized bucket—Wolfman • Gold & Good Company, 116 Greene Street. Engraved goblets, circa 1880; table croquet set, circa 1900—James II Galleries, 11 East 57th Street. Glass pitcher—William-Wayne & Co., 850 Lexington Avenue. Oak and silver-plate biscuit box, circa 1880—S. Wyler, 941 Lexington Avenue. Wicker arm chair—Newel Art Galleries, Inc., 425 East 53rd Street.

The Menu Collection
Table Setting (page 10): See Table Setting credits for Autumn Dinner for Two below.

A Southern New Year's Day Buffet
Table Setting (pages 12 and 13): Ceramic dinner plates from the Mulberry at Home collection; "Dot" ceramic casserole; "Mallards" cotton tablecloth—ABC Carpet & Home, 888 Broadway. Austrian sterling flatware—F. Gorevic & Son, 635 Madison Avenue. Wineglasses; rattan tray with brass trim; willow basket; lacquered wood tea caddy and papier-mâché tray (on wall), both one of a kind—William-Wayne & Company, 850 Lexington Avenue. Cotton napkins; iron basket—Pottery Barn, 117 East 59th Street. Flowers—Zezé, 398 East 52nd Street. "Gothic" handmade wrought-iron armchairs (seat cushions not included)—Briger Design, tel. (212) 517-4489. Limoges fish platter and plates, 1868; nineteenth century lithographs—The Bespeckled Trout, 422 Hudson Street. Painted wood bookcase with faux bamboo trim, circa 1810—Kentshire Galleries Ltd., 37 East 12th Street.
Mocha Rum Cake; Benne Seed Raisin Bars (page 15): Vintage terra-cotta leaf plates—William-Wayne & Company, 850 Lexington Avenue.

New Year's Eve Supper for Two
Chocolate Almond Sherry Cake (page 16): "Goldie" Champagne flutes designed by Ulrica Hydman-Vallien for Kosta Boda—Galleri Orrefors Kosta Boda, 58 East 57th Street. Handmade

56- by 40-inch reproduction Gobelin tapestry—ABC Carpet & Home, 888 Broadway.
Leek, Prosciutto, and Cheese Empanadas; Mixed Greens with Walnut Vinaigrette (pages 16 and 17): "Metropoles" porcelain salad plates and service plates—Bernardaud, 777 Madison Avenue. "Viva" Champagne flutes designed by Anna Ehrner for Kosta Boda—Galleri Orrefors Kosta Boda, 58 East 57th Street. "Arc-en-Ciel" plaid cotton fabric (on chairs, available through decorator)—Brunschwig & Fils, 979 Third Avenue. Edwardian sterling napkin rings; red glass and silver-plate castors, circa 1910; glass jug, circa 1870; Art Nouveau copper and brass candlestick by Benson, circa 1880 (one of a pair); nineteenth-century brass pail—James II Galleries, Ltd., 15 East 57th Street. Handmade wrought-iron and steel drum tray table—Briger Design Ltd., tel. (212) 517-4489.

Chicken Dinners in the Kitchen
Table Setting (pages 18 and 19): Porcelain trays, "Toucan" wineglasses and water goblets, cotton napkins by Paula Sweet; gold-leaf napkin rings, bamboo place mats by Chateau X; ceramic tray, pewter and glass pepper mill, pewter candlesticks—Frank McIntosh Shop at Henri Bendel, 712 Fifth Avenue. "Cardinale" sterling flatware—Puiforcat, 811 Madison Avenue. Flowers—Zezé,

398 East 52nd Street. Corian countertop—tel. (800) 4-CORIAN.

Chicken and Dumplings (page 20): "Empire" bone china dinner plates—Polo Ralph Lauren, 867 Madison Avenue. Faience soup bowls, cotton tablecloth by Paula Sweet—Frank McIntosh Shop at Henri Bendel, 712 Fifth Avenue. Flowers—Zezé, 398 East 52nd Street.

Roast Chicken with Mashed-Potato Stuffing and Root Vegetables (page 21): Ceramic and stainless-steel servers—Frank McIntosh Shop at Henri Bendel, 712 Fifth Avenue.

Après-Skate Danish-Style

Curried Herring on Pumpernickel (page 22): "Ursula" faïence cake plate; "Palm Tree" *snaps* glasses by Kosta Boda—Royal Copenhagen Porcelain/Georg Jensen Silversmiths, 683 Madison Avenue.

Buffet Spread (page 23): Fioriware ceramic dinner plates and bowls—Barneys New York, 660 Madison Avenue. "Polished Stonehenge" stainless-steel flatware; twig window basket with flower pots; silk sunflowers—The Pottery Barn, 117 East 59th Street. "Aarne" beer glasses by ittalia—Royal Copenhagen Porcelain/Georg Jensen Silversmiths, 683 Madison Avenue. Pine tree candles; vintage Beacon cotton blanket—Whispering Pines, 516 Main Street, Piermont, NY 10968, tel. (914) 359-6302.

Bright Lights Big City Dinner

Table Setting (pages 24 and 25): "Les Nacrés Sable" Limoges service and soup plates; "Variations Sable" Limoges dinner plates; "Biarritz" sterling flatware—Puiforcat, 811 Madison Avenue. Handmade Murano wineglasses; "Leaf" handmade Champagne flutes—Avventura, 463 Amsterdam Avenue. "Constantine" hand-painted napkins—

Leslie Pontz, tel. (215) 242-3366. "Column" candles—Keesal & Mathews, 1244 Madison Avenue. Tole palm tree, available through decorator—John Rosselli International, 523 East 73rd Street. "Imperia" viscose and cotton fabric (tablecloth), available through decorator—Schumacher, tel. (800) 332-3384. Arch Sheers "Bronze" polyester fabric (at window)—(through decorator) Agnes Bourne, Inc., 2 Henry Adams Street, Showroom 220, San Francisco, CA 94103 or (retail) MIKE Furniture, 2142 Fillmore Street, San Francisco, CA 94115.

Pavlovas with Kir Royale Sorbet and Kiwis (page 27): Painted variegated leaf background—Richard Pellicci, tel. (914) 271-6710.

An Early Spring Dinner

Mixed Baby Greens with Aniseed Vinaigrette and Goat Cheese Crostini (page 28): Tunisian porcelain salad plate by Nelly Reynaud—Barneys New York, 660 Madison Avenue.

Marinated Lamb Chops; Yellow Pepper Risotto; Pencil-thin Asparagus and Scallions (pages 28 and 29): Tunisian porcelain dinner plates by Nelly Reynaud—Barneys New York, 660 Madison Avenue. Bronze asparagus centerpiece by Donald Reed—River's Edge Foundry, R. R. 2, Oregon, IL 61061. "Lattice" wood cachepots—Treillage Ltd., 420 East 75th Street. Flowers—Zezé, 398 East 52nd Street.

Easter Dinner

Table Setting (pages 30 and 31): Coalport porcelain dinner plates, circa 1840—Bardith Ltd., 901 Madison Avenue. "Laura" hand-crafted sterling flatware—Buccellati Inc., 46 East 57th Street. "Isadora Lilac" waterglasses and "Fenix" wineglasses by Kosta Boda—Orrefors Crystal Gallery, 58 East 57th Street. Linen napkins by Archipelago—

Barneys New York, 660 Madison Avenue. Flowers—Zezé, 398 East 52nd Street. George III painted armchairs, circa 1812—Kentshire Galleries, 37 East 12th Street.

Entrée and accompaniments (page 33): English Sheffield tray, circa 1790; vintage Tiffany sterling sauceboat; silverplate shell and bowl; vintage Reed & Barton sterling carving set—F. Gorevic and Son, 635 Madison Avenue.

Sunday Supper

Old-Fashioned Meat Loaf; Scalloped Potatoes; Buttered Peas (pages 34 and 35): North Carolina pottery plates; unmatched silver-plate flatware; glass goblets; cotton napkins and place mats; baluster candlesticks; colander; milk-painted pine farm table; vintage painted chairs; television cabinet made to order from old pine by Martina Dörr—Henro, 525 Broome Street. Nineteenth-century oil painting—The Barking Dog Antiques, Firehouse Road, High Falls, NY 12440, tel. (914) 687-4834.

Red-Leaf Lettuce and Watercress Salad with Buttermilk Dressing (page 35): Wooden bowl and glass pitcher—Simon Pearce, 500 Park Avenue. Old pine tray by Martina Dörr; North Carolina pottery bowls—Henro, 525 Broome Street.

A New Orleans Courtyard Dinner

Table Setting (pages 36 and 37): "Carnival" Portuguese hand-painted earthenware dinner plates—Keesal & Mathews, 1244 Madison Avenue, tel. (800) 624-8400. "Dot" hand-painted wineglasses—MacKenzie-Childs, Ltd., 824 Madison Avenue. "Palmette" sterling flatware, "57th Street" crystal wineglasses—Tiffany & Co., 727 Fifth Avenue. French damask napkins, circa 1880—Lucullus, 610 Chartres Street, New Orleans, LA 70130. "Palm" hurricane lamps—Frank McIntosh Shop at Henri Bendel, 712 Fifth Avenue.

Grilled Spiced Chicken Breasts; Creole Sauce with Yellow Peppers; Tasso Grits Batons; Haricots Verts (page 38): Blue glass dinner plate by Jay Camp—Bergdorf Goodman, 754 Fifth Avenue. *Praline Pecan Tarts* (page 39): "Ivy" fused glass dessert plates—Keesal & Mathews, 1244 Madison Avenue, tel. (800) 624-8400. Belgian linen and lace napkins, circa 1920—Françoise Nunnal-lé, 105 West 55th Street, tel. (212) 246-4281 (by appointment only). Resin urn—Treillage, Ltd., 418 E. 75th Street. Flowers—Tommy's Flower Shop, 1029 Chartres Street, New Orleans, LA 70116.

A Pan-Asian Luncheon on Maui

Table Setting (pages 40 and 41): Haviland "Océane" Limoges dinner and salad plates—Baccarat, 625 Madison Avenue. *Pâte de verre* and silver-plate flatware; *pâte de verre* and crystal wineglasses, both from the Trapani Collection by Garouste & Bonetti—Daum Boutique, 694 Madison Avenue. Cotton napkins—Pottery Barn, 117 East 59th Street. "Sea Urchin" plaster napkin rings designed by Jane Krolik—Chateau X, tel. (212) 477-3123. "Tiki" glasses (with flowers)—Frank McIntosh Shop at Henri Bendel, 712 Fifth Avenue. Flowers—Maui North Shore Farms, Maui, HI, tel. (800) 301-7111. "Les Algues" cotton fabric (tablecloth), available through decorator—Brunschwig & Fils, 979 Third Avenue. "Les Feuilles" cotton fabric (on chairs), available through decorator—Grey Watkins, 979 Third Avenue.

A Taste of Thailand

Table Setting (pages 44 and 45): "Soliel" porcelain dinner and salad plates—Lalique Boutique, 680 Madison Avenue. Glass bowls—Mayhew, 507 Park Avenue. French bamboo-handled flatware—Bergdorf Goodman, 754

Fifth Avenue. "Bamboo" crystal wineglasses by Justin Tharaud—Cardel, Ltd., 621 Madison Avenue. Cotton napkins; metal vase; wooden folding chairs—Pottery Barn, 117 East 59th Street (chairs hand-painted by Richard Pellicci, tel. 914-271-6710). Napkin rings designed by Jane Krolik for Chateau X—Neiman Marcus, all stores. "Ming Garden" linen and cotton fabric (available through decorator)—China Seas, 979 Third Avenue. Orchids—Maui North Shore Farms, Maui, HI, tel. (800) 301-7111.

Dinner from the Grill

Grilled Rosemary Garlic Shrimp, Grilled Tortilla and Onion Cake, Wilted Red Cabbage and Bell Pepper Slaw (pages 48 and 49): Italian ceramic dinner plates; glasses; cotton napkins—Pottery Barn, 117 East 59th Street. "Palette" stainless-steel and acrylic flatware (from a 20-piece set)—Oneida, (800) 877-6667. Solid teak game table and dining chairs by McGuire (available through decorator)—Baker, Knapp & Tubbs, 200 Lexington Avenue or McGuire showrooms nationwide. *Baked Alaska Peanut S'mores* (page 49): Glass dessert plates—Kitchen Classics, P. O. Box 1281, Bridgehampton, NY 11932.

Fourth of July
Family Reunion Picnic

Table Setting (pages 51 and 52): "Sunflowers" hand-painted wood platter (with carrots) and bowl (with chips), designed by Esther Katz—Mariposa, (800) 788-1304. Ceramic bowl (with dip)—ABC Carpet & Home, 888 Broadway, "Fleur" glass bowls (with *salsa*) by Durand (from a set of 4)—The Alley, 490 South Palm Canyon Drive, Palm Springs, CA 92262, tel. (619) 320-5664. Metal pails—Pottery Barn, 117 East 59th Street.

Picnic Setting (pages 52 and 53): "Sunflowers" hand-painted wood tray (with burgers and sausages) designed by Esther Katz; *brillante* aluminum bowl (with pasta) and servers by Michael Updike; "Cambridge" nylon flatware by SCOF—Mariposa, tel. (800) 788-1304. Hand-thrown and hand-painted ceramic dinner plates and pitcher (with flowers), by Ellen Reznick—Avventura, 463 Amsterdam Avenue. "Cordoba" recycled glass carafes, pitcher, and glasses—Global Guzzini, 2465 Coral Street, Vista, CA 92083, tel. (619) 598-0188. "Corn" ceramic platters (with vegetables); hand-painted ceramic mustard and ketchup pots by Eigen Arts; wire trivet (under bowl of chips)—ABC Carpet & Home, 888 Broadway. Cotton napkins—Pottery Barn, 117 East 59th Street.

Cocktails After Tennis

Lemon Fennel Shrimp with Tarragon (page 54): Frosted glass bowl with glass insert—Barneys New York, 660 Madison Avenue.
Orange Rum Rickeys; Vodka Coolers; Spicy Cumin Cheese Straws; Tomato and Bacon Salad in Bibb Lettuce Cups (pages 54 and 55): Italian ironstone platter (with lettuce cups)—Williams-Sonoma, 20 East 60th Street. "Bellini" Italian wineglasses by Mariposa; "Mosaic" ceramic platter by Vietri—Zona, 97 Greene Street. Glass flowerpots (with cheese straws)—Ad Hoc Softwares, 410 West Broadway. "Harlequin" highball glasses—Barneys New York, 660 Madison Avenue. Reproduction nineteenth-century French wrought-iron table base with glass top—T & K French Antiques, 120 Wooster Street. Lloyd Flanders all-weather wicker sofa, lounge chair, and glass-topped end table (available through decorator)—Triconfort, 200 Lexington Avenue.

A Moroccan Feast

Orange and Radish Salad; French Bread (page 56): Annieglass Color Series "Triangle" platter—Annieglass, tel. (800) 347-6133. Murano glasses—Avventura, 463 Amsterdam Avenue. Moroccan hand-painted wood table—ABC Carpet & Home, 888 Broadway. Wire globe basket—Mottura, tel. (800) 257-5300.

Table Setting (page 57): "Biskra" hand-painted porcelain dinner plates by Palais Royal—Garson Goodman, 1244 West Paces Ferry Road, Atlanta, GA 30327, tel. (404) 841-9111. Glass salad plates—Annieglass, tel. (800) 347-6133. "Orbit Gold" stainless-steel flatware—Sasaki, tel. (212) 686-5080. "Morocco" wineglasses by Stephen Smyers—Avventura, 463 Amsterdam Avenue. Brass goblets; ceramic and metal bottle—Adriana's Caravan, tel. (718) 436-8565. "Donatello" cotton and linen napkins; cotton and rayon tassels—ABC Carpet & Home, 888 Broadway. Hand-painted tabletop by Richard Pellicci, tel. (914) 271-6710. "Victoria" cotton fabric on pillows (available through decorator)—Clarence House, 211 East 58th Street. "Kilim" linen fabric and "Zamora" cotton fabric, both on pillows (available through decorator)—Brunschwig & Fils, 979 Third Avenue. Poppies—Village Florist, 435 North Palm Canyon Drive, Palm Springs, CA 92262, tel. (619) 325-2577.

Honey Nut Candies; Melon, Grapes, Dates; Moroccan Mint Tea (page 59): Glass platter—Annieglass, tel. (800) 347-6133.

Supper on the Porch

Watermelon Sorbet with Chocolate Seeds (page 60): Ceramic platter—Bloomingdale's, 1000 Third Avenue.

Grilled Rib-Eye Steaks with Béarnaise Butter; Corn Boats with Zucchini and Pepper Jack Cheese; Potato Salad with

Garlic Mayonnaise and Chives; Vine-Ripened Cherry Tomatoes (pages 60 and 61): Ceramic buffet plates and bowl; wooden farm table with original paint; four- by six-foot kilim rug; deconstructionist wooden console; screen doors—Wolfman • Gold & Good Company, 116 Greene Street. "Cheyenne" stainless-steel flatware—Zona, 97 Greene Street. Wüsthof-Trident steak knives; Dansk crystal wineglasses—Bloomingdale's, 1000 Third Avenue. Cotton napkins—Pottery Barn, 117 East 59th Street.

A Small Garden Wedding

Cold Shrimp and Vegetable Spring Rolls with Cashew Dipping Sauce; Smoked Chicken with Mango and Mint; Salmon Caviar Torte with Toast Points (pages 62 and 63): Silver-plate serving dish and sauceboat, circa 1870; English pottery platter, 1870; glass and silver-plate dish (cover not shown), circa 1865 (with toast points)—James II Galleries, 11 East 57th Street. Vintage glass cake stand—Wolfman • Gold & Good Company, 116 Greene Street. Marquis "Bermuda Clear" water goblets by Waterford Crystal—Waterford Crystal, tel. (800) 677-7860. Composition urns (flower containers)—Treillage, 418 East 75th Street. Flower arrangements and rose standards—Castle and Pierpont, 401 East 76th Street. Iron console with composition top—Lexington Gardens, 1011 Lexington Avenue.

Buffet Spread: (pages 64 and 65): Fossilglass platter by Cristina Salusti—Frank McIntosh Shop at Henri Bendel, 712 Fifth Avenue. "Heartland" hand-blown footed glass bowls—Simon Pearce, 500 Park Avenue (entrance on 59th Street). Silver-plate basket, circa 1865—James II Galleries, 11 East 57th Street. Schott-Zwiesel glass bowl (with roasted garlic vinaigrette)—Cardel Ltd., 621 Madison Avenue. "Fiddle Thread

& Shell" sterling serving spoon and ladle—Tiffany & Co., 727 Fifth Avenue. "Tramezzo" painted wood screens by Niermann Weeks—Treillage, 418 East 75th Street.

A Hikers' Picnic

Granola and Dried Cranberry Chocolate Chip Cookies (page 66): High Sierra backpack—Innovation Luggage, 866 Third Avenue.

Chilled Yellow Pepper and Scallion Buttermilk Soup; Azuki Bean and Vegetable Salad in Pita Bread (page 67): Enamelware plates—ABC Carpet & Home, 888 Broadway. Stainless-steel cups—Sierra Club Bookstore, (800) 935-1056. Swiss Army knife—Hoffritz stores nationwide. Denim shirt—Gap stores nationwide.

Oktoberfest

Table Setting (pages 68 and 69): Hand-painted ceramic dinner and soup plates; staghorn flatware—The Design Museum Shop at the Cooper-Hewitt, 2 East 91st Street, (212) 860-6933. Beer glasses—Pottery Barn, 117 East 59th Street. "Saturn" cotton and linen napkins; "Autumn Leaves" napkin rings—ABC Carpet & Home, 888 Broadway. Antler candlesticks, circa 1840—J. Garvin Mecking, 72 East 11th Street. "Colmar" cotton fabric (tablecloth and pillows); "Davington Stripe" linen and cotton fabric (banquettes and pillows), both available through decorator—Cowtan & Tout, 979 Third Avenue. Nineteenth-century iron and ostrich-shell owl flask; nineteenth-century porcelain beer steins with pewter tops—Newel Art Galleries, 425 East 53rd Street.

Autumn Dinner for Two

Caramelized Pear Charlotte with Persimmon (page 72): Porcelain dessert plate (from a set of six plates and two compotes), circa 1890—Bergdorf Goodman, 754 Fifth Avenue.

Sautéed Quail with Shiitake Port Sauce; Bulgur, Pine Nut, and Red Pepper Pilaf; Broccoli Rabe with Sherry Vinegar (page 73): Puiforcat "Klimt" hand-painted porcelain dinner plates; Puiforcat "Normandie" silver-plate flatware—for stores call (800) 993-2580. Wineglasses with bronze leaf decoration—Bergdorf Goodman, 754 Fifth Avenue. Anthony Stern water glasses and glass vase with silver-plate copper bands; gold-leaf candlesticks by the William Howe Studio—Barneys New York, Madison Avenue at 61st Street. Taffeta napkins; "Marble" six- by nine-foot pressed jute rug—ABC Carpet & Home, 888 Broadway. Orchid plant and calla lilies—Zezé, 398 East 52nd Street. French sycamore tea table by André Arbus, circa 1940; hand-painted smoked mirrored screen, circa 1935—Newel Art Galleries, 425 East 53rd Street. Nineteenth-century French wrought-iron park chairs—T&K French Antiques, 120 Wooster Street. "Kipling" linen and cotton fabric (on chair seat, fabric available through decorator)—Cowtan & Tout, 979 Third Avenue.

Thanksgiving Dinner

Table Setting (pages 74 and 75): Christian Dior "Beau Rivage" porcelain dinner and salad plates—for stores call (212) 679-3169. Nineteenth-century "Old English Bead" sterling flatware—Hancock's, 1 Burlington Gardens, London, England W1X2HP. Victorian cut-glass and enameled wineglasses, circa 1860; Ridgway porcelain candlesticks, circa 1840—James II Galleries, 11 West 57th Street. "Malmaison" crystal wineglasses—Baccarat, 625 Madison Avenue. Linen and velvet napkins by Paula Sweet; beaded hand-loomed straw place mats by Jane Krolik for Chateau•X—Frank McIntosh Shop at Henri Bendel, 712 Fifth Avenue. Victorian silver-plate butter tureen (with

nuts)—S. Wyler, 941 Lexington Avenue. Vintage sterling trophies—F. Gorevic & Son, 635 Madison Avenue. Paneling and scenes hand-painted by Betsy Arnold—for information call (804) 273-0869.

Entrée and accompaniments (pages 76 and 77): Donovan ironstone platter (with turkey), circa 1850; Spode green and gold vegetable dishes, circa 1820; Victorian silver-plate serving pieces (from a service for 18)—S. Wyler, 941 Lexington Avenue. Vintage Tiffany sterling sauceboat; vintage hexagonal silver-plate basket by Walker & Hall; Victorian silver-plate revolving dish (with chutney), circa 1885—Fortunoff, 681 Fifth Avenue. Christian Dior "Beau Rivage" porcelain vegetable dish—for stores call (212) 679-3169. Anglo-Indian rosewood console, circa 1845 (available through decorator)—Yale R. Burge Antiques, 305 East 63rd Street. "Marlborough" wallpaper by Colefax and Fowler (available through decorator)—Cowtan & Tout, 979 Third Avenue.

A Bird of a Different Feather

Grape and Rosemary Focaccia (page 78): Patrick Frey "Paniers Fleuris" Limoges dessert plates—Bergdorf Goodman, 754 Fifth Avenue.

Table Setting (pages 78 and 79): Patrick Frey "Sorgues" Limoges dinner plates and "Paniers Fleuris" cotton place mats—Bergdorf Goodman, 754 Fifth Avenue. "Montana" wood-handled flatware—Pottery Barn, 117 East 59th Street. Wineglasses and cotton napkins—William-Wayne, 850 Lexington Avenue. Flowers—Zezé, 398 East 52nd Street.

Christmas Dinner

Table Setting (pages 80 and 81): "Sylvan Nocturne" porcelain plates by Lynn Chase—for stores call, tel. (800) 228-9909. "Malmaison" silver-plate

flatware—Pavillon Christofle, 680 Madison Avenue. Wineglasses by Union Street Glass—Barneys New York, Madison Avenue at 61st Street. Hand-painted linen napkins by Liz Wain—special order from Scully & Scully, 504 Park Avenue. Napkin rings—William-Wayne, 850 Lexington Avenue. Hand-painted glass votives; tole Gothic chairs—Briger Design, tel. (212) 517-4489. Floral arrangement and topiaries—Zezé, 398 East 52nd Street. "Napoleonic Bee" viscose rayon fabric (available through decorator)—Schumacher, 939 Third Avenue. Iron and cane chairs—Bergdorf Goodman, 754 Fifth Avenue.

Entrée and accompaniments (pages 82 and 83): Victorian silver-plate platter, cake basket, sauceboat (one of a pair), and ladle—S. Wyler, 941 Lexington Avenue. Old Newbury Crafters "Classic English" hand-forged sterling carving set and "Moulton" hand-forged sterling serving fork and spoon—Cardel, 621 Madison Avenue. Sadek porcelain baking dish (potato gratin) and Resista porcelain baking dish (broccoli and cauliflower)—Mayhew, 507 Park Avenue.

A Caroling Party

Nose-Warmer Punch and Crispy Spiced Nuts (page 84): Glass punch cups; Vietri ceramic leaf bowl and stand—Mayhew, 507 Park Avenue.

Hearty Goulash Soup; Viennese Cucumber Salad (pages 84 and 85): Laure Japy "Louisiane" porcelain dinner and soup plates—Cardel, 621 Madison Avenue. French acrylic and stainless steel flatware—Barneys New York, Madison Avenue at 61st Street. Vietri "Puccinelli" wineglasses—for stores call (800) 277-5933. Cotton napkins—Frank McIntosh Shop at Henri Bendel, 712 Fifth Avenue. Brass "pinecone" candlesticks; twig napkin rings—Keesal & Mathews, 1244 Madison Avenue.

Barley-candy deer and assorted tree ornaments made in antique molds—Dorothy Timberlake Candies, Main Street, Eaton Center, NH 03832, tel. (603) 447-2221. Handmade cherry dining table with tiger-maple star inlay and pedestal base with maple rondels; handmade French cherry side chairs with natural rush seats—Malandra Funderburke, tel. (212) 410-2023.

A Recipe Compendium

Table Setting (page 86): See Table Setting credits for Chicken Dinners in the Kitchen above.

Almuerzo

Café con Leche; Chocolate Mexicano; Pan Dulce (page 276): Floral tiles, tin tray, cocktail napkin, cup and saucer, handblown highball glass and wooden spoon—Pan American Phoenix, 153 East 53rd Street.

Chilaquiles al Horno con Salsa de Chiles y *Tomates; Frijoles Negros; Bolillos; Machacado con Huevos* (page 277): Floral tiles, bread basket, and wooden utensils—Pan American Phoenix, 153 East 53rd Street. Terracotta tiles—Elon, Inc., 5 Skyline Drive, Hawthorne, NY 10532, (914) 347-7800.

Comida de Oaxaca

Loma de Cerdo Asado con Mole Coloradito; Calabacitas Salteadas con Menta; Arroz Blanco con Fajas de Chile Poblano en Escabeche (pages 284 and 285): Tin charger—Pan American Phoenix, 153 East 53rd Street.

A Mexican Buffet

Buffet Spread (pages 294 and 295): Mexican rug, large clay pot and white shawl (both on chair), wine goblets, and large green casserole—Pan American Phoenix, 153 East 53rd Street. Flowers—Zezé, 398 East 52nd Street.

CREDITS

———

Grateful acknowledgment is made to the following for permission to reprint recipes previously published in *Gourmet* Magazine:

Rozanne Gold: "Chocolate Pistachio Log" (page 248). Copyright © 1994 by Rozanne Gold. Reprinted by permission of the author.

Jeanne Lemlin: "Golden-Raisin Irish Soda Bread" (page 102); "Irish Brown Soda Bread" (page 102). Copyright © 1994 by Jeanne Lemlin. Reprinted by permission of the author.

Paula Wolfert: "Paula Wolfert's Seven-Day Preserved Lemons" (page 92) Copyright © 1994 by Paula Wolfert. Reprinted by permission of the author.

Zanne Early Zakroff: "Duck Confit and Mashed Potato Ravioli with White Truffle Sauce" (page 160); "Raspberry Chocolate Meringue Icebox Cake" (page 220). Copyright © 1994 by Zanne Early Zakroff. Reprinted by permission of the author.

Mark Ferri has generously given permission to use the following photographs, previously published in *Gourmet* Magazine: "Thanksgiving Dinner" (pages 74 through 77). Copyright © 1994 by Mark Ferri. Reprinted by permission of the photographer.

If you are not already a subscriber to *Gourmet* Magazine and would be interested in subscribing, please call *Gourmet's* toll-free number, 1-800-365-2454.

If you are interested in purchasing additional copies of this book or other *Gourmet* cookbooks, please call 1-800-245-2010.